# *Contents*

# Acknowledgements

I am indebted to many people for their help in correcting my draft of this book. Each of them, listed below in alphabetical order, kindly took the time and trouble to read through part or all of the draft chapter relevant to their personal experience of the events described, and to verify its accuracy and identify any mistakes, without sight or knowledge of the other chapters of the book. Only two of them read through the whole book before it's publication, I owe a special thanks to my English teacher and friend, Gillian Howarth, who painstakingly vetted the whole draft, corrected the typing and grammatical errors and advised me during the preparation of this book: I also wish to thank my distinguished apprentice and artificer contemporary, Rear Admiral Mike Simpson CB, for kindly writing the Foreword.

Captain Richard Channon RN
Margaret (Peggy) Chapman, née Murdoch
Barry Elliott Esq
Lieutenant Malcolm Howard RN
Mrs Gillian Howarth
Mrs Anne Kanavan
Mr Ron Kelbrick BEM
Mrs Eileen Lewis née Murdoch
Rear Admiral Guy Liardet
Lieutenant-Commander Jack Limburn RN
Lieutenant Terry Liming RN
Ms Sally Murdoch
Miss Victoria Murdoch
Admiral Sir William O'Brien KCB, DSC
Dennis O'Neil Esq
Lieutenant Fred Pointer RN
Commander Ron Short RN
Rear Admiral Mike Simpson CB

# Don's Story

## The life and times of Lieutenant-Commander D.W. Murdoch MBE, RN.

A personal account of life as a sickly child, evacuee, 'tiffy', naval officer, chartered engineer, project manager and pensioner, during 80 years of great social change.

# Dedication

This book is dedicated to my dear wife Eileen who not only had to contend with my absences during my naval and civilian careers, but also with some later pre-occupation in writing about them.

God bless you Darling and all my love and heartfelt thanks for your love and devotion throughout our long and happy marriage.

John Stupples Esq
Captain Tony Wardale RN
Frank Wootton Esq

I did not keep a diary during the 80 years covered by this story, except to record future appointments. I have a poor recent recall but fortunately, have a good memory for long past events. I most gratefully acknowledge the help given me by the following publications in confirming the dates and details of incidents and events to which my personal story is related, and to some of which, I contributed the original story.

'Evacuees 60 Years On' published 1999 by the Portsmouth News
'A Trevolier's Tale' serialised in The Fisgardian Magazine 2006
'HMS Theseus Goes East' published in 1951
'HMS Cheviot – The Last Commission' published in 1959
'HMS Nubian 1962-64 First Commission' published in 1964
'The Falmouth Packet' by Richard Channon, all issues 1971 – 72
'UZZ' published weekly in HMS Falmouth 1971-72
'The CE Bulletin' issues 1 to 4 published by HMS Collingwood
HMS Bulwark's 'Weekly Bee' Issues 1 to 8 published in 1979
"Second to None 100 Years of the Artificer Apprentice" 2003

I also wish to thank my daughter Sally, not only for vetting all of Chapter 24 and the family elements of Chapters 13 to 23, but also for secretly having Chapters 1 to 12 published as a surprise 80th birthday present and then for encouraging me to complete the whole book.

Finally, I am most grateful to everyone mentioned, or quite unintentionally omitted, from this history, who helped shape the life I have enjoyed and which I have tried to describe.

The opinions expressed in Don's Story are those of the author and are not necessarily shared with the above-mentioned friends who collectively and kindly checked the story.

# Foreword

by
Rear Admiral Michael F Simpson CB
Director General of Aircraft (Naval) 1982 -85
Chairman-Aircraft Engineering Division Hunting Aviation 1992-98

This is a warm and engaging story of Don's life from childhood to old age, told with great accuracy and sincerity. As well as a personal story of selfless family life, it also reveals just how much the Royal Navy depended on the dedication and skills of its Artificers, who formed the hard core of the Navy's engineering capability.

Intrinsic to providing this capability was the four year Artificer Apprenticeship. In Don's time this was carried out between the ages of fifteen and nineteen and Don's detailed narrative of his four years at HMS Fisgard probably describes the reality of life there for the first time. The exposure of youngsters to both advanced education and naval discipline could only influence their development, and the rest of Don's story shows how the culture of this intensive training flowed into the veins of naval engineering potency.

As shown in Don's story, Artificer Apprentices were selected from candidates who sat a competitive academic exam about the same standard as the old School Certificate. In Don's time, if selected, their commitment was to sign on for at least fifteen years and their reward was promotion to Senior Rate one year after completing their apprenticeship. Artificers were an elitist branch which experienced a major extraction of Engineer Officers, one of the Navy's own rewards for a considerable training investment.

A large part of Don's story follows the logical path from Artificer Apprentice to Engineer Lieutenant Commander, embracing an active naval career of 35 years. For economic reasons, the Navy has just abandoned the recruitment and training of

Artificers. In the longer term, the risk that this drastic policy change will bring to future weapon system availability will not become evident until the existing Artificers retire.

Don's retirement was followed by a successful fourteen year career with Marconi Defence and Underwater Systems where the differences in dedication and leadership soon became apparent. Don sums up his two careers by saying "the former was a complete way of life and not just a good job, and it gave me the experience to tackle the second one with confidence"

As a contemporary of mine, I respect Don's profound dedication to his family life, his mature Christian views and his ungrudging contribution to the Royal Navy. This book is about the success of a generous, talented and modest gentleman who achieved what he did entirely by his own efforts, which were initiated in an era of unhelpful social prejudice.

# Chapter 1

## Early Days - 1929 – 39

I was born 'under a caul' at 1-15 am on Monday 18th January 1929 in the middle bedroom of my paternal grandmother's house, No 13, Tokar Street in Eastney, a part of Southsea, the holiday resort district of Portsmouth. It was snowing as I made my first appearance and doubtless somewhat chilly in that small room, heated as it was only by a small coal fire, as my petite mother gave birth to her second child and first son who weighed a whopping eleven and three-quarter pounds. It was a difficult birth and, apparently, I was considered, by the doctor to be in great danger of failing to see the dawn. Thus I had my first encounter with practical Christian ecumenism at a very early age when, at my mother's request, her Ulster-protestant doctor baptised me. I was formally christened at St Swithun's Catholic Church Southsea three weeks later. At that time, the possession of a caul was thought to protect the holder from a watery grave and cauls were much sought after by superstitious sailors and fishermen. Years later, my mother expressed confidence that I had chosen the right career when I joined the navy for, although my caul had long since disappeared, the sac which had covered my head at birth, would keep me from drowning.

Needless to say I have no recollection of this event or of the next few years but from family photographs and memories it seems I was a blond, curly-headed child who, as an infant suffered from whooping cough. Until I was nine years old my parents, William John (known as John) and Eileen Murdoch, who were married in 1926, were really rather poor. My father, who had left the army in 1925, was, throughout the 1930s' depression, either unemployed or in poorly paid temporary seasonal jobs. We lived with his Scottish mother whom we called Nana, in a terraced house

quite close to Eastney beach. My mother helped supplement the family's meagre income by doing cleaning jobs and helping Nana to 'look after' her 'summer visitors' who regularly came every year for a holiday by the seaside. Nana was a Royal Marine's widow with a tiny pension and relied on the modest rent paid by Dad and on her 'bed & breakfast and evening meal' holidaymakers In the summer, Nana slept in the

parlour, my parents in the kitchen and we children slept in a wooden lean-to built by my father on to the back of the house. It was quite cosy and we were happy and the 'visitors' were friendly and kind to us. They ate in the 'front room' downstairs, but otherwise lived upstairs. The house had no bathroom or running hot water so they washed in their bedrooms using china basins filled from large jugs of hot water brought upstairs from the kitchen. The only lavatory in the house was downstairs, so the holidaymakers had to use chamber pots which were emptied by Nana or Mum while the visitors were having breakfast. We washed in the kitchen and bathed there once a week in a galvanised bath, normally hung up in the rear lobby, and scoop-filled from the kitchen's coal fired washing boiler.

My parents never had a holiday together in the 16 years they were married, although Mum took us twice to Ireland in the summer to her mother's home. Our Irish grandmother, who was a District Nurse and Midwife, paid for the tickets. We were a happy and close-knit family, we children being fortunate that both of our parents were teetotal and didn't smoke or gamble, dedicating all of their small income to bringing us up. This utter devotion proved particularly important to my younger sister and me.

My first memory is of being taken into the house by my aunt, with my elder sister Margaret, (known as Peggy), to be shown my new baby sister Eileen who had just been born in the same bed as I had been some four years earlier. Eileen and I were destined to be very close from that day forward. I later learned that my mother had given birth to a still-born son, two years before Eileen's birth completed the Murdoch Family.

I started school in September 1933 at Reginald Road (mixed) Infants School and almost immediately fell in love with the girl with whom I shared a double-desk. Her name was June Vincent; she had long curly hair and lived in a house called 'Tredegar' in Winter Road on the corner of Tredegar Road. I wonder whatever happened to her? The house still stands as a reminder of my first love. I recall the excitement at finding that the two men who were working in our house while I was at school, were installing electric lighting and two-pin sockets, and delighted when Dad bought an Ultra wireless set and we could listen to Childrens' Hour on the BBC and to Radio Luxembourg. Mum bought an electric iron, but I remember Nana still continued to use her gas hob heated flat iron. The gas lights were not removed and proved invaluable during the blitzes seven years later when electricity supplies were cut by the bombing.

We started to write using small hand-held slates and slate-pencils and when we had mastered the alphabet and basic writing we graduated to using pencil and paper. Every morning we would arrive at school clutching our greaseproof paper-wrapped lunches which our lady-teacher would label before storing them in a huge hinged desk-like cupboard, to be opened at noon. We were given a free issue of one-third of a pint of milk which we drank through a straw pushed through a hole in the bottle's cardboard top.

I travelled to school on foot with my sister Peggy and soon made friends with classmates. I will always remember, to my lasting shame, and because she always took great delight in recounting the story, that at one of my friends' fifth birthday party in a house near the school, loath to miss any of the party and too shy to ask where the lavatory was, I had a most embarrassing accident and had to beat a hasty and uncomfortable retreat home. I  don't remember much more about my time at the Infants' school except that in 1935 we received a blue hardback souvenir book on Portsmouth and a china mug to commemorate the Silver Jubilee of King George V.   We also had a party in our street at which my Uncle Will played the drums. I still have the book and mug. One thing I do recall is that I was happy in the Infants School, made good progress and, in common with all of my classmates, when I 'went up' to the 'Juniors', I could read and write.

I remember the great excitement of joining the boys-only Junior School at Reginald Road. For the first time I was being taught by a schoolmaster, a kindly man named Mr Hosmer whom we called "Sir". We sat in a tiered classroom where the windows were too high to look out, but where the whole class could see the teacher and the blackboard and he could see every pupil. Each desk had an inkwell and on the first day we were all issued with wooden pens with a small replaceable metal nib and introduced to writing in ink in 'joined up' letters. We quaintly called this "ladies writing".

Discipline was firm and fair and we all respected the teachers. We were encouraged to join the local public library and most of us became avid readers. The school had a very good orchestra and the concerts given by successive groups of musically talented youngsters of between seven and eleven were always well attended by parents and pupils. I recall happily joining the whole assembly in singing "Land of Hope and Glory" at the end of these popular evening events. We were all very proud of our school and our country.

Naturally, as boys we all aspired to play football for the school. Our First XI was one of the best in the city and you had to be very good to be chosen to play, an honour I never achieved. Inter school matches were well supported by all of the teachers and pupils.

I enjoyed my childhood at Eastney, at school and at play. I belonged to a gang of boys of the same age who learnt to swim in the sea and amassed great collections by asking holidaymakers if we could have their cigarette cards. I was never bullied and cannot recall anyone else being badly treated. Our street seldom saw a vehicle and we were able to play marbles in the gutter and cricket and football against the end wall of the terrace, without any danger to ourselves or complaints from the neighbours. We walked everywhere ranging as far as Clarence pier, Hayling ferry and Milton Park. It was just as well that, because my family was considered to be 'poor', we were given free boots, which we collected from a depot in Goldsmith's Avenue opposite Fratton station. My chums and I spent a lot of time on the beach or in Eastney Barracks, which we entered unchallenged by the small gate to the north of the main gate, our frequent presence being tolerated by the marines since we posed no security threat. My mother regularly gave me 3d to have a haircut but I used to get one in the barracks for 2d and have a penny to spend on hot chestnuts from a stall or an ice cream from the Stop Me and Buy One man on his tricycle. I remember our gang, led by older lads from the street, scouring the butts of the pistol range for lead bullets and taking them home, melting them down and making fishing weights. Occasionally, fishermen would row out from Eastney beach in a semi-circle letting out a net. When they reached the shore further along, the fishermen asked everyone on the beach, including us boys, to help them pull in the net from each end and to land the catch. We were rewarded with a fish to take home to our parents. I remember seeing the giant towers being erected along Eastney promenade. We didn't know that they were to become a part of history when they were used for the first trials of radar. After school in the summer, my sister and I used to collect the abandoned deckchairs from all over Eastney beach and return them to the attendant to stack neatly above the high water line. This was hard work for seven and eight year olds but we were given a penny each for our labours and always spent it on a 'lucky dip' at a shop near Bransbury Park. If we were lucky we would win tuppence or even thruppence worth of sweets for 1d.

My sister kept watch from Nana's front room on the Bubble-

gum machine outside the corner shop opposite. It gave two packets of gum to every 4$^{th}$ customer. She would alert her friends or us when it was due to 'cough-up'. As we did not attend a Catholic school Margaret and I went to St Swithun's school every Saturday morning and Sunday afternoon for religious instruction. We walked there and back with an older girl called Monica Baker who went to the Southern Secondary school. Every Sunday morning we again walked that not inconsiderable distance again with Mum to attend mass. Although we seldom if

*Nana, Peggy, Eileen, Don, in 1936* ever missed Saturday and Sunday school, we did not fare well at the annual prize-giving. All of the good prizes had been taken by the time our names were called. One year my prize was a Japanese Box, which I thought was full of sweets. When I opened it on the way home I found it was empty! However, that box, now rather battered, has held my toilet gear through 70 years of travel and I would have felt lost without it. It served to remind me of the first time I was 'seen off' and I doubt that any of the other children at that prize-giving still have their prizes.

During my second year in the junior school, just after Christmas 1936, my happy young days at Reginald Road School came to an end. I was taken to hospital to have my adenoids removed and then suffered from mumps, measles and several other childhood illnesses including scarlet fever. I vaguely remember spending my eighth birthday in hospital and, on various other occasions when I was taken away by ambulance, I recall my friends waving me off. I understand I was rather poorly during this period and caused my parents much anxiety. This bout of ill health required a total of nine months in various hospitals and left me in a weak state, further more, an X-ray had revealed that I had a scar on one lung. By the time I was finally discharged from hospital, I had gone from a chubby little boy to a skinny lad and, as I was considered to be a 'delicate' child, I was sent directly to a local sanatorium for a further six months. During that year and three months 'out'. I had no schooling at all. However, I could read well, there were plenty of 'good' books and I was able to make some academic progress on my own.

Langstone Sanatorium was situated close to the Western shore of Langstone harbour at the end of Locksway Road. The children's wing was in the north-east corner of the sanatorium site, occupying 'Beach Lodge' a detached brick-built Edwardian house. The adult patients were accommodated in individual wooden chalets, some of which could be turned to face the sun and all were of 'open' construction. This spartan accommodation remained in use until just after World War 2 when the sanatorium was closed, the chalets

were demolished and the site was sold, for private housing
However, 'Beach Lodge', (shown below) and the main building of
the sanatorium, 'Langstone Lodge',
were still in use in April 2006 as
private homes and sections of the
railings around the sanatorium
were still standing, though they
were rather dilapidated.

I remember that at Langstone
we slept with all of the sash
windows open, winter and summer and at low tide could smell the
awful, but allegedly healthy odour of the mudflats just beyond the
iron railings around the sanatorium. There was a Matron in charge
of the house, whose name now escapes me, but I do recall a Nurse
Marsh. This lovely auburn-haired lady looked after us very well,
showing a personal interest in all of the boys and girls in her care
and we were a happy bunch of children. Although part of it, we had
little contact with the sanatorium, living, sleeping and taking our
wholesome meals in Beach Lodge. However, on several occasions,
for reasons unknown to me, we had our lunch in the main part of
the sanatorium with the adult patients not confined to bed. On
these occasions we walked in a 'crocodile' to the main dining hall
escorted by our matron and nurses. On the way we passed chalets
on whose verandas men and women patients slept in all weathers. I
also vividly recall seeing rats scurrying along the side of the path as
we made our way to lunch.

At Langstone we didn't do any 'outside activities' or physical
exercises. However there was a plentiful supply of games and jig-
saw puzzles and lots of 'good' books, most of which I read during
my six month long sojourn.

I was at Langstone in December 1937 when the comics 'Dandy'
and 'Beano' were first published. Although I was not quite nine

years old I found them too juvenile for my taste. In retrospect, I wish I had kept those first issues, which are now worth a fortune. I also recall lying in bed on the evening of Christmas Eve 1937 and overhearing my parents handing my Christmas presents to the Matron at the front door. I then went happily to sleep. By April 1938, the scar on my lung was identified as stemming from the Whooping Cough I had suffered from as an infant and not  indicative of a serious problem and my discharge was imminent. I am eternally grateful for the kindness and professional care shown me at Langstone by the staff of the childrens wing, in particular Nurse Lilian Marsh. I was very sorry to hear, in 2006 that this truly dedicated children's nurse had died of Tuberculosis in 1940, at the early age of 40.

My final memory of Langstone was destined however to be the least pleasant because I had the misfortune to catch a hospital infection in the shape of Impetigo and was isolated from the other children at Beach Lodge for two weeks whilst this nasty very contagious complaint was cured. I was then transferred to Futcher's Open Air School of Recovery at Drayton, as a resident (i.e. boarder).

Futcher's School, named after its founder, a local philanthropist called Thomas Futcher, had opened in 1927 and was the (Portsmouth) Council School of Recovery (CSR). It specialised in teaching "crippled and delicate children" and accommodated 70 day and 10 resident pupils, providing them with a "healthy environment, plenty of fresh air, exercise and good food". The pupils, whose ages ranged from five to fourteen years, were allocated to one of three classes by their academic ability rather than age and the school's aim was to advance their education, whilst restoring them to full health so that they could return to mainstream schools.

The school stood in the extensive grounds of a Victorian house, on the North side of the Havant Road at Drayton. The school buildings also included a cottage and former stables and classrooms whose glass walls opened outwards on to verandas on all sides. As I recall, the

curriculum was divided between lessons in the '3 Rs', rather a lot of instruction and practice in handicrafts, such as cane basket and wool rug making and regular PE. School hours were 0845 to 1545 daily, special buses carrying the day pupils to and from school. Day and resident pupils were given a cooked lunch including fresh vegetables and fruit from the school gardens. Every

day all pupils had to take half an hour's post-prandial rest on a stretcher laid out on the lawns or the verandas, depending on the weather. Pupils placed their own stretchers in position, and in the winter were provided with a blanket but never with a pillow. Quite incredibly this daily period of rest was spent in silence, and at the end, the pupils folded up their stretchers and returned them to the stowage. The children also took part in School plays and I recall playing a minor role in 'A Midsummer Night's Dream' with the stage-set hand painted by one of the teachers. At the South-east corner of the school grounds stood a large diagonally-striped wooden summerhouse in which we were taught the rudiments of photography and botany. I was a resident in the 'House' for the summer term of 1938 and remember sleeping in a boys dormitory with all of the windows open. One of my cherished memories of that time is listening to a solo-violinist busker outside the Drayton

Institute opposite, playing Dvorak's 'Humoresque'. I am sure my love of classical music stems from the efforts of that be-medalled ex-soldier.

The food at Futcher's was wholesome and doubtless very nourishing but as a child, I hated certain things such as Pigeon Pie, figs and the skin on top of rice pudding. I used to skim off the top, wrap it surreptitiously in my handkerchief and later secretly drop it down the grill of the drain on the veranda. The same fate awaited the skin off the nightly cup of Horlicks. Just before the end of the summer term of 1938 I was considered fit enough to become a day pupil and thereafter travelled to and from home in one of the special buses.

I recall that my parents purchased a cane waste-paper basket and a raffia bag I had made at school, for a total of two shillings. This modest charge, not inconsiderable to them, was made to cover the cost of the materials used. I also made several 4 by 2 foot wool rugs to order and understand they were sold to defray the cost of the Paton and Baldwin wool, the paper pattern and the canvas used to produce these quality, deep pile, hook-knotted, long lasting wool rugs. Though laborious, making these attractive goods gave us youngsters a pride of achievement, particularly when the purchaser enthused about our workmanship. Years later, when away at sea, I made a number of rugs which graced our home for more than twenty years.

As 'delicate children', we did not play team games, but probably had much more PE than most children. We did not have a school uniform but wore a small circular tin badge bearing the words 'Futcher's School' in black letters on a white background. I remember playing football at Eastney with my old chums from Reginald Road who were wearing the school strip. I was the butt of some ribald comments when I turned up in a gym shirt emblazoned with a tin badge. During the summer holidays of 1938 my Uncle

Will Elderfield, a painter and decorator who owned the only car in our street – there's posh for you, took his wife, who was my Dad's sister and my Auntie Kate, their son Stanley and me to Reigate for the day to visit his brother and family. This was the first time I had ever been in a car and I enjoyed the trip very much and recall that I 'hit it off' well with my new-found 9 years old distant cousin Jean.

Shortly afterwards my Dad secured his first permanent job in 13 years, as a sorter at the GPO close to Portsmouth Guildhall. At the same time, possibly because 'the Authorities' thought our summer accommodation was not really ideal for 'delicate' children, my parents were offered the tenancy of a three-bed-roomed, semi-detached council house at Hilsea for a rent of 10 shillings and sixpence per week. They jumped at the chance of having their own home for the first time and Dad was delighted as it had a large garden. He gave up his allotment at Milton and on the 25th August 1938, we moved into our 'new' home. I remember Nana encouraged the three of us children to buy 'Something for the new house' from our pocket money and for some strange reason I bought a lavatory cleaning brush and stand with which my parents affected delight. The new house had a bathroom with hot running water, a real luxury, and we had the whole house and garden to ourselves. We soon settled down at Hilsea but found we had little in common with the local children. I missed my friends at Eastney but made friends with four boys from St John's College who served mass at the garrison chapel in Hilsea Barracks. These lads, Teddy and Pat Fitzgerald, Bernard Seabourne and Dennis O'Neil encouraged me to join them as an altar server for, and under the Latin tutelage of, the legendary and saintly Chaplain, Father Freeley. Forty years later I was honoured to be able to assist, in a small way, the author Mrs Danielle Miles, with some research for the biography entitled 'Knight of Sport, Champion of the Underprivileged, Father Frederick Freeley CF, MC', published in 1981. Sadly Father Freeley died in 1942, his Senior Server Teddy

Fitzgerald was killed during the D Day landings and his No 2 Server Bernard died from wounds sustained at Anzio.

In 1939, my six year old sister Eileen, who had also suffered a succession of childhood illnesses, joined me as a day pupil at Futcher's and travelled to and from school with me in the bus. By then my father had 'licked his new gardens into shape', was growing almost all the vegetables we ate and rearing rabbits for the table. Eileen and I did not have to travel so far to school; she was in the 'Infants' class taught by Miss Cat. I was generally taught by the other teacher, a Mrs Turton but often, the head teacher Miss Cooke took a group of us for more advanced work. I recall having Miss Cooke's permission for a day off school to accompany my father to Goodwood on 25th July 1939 to watch the 'Stewards Cup'. Next day she made me give her and the class a talk on my day at the races. I recall that she asked me if my father had won anything on any of the horses and was incredulous when I said "No, he is not a gambler". That incident was to be my penultimate memory of Futcher's School at Drayton for on 1st September 1939, the world turned upside down.

# Chapter 2

## *Evacuation Part 1- Bishopstoke 1939 – 40*

Two days before the outbreak of the Second World War, I was evacuated at the age of ten, from home in Portsmouth to Bishopstoke, near Eastleigh with some 60 pupils of the Futcher School. Blissfully unaware of how long we would be away from home we excitedly boarded a convoy of three brand-new Corporation single-decker buses for the 23-mile journey. At the same time my older sister Peggy, who attended Northern Parade School, was evacuated to the village of Bramshaw in the New Forest.

The 11 to 14 year olds of Futcher's school travelled in the lead bus with Miss Cooke the Head Teacher, the juniors, including myself in the second bus with Mrs Turton, and infants, including my six-year old sister Eileen, in the third with their teacher Miss Cat.

In those days the Futcher's School at Drayton was an 'Open-

Air School of Recovery', most of whose pupils were considered to be in need of a special healthy regimen after having spent long periods in hospitals and/or sanatoria. In our case we were considered to be 'delicate children' who would benefit from attending this special school. Several of our fellow pupils suffered from Asthma and a few of the children who were accompanied by carers, wore iron leg calipers following Infantile Paralysis (Polio) or Rickets but the rest were not at all disabled.

We arrived at the village school around 11am. After being counted, given lunch and arranged in groups, we were each given a brown paper carrier bag containing an apple, chocolate biscuits, and a tin of corned beef and condensed milk before setting off in a crocodile to our new homes.

My sister and I were allocated to a friendly retired couple, Mr. Hayes and his housekeeper Mrs. Cox who had an 18 year old son. I recall gulping down my tea on that first day in my eagerness to get out, leaving my young sister in Mrs Cox's care, while I went out to explore my new 'playground', the nearby woods.

We were taught separately from the village children in two rooms of an old hut in the school playground. This building was still standing in 1999. There was no facility to practise the handicrafts raffia weaving, cane basket-making and rug-making, which had featured large in the curriculum at Drayton. Furthermore there was no space to carry out the Futcher's daily routine of set exercises or the compulsory rest after lunch. Fortunately this shortcoming was more than compensated for by the fresh air and exercise received naturally in our new environment. However in retrospect, replacement of these activities by academic subjects clearly led to an improvement in the career prospects of the pupils. The most academically able pupils were taught more advanced subjects by the Head teacher and at least some of them would have stood a good chance of passing the scholarship examination for the Portsmouth Secondary (grammar) schools had they been entered for it. However, the educational authorities at the time did not consider this option and our chance was lost.

Several of my sister's school friends were billeted nearby but the other boys in my class lived at the far end of the village so I soon made friends with some local lads, joined their 'gang' and with them the local Scout troop. They taught me how to enjoy country life and, to a city boy, Bishopstoke and the surrounding area was a paradise. I enjoyed fishing, swimming and rafting on the river, camping, tobogganing on Shawford Downs, go-karting and roller skating scarily down steep Spring Lane, 'bird-nesting', not considered taboo in those days, and building a series of secret dens in the woods from which we could observe the abundant wild-life. Every Sunday morning my sister and I walked to Eastleigh to attend mass. Abiding memories of my time at Bishopstoke include:

The comforting sound, at dead of night, of the grandfather clock downstairs.
The bells of St. Mary's church ringing out on Sundays.
Listening to Neville Chamberlain announcing that we were at war.
Recording the arrival of each of the species of migratory birds unknown to a city boy.
Buying a pennyworth of yesterday's cakes or broken biscuits at a confectioners in Eastleigh before going to the cinema children's matinee for twopence.

The winter of 1939 was very cold and there was much more snow than I had ever seen before. I remember the tragic death of one of the local boys who was trapped under the ice on a frozen pond 'our gang' had been playing on the day before. Eric, the son of the house was an apprentice at the Eastleigh railway works and, during the long winter evenings taught me how to make various useful things including a short-wave valved wireless set. I remember the thrill of hearing broadcasts from distant places including the Falkland Islands. Little did I realise that this new hobby was a portent of my future career.

In February 1940 our dear landlady Mrs Cox was taken to hospital and we were moved to the nearby home of Mr. Waters an old -soldier who had won the Croix de Guerre and Medaille Militaire during the Great War. He and his wife were kind to us and he was a splendid old countryman who was a fount of knowledge of matters rural. I enjoyed his stories and helping him in his productive garden during the spring and early summer of 1940 whilst still fully participating in my boyhood adventures with the local lads.

Mum and Dad came to see us several times and letters were frequently exchanged. Our parents were content in the knowledge that we were being well looked after and were happy. In their final visit we were thrilled when they brought with them a mongrel puppy they had named Bob. However, not everyone at our school was happy at Bishopstoke. Two of the younger boys ran away and were caught at Botley on their way home to Portsmouth. Because I was erroneously thought to have been aware of their intention and did not inform on them I was given six of the best on each hand with a thick cane, by the head teacher, in front of the whole school. A later public apology for this miscarriage of justice did something to alleviate the lingering pain.

Other less painful and indeed fond memories I have of Miss Cooke at Bishopstoke include her teaching a small but fascinated group of us the basics of Constitutional History from Anglo-Saxon times to 1914 and examining Current Affairs. The latter, based on a text book published in 1938, contained a Chapter on the British habit of families leaving the comfort of their homes for a week every summer to spend a holiday in less affluent accommodation by the seaside. I recall that this struck a particular chord with me since my family had boarded relatively well-off visitors to supplement a meagre income. I had to write an essay on this phenomenon and widened the subject by adding my experiences as a child member of a host family who had to 'camp-out' in a lean-to shed during the summer season to allow the visitors to use our rooms. Miss Cooke read my effort with surprised interest and questioned me searchingly but sympathetically, in front of the class, on various points I had made. Her reaction and that of my classmates to my answers were to bring home to me, for the first time, just how relatively poor my family had been until 1938.

Following the withdrawal from Dunkirk, the war situation began to look serious We helped the village schoolchildren dig-up the playing fields for air raid shelters and to plant vegetables. The many grandchildren of our foster parents came from Southampton to stay and the resultant overcrowding led to friction between them and us. My sister and I became unhappy and homesick and at the end of the summer term we came home to Portsmouth for the summer holidays and never returned.

The healthy open-air life I enjoyed at Bishopstoke undoubtedly completed my recovery for, when I returned home at the end of July 1940, I was as fit as a fiddle. I am eternally thankful to Mr. Hayes, Mrs Cox and her son Eric, and to Mr. & Mrs  Waters for looking after my sister and me, and to my local friends, specially Desmond Hutchings, for making my first experience of country life so enjoyable. Unfortunately it was difficult to get films during WW2 and I have very few pictures of that period. The picture shown on page 18 is of Mr. & Mrs Waters taken on their 25<sup>th</sup> Wedding Anniversary in 1945. They kindly gave it to me during a visit I made to them in 1949.

Clearly this period of my formative years had a profound and beneficial effect on my health and thus my future. I am also extremely grateful to Miss Cooke and Mrs Turton who, under difficult circumstances, advanced my education so that, by the time I came home from Bishopstoke in July 1940, I had caught up much of my lost schooling.

# Chapter 3

*"Put that book down and pay attention to the air-raid"*
*Portsmouth July 1940 – September 1941*

I returned to Portsmouth from Bishopstoke with my younger sister Eileen on the 26th July 1940, just after the first air-raid on the city. I remember showing a somewhat morbid interest in the damage caused at Kingston Cross and the list of casualties posted on the Police Station notice board. A few weeks later, during a family picnic on Portsdown Hill I watched in fascination as German Me109 fighters shot down a number of barrage balloons with short bursts from their cannons, the blazing balloons falling lazily to the ground. Shortly afterwards I saw Ju 87 Stukas dive-bombing the harbour area and Ju 88s dropping bombs on the city. It was strange to be witnessing this raid from a vantage point without any apparent risk to ourselves. We were to learn when we got home that the Prince's cinema had been hit during a matinee; killing a large number of children. This quickly brought home to me the seriousness of what I had witnessed.

Throughout the remainder of the school summer-holidays of 1940 the Battle of Britain raged overhead, the blue skies streaked with interwoven vapour trails as the 'few' of the RAF battled with the enemy hordes. During this period there were several air-raids on Portsmouth. The authorities quickly offered to re-evacuate all of the many children who had returned to the city from the relative safety of the countryside. My parents decided that my two sisters Peggy (12) and Eileen (7) should go to Petworth. Before they left, my sisters and I had the only photograph taken of us together during the war. I prevailed upon them to let me stay in Portsmouth and return to the school I had attended until I was nearly eight years old, when I began my long illness and convalescence. As this was close to where my grandmother lived alone, it was agreed that I would rejoin Reginald Road School and move in with Nana, returning every Sunday to my parents at Hilsea for mass and lunch before catching the bus back to Eastney.

Many of the Portsmouth schools had by this time been commandeered for war use as First-Aid posts, stores etc and so those still open had to double-up. We had to make do with half-time schooling, attending school mornings one week and afternoons the next. Later on we had an extra 'holiday' when an unexploded bomb landed in the playground and took several school days to make safe.

One of the features of all of the air-raids on Portsmouth was the terrific noise, for the city was very well defended by Anti-Aircraft guns. There were fixed mountings at Fort Cumberland and Southsea Common and lots of mobile guns scattered around the city in addition to those mounted on the ships in the harbour and the Solent. During the three great Blitzes and other less destructive raids, the almost incessant noise of the barrage, not to mention the loud explosions of bursting bombs, was sometimes strangely broken by short periods of eerie silence when all you could hear was the throbbing drone of the bombers. I well remember the night of the first Blitz on 10th January 1941, Nana and I were finishing our evening meal and listening to the 6 o'clock news when the air raid siren sounded and almost at once the nearby AA guns opened fire, bombs began falling and there was a complete electricity failure. We took cover under the dining table but shortly afterwards, a loud banging on the front door signalled my uncle Will Elderfield who said "This looks like it is going to be a heavy raid, you had better come to our shelter". We kept close to the front wall of the terraced houses to avoid the falling shrapnel as we made our way to his house three doors down the street. As we stepped out of the conservatory door to run down the garden to the Anderson shelter during a lull in the bombardment, the deathly silence was shattered by the piercing shriek of the double-barrelled Lewis gun on the top of the nearby Eastney barracks tower attempting to extinguish a German flare which was brightly illuminating the area. I nearly jumped out of my skin at this sudden and unexpected sound! We took shelter with my Auntie Kate, Uncle Will and a friend of theirs from Cardiff who told us that during a recent raid on the Welsh capital "The fires had been so bright that you could read a newspaper by the glare"! Uncle's shelter was luxurious compared to ours but their heating and lighting was useless without electricity and we had to leave the door ajar. Within twenty minutes we too were able to read by the red glare of the fires caused by the thousands of incendiary bombs and many HE bombs dropped on the city!

The first phase of the blitz lasted a couple of hours and then there was a lull of about two to three hours while the German bombers returned to their bases in Northern France to refuel and re-arm before coming back to further hammer the burning city. During this lull, while fire fighters and servicemen fought desperately to extinguish the many fires threatening to engulf the city, my Auntie Nell Murdoch and her daughter Jean returned home to Reginald Road to find their home badly damaged. They had been watching a film at the Odeon Southsea and had taken shelter nearby during the first phase of the blitz. A bomb had struck the house directly opposite theirs killing a whole family, including one of my classmates at the nearby school. My cousin Jean, who was on leave from the WRNS, and her mother, came around to us in Tokar Street in some distress, just in time to join the five of us in

Uncle Will's shelter for the second phase of the blitz in which the bombers, using the raging fires as markers, rained HE bombs down on the city. By then we had two oil lamps burning and kept the shelter door firmly closed. Family folklore has it that during the worst of those two hours of incessant bombing, the only child in a shelter full of adults and fully engrossed in my book, I was famously told by my grandmother to "put down that book and pay attention to the air-raid"!

Next morning I went with my aunt and cousin to their severely damaged house and helped them to recover some of their treasured items from the ruins. I recall the utter chaos of the scene, debris, soot and broken glass all over the road, a ruptured gas main still burning and the bomb crater full of water from a broken water main.

My father, a former soldier and a member of the Home Guard, was a Sorter at the GPO and just before Christmas 1940 was working in the Connaught Drill Hall, which was being used as an overflow sorting office, when a bomb landed nearby. He was buried under a collapsed wall and was dug out bruised and bloodied. Two weeks later as duty 'Fire-watcher' on the roof of the GPO during the 10th January blitz he helped save the building by extinguishing several incendiaries with sandbags and a stirrup pump but, from his isolated position, had to watch helplessly as the adjacent Guildhall and shops in Commercial Road went up in flames. Geoff Elderfield, a cousin by marriage, who had been bombed out of Ariel Road in Fratton, came to live with Auntie Kate and we went to school and often played together. We collected wickedly jagged pieces of shrapnel and the occasional burnt-out incendiary bomb and took them to Milton Police station and otherwise generally made the most of our limited recreational facilities, the nearby beach being fenced off. Another uncle, Harry Elderfield, who taught woodwork at our school, took us both under his wing and, since we only had half-day schooling, set us extra homework to prepare us for the

March 1941 'Scholarship' exams. Geoff was hoping to get into the city's Southern Secondary school and I aimed to grasp my only chance of a secondary education by passing the '12 plus' entrance exam for the Junior Technical School.

I was also a member of Eastney Boys' Club in Prince Albert Street. I remember being caught at the club during a raid and taking shelter under a billiard table with a crowd of lads all loudly singing songs to drown out the noise of the AA barrage and bombs. When the raid ended I ran home to a very anxious grandmother. At the club we were instructed in First-Aid and I came first in the final exam and won the prize of 10 shillings! I was delighted, and somewhat amazed, and ran home to tell Nana of my good fortune. She, being a thrifty Scot, insisted that I banked all of it!

On March 10th there was another heavy two-part blitz on Portsmouth and this time Nana and I were alone in our Anderson shelter. It was heated and lit by paraffin and was reasonably cosy and I spent most of the time reading. Towards the end of the first phase of the blitz, we heard the unnerving whistling scream of an approaching bomb and felt the violent shaking of the ground and the very loud bang of a nearby explosion. My grandmother cried out "The house has gone"! I turned down the lamp and opened the door but couldn't see the house because of a thick pall of brick dust and had to shut the door quickly as debris, thrown into the air by the explosion, began to fall. With the naivety of youth I confirmed Nana's worst fears at which she went into a sort of trance, moaning and crying. My first-aid training hadn't covered this sort of thing and, unable to bring her round, I opened the door to seek help. Straight away I saw, now that the dust had settled, that the house was still standing, indeed, apart from some fallen ceilings, broken windows and lots of soot all over the place, it was undamaged. I tried to reassure Nana but to no avail and, unable to alert the neighbours whose shelter door was firmly closed, I climbed over the three low garden walls to reach my Uncle's shelter, knocked on the door and asked my uncle to come to Nana's aid. He did so bringing with him a small flask of brandy which quickly restored my hitherto life-long teetotal grandmother to normal! Shortly afterwards the mid-blitz lull commenced and we all went into our house and, finding the gas still available made a pot of tea. In the dark, there being no electricity, we hadn't noticed that some of the soot and ceiling plaster had managed to get into the kettle via the spout and the longed for cuppa tasted absolutely foul. We then went out into the street to watch the Royal Marines fighting a huge fire raging in Eastney bus depot and saw burning buses being driven out of the depot. We spent the second half of the blitz in Uncle's shelter, Nana sleeping and me revising for the imminent exam.

A few days later the exam day dawned and being keen and because the trolley buses were out of action due to the lines being down, I set off early, before the morning post arrived, to make my way to Penhale Road School where I was to sit the exam. On arrival I found the school had been bombed during the blitz and the staff were feverishly burrowing in the debris to salvage books. On enquiring "Where is the scholarship exam being held?" I was told that all candidates had been informed by post that, because of enemy action it had been moved to Lyndhurst Road School. Not knowing where that was, I must have looked devastated for a kind lady teacher told me how to get there and gave me sixpence for the bus fare and wished me luck. With the help of an incredibly old single-decker petrol bus I reached the new exam venue with seconds to spare.

Halfway through the first exam paper the siren sounded and we were ordered to stop writing and to file silently out to the air-raid shelter and to sit mutely with our arms folded while the AA guns engaged a photographic reconnaissance aircraft. At the 'all-clear' we marched back silently to our desks and resumed the exam. During the lunch-break I remember visiting the new branch of Woolworths opened that morning on the corner of London and Chichester Roads to replace the branches in Commercial and King's Roads destroyed in the January blitz. I have some other vivid memories of Portsmouth's darkest days:

Walking to my parents home after serving mass on the Sunday after the 10th January blitz and seeing a line of fire-engines in the liveries of the 'City of London, of Oxford' and of Birmingham' parked along the Old London Road at Hilsea while their crews took a well-earned rest. Hearing fulsome praise of their heroism from the First World War hero and saintly priest Fatherm Frederick Freeley MC. Being given two shillings by my grandmother to buy 'war-damaged' tins of food sold for a penny or two each in a special shop opened after every blitz. Many tins had no labels and whilst tins of herrings or sardines were obvious from the shape,  ordinary tins could contain carrots or plums or anything. I recall I was not particularly lucky in my choice.

Seeing armed soldiers, patrolling the streets around the badly damaged Co-Op Department Store in Fratton Road, to prevent looting. Being sent home from school one day in May 1941 when the news broke of the sinking of HMS Hood, because so many of the boys had fathers or brothers serving in her.

The third and last great blitz on Portsmouth took place on the night of 27th April 1941. This time the city was attacked by HE bombs and a new weapon – a parachute bomb, rather oddly called a 'land mine', presumably because it was spherical like a sea mine, although it was not detonated underground or underwater but in the air on first surface contact. This inaccurate weapon gave no warning of its approach and its distinctive loud 'whooshing' explosion, caused enormous surface blast damage. It was of course an indiscriminate weapon of terror and it was very fortunate for us that shortly afterwards, the bulk of the Luftwaffe was moved East to prepare for the German invasion of Russia in June 1941.

In early July the scholarship examination results were published in the Evening News and Geoff and I had passed. I came 18th in my Exam and would be leaving Portsmouth in September for Salisbury to join the evacuated JTS. Just before then my parents took me to Petworth to see my sisters. Looking back on the period described in this Chapter I often think how lucky I, and my family were to survive the blitzes and also wonder how different my subsequent life would have been if that kind teacher at Penhale Road had not come to my rescue – bless her!

# Chapter 4

## *Evacuation Part 2- Salisbury, September 1941 – July 1944*

In early September 1941, I set off by train to Salisbury proudly wearing my new school uniform. This comprised a white shirt, blue, black and white striped tie, black blazer and cap each with gold wire badge depicting a galleon and the motto 'Veritas Honor, Virtus' and the name Portsmouth Junior Technical School.

My first billet at Salisbury was a rambling old house next door to a brewery whose revolting and pervading smell very nearly put this son of a teetotal family off beer for life! Six or seven boys from my new school were billeted there and it was overcrowded. There was insufficient food for growing lads and I and others had to sleep on the landing. The couple owning this establishment ran it as a business and I didn't get on at all well with either of them. At the first half-term, at my request, I was moved to another billet in an old part of the town to the home of a soldier and his wife. Mr and Mrs Pragnell were kind to me and I settled down and was briefly joined by my younger sister while my mother, who was nursing my father, was herself taken seriously ill.

I was happy at school, had a lot of respect for the teachers and enjoyed the camaraderie of an all-boys senior school. In the mornings we attended classes in a collection of church-hall rooms; in the afternoons lessons were held in the classrooms and laboratories of the Bishop Wordsworth School. We worked from 8-45 am to 4-45pm daily and until noon on Saturdays, to make up for one afternoon of sports. At Salisbury there were no facilities for the teaching of metal or woodwork and so the time that would have been spent on practical technical instruction was devoted instead to academic subjects. In fact the 'A' stream followed the wide curriculum of the secondary (grammar) schools.

The Headmaster 'Dan' Dunne was a remote figure and boys only saw him when they were in trouble. My only encounter with him was in the second year when he learned that I was delivering newspapers in the morning before school. Although I told him my school uniform was not visible under my coat he told me to pack up the job because "it was unbecoming of a pupil of this school". Such social attitudes were the norm in those days!

The day to day running of the school was in the able hands of 'Cherry' Mead the Deputy Head who also took our class for English. Throughout the three years, my Math's teacher was the renowned W 'Gus' Gates, my Science teacher and Form Master was 'Bill Blood'. Our French teacher was the fearsome 'Pongo' Partridge and we were taught art by the rather tattily gowned and black-bearded giant 'Ronnie' Redpath, whose terse and damming final report on my art was that I "had no ability and showed no interest". Fortunately the other teachers were more appreciative of my efforts.

I was the only Catholic in my class and was often publicly ribbed by one of the masters because his hero Galileo had been persecuted by a XV11th century Pope. One Sunday, after I had stepped-in at the last minute, for the nominated server at mass in St. Osmunds church, I was severely rebuked by the priest for wearing plimsolls. Possibly, out of innate contrariness, I didn't let these incidents rock my faith, for I continued to attend musical concerts in which my tormentor played the violin, and carried on regularly serving mass.

We had little contact with the local schoolboys except at sports and in the Scouts, forming groups of friends from within our own school. My form mates at school were Ray Dixon, Bob Gilbey and Bob Forsyth. At the end of each term we all returned to Portsmouth for the holidays in a special train with the girls of the Southern Secondary School, the teachers enforcing a strict segregation between them and us. Two of us boys were once publicly thrown out of the girls' half of the train by one of our masters, to the amusement of both schools! Most of us also went home for the half-term long-weekend breaks.

My memories of Salisbury include many weekend scout camping expeditions to Woodford and Great Yews; collecting waste paper for the war effort; guiding Allied troops around the historic city; milking the cows brought overnight to market on Tuesdays and bellowing for relief in the auctioneer's yard; sketching the cathedral from every angle during al-fresco art lessons; French lessons from 'Pongo' Partridge; experiments in the chemistry lab with 'Sep' Philips; being ordered to write the definition of potential energy 80 times by Bill Blood, I still remember it to this day; learning to waltz in a church hall with girls of the Portsmouth South and South Wilts Secondary schools to a gramophone record of 'The Blue Danube' and the whole school lustily singing patriotic songs during the last period of the half-term Friday before we dashed off to catch the always late 5-05 train home to Portsmouth.

In January 1943 my dear father passed away at the age of 45 after an eighteen months battle with cancer. A lifelong teetotaller and non smoker, he died from cancer of the bronchus after a hard life with little comfort. In fact he never had a holiday or ever had a ride in a car. He was a good Christian who, undemonstrative, as most Britons of Scottish origin were in those days, loved his children, never raised his voice or hand against us, or swore. He dedicated all of his modest income and spare time to the welfare of his family. I wish I could have given him some of the good times I have subsequently enjoyed in abundance. My mother, by then recovered from her illness and left to provide for three children alone, went out to work and decided it would be best if I continued with my education. In the summer of 1943 my landlady Mrs Pragnell, whose genial husband was, by then serving in Burma, gave birth to her first child which, tragically, was stillborn. She was absolutely devastated and went to live with her mother. I moved to my final evacuee billet with a jolly couple formerly from London. My new landlord Mr Lowe was a postman with two grown-up daughters who rather spoiled me. I was treated as a member of the family and had a happy last year at Salisbury.

My Irish grandma, then 68, took a break from her busy job as District Nurse and Midwife, and risked two wartime crossings of the sea to visit her sons' families in Manchester and her only daughter's family in Portsmouth also travelling to Salisbury to see me. Granny was a lovely, lively, relatively well-off lady who liked the finer things in life and she took me out to the best café in town, the Cadena where, in the company of a number of other well dressed ladies and officers in uniform, I enjoyed a fabulous  tea with dainty sandwiches and quite delightful cakes, with the tea poured from a silver teapot by a uniformed waitress wearing a white lace cap. I later wondered how such a feast was available, in those days of severe rationing, in the middle of the war. By then Granny had two sons in POW camps in Germany and Malaya and her youngest, my Uncle Olly, who was only six years older than me, having survived the Arctic sinking of HMS Trinidad and the loss of HMS Quayle in the Med, was on his way out to the Pacific from where he later returned after Okinawa in the kamikaze-damaged HMS Ulster.

The great Depression of the 1930s, with its mass unemployment, led to teenage boys being advised by their elders that they should learn a trade so that they would have something to fall back on if hard times returned after the war. The prevailing wisdom among teachers was that the post war employment market would return to the pre-war pattern.

In broad terms this was:

10% Professionals recruited from university graduates
25% Skilled, workers who had completed an apprenticeship
65% Semi. or Unskilled, lowly paid workers in insecure jobs.

As there was no 6th form at my school, there was no chance. or expectation of going to university, so my career aspirations were limited to the only two options available during wartime, that provided further study and an interesting paid job, viz :

An RN Artificer Apprenticeship with 4 years guaranteed further academic and technical study

A Dockyard Apprenticeship with technical study of up to 4 years, depending on yearly progress

Access to either of these well respected apprenticeships was by the Civil Service Commission Open Competitive Examination for entry to the Royal Navy as an Artificer Apprentice, or to any of the four Naval Dockyards or Admiralty Weapons Factories as a Craft Apprentice. The exam was held every April at various centres throughout the country.

I understand that I had shown some interest in joining the navy after seeing, at the age of six, a poster saying, "Men and Boys Wanted for the Royal Navy". However, I had never been aboard a warship, or been inside Portsmouth Dockyard, even to visit HMS Victory. I had enjoyed witnessing the 1935 and 1937 Spithead Fleet Reviews from Southsea front and had been aboard the liner Berengaria during a day trip to Southampton with my parents in 1935. I had also visited Ireland twice before the war. In 1944, the navy was very highly regarded by British society and so, with all the patriotic fervour of youth and little real thought of the consequences, I decided that a life on the ocean wave held the greater attraction for me and applied to take the examination. In previous years this had comprised 5 subjects, reportedly at School Certificate level but, in

1944 and subsequent years, History and Geography, two of my best subjects, were dropped for some reason. I stayed behind at Salisbury for the first week of the Easter holidays, to sit the papers in Mathematics, Science and English, each exam lasting three hours. I then went home to Portsmouth for the rest of the holiday,

During the second week of that holiday, after getting special permission to travel, I crossed to the Isle of Wight with my mother to visit my sister Eileen who was recovering from TB in the sanatorium at Haven Street. I recall seeing lots of Italian former POWs wearing chocolate-coloured battle-dress with yellow patches on them cheerfully working in the fields around the sanatorium, I also vividly remember the trip across a Solent packed with shipping, landing-craft and lots of strange looking floating concrete platforms, all protected by water-borne Barrage balloons We wondered what these strange 'vessels' were. We were to realise later that they were parts of the famous Mulberry Harbour.

Back at school I witnessed the incredible build-up of troops around Salisbury and the mass movement of tanks. On the night of 5/6th June, Mrs Lowe woke me to look at hundreds of aircraft towing gliders passing low overhead with their navigation lights switched on. We had often heard great numbers of allied aircraft before, but they had never flown so low or showed lights so we assumed it must be an exercise Next morning we realised from the news that we had seen the spearhead of the invasion setting out for France.

A few days later, I was notified that I had been placed 18th in the examination for entry to the navy as an Artificer Apprentice. The letter enclosed a copy of the following recruitment advert describing the role of Artificers in the Royal Navy and, since my position in the order of merit enabled me to choose, asked me, which branch I wished to join.

"The best paid branches in the Navy are the Artificer branches, of which there are three: Engine Room Artificers, Electrical Artificers and Ordnance Artificers. Known respectively as ERAs, EAs and OAs, the artificers are the petty officers and chief petty officers responsible for the operation and maintenance and repair of engines, electrical equipment and torpedoes, gun machinery, and fire-control equipment. The work is highly skilled and responsible, and the pay is correspondingly higher than in other branches".

I made my career choice at the age of 15 ½ at the prospect of being responsible for torpedoes, and joined the navy as one of the first class of EAs not to be trained in their maintenance, this being taken over by OAs in exchange for weapons fire-control equipment!

I travelled to Southampton to take the medical examination. Bearing in mind my earlier medical problems, it is noteworthy that I was one of only 8 of the 16 candidates that day who passed this final hurdle! At the end of the summer term, after a tremendous farewell party given by my 'foster parents', I left school and Salisbury and on the 2nd.August 1944 began a naval career which was to last 35 years.

Looking back, I was reasonably happy and certainly contented in four of my five 'foster' homes at Bishopstoke and Salisbury. I was well looked after and generally treated like one of the family. My mother was particularly thankful for their kindness to me during her illness and the harrowing eighteen months she had nursing my father until his death.

My two sisters, who were evacuated to Petworth in 1940, and several of my classmates, and my Godmother's daughter, were billeted in grand houses at Salisbury but saw little of the host families. The 'upstairs and downstairs' social division was de rigeur at that time and the evacuees were relegated to the servants' quarters. I was fortunate to have been treated as one of the family in all but one of my modest foster homes.

It could be argued that in my case evacuation was a complete waste of time since I was back in Portsmouth for the heavy air raids and Blitzes of 1940 and 1941 and the later holiday-time raids. This view ignores the benefits I gained from spending some of my formative years in the country and having a sound and uninterrupted secondary education in the 'A' stream at the 'Tech'. There, I more than made up for having missed fifteen months of schooling before the war, having two years of education with a limited academic content and a year of half-time schooling during the blitzes. In fact, none of my age group who had attended either of the Portsmouth Secondary (later Grammar) schools, was placed higher than 17th in the National Civil Service Commission examination in 1944. I owe this modest success to the schooling I received at Reginald Rd, Futcher's School, and especially at the JTS.

After the war I visited my former 'foster parents' and kept in touch until they passed-on. On the lst September 1989 my sister and I took Eric Cox, the son of our first evacuee home out to dinner and had a fiftieth anniversary reunion with Des Hutchinson and several other old village friends. I have retained a love of the countryside and a particular affection for Salisbury.

I am eternally grateful to those kindly couples who took me into their homes, shared my joys and sorrows and made me a temporary member of their families at a time my own family was under tremendous pressure. My subsequent life and career was, I believe profoundly influenced for the better by my experiences as an evacuee. Perhaps, one day Britain will acknowledge the thanks it owes to the many thousands of good-hearted ordinary country folk who, for scant reward, upset their homes to take in city children.

# Chapter 5

## Royal Navy Artificers' Training Establishment (RNATE) / HMS Fisgard – August 1944 – August 1948

On 2nd August 1944, after a nine hour rail journey from Portsmouth a crowd of 15/16 year olds arrived at Plymouth North Road station at about 6 pm and were met by a 3 ton lorry, a cheery, rotund Seaman Petty Officer called Trigg and an enthusiastic Scottish PO Physical Training Instructor named Merrillees. PO Alfie Trigg ordered us to "fall in" and told us we were joining Anson Division and that he was our Divisional Petty Officer. PO Jock Merrillees our Divisional PTI, then spoke to us of a mysterious quality called 'Esprit' which he pledged to instill in all of us and which would make us, like our predecessors of Anson 1940 entry, who had just completed their apprenticeship, the best division in RNATE. The lorry took us through the devastation of what had been Devonport before arriving at the Torpoint steam-driven chain ferry. As we crossed the Tamar we marvelled at the sight of every type of warship in Devonport Dockyard.

At about 7pm the lorry entered the near-deserted RNATE, almost all of the apprentices were on leave, and made its way up the East side road. We were allocated to Trevithick 4, 5 & 6 huts. This first muster of the class, and all subsequent musters during the next four years, were carried out alphabetically within the sequence: Engine-Room, Electrical and Ordnance Artificers (ERAs, EAs and OAs). Sixty years later I can still remember the names of my original classmates in that order.

We EAs were allocated T5 hut and I was given a bed below another Portsmouth lad, Eric Lemmon. After unpacking we were ushered down to the Apprentices Dining Hall for a supper comprising the wartime favourite sausages, onions, rich brown gravy and mash. By then all 78 of us lads were starving having had little to eat all day and this first naval meal was devoured with great gusto.

After supper, while we were making our beds, we were visited by a fatherly 'old' Engineer Lieutenant-Commander who gave us a pep talk extolling the importance of the Artificer branches. He told us that we should all aim to become Chief Artificers at an early age and should even aspire to become Engineer Officers. He ended his homily with the words: "Don't worry if you feel homesick on the first night, just have a good cry and then forget it". I don't recall anyone being that upset, perhaps because most of us had already experienced separation from our families by being evacuated.

Next morning, after reveille, we lads leapt keenly out of bed and dashed off to the Ablutions block and later eagerly rushed down to the dining hall for breakfast. We then mustered outside the clothing store, known as the 'Slop Room', and were issued with our uniforms and other kit. We returned to our huts and spent the rest of the day marking our kit. We then changed into our new serge suits and fell in again, this time as the lowliest of the elite Artificer corps – 'A' class Apprentices.

For the next three weeks we underwent much 'square-bashing', physical-training and indoctrination into the ways of the navy, in addition to medical and dental checks and such treatment as found necessary. Whilst having fillings from a dentist, aptly named Payne, I recall that he touched a nerve while using his relatively slow pedal-driven drill and had me writhing in agony as I wished I was with my new classmates marching up and down the parade ground outside the surgery. I have to say however that I still have those fillings, for although now unpopular, Amalgam was good stuff and he was a great dentist. On the first Friday we all received the cocktail of jabs associated with joining the navy, lining up and getting the needle in both arms. I remember going ashore the next day to see the epic film 'Gone With the Wind' in Plymouth. I had read the book at school and was eagerly looking forward to seeing the film, which had only just been generally released. I wasn't feeling too great when the film started, by the half-way intermission I was feeling lousy and by the end I was feeling dreadful. I somehow staggered back to RNATE and at about 6pm, went straight to bed, remaining there and feeling wretched until the Monday morning. Like many of my classmates I was suffering from the aftermath of the TAB jab.

Our uniform comprised a plain navy blue serge suit with black horn buttons, a black cap with flat red badge, white shirt with separate rounded stiff collar, black tie and black boots and socks. In common with qualified artificers, we wore no branch badge and since we had no rank we had bare sleeves. This distinguished us from Junior Supply and Medical ratings who (then) also wore 'fore and aft rig'. For work and square-bashing we wore blue and white striped shirts with separate collars as worn in those and 'Porridge' days by inmates of HM Prisons. Alone of all junior ratings, we were issued with pyjamas. For PT and games we wore yellow sports shirts, Anson's colours, and white shorts and gym shoes.

During our pre-technical training, we were taken to Devonport Barracks Swimming Pool to take the swimming test. This comprised jumping into the deep end wearing a canvas suit, swimming two lengths, treading water for five minutes and swimming one length. Of the 78 in our class, only 15 of us passed. Oddly two of the 15 came from Sutton Coldfield and one of these was to drown in 1945. In those days it was not uncommon for lads, even those living near the sea or sons of sailors and fishermen, to be non-swimmers. Four years later, only those of us who had passed in 1944 were able to pass this test, there having being no swimming facility at Torpoint during the intervening years. On another outing, the class was shown around Devonport Dockyard, saw a cruiser in dock after it had been hit with a torpedo in a boiler room and were taken down a dry dock and under the battleship HMS Anson.

Those first three weeks at Torpoint were bewilderingly hectic and exhausting for all of us and we had no trouble getting to sleep after 'lights out'. At the end of our induction course and just as the other 750 apprentices returned from summer leave and our apprenticeship was about to commence, I took what proved to be 'the wrong path'. On my third Sunday at RNATE I went ashore for a walk with Ian Black, the only other old boy of my school in our class. It was a hot summer's day and after three pennies' worth of baked beans on toast in the YMCA in Torpoint we made our way back to the camp, as we called RNATE. We must have looked like the sprogs we were, dressed in No1 serge suits, with boots and undistorted caps, (we hadn't yet been shown how to mould a 'Tiffies' cap). As we came up the last hill before RNATE we spied, on the right-hand side of the road an orchard in the grounds of a rather nice house. We failed to notice that a pennant was flying from a flagpole in front of the house but saw that some of the apples seemed ready for plucking. We climbed over the low wall and started to help ourselves when a very irate chap dressed like the pensioner attendants who were so kindly looking after us at RNATE and whom we were soon to know rather unkindly as 'gobbies', suddenly pounced on us. He told us he knew we were new recruits, took our names and said he would report us for stealing apples from the Commodore of RN Barracks Devonport's orchard. That evening we were arraigned before the Officer of the Day and in due course, and after much hectoring from several officers, received 5 days 8A punishment and 14 days 'Off Privileged Leave' (OPL). 8A involved sleeping on wooden boards on the floor of T7 the Punishment Hut, getting up at 0600, 30 minutes before Reveille, standing outside the Regulating Office for 30 minutes before breakfast and during dinner time. In the evening after supper, doing 45 minutes 'Jankers', doubling around holding a rifle above one's head or doing strenuous exercises on the parade ground and turning in at 2100 with 'Lights-out' at 2110. OPL meant confined to camp. When Ian and I started our punishment we were joined by a number of apprentices of all classes who had come back adrift from leave or had committed offences on return. These included several of RNATE's renowned defaulters, known in the navy as 'skates'. After T7 'lights-out' we sprogs were regaled with stories of past escapades by the 'old lags'.

Although I had attended a Technical school, I had received an academic education with no instruction in metal work and I was a complete ignoramus on the use of tools and had never even visited a workshop. I was therefore somewhat mystified as to what use I would make of the centre punch, scriber, hammer and chisels - the total contents of the wooden toolbox with which I had been issued.

We began our apprenticeship proper in the 'A' and 'B' Class Fitting Shop. On arrival with our wooden toolboxes, we were each issued with a 4-inch diameter by 6-inch long mild steel cylinder and allocated a vice and space on a long bench. Down the middle of the bench stood a zinc gauze screen designed to prevent the chippings from one side hitting the apprentices on the other side. After a brief demonstration by the instructors, all of whom were senior serving or ex Artificers, we marked out the ends of our cylinders in a hexagon, using the centre punch and scriber and then put them in our vice with the top edge of the hexagon uppermost. We watched in awe as the instructors effortlessly chipped the top of their cylinders flat to the scribed line and were then told to start chipping ours.

With all the enthusiasm of youth, all 78 of us picked up our 1¾ pound hammers and flat chisels and started to attack our cylinders. For almost two hours we toiled without pause until 'Stand Easy' was sounded. By this time my left thumb and knuckle were a bloody and bruised mess and my right fingers and palm bore an array of blisters. The silence coming after two hours of the incessant noise of hammering metal on metal, interspersed with yells of pain and the odd curse, was eerie and somewhat reminiscent of the lull in an air raid – blessed relief but tinged with the fear of further agony. During the short break we tended our wounds and compared our handiwork. It wasn't anything like as much or as good as our Instructor's but I was pleased to see I had made some impression. During the next few days of similar toil, we all managed to produce a recognisable rough-hewn hexagon, some of them being rather smaller than intended. Of course the main purpose of this task was to harden-up our soft hands and it certainly succeeded in doing that. Furthermore it taught us all how to chip, an ability which proved invaluable to me on a number of later occasions, even in retirement. We were then taught how to file the block into a smooth regular hexagon. This exercise took many days but by the end we had all mastered the basic elements of filing.

In addition to our travails in the workshop we faced the traditional 'ragging and fagging' from the senior class, 'H' Class – 1941 Hawke Division. One evening after supper our hut was entered by a group from 'H' Class who pointed out to us that we were the lowest form of apprentice life. Besides following strict codes of personal hygiene, we would be required to provide valeting services for our elders and betters. Having recently completed my first spell of '8A' punishment, I was a bit cocky and a tad disrespectful during this 'lecture' and was adjudged by a PO Apprentice, to have been insolent. He called me "stroppy" and, making the punishment fit the crime and 'pour encourager les autres', he stropped my trousered backside. This was not unusual in those days and I bore him no ill will, indeed we became friends a few years later and remain so today.

Fortunately for us, the arrival of K Class, Keppel Division on 1st September 1944, raised our status minutely and deflected some of the torment we suffered from our elders towards the new sprog Fleet Air Arm Artificer Apprentices.

A stream of momentous events occurred between August and December 1944. We avidly listened in the Junior Recreation Room to all news bulletins and followed, on a regularly updated map, the daily progress of the Allied armies as they advanced towards the German border and overran the V1 'Doodle-bug' launch sites. On a more sombre note we saw the new names of ex-Apprentices added to the Roll of Honour displayed on the East wall of the Dining Hall. We were saddened to see more ex-boys had lost their lives and more ships had been sunk but, with youthful heroic fervour, thrilled to see new awards to those who had shown bravery or distinguished service in action. I recall the RC Padre coming into the weekly Religious Instruction he gave to all 80 Catholics in RNATE, with the news, "Paris has been liberated". On another occasion he arrived late and apologised saying that he had been waylaid by the Commander who had demanded to know why, with only 10% of the total number of apprentices, the RCs provided more than 50% of the men under punishment. The padre devoted the whole session to a debate on the subject. The conclusion from this frank and lively discussion was that most Catholics in the UK owed their religion to an Irish parent or grandparent and the Irish are well known to be natural rebels against authority. I remember that the most eloquent speaker during that debate was 'Paddy' O' Grady of 1942 Exmouth, RNATE's leading skate at the time. Later he was discharged after purposely failing his passing-out test job, went to Bristol University, studied law, became Chairman of the Student Union, stood (unsuccessfully) against Sir Stafford Cripps, Chancellor of the Exchequer, in the 1950 General election and later became a solicitor.

In those days the accommodation at Torpoint was pretty basic. The huts were only heated by a single coal-burning stove which roasted the occupants of the nearest two-tier beds and gave the rest of the occupants little comfort. The interior walls were of unpainted breeze blocks and there was no covering on the black concrete bitumen-coated floor. The roof was corrugated asbestos. There was no Radio speaker, only a 'Tannoy' to broadcast orders. We wore pyjamas but had no sheets and relied on two 'pusser's' (naval issue) blankets, kept in place by a tucked-in hammock used as a counterpane, supplemented when the weather became really cold, by our greatcoats. In winter the morning dash to the ablution block soon woke us up, for the 'covered way' was just that. It had no walls and was open to the elements. However, as none of us had previously enjoyed the luxury of central heating we accepted this situation as pretty normal.

Envy of our 'Tiddly Tiff' elders and betters led us to seek instruction from old school friends in 'B' and 'C' Class in the traditional art of 'soaking a goss' (distorting a cap). Overnight the Trevithick drying room was filled with soaking black caps with their backs cut down and their sides bound. We all made and henceforth carried with us, a short grommet extension to restore our cap to something like its former shape in the event of an inspection. Peer pressure, personal pride and comfort ashore also encouraged us to invest a chunk of our meagre pay on an embossed red cap badge, white semi-stiff collars and black shoes to replace the ghastly flat cap badge, Edwardian rounded stiff collars and boots with which we had been issued. The pinnacle of sartorial elegance for 'Boy Arts' was to wear brown leather gloves and a just visible white silk scarf with one's greatcoat. I couldn't afford these 'must-haves' in 'A' Class but, having dropped a few hints to my family, hoped to receive them as Christmas presents.

All of us had played soccer and/or rugby, hockey and cricket at school but with little or no experience or desire we all became cross-country runners. Whenever the playing fields were unplayable due to rain, recreation afternoons were given over to X-Country and we padded (or paddled) around the 3½ mile road course encircling RNATE or the gruelling 5¼ mile Millbrook course. Although I was a good sprinter, and enjoyed playing soccer and.

rugby, I hated X-country and seldom came in the first half of the runners to finish.

In November all apprentices were required to take part in public PT Displays in the Gymnasium in HMS Raleigh. The programme of synchronised exercises was carried out rhythmically to the popular music of Waldteufel's Skaters Waltz. We took part in the Junior Display and didn't make too much of a hash of it. Next day the Senior display was thrown into chaos when 'H' Class (1941 Hawke) sat down on the floor and refused to take part. A light-hearted account of this legendary 'mutiny' is given in 'Second to None'.

Captain 'Tiny' Dalton our 18 stone ebullient Captain, had a love of boxing and, like all of my classmates, I was coerced into taking part in a sport in which I had no interest and, it was soon obvious, little or no ability. In my first bout I was paired with a chap who had less of a reach than me and I was able to keep him away and land a few punches to win the bout. That was a mistake for in my second fight I faced 'Butch' Munday who had no trouble overwhelming me with a flurry of painful and bloody blows. Unfortunately, this was not my last appearance in the ring because, as I had won my first fight, I was 'selected' for the dreaded Melée. This was a barely legal form of boxing, put on during the interval between the junior and senior competitions of the annual Boxing Championships. Before a packed audience of apprentices in the main dining hall, I was pushed into the ring wearing a red sash and in a ferocious two minute punch-up with a fellow sprog from Keppel. I was battered to a pulp before staggering out of the ring to hear Tiny Dalton announce "Well done Red, Green wins". That definitely ended my boxing career.

In December 1944, we undertook the end of term exams in Maths, English, and History and the 'A' Class test job. When the results were announced I had done reasonably well, coming 12th in the class overall. We then became 'B' class and shortly afterwards went home on Christmas leave very smartly dressed in uniform, wearing greatcoats and big smiles and carrying pusser's green suitcases, looking forward to a break after an exciting and very busy first 4½ months in the Navy.

During Christmas leave 1944, I rendezvoused with five or six Pompey classmates at a Southsea hostelry where, although we were well under the legal age, our uniforms 'allowed' us to drink without being challenged. This event became a ritual and was repeated on the first Saturday of every seasonal leave until August 1948.

On the train back to Plymouth in early January 1945, it was amazing how relaxed (downright scruffy) the senior apprentices appeared returning from leave compared with their immaculate turnout on the journey home. We duly followed their lead on subsequent returns from leave.

We watched in wry amusement as the new 'A' Class (1945 Hawke) underwent their painful baptism of chipping and received most of the attention of the new 'H' Class, 1941 Grenville. In 'A' Class I had only occasionally been required to fag for a member of 'H' Class, cleaning his shoes and pressing his suit. This minor chore was no great pain since he 'protected' me from the rest of his class. In 'B' Class I enjoyed freedom from harassment by 'H' Class but burdened myself by earning periods of '8A' punishment for 'slack hammocks' (tardiness in getting out of bed) and other minor transgressions.

All Apprentices fell in by Divisions every morning at 0745 on the parade ground facing the 'factory' as the main workshop was called. H,G F and E classes on the West (Senior) side and D, C, B, A classes and L and K, the two FAA classes, on the East or Junior side. We all wore (originally dark blue) overalls over our blue and white striped ('check') shirts with detachable collars and black ties, jackets and caps and, in winter, 'Burberrys' or greatcoats. Frequent laundering of the overalls and shirts resulted in their gradual fading and shrinking as the former became a pale grey and crept up the legs to the knees. The collars became impossible to do up leaving a great gap which could not be hidden behind the thin black 'bootlace' tie and the shirts almost lost their stripes and assumed a plain dirty white hue. Together with the battered cap the degree of scruffiness gave a rough indication of the seniority of the wearer, and was a sartorial characteristic of Boy-Art tradition in those days. Another indication of an apprentice's seniority was the number of small red inverted 'war service' chevrons he wore. H and G class wore 3, F and E 2, D and C I and B and A, K and L none. My class hoisted their first and only chevron 13 days before the end of WW2 and some time later their wearing was disallowed.

We were paid every other Thursday. Our rate of pay was 9 pence per day plus 6 pence 'war excess'. However, nine shillings and sixpence was withheld to cover laundry, tools and clothing in excess of the Kit Upkeep Allowance (KUA). Thus, for almost 3 years, we drew just 8 shillings (40 pence) a fortnight. Often a pretty Wren would be stationed at the pay table in the forlorn hope of collecting money for some worthy cause. Needless to say apprentices having just been rescued from rock-bottom by 4 two-bob bits were not very keen on parting with at least half a week's pay and should be forgiven for adopting a hard-hearted attitude to charity, whatever the cause.

From time to time, generally during daily or Sunday Divisions, a Warrant Punishment was publicly awarded, preceded by a selection of sombre excerpts from the 'Articles of War' including that covering the relevant offence and always sandwiched between the chilling introduction and conclusion:

"Anyone subject to this act who shall commit ----shall suffer death
or such other punishment as is hereinafter mentioned".

The warrant reading generally ended with the words:

"He bringing no one in his defence, I find him guilty and, this being the umpteenth offence recorded against him, I sentence him to 42 days detention in the RN Detention Quarters.

Signed, Roland Palmer Dalton, Engineer Captain, Commanding Officer

On caps, prisoner and escort about turn, quick march".

Most of the Apprentices publicly sentenced in this way had been charged with persistent leave breaking and some received longer sentences for 'Desertion' or 'Direct Disobedience'. They were temporarily re-categorised as ODs (Ordinary Seamen) whilst in RNDQs, becoming apprentices on return and being given a new Ship's Book Number which ensured they were last to be paid. The Articles of War read out on these occasions often included the offence of Buggery or Sodomy. However, in my 4 years at Torpoint, during which some 1600 apprentices served there, no one was publicly charged with these offences and I never heard of anyone suspected of such offences. This suggests that the incidence of homosexuality in the navy during the 1940s was very much lower than is currently claimed by its proponents.

We were always referred to as Apprentices and never as ratings and enjoyed a number of privileges not given to young ratings. We had our living huts, dining hall, recreation rooms, canteens and ablution blocks cleaned by pensioners and most of our washing and ironing done by a laundry. We were served our meals and had an extra week of leave in the summer. When duty-watch, (one in four), we were required to sweep up our huts before night rounds but otherwise had no extraneous duties or communal chores. We did however have to toil in the workshops from 0805 to Noon and 1300 to 1600, (Saturdays until noon, or until 1600 if you had failed a test job). We had evening instruction on three evenings a week from 1700 to 1900, (four evenings if you had failed a subject at the previous end of term). One afternoon a week was devoted to sport and we had an hour in the Gym and on the parade ground during working hours. If you were under punishment you had very little spare time at all what with 'jankers' and mustering at the Regulating Office and standing outside it before and after all meals.

There was no cinema in RNATE and Apprentices wishing to see a film fell-in after supper in 'night clothing', generally carrying raincoats and marched across to the 'Bucko' as HMS Raleigh's cinema was known. In the absence of other entertainment we could see a 'B' movie there for 2 pence. Occasionally we were entertained in the 'Junior Rec' by an ENSA show and once enjoyed a demonstration of Snooker and Billiards by Joe Davis and Walter Lindrum, the World Billiards Chaampion 1933-51.

The Spring term of 1945 passed very quickly. Von Runstedt's offensive in the Ardennes in January soon gave way to the Allied counter attack and advance to, and across the Rhine and into Germany. There was an air of excitement as we went home on Easter leave – the war in Europe was clearly coming to an end and morale throughout the country was very high. We all enjoyed a happy leave and returned in great form. On the evening of 7th May we learnt that the Germans had surrendered and that tomorrow would be Victory in Europe, VE Day.

After supper, all of the Apprentices spontaneously assembled on the Parade Ground in high spirits, not, I hasten to add, fuelled by alcohol, at least not the juniors who had no access to the stuff. The apprentices' band climbed up on to the roof of the factory offices with their instruments and, sitting on either side of the clock played a selection of patriotic songs which were sung with great gusto if not harmoniously, by almost 800 happy young men. This un-rehearsed celebration was ended by the Duty CO, a Lieutenant-Commander known as 'Monkey' who ordered the apprentices to fall in by classes as for Divisions and the band to come down from the roof. He then brought us all down to earth with a homily beginning with the statement:

"I don't know what right you have to celebrate. You didn't contribute anything to the defeat of the Nazis"

Next day we were undergoing an English exam when it was interrupted at 3pm so that we could listen on the Tannoy to Mr Churchill's famous end of war speech live. When it ended we were ordered to resume our exam.

That night a crowd of us uniformed but underage 'B Class' apprentices enjoyed a free pub crawl of the packed Torpoint pubs. We enjoyed the company and hospitality of some generous allied sailors, including Dutch and Americans and friendly bar staffs, and shared with them a memorable and deliriously happy evening.

The following day was declared a holiday but I was in the duty watch. It was an unusually fine hot day for early May and whilst we who had to remain onboard sunbathed on the playing field, the rest of our class made for Whitsands Bay. During the afternoon, one of them, Jimmy Carter, who was a good swimmer, was tragically drowned there. This brought to a sad end our euphoria over the end of the war in Europe. The following week we all marched sombrely at his naval funeral.

The highlight of every summer term at Torpoint was Sports Day when Apprentices took part in the full gambit of athletic and track events. The standard achieved, particularly by the seniors, was very high and I recall the great excitement during the 1945 event when one of the seniors broke the RN record for the pole-vault and another that for the 440 yards. I took part in the junior 440 yards that year but came nowhere near to winning a medal. Nevertheless I thoroughly enjoyed a well organised and fiercely competitive but truly sporting day.

The rest of our first year in RNATE passed quickly. The B Class Test Job, the keyed L Block and plate shown on page 49,, was undertaken and passed as were the B Class Academic Examinations and, at the end of July 1945, newly elevated to C Class, and cheered by the great news of successive allied victories in the war against Japan, we excitedly prepared to go on three weeks, well-earned, or so we thought, summer leave.

For me, Summer leave in 1945 was truly memorable, but not for the best of reasons. Taking advantage of the chance of a free travel warrant all the way, I decided to spend all of it in Southern Ireland where my younger sister was living with my grandmother and where my mother intended to holiday at the time. The small group of Boy-Arts of all ages travelling to Eire, stood out at supper the night before leave officially started, as we were dressed in civilian clothes. We were taken to North Road station where, like all of the servicemen and officers waiting for overnight trains, we were given a sandwich and a jam-jar of tea by ladies of the WVS. Around midnight we all piled on to an overcrowded train which set off for Holyhead via Exeter, Bristol, Hereford, Shrewsbury, Crewe and

Chester, arriving just in time to catch the next night's 'Mail Boat' to Dun Laoghaire. After an uneventful crossing and 36 hours after leaving RNATE, the ship berthed and I took a horse-drawn cab to my grandmother's house and was soon enjoying a sumptuous breakfast.

During the first few days I gorged myself on the abundance of unrationed food, enjoying the long forgotten taste of many pre-war luxuries. Soon news came of the first Atom bomb being dropped on Hiroshima and a few days later the second one on Nagasaki. On 15th August, VJ Day, in high spirits I took the tram to Dublin and set off looking for a big party to celebrate the end of WW2. Forgetting this was neutral Eire, I naively assumed I would find it in one or more of Dublin's famous pubs but despite visiting many of them I was disappointed to find them all lacking in party spirit. None of the locals seemed to share my joy at the end of the longest and most bloody of World Wars, although many of them doubtless had relatives serving in the British forces. I felt deflated and wished I were in England where everyone was reportedly having a whale of a time. As I returned from leave, passing through Welsh and English towns still decorated in flags and banners, I realised that I had just missed the greatest party of the 20th Century.

Back at RNATE the end of the war brought little change. True, the blackout curtains were taken down and the 'Camp', as it was generally known, was lit up at night, but food and sweet rationing was still in force and shore-leave was as restrictive as ever. The meals provided by the galley were poorly cooked and inadequate in quantity for growing lads living a pretty active life. I recall that even the roast potatoes on a Sunday were case-hardened. and in 1945 we were perpetually hungry and sought sustenance from bread filched from the dining hall at Breakfast and toasted on the workshop furnaces at 'Stand-Easy' and from penny dough buns at the canteen. Ashore, we enjoyed three penny's worth of beans on toast at the YMCA in Torpoint and it proved well worth the walk to Millbrook for a tasty sixpenny two-course meal cooked by the dear ladies in the canteen there, particularly as, despite being underage, we could wash it down on the way back with a half-pint of Scrumpy for 4d at the Inn at St John's.

Now in C Class, we moved into the main workshop or Factory as it was known, spending most of the term honing our fitting skills. As EAs we generally made smaller versions of the tools manufactured by the ERA (Fitter&Turners) and OAs and undertook 'production' jobs for ships in Devonport Dockyard. This gave us great job-satisfaction. Later we learnt how to set up and operate a shaping machine. At first we were not entrusted with one of the brand new Ormerod machines but had to use one of the three awesome pre-WW1 belt driven monsters affectionately known as 'Petrifier', 'Perisher' and 'Pulveriser'. Meanwhile the ERAs 'selected' for the 'Outside Trades' began their training as Enginesmiths, Coppersmiths and Boilermakers. With typical logic, our smallest classmate became an Enginesmith. 'Tiny' as he was known, could hardly lift a 14lb sledgehammer let alone swing it!

Geoff Cook was the only one in our class who could dance when we joined and during our first year as Boy Arts he patiently taught all of us (in the Junior Rec) to do the Quick-Step, Foxtrot and Waltz and lent us moral support as we made our first foray on a public dance floor during successive Saturday Tea Dances in Union St. Plymouth. I had my ego shattered at the start of my terpsichorean debut when the first lady I asked up to dance towered over me as she stood up and disdainfully turned me down as "a mere boy". Geoff gave me a pep talk and I was soon moving reasonably smoothly around the floor with a young lady who was closer to my 16 years of age. By the end of that afternoon, I and my classmates were hooked on dancing and, since this was the only way (in those days) to meet the fair sex, dancing became our principal leisure activity. As we gained in confidence, being Tiffies, we sought a better class of dance hall. As Juniors we were unable to attend

'Green and Whites' so in preparation for the day we would be eligible, we practiced at home on leave and at up-market Plymouth dances.

As the senior class on the Junior (East) side of the camp we were no longer pestered by H Class, and in a minor way ruled the roost without of course the ragging and fagging 'rights' of the senior class. Our new status did not increase our pay from the miserly 8 shillings a fortnight (40 pence) or improve our shore leave entitlement. We were still only entitled to leave on a Friday and Sunday until 2200 and until 2230 on a Saturday, if not on extra study or in the duty watch. It was therefore impossible for non-natives to attend a dance in Plymouth. So, on the Friday of a 'pay week', we would climb the fence behind the playing fields and walk down the back road to Torpoint, cross the ferry and make for Mutley Assembly Rooms.

One night after a dance there, returning on the last ferry to Torpoint with my ginger-headed six foot three chum Jack and dying for a smoke we found we had no matches. Recklessly as was his wont, he approached the embarked Naval Patrol and asked one of them for a light for his 'Tickler'. He then nonchalantly returned to me and, in full view of them, gave his rather scared 'Oppo' a light. Not content with risking being caught over the wire, Jack sought the extra rush of Adrenalin from another act of daring. Safely back over the fence we assumed the patrol thought we were 'Sick Bay Tiffies' or S&S ratings who enjoyed all-night leave..

Like several of my classmates, I suffered from the curse of adolescence – Acne and its source – Blackheads. Although the fortnightly pay parade provided plenty of candidates for a haircut, and there was a barber in Raleigh, I don't recall there being one in RNATE. I do however remember we used the tonsorial artist in

Fore Street, Torpoint. Included in his modest charge for an a la mode trim, he painlessly and neatly removed any blackheads on our necks, giving this service free to Boy Arts despite his barber's pole having been earlier nicked by 41 Grenville on their passing-out night, although it was returned promptly the following day.

During the Autumn term we took part in the Winter Games of Cross-Country, Soccer, Rugby and Hockey, the annual display of Gymnastics, (this time minus the mutiny) and, for the few still interested in pugilism, the finals of the boxing. We sat the C Class scholastic exams and, six-months earlier than in previous years, undertook the Large Offset Double-Hexagon Test Job, EAs tackling the same size as ERAs and OAs. Although we were due to undergo another term of precision fitting in G Class, this landmark test signified that we were reasonable Fitters.

The female section of the Double-Hexagon Test Job was manufactured from cast-iron, the male Hexagon from mild steel. It was first necessary to mark out the external hexagon on each end of both the female and male cylinders and the offset internal hexagonal hole in the female cylinder Then came the tricky bit, we had to chip out the internal hexagonal hole.

Cast-iron easily shatters when chipped and had to be chipped inwards from each end. After this nail-biting task was completed, the internal hexagon hole had to be filed to near the prescribed size, offset to a specified distance from one of the marked out, but not yet completed, external faces. When this was complete, the female cylinder was set up on one of the modern shaping machine, and the external hexagon was carefully machined, every stroke of the shaper ram being nervously watched in case the cast-iron edges broke. The subsequent shaping of the male hexagon to the marked lines was no sweat. The male was then filed to the precise size and polished before being 'offered-up' to its female counterpart. The internal hexagon on my test job then required quite a lot of dressing before the male hexagon finally passed through it. We were allowed 40 hours to complete this test job. I went five hours overtime but my dimensional accuracy and finish were reasonable and I was pleased to get over 60% for my efforts. OA Apprentice Terry Liming, easily the best Fitter, and later Turner, in the class, produced a legendary test job whose male hexagon took several hours to slide vertically through its female without help when the assembly was stood on a face plate. Terry's efforts completed inside the prescribed time, earned him the prize for craftsmanship with a mark of 90.6%, some achievement with the tight marking regime in force!

The Authorities did not consider it necessary to keep any of the apprentices back from leave to form a duty watch so all of the Boy Arts at Torpoint enjoyed the first post war Christmas at home with their families.

In the autumn of 1945, when we were 'C' Class, and the most senior class on the East (Junior) side of the Camp, improvements were introduced to make the accommodation less spartan. The so-called covered ways between the huts and Ablution blocks (the 'Blu' rooms), previously just a narrow corrugated asbestos roof supported by 4"x 4" wooden beams and open to all weathers, were converted into unheated breeze-block corridors. Contractors also began to colour-wash the bare breeze block walls of the living huts. Furthermore a strip of coconut matting was run down each side of the huts, under the lower berths of the two-tier beds so that apprentices no longer had to stand on the bare bitumen-covered concrete floor when getting in and out of bed. This sheer luxury was of course welcomed but, human nature being what it is, we ungrateful Trevoliers, aware of the palatial conditions enjoyed by our fellow Apprentices at Rosyth, demonstrated our dissatisfaction by various acts of group lawlessness.

At about this time, members of 1942 Exmouth, then 'G' class, were responsible for the famous "Explosion believed to be engineered by Apprentices" which awoke the whole camp one Sunday afternoon. This legendary event in Boy-Art folklore is described on pages 83 and 84 of 'Second To None'. Just before we left the east side several of us, led by Jack Palmer and including Mike Roberts and Peter Hodges climbed to the top of Trevithick Ablution Block Tower and, leaning over the parapet, painted our division's name in large white letters. This self- publicity stunt declared that we were the top dogs of the Juniors, even though we were about to move over to the Senior side of the camp, where for another two years, we would count for little. Unfortunately, we graffitists painted the letter S in reverse and thereafter lumbered the class with a prominent advertisement of our dyslexia that was mocked by the other classes. Naturally we pretended that we had intended to spell Anson that way and brazened out the embarrassment by using this Just William like version forever after.

One day the Master-at Arms broadcast an appeal to the apprentice(s) who stole a box of 144 prophylactics to return them immediately to the unmanned Sick Bay and promising that if this happened in the next half an hour, no further action would be taken. The rubber goods were duly returned and the MAA was true to his word. It must have been the work of senior apprentices, juniors in those days wouldn't have known what to do with them.

In early 1946, the daily breakfast menu was suddenly enhanced by the addition of Marmalade but after several days no apprentice had seen any. So a group of us 'D' Class malcontents called upon the CERA Mess President, whilst he was tucking into a full English breakfast with toast and marmalade, only to be given the run around. That night 'Dinger' Tripp and I wrote in large white chalk letters on the West Side Fire pump wall "Where's Our Marmalade". At morning Divisions next day the Duty CO, assuming that this outrage was the work of 'H' Class, ordered them to scrub off the offending words, during their dinner-time. Needless to say the senior class was not best pleased at this and to avoid their wrath we had to keep very quiet about it. Sorry chaps, honest.

In D class we spent about two months learning to turn on ancient Lang Variable or Lang cone lathes. The latter posed a safety hazard in that one changed speed by 'patting' the moving belt drive to the necessary cone to achieve the required speed, hoping the metalled joint in the belt didn't catch and lacerate one's hand. The rest of the 6 month term was spent in the Enginesmith's, Welding and Coppersmith's shops learning the 'Outside Trades'. This included forging and hardening our own tools, making our own adjustable toasting forks, brazing, oxy-acetylene and electric arc welding, sheet-metal work and plumbing, using copper pipes. This was very interesting and proved most useful to us all. I still have my 'Soap Tin', used for its designed purpose for years at sea, and now holding my small precision tools. At the end of our second year as apprentices we all sat the Admiralty Part 1 Examination in Mathematics (2 Papers), Heat and Electricity, Mechanics, English and Naval History. These were roughly at modern A level.

Until mid 1946, apart from the First Lieutenant and PT Officer, all of the officers in RNATE were either Engineers or Naval Schoolmasters known as 'Schoolies'. The title Engineer was only borne by graduates of the Royal Naval Engineering College at Keyham , and by officers promoted from ERAs as Mate(E)s , (Upper Yardmen) or Warrant Engineers. Electrical and Ordnance Officers were not then designated Engineers and, like Schoolies and Shipwright Officers, could only rise, (via Warrant and Commissioned Officer), as far as the rank of Lieutenant. Indeed, the Headmaster was the only Schoolmaster Lieutenant in the camp. Depending on their position in the entrance examination and the relative popularity of each specialisation with schoolboys, Boy-Arts joined the navy as EA, ERA or OA apprentices, with no real idea of the role or career prospects of the different branches. The specialist technical training of Apprentices did not commence until 'E' Class. For the first two years of their apprenticeship, ERA (Fitter & Turner), EA and OA Apprentices received the same academic instruction, took the same exams, received the same workshop training and did the same test jobs. Furthermore all of the production work carried out by them for ships was of a Marine Engineering nature. Thus, at the end of our second year at RNATE, all of our class theoretically became eligible to try for the one available Cadet (E)-ship at RNEC, the path to the top in naval engineering.

Normally only the five or six 'D' Class apprentices with the highest average marks for their A, B and C class scholastic exams and D Class Admiralty Part 1 exams were considered for the 'Keyham Stag', as the selection process was called. In our case, as the top nine in the class were EAs and OAs, the top twelve were considered. That is how, to my astonishment, and that of everyone else, I found myself on the list of Keyham candidates. Our behaviour was closely monitored to assess our 'Officer-like Qualities' (OLQs) but, needless to say, with my record for waywardness and other negative qualities, I didn't make the short-list. Gradually all ten of the boys in front of me in the Stag were eliminated including Philip Snell, whose average mark was 20% more than the runner-up and who was absolutely brilliant and Captain of Rugby to boot. This left No 12, Eric Ball the oldest and most mature member of the class. He had the necessary OLQs , (a quality in rather short supply among Boy Arts half-way through their apprenticeship), and happened to be one of the two ERA apprentices in the Stag, (the other was No 10). The winner was a popular choice with all of us and we wished Eric every success, but it did seem unfair that our genius Phillip had been deprived of the one chance he had of reaching senior rank, while ERA Apprentices would have another bite at the cherry as Mate(E) candidates five years later, (an avenue not then available to the others). It is thus not surprising that the apparent bias in favour of ERA Apprentices, also evident in all but one of the classes' senior to us at Torpoint, was perceived by EA and OA apprentices to be rather Orwellian. "All D Class apprentices may have had an equal chance of becoming a Cadet (E) but ERA Apprentices had a more equal chance than the others". Fortunately later that year, the huge expansion of the Electrical branch and creation of the Ordnance Engineering sub-specialisation, gave all ex-boys the chance of becoming Upper Yardmen and a commission as a Sub-Lieutenant at the age of 22. The top three of our Stag list did just that and six more of them, and later 12 other Ansons, were also commissioned as Weapons and Electrical (WE), or Marine (ME) Engineer Officers.

Just before summer leave during a Saturday afternoon swim at the Mount Wise swimming pool, my chum Jack dared me to follow him in a dive into the Hamoaze off the top of the high wall dividing the men's and women's pools. The tide was ebbing and when I surfaced I found myself being swept rapidly out into the Sound. I had to swim back to an iron ladder on the sea wall and only just made it after a long, somewhat frightening and extremely exhausting swim against the tide. Being a stronger swimmer, Jack had reached safety long before I finally made it to the ladder. I swore I would never again take part in any of his madcap stunts.

My widowed mother remarried at the end of September so I put in for 'Compassionate Leave' to attend her wedding. When I went to the Regulating Office I found myself the butt of ribald remarks and much hilarity when 'Pusser' Dadd and 'Pincher' Martin read my request "to attend my mother's wedding". Chief Stoker Dadd, (with whom I had experienced many encounters in which I had come off worse), declared in his nice quiet and friendly manner that he had always suspected my legitimacy, or words to that effect. Some time afterwards, he got his come-uppance. The Chaplain called at the Reg Office one evening to ask the staff not to broadcast anything on the Junior Rec speaker next morning because the Bishop of Plymouth was conducting a Confirmation service for a number of apprentices. At the most solemn part of the service the Tannoy came on and Pusser Dadd was heard to shout " Hey Pincher, what 'effing' place 'aven't we got to pipe in this morning". Needless to say, this infamous Chief Stoker, who had introduced numerous well-brought-up young apprentices to the Anglo-Saxon expletive and other vulgar words, was not very popular with the Captain, or the Bishop, and soon afterwards he was off back to Chatham Depot for a long overdue sea draft.

Now E Class Senior Apprentices, we began our specialist training. As EAs, we moved into the exclusive EAs shop which was so much quieter than the main shop, had very pleasant Instructors and the best Heads in the camp. In this haven we began using Myford lathes to produce miniature versions of the screwed spindles made by our ERA and OA colleagues. Having already completed our academic education, we started our technical instruction with night classes in Electrical Engineering, Workshop Practice, and Mechanical Drawing.

E CLASS
Screwed Spindle
(E.A's only)

One morning our class was diverted from the workshops to a classroom where we were addressed by a gorgeous young Wren Officer who told us that she was going to conduct a series of new fangled tests on us to assess our all round suitability for an Artificer Apprenticeship. Spellbound by her beauty, we failed to listen to the purpose and significance of these pioneer tests and, as we were already half-way through our 'time', we didn't see the point of the exercise. Being typically 'Bolshie' senior apprentices of the time, most of us treated it as a big joke and generally 'messed about' during the written and practical tests, some even giving ridiculous answers. When the clearly disappointed 'Vision of Loveliness' announced the results, the class had performed pretty poorly and a few members had even indicated a marked unsuitability to be Tiffies! Years later I realised that my frivolous response to some of the questions in these tests had resulted in the recorded T2 (IQ) figure on my confidential record being assessed at a considerably lower value than I later achieved when I joined Mensa. I am ruefully sure that fooling around that day in 1946 did my subsequent career no great favour. The following year Psychometric testing was introduced for all candidates who had passed the entry examination. They were treated with proper respect by the keen young aspirants and were doubtless responsible for ending the 'Square Pegs in Round Holes' syndrome which had earlier led to the discharge of numbers of apprentices who were found to be unsuitable.

On 31st October 1946 I was on 8A punishment. After the final session of Jankers and muster, us men under punishment left T7 hut and, dressed in seamen's jerseys, went over the fence and took part in a Halloween stunt at Scraesdon Fort overlooking Antony. An apocryphal account of this appears on pages 85-87 of 'Second to None'.

November saw several major changes at Torpoint, first the departure of Engineer Captain 'Tiny', Roland Palmer Dalton RN after eight years in command of the Fisgard apprentices. We all turned out to bid farewell to our popular, larger than life CO as he left the camp, and the service. Next day his replacement Captain (E) RP Chapman RN, who really was tiny, took over. An ex POW in the hands of the Japanese after his ship was sunk, he now became responsible for the conduct, training and welfare of 800 fit, high spirited and sometimes unruly 15 to 20 year old apprentices. Shortly afterwards, RNATE Torpoint became HMS Fisgard, restoring the proud title lost when apprentices left the hulks in Portsmouth harbour for Chatham in 1931.

About this time, major changes occurred in the status of junior officers and Schoolies and the Electrical branch was formed. Warrant Engineers and Commissioned Engineers were re-designated Commissioned and Senior Commissioned Engineers and moved into the Wardroom, though they continued to wear a single thin or thick ring respectively and to be addressed as 'Mr'. Overnight the Headmaster Lieutenant was elevated to become an Instructor Commander, the Commissioned (i.e. one thick stripe) Schoolies became Instructor Lieutenant-Commanders and the Warrant Schoolies Instructor Lieutenants. Furthermore RNATE's first Electrical Officer, Lieutenant Tom Loosemore, and first Ordnance Officer Mr Tommy Boustead, both of whom were ex Boys, joined the staff, providing a great fillip to the EA and OA Apprentices.

All of the apprentices at Fisgard who had joined before 15th August 1945, were rewarded by a grateful nation for their 'invaluable' contribution to the defeat of Hitler and Tojo by the award of a 'Victory' medal ribbon. More importantly, for ever-hungry growing lads, we also received a Post Office Savings Book containing a War Gratuity. Each of my class received 12 Guineas (£12.60) for their 12 ½ months 'distinguished' service and many of us blew the lot on slap-up meals on successive weekends at 'Tony's Imperial Restaurant' in the Octagon at Plymouth or in the Greek Restaurant in Union Street, generally managing to scoff two meals in one run ashore. *How one's priorities change with age! Six years later I was given 14 Guineas (£14.70) for my more 'active service' during the Korean War and spent it all on an eiderdown and bedspread for the matrimonial bed.*

After successfully completing the E Class Test job, a screwed spindle with a double-start square thread on one end and a Vee thread on the other, shown on page 60, and the technical exams, we prepared to go on Christmas leave. There was an added air of excitement this time as we felt that our living conditions and future prospects had markedly improved during a memorable year. Things were on the up and we looked forward to 1947.

As we returned from Christmas leave it was snowing and Britain was already experiencing the beginning of what proved to be, and still is recorded as, the coldest winter since 1880. As it continued to snow and lay deeply on the ground, public transport ground to a halt, coal stocks dwindled and power cuts brought the country almost to a standstill. At HMS Fisgard, the workshops were only without power for a few days of the three months the exceptionally cold winter spell lasted. During the first of those days we all sat on our toolboxes wearing greatcoats and gloves and read books or played cards in the unheated workshops. This unwelcome inactivity was soon replaced by organised activities such as snow clearing, enlivened by the odd snow fight. The Dining room, Recreation rooms and Studies were uncomfortably cold and the food was even less appetising than usual. Coal for the single 'pot-belly' stove, that provided what passed for 'central heating' in our accommodation huts, was limited to enough for one evening at a time, fires being lit after Tea and banked before night rounds. There was no SRE in the huts and shore leave was out of the question, we were cut off from Torpoint and Antony. In fact our routine was now little different from that of the inmates of HM Prison at Princeton on Dartmoor. We wore the same blue and white striped shirts, slept in the same type of two-tiered beds and had the same sort of food. Since the end of WW2 there had been a spate of German Prisoner of War films and thus Fisgard now became colloquially known as 'Applag VIIIA'.

Now in F Class, most of that bitterly cold period coincided with a very interesting part of Anson's workshop and technical training.

This was conducted by a new generation of WW2 veterans who had quickly established themselves as sterling characters, following the departure of most of the original Ex Chatham stalwarts (or stanchions?) The new Senior Engineer, Lieutenant-Commander(E) John Shoring, an ex-Boy, who coined the immortal phrase "Never Associate Yourself With a Shoddy Job", led a keen staff from the front First we enjoyed a spell with a civilian craftsman called Quentin Edward Dowrick in the Tool Room. Under the expert tutelage of QED, as he was aptly called, we had instilled in us, a sense of the professional standards expressed in the Boy Art maxims, quoted on page 84 of '2$^{nd}$ to None'. This genial fount of knowledge also had the knack of jumping up and suspending himself by the finger tips of one hand from the narrow ledge of a girder running across the tool room. He offered each member of every of class 2/6d if they could do this to a count of five. No apprentice ever won this challenge. Then followed another entertaining period with Chief OA 'Codder' Cownden, who taught us how to use a milling machine and to set up a dividing head and to cut gears. At every opportunity he drew our attention to his "perfect sense of balance" as he tightened up securing nuts with a spanner, hence his nick-name. He also had a blood-stained finger nail, reputedly his own, hanging over his desk to warn us of the dangerous sharpness of milling cutters. In the classroom we were taught Electrical Engineering by a fierce Lt Cdr Schoolie called Ennor who ruled us with a rod of iron, and by Lieutenant(L) Tom Loosemore and two genial Chief EAs Bill Coulson and 'Donkey Bray' all of whom kept our attention and interest without difficulty. Half-way through March the first signs of a thaw appeared and gradually Fisgard and the rest of the country came back to normal, sport was resumed and it became worthwhile to go ashore again for night leave and to look forward to Easter leave.

After completing our Milling course we EAs were allocated the best lathes in the whole Factory - the American precision 6 inch Ward-Haggas lathes. Bill Haddon and I were given a rush job to do for the Dockyard – to produce six valve spindles with a double-start square-thread on one end and a Vee thread on the other, from monel-metal, a material which requires resolute and accurate machining. By working our butts off we completed three each in the time allowed and felt a real sense of satisfaction. Monel is notoriously difficult to turn and tools have to be kept sharp and their height set accurately, if you are to avoid the job 'riding' over the tool, particularly when screw-cutting or parting.

Fortunately for all of us poverty-stricken Boy-Arts, as the Bard might have said, "Now is the winter of our discomfort become glorious summer by the sums of money we suddenly received "for that year, the Armed Forces received a huge pay rise. Although we had contributed little to the defence of the realm, our 'take-home' pay, after deductions for laundry, tools and kit, staggeringly increased by 400% from 8 shillings to 40 shillings (£2) a fortnight. All of a sudden we were in possession of riches beyond the dreams of avarice. Now 18 years old we could afford to drink in the Senior Apprentices' Canteen and, legally at last, ashore. We could also afford to have a local girl friend as long as she was prepared to 'go Dutch' and of course, providing her mother was a good cook. "Viva Up-'omers".

The summer of 1947 was quite hot and there was no Swimming Pool in Fisgard or Raleigh. However, some bright spark persuaded the camp authorities that, with a good clean-out and minor modifications, the large Static Water Tank, a WW2 Fire-Fighting aid, near the Senior Rec Room could fill this role. Volunteers eagerly cleaned out the tank and bent some of the internal struts to minimise the obstructions to free swimming before it was filled, first with clean cold water and then with hordes of perspiring apprentices. Fisgard's first Swimming Pool provided a lot of fun for a day or two until the Command Medical Officer carried out an inspection, declared it dangerously unhygienic and banned it.

The CinC Plymouth decided to visit Fisgard and chose a very hot day to do so. Daily Orders showed that we would be on the parade ground for an hour before he even arrived and goodness knows how long afterwards. So Ian Black, Bob Weedon and I decided to cut our presence down to a minimum by one of us pretending to faint and the other two to carry him off. I drew the short straw so I fell in between Ian and Bob in the middle rank of our class. Shortly after we were reported "Present and Correct", I duly swooned and was 'saved' from hitting the gravel by my co-conspirators and was ostentatiously carried off the parade and back to our hut. Once inside we rolled 'Ticklers' (hand-rolled naval cigarettes) and were just congratulating ourselves on having escaped from a tiresome parade when in came an 'H' Class PO Apprentice. Observing my miraculous recovery and then hearing my candid admission that the fainting had been a put up job, he declared that he was running us in. Since we were only a year behind him in seniority we were taken aback by his attitude and on the way down to the Reg Office we decided to claim that I genuinely had felt faint. The OOD heard his pretty accurate account of what had happened and then each of us denied the charge of planning to avoid divisions by faking a faint. Since it was his word against the three of us the OOD had little option but to dismiss the case. As we replaced our caps he said "Wait a minute, Off Caps, let me have a look at them". We were then placed in the Commander's report for wearing distorted caps and subsequently received 14 days 8A and 28 days OPL from the Captain. Justice was done although we didn't see it that way at the time. Years later I met the PO App concerned socially and having long realised what a fine line had to be trod by Hook Boys and how difficult their job had been, I no longer held a grudge against him and we are now friends.

As we toiled away that summer at the F Class test job and the technical examinations there were rumours that major changes to the training of Apprentices were in the offing. However we had no details or any idea how vital these exams would prove to our immediate future. When the results were announced we learnt that the lower third of each of the specialisations within our class, together with the upper third of E Class (45 Hawke), were to be transferred to Caledonia where they would join their 'opposite' numbers to form Interim 1 Class. Thus our class, originally 78 strong but already reduced over the years to 63 by the discharge of those who had failed exams, test jobs or both, by being invalided, dying or being made a Cadet (E), would dwindle to 42. Interim 1 Class, created to start a 3-Entry scheme from the former. 2-Entries per year would pass out at Christmas 1948. However, the ex-Ansons were assured their seniority as 5th Class Artificers would be back-dated to that of their former classmates.

Earlier in 1947, Fisgard's team led by Harold Brickwood of 1943 Collingwood, had become RN Cross-Country champions and had also won the Exter to Plymouth 48 mile Road Relay race. A few months later the annual Sports Day was the last time that Senior Apprentices competed against each other in Fisgard at, or near RN and Devonport Command Athletics standard, ending a proud history of sporting achievement, going back 42 years. The winners of several of the senior track and field events on this historic Sports Day also set new records.

Just before summer leave with the first moves in the geographical separation of the specialist technical training of senior Apprentices from the general engineering training of junior Apprentices. This was closely followed by the introduction of a House system in place of the traditional Class/Division system and a three entry per year scheme aligned to the school terms.

I sadly bade farewell to 21 classmates and long time friends, including Ian Black, Don Fraser, as they set off with 1945 Hawke and some of Grenville and Frobisher on a horrendous 35 hour rail journey to Rosyth. 1944 Anson ceased to exist and the 42 of us left were spread between the 8 'Houses' scattered around the camp. I now shared an Exmouth hut with 10 ex Blakes, 4 ex Ansons and 8 Ex Grenville/Frobishers of 12, 10 and 6 Class respectively.

Our old Anson esprit was at low ebb as we set off on summer leave, bewildered and apprehensive as to what the next term would bring.

On return from leave we had to accustom ourselves to a hybrid system comprising two senior classes, our immediate seniors the former 'H' Class-1944 Blake who were re-designated 12 Class, as they were in their last term as apprentices, and our class now called 10 class, because we faced the Spring and Summer terms of 1948. The remaining occupants of Fisgard were junior apprentices now designated 6, 5, 4, 3, 2 & 1 Class. The latter, Series 1, was the last class to join as EA, ERA, OA and Air apprentices, after passing the Civil Service Commission entry examination. Each of the 8 classes were divided, for the purposes of accommodation and recreation, between 8 'Houses' which bore the same names of famous Admirals as the previous Divisional system. This arrangement more evenly distributed the sporting talent throughout the camp, but did little to maintain the identity and esprit of the senior classes, built up over more than three years together. Paradoxically it also facilitated fagging and unauthorised absences, as all huts contained members of several classes who might quite legally be elsewhere at the time of rounds.

It was strange falling-in by Houses in fairly close proximity to a lot of sprogs because we senior 12 and 10 Class Apprentices were pretty scruffy, wore distorted caps and were at least three years older than them. From the disciplinary point of view we were hardly suitable role models for these keen 15 ½ to 16 ½ year-old youths. I bet the authorities wished they had been able to send us away with the other senior apprentices at the end of the previous term to avoid our bad influence, and probably looked forward to our passing-out as much as we did. With our age and relative experience however, we naturally dominated the ship's and house sports teams and even pretty ordinary Rugby and Soccer players like me managed to regularly play for their House.

My step-brother George, who was doing his National Service as a Naval Air Mechanic at RNAS Ford, Sussex, contracted Pleurisy and was sent to the RN Auxiliary Hospital at Sherborne. Although sprog Stokers in Raleigh enjoyed all-night and weekend leave, non-native senior apprentices in their fourth year of training had no such privilege. So in order to visit George I had to go 'over the fence', which I did in uniform early one Saturday afternoon, and made my way by ferry, bus and train to RNAH Sherborne. I found George in good spirits, the hospital routine relaxed, and the staff kind and helpful. They gave me tea and supper and recommended a nearby B&B where I spent a comfortable night and enjoyed a good breakfast before going back in to see George. I spent the rest of the Sunday in with him, leaving him after Tea. As the train pulled in I saw my stepfather on board and joined him for the journey back to Plymouth, giving him the news of George's improved state. He was returning to RAF Mount Batten after a weekend at home and gave me the news of my mother and sisters. Being in the well-disciplined RAF he assumed I was on weekend leave and I didn't correct this misunderstanding. We parted at Plymouth North Road and I made my way back, via the back road to the north fence of Fisgard. It was a moonlit night and as I approached the fence down the path past the old AA Gun battery I saw the Perimeter Rounds coming across the playing fields towards me. I darted through a gap in the hedge on the east-side of the path and almost stumbled over a couple in what I later learned was known as the 'Missionary position'. The young lady was looking straight up at me with an expression of shock and embarrassment at having been caught in flagrante by a man in uniform who must have appeared somewhat surprised and not a little alarmed. I put my finger to my lips to indicate she should not say anything to her lover, who was too preoccupied at the time to look round, and I averted my gaze to save her blushes until the Rounds party had disappeared. I then gave her a nod and left the scene, climbed the fence and made my way back to my hut where I was relieved to find that my absence over the weekend had not been noticed. This was one of the odd benefits of the House system where huts contained members of three different classes and it was difficult to check if anyone was missing. I wonder if the young lady concerned, who must now be about 80, still remembers her most embarrassing moment?

Later that Autumn term we underwent 4 weeks 'Afloat' training in HMS Vanguard, newly returned from its royal visit to South Africa. We were accommodated in a mess deck aft and found life onboard so much better than back in Fisgard. The food was infinitely superior and we were well treated by the ship's electrical staff with whom we worked for 2 weeks on both the High Power (electrical) and Low Power (weapon/electronic equipment). An abiding memory of this first happy taste of life afloat is of one of our class, later an Upper Yardman and commissioned at the age of 22, letting slip the Anglo-Saxon expletive and being run in to the Captain, by the ship's Commander(E), charged with "Using language unbecoming to an Artificer Apprentice". My! How standards have changed since those innocent days! Devonport Dockyard had a terribly class conscious passenger train running between North and South yards through a tunnel under the road to the Torpoint chain ferry. Foremen rode in relative luxury, Inspectors in pretty good comfort, chargemen in the equivalent of 3$^{rd}$ class and the workforce in little better than cattle-trucks. It was our first experience of how status seems to mean more to the Civil Service than it does to the navy. On a happier note I recall buying an 'Oggie' (Cornish pasty) for 3 pence at the Albert Gate from a man who kept them hot in a hay-box, and enjoying eating it on the way back to the ship.

Our workshop training followed the old 'G' class syllabus and was dedicated to making small tools for our future personal use such as a tool-maker's vice, pin vice, and various gauges, all of which I still have. At the end of term we undertook the ½ inch Double-Cube and Split Plate whose fitting by every one of the 128 combinations was marked to half of a thousandth of an inch. We were allowed 25 hours to complete this acme of all fitting test jobs. It had long been a tradition in the EAs Shop for G Class to act as mates for the H Class EAs doing their passing-out test job, by manufacturing minor pieces such as pins, bolts and nuts, thus allowing the H Class apprentices to concentrate on the major items. I enjoyed my part in this for it gave me a taste of what was to come six months later, although our test job would be different, would remain a mystery until then, and we would have no mates.

On 12th December 1947 our immediate seniors, the 80-odd strong former 1944 Blake Division passed-out of Fisgard. About the same time, the newly elevated 7 Class, (comprising parts of the former 1945 Grenville and 1946 Frobisher) and now senior apprentices, were sent to Rosyth. This left all of 1946 Exmouth and 1947 Duncan divisions, now 6,5,4 and 3 Class respectively, and Series 1, (now 2 Class) as the Junior Apprentices. The 42 of us remaining ex 1944 Ansons thus became the only senior Apprentices in Fisgard. We were re-designated 12 (rather than 11) Class and went off on Christmas leave as 'Top Dogs', eagerly looking forward to the privileges this would bring after our 3 ½ year-long wait.

The total January 1948 Artificer Apprentice intake was made up of a huge number of unspecified apprentices, who had passed the new RN-run entry exam and three days of aptitude and IQ tests, before joining HMS Fisgard as a common entry known thereafter as Series 2. They were destined to become Air, Electrical, Engine-room, Ordnance or Shipwright Artificer Apprentices at the end of their first year at Fisgard and, after being kitted-out and completing parade training, began their common technical training with woodwork. They were evenly distributed between the 8 Houses and though accommodated close to the senior apprentices in their House, they shared huts with the other junior apprentices.

One evening in mid January 1948, I was with nine of my classmates busy addressing about 40 of the 120 strong newly-joined I Class (Series 2). We were explaining to them that they now occupied the lowest level in Boy-Art society and would, until relieved of this stigma when Series 3 joined in May, be required to render due obeisance to and fag for us, their undoubted elders and betters. At this point in a time-honoured Boy-Art rite of passage the door flew open and a clutch of RPOs and POs, obviously acting on a tip-off, burst in grabbing the nearest two of us 12 Class apprentices, while the other 8 managed to escape unidentified through the other door. Although we had not played a particularly prominent role in the 'lecture', Ernie Ware and I were the two fall guys and found ourselves arraigned before the Captain. There was no question or charge of us using physical abuse on the junior apprentices but the Captain, an ex POW of the Japanese, who abhorred bullying, decided to punish the two of us severely as a deterrent to our classmates. We were given 14 days 8A, a Captain's Warning for Conduct and Indefinite Leave Stopped. 'Skipper's Lobs' was usually given to apprentices when the aggregate of their 8A exceeded 100 days. Since Ernie and I had only notched up about 60 days each by then we were somewhat gob-smacked and also felt that 'Indefinite Leave Stopped' was totally out of order and surely an illegal punishment.

We were 'weighed off' just before noon on the morning of Saturday 18th January 1948, my 19th birthday, what a present! I figured that the Captain's Office would be closed until the Monday, so if I wrote and posted my "- - - - -don't worry Mum every one gets one of these warnings" letter before the Sunday post was collected, she would get my explanation before the warning arrived. Mistake! I didn't realise then that the outcome of a summary trial and the consequent punishment was more or less decided before the 'Accused' even appeared before the Captain. My mother received the Captain's letter, typed and signed before the trial, on the Monday morning whilst my reassuring apologia, buried half-way through the loving letter of a dutiful son, arrived on the Tuesday. When my Mother opened the Captain's letter it was folded showing just the last paragraph which read "If this warning is not heeded it will be followed by an Admiralty Warning and discharge from the Royal Navy, signed R.P.Chapman, Captain (E) Royal Navy". My tiny Irish mother went mad, said I was a disgrace to the family, told me not to come home at Easter and threatened to disown me.

Three weeks later, having completed our 8A, Ernie and I went with 8 of our class for 2 weeks 'Afloat training' in HMS Implacable. Whilst aboard her, four of our class, including two PO Apprentices, were run in for "humiliating a junior apprentice", by making him trace the route of a snooker ball under the table. During the investigation into this offence, and in a classic display of Anson esprit de corps, all 32 members of 12 Class present in Fisgard at the time, including the CPO and PO Apprentices, stepped forward and accepted collective responsibility for this heinous crime. The Captain angrily railed at them for bullying the poor lad and awarded the whole class one month's stoppage of leave and daily 'jankers'. Defiantly 12 Class withdrew from all of the ship's teams. As they provided their backbone, the Rugby XV and the Soccer and Hockey X1s suffered successive unexpected defeats until, after negotiations involving the Captain, Padre and the father of one of the PO Apprentices, the stoppage of leave and Jankers were rescinded and the sports teams returned to full strength. Ernie and I also had our normal leave restored though the Captain's warning remained in place. Tactfully, the Authorities then allowed our class to continue to enjoy the valeting and messenger services of 'voluntary' Fags and the privilege of being addressed as "Senior Apprentice" until we passed-out in August 1948.

Shortly after my return from an instructive fortnight onboard HMS Implacable, during which I realised that the life of a Tiffy in the navy was really something worthwhile and rewarding, I was among a number in our hut run-in for slack- hammocks. This minor offence was normally dealt with by the OOD but as I was on 'Skipper's Lobs' I was put in the Captain's Report. He gave me a right rollicking and threatened that if I appeared before him again I would get Admiralty Lobs and be chucked out. As I walked back up the road to the factory, I literally 'saw the light'. I decided there and then that I would no longer swim against the tide but would toe the line, buckle down to discipline and make a go of a naval career. To be honest this sudden 'conversion'. or perhaps growing-up? owed much to the influence of my mother and to the fact that I had met a nice girl from Torpoint and had grown used to seeing her as often as I could. However, the principal reason for this step-change in my attitude was that I realised how dangerously close I was to wasting all of my training over the past 3 ½ years and of ruining a career that showed some promise. For the rest of that Spring term I did my damnedest to keep out of trouble and even earned from my classmates the sobriquet 'All – Pusser Dan', ie obeying all orders to the letter. I bought an ex GPO bicycle for 10 shillings and though it only had one gear, I used to ride it down to Torpoint, walking up the hills, to see my girl-friend Jessie. One Saturday night I was stopped by a policeman just short of the Fisgard gates because my rear light wasn't working. I told him that my leave was up in a few minutes and I would be in deep trouble if I was adrift so, having taken my details, he let me remount and dash for the gate which I made just in time. Phew! On hearing my solemn promise that I was a reformed character my dear Mother welcomed me back into the family and I enjoyed Easter leave during which I bought a new rear light and mudguards for my bike.

The day we returned for our last term as Apprentices, I found that my bike had been stolen from the Air Raid Shelter near my hut where I'd left it. That afternoon I was called to the Factory office where a policeman handed me a summons for riding a bike with a defective rear light, I wish I had kept that ornate document.

Anyhow to avoid the loss of a day's pay I wrote and pleaded guilty but said my bike had since been stolen. The Torpoint Magistrates, including one of our Factory Instructors, could have fined me 5 shillings but they docked me 10 bob, the rotten So and Sos. A couple of days later, being now dead keen, I went up to the Main Factory early after dinner and started work before the staff arrived but had a sudden call of nature. Since the EAs' Shop had the only civilised Heads around I went there and was a couple of minutes late for the muster. The Instructor reported me absent to the Senior Engineer and very soon I was up before the Captain again. I really thought that this is it, I'm for the chop. However, my recent strenuous efforts to keep out of trouble had not gone unnoticed and with a Final, Final warning my absolutely true excuse was accepted and I was mercifully cleared.

On the following Monday we began the Admiralty Part 2 Examinations. These comprised 5 three-hour papers and ended at noon on the Wednesday. That afternoon we met in a classroom where the secret plans of our Passing-out Test job were unveiled and our questions answered. We were then each handed a copy and given the rest of the day to manufacture our own special tools for cutting the internal and external threads. We also drew lots for lathes and shaping and milling Machines. Luckily I drew a Harrison lathe, an Ormerod Shaper and a Miller. We were given 120 hours to complete our half-size version of the OAs and ERA(F&T)'s 135 hour Test Job and next morning we got cracking. After more than three weeks of blood, toil tears and sweat, I finally handed in my completed test job at four o'clock one afternoon, confident that although I had gone three hours over time, I had passed. I rushed out of the Factory, down to the 'blu room', showered and changed into No 1s and was ready for the official Passing-Out photo taken at the time shown on the Fisgard clock. I already knew I had passed the Part 2 technical exams and my captured smile testifies to my relief and joy, see smile on 2nd from right in 3rd row from front in the photograph shown on the next page.

Our happiness at completing the apprenticeship was tempered by the departure of Mike Roberts our popular leading 'skate', who had earlier 'earned' a Captain's Warning for conduct on achieving 100 days 8A and was then given an Admiralty Warning for Conduct for his failure to salute an officer in Devonport Gunnery School. This proved to be the straw that broke the camel's back, He had taken and passed the Part 2 Exams but was discharged before completing his Test Job. I personally felt gutted by his cruel fate at the Eleventh Hour, and realised it could so easily have been mine.

*Anson 2<sup>nd</sup> August 1944-12<sup>th</sup> August 1948  the last class to*
*omplete all of their Apprenticeship at RNATE/Fisgard, Torpoint*
*Stephens, Ellis, Hodges, D.Smith, D. Taylor*
*Rouse, Field, Dolley, E. Smith, Cross, Liming, Haddon, Murdoch, Grant*
*West, Rowlands, H.Taylor, Bishop, Weedon, Bond, Watts, Cann, R.Westlake, Poole*
*Hoskins, Snell, Cook, Ware, Selves*
*Partridge, Broome, Muller, King, Wooden, Cdr. Gatey, Capt Morrell,*
*CERA Short, Crewe, Lemmon, Edwards, Wakeham, Butler, Alp*

Then followed, three weeks of unwinding. We enjoyed the challenge of a Royal Marine Commando course at Bickleigh, went to sea for the day in the destroyer HMS Wizard and, after years of indifferent marching, but in accordance with Boy-Art tradition, performed incredibly well at our ceremonial Passing Out parade. We held our Passing-out Dinner at the Continental Hotel in Plymouth after receiving our final results, our advancement details and Port Divisions. All 41 of us had passed but the six weeks advancement I had earned for my workshop and classroom efforts were forfeited because of my punishment record. However, I was delighted, and lucky, to get my preferred port division for though I came 12th in the class and 8th EA, I grabbed the 6th and last Pompey place for EAs. Number 13 another Pompey EA was condemned to Chatham. On 12th August, after saying farewell and thanking my Torpoint girl friend, and her Mum, for looking after me during my final year as an apprentice, I set off for HMS Collingwood with a killick, (anchor), on my arm and a twinkle in my eye. I had survived, my conduct sheet had been wiped clean and I could now look forward to a spell at home with reasonable spending power.

In 1944, RNATE Torpoint was in all respects a naval boarding school whose pupils were selected by academic ability alone, in the hope that as apprentices they would prove receptive to a largely practical training and become both skilled craftsmen and sound engineering diagnosticians. It says something for the standard of training received that 80% of my entry of 78 achieved this aim. Furthermore and surprisingly, the Civil Service Open Competitive Academic Exam by which we gained entry, pretty accurately predicted the final combined academic, technical and workshop order of merit at passing-out four years later.

Although subject to the Naval Discipline Act we Apprentices were not treated as strictly as other young naval trainees. The task of maintaining good order and discipline among over 800 young men of between 15 and 20 years of age, confined for four years in one place with low pay and little leave was beyond the capability of the small staff of mostly retired officers and senior ratings. They relied upon the help of the Chief and Petty Officer Apprentices (Prefects) and the controlled 'assistance' of the senior class. Together they managed to ensure the smooth running of the establishment. I must say that when we were 12 Class, the 'Hook Boys' (Prefects) in my class steered a steady course between two often conflicting loyalties. They must have been aware of most of the 'law-breaking' being carried out by their own classmates, particularly the 'ragging and fagging' and leave-breaking. I now believe that the staff were also aware of this but if not specifically alerted they too chose to 'look the other way', in the interests of harmony. This traditional public school approach avoided the application of the normal heavy-handed discipline applied to other young naval ratings, whose training lasted less than one fifth of the time Artificer Apprentices spent at RNATE. It also avoided the long-term affect on careers that might otherwise have been irrevocably ruined as a result of youthful misdemeanours made by high-spirited lads in a boarding school environment.

It was not all work and study at Torpoint. We also had a lot of fun. To occupy the many hours we were confined to the camp and to avoid boredom, we enjoyed playing all kinds of competitive team or individual sports and indoor games to at least a 'social' standard. This of course included card games, Chess, Draughts, Uckers, Snooker and Billiards. We were also encouraged to enjoy the finer things in life such as, Classical, Jazz and Swing Music, Art and Literature. Those of us not blessed with natural prowess on the playing field, snooker or card table, in the band or madly in love with a local maiden, got our kicks by taking part in illegal (but never criminal) activities like 'going over the fence' to attend a dance in Plymouth. Unfortunately we also learned how to swear like sailors! However, bonded together as a division by esprit, we forged friendships that have lasted for 65 years.

Our four years training at Torpoint comprised 80% workshop to 20% technical Instruction, although I received another nine months full-time technical instruction at HMS Collingwood immediately afterwards, before I was let loose on the fleet. The academic and technical instruction received in Fisgard was of a high standard (apart from some risible English Grammar lessons given by a Schoolie who was more at ease with Science), and reinforced the foundation given me at school. The sound platform of academic and technical knowledge provided, gave most of us a thirst for more and made it possible for many of us to achieve university-entry qualifications and Chartered Engineer status by private and assisted study and by the exercise of charge responsibility at sea. This proved very beneficial to those of us who remained in engineering after we left the service.

One is supposed to reach one's physical peak at the age of 19 and thereafter to suffer in varying degrees from the 'over 19 disease'. Thus in the last year at Fisgard, my classmates and I were pretty fit. Whilst none of us had reached the peak of our mental capacity most of them had reached a level of adult maturity consistent with our age. I have to admit that I was lagging behind in this respect until I received a 'Wake-Up-Call' in the shape of a Captain's Warning for Conduct. I have long forgiven the unknown 'grass' whose tip-off led to my 'lobs' for, in retrospect, that was the best thing that

**Screw-Operated Piston Valve**

(The Passing – Out Test Job of the last Artificer Apprentices to serve the whole of their apprenticeship at RNATE/HMS Fisgard, Torpoint)

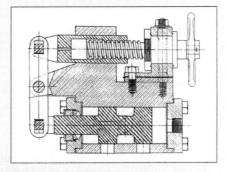

This Test Job, unique to the Fisgard and Caledonia Ansons passing-out in August 1948 and unseen by them until the start of the job, comprised 53 pieces. The valve body, valve cover and control spindle bracket were made from Gunmetal, the remainder from mild steel. ERA (F&T)s and OAs were allowed 135 hours and EAs (whose test job was identical but half-size) 125 hours to complete the task. This test job involved turning, boring, milling, shaping, slotting, double-start screw cutting, drilling, hand fitting, and the manufacture of the special tools and gauges necessary to carry out the various machine-tool operations. The final task was to file and scrape the lever stop faces to adjust the travel of the valve to 0.1825 inches either side of the centre line.

OA Apprentice Terry Liming, who had led the class in craftsmanship throughout the four years and had achieved 90.6% for the "C" Class Double-Hexagon, came top again with over 85%. Regrettably no example of this test job remains in existence.

could have happened to me. Where Gunnery Instructors and Regulating Petty Officers had failed for nearly four years, an angry reprimand from my tiny Irish mother succeeded in making me 'see the light'. Perhaps the Civil Authorities would have more success today in curbing the wild excesses of wayward youth if they tackled them through their parents?

Called Apprentices and never Ratings, we were treated as a breed apart, an elite who were destined to become Chief Petty Officers at a very young age. It is small wonder that we really thought we were the 'cat's whiskers'. However, we were all treated as school-boys and this rankled especially when over 18 we still had less liberty than the young trainee Stokers in adjacent HMS Raleigh. It is fair to say that all Boy Arts longed for the day that they would 'pass-out' and become 'Ex Boys'.

## So, was our Artificer apprenticeship worth it?

Like most ex-Boys, after my 'passing-out' test job, I was rarely called upon to use the fitting and turning skills given me by a number of dedicated instructors. I never served on a Depot Ship and, apart from a lot of commutator skimming and undercutting and contact dressing in my first 4 (dc) ships, it was eight years, later, as a Chief EA, before I actually undertook a real F&T job. I was asked by the anxious MEO of my new frigate if I could urgently make an ignition adaptor so that he could flash-up the boilers, because no one in his staff was happy to cut a screw-thread on the Harrison lathe. I enjoyed the challenge, the job went to plan and the ship sailed on time. My long expensive workshop training was not however only justified by this single job but by the engineering know-how my apprenticeship, and later 'hands-on' experience had given me that allowed me to make sound judgments on the practicality of repair options. This was invaluable when at sea with charge responsibility, and while serving in the FMG and as a FOST Staff Sea-Rider. In my last job and ship in the RN, I was tasked with bringing all of the weapons, radio and electrical equipment, including the electrics taken over by then in all other ships, by the ME department, out of mothballs and get her to sea as a front-line carrier for two years. Allowed just over six months and £1 ¾ Million (in 1978) to accomplish this, I had to look at every piece of equipment and allot the limited funds to those jobs that only the Dockyard could do, leaving the major part of the work to my own ship's department and the FMG. Repair by replacement of the machinery and equipment in that 33-year old ship was not an option and almost every job needed the skills of an old-fashioned Artificer. After much effort by all concerned we carried out sea-trials, commissioned and worked up at Portland on time and met the subsequent demanding operational programme. This success was largely due to the 'hands-on' engineering skills and professional pride instilled at Fisgard and Caledonia in the many ex-boys involved in that venture. I very much doubt that a less practical apprenticeship would have provided us with the wherewithal we were required to demonstrate during that busy period.

Finally I would like to pay tribute to all of my classmates, my Divisional and other Officers, the Chief and POs, PTIs, Schoolies and Instructors and even 'hated' figures like Pusser Dadd, for their part in shaping my formative years. Knowingly or unwittingly and for better or worse they became a part of me and I thank them all for the help they gave me during those four years. I thoroughly enjoyed my subsequent naval career but look back on my apprenticeship at Fisgard with particular pride, affection, and gratitude.

# Chapter 6

## HMS Collingwood August 1948 – July 1949

The 14 Electrical Artificers 5th Class ex HMS Fisgard's 12 Class joined HMS Collingwood at Fareham on 12th August 1948, carrying their kit and toolboxes, having travelled by train from Plymouth. We were shown to wooden huts in the EAs Qualifying Block at the extreme western end of the camp, seemingly several miles from the main gate, where we met our 14 HMS Caledonia fellow ex-Ansons for the first time. Among these were Fred Pointer and Barry Elliott with each of whom I was destined to become a life-long friend. After unpacking we filled in our leave applications, collected our railway warrants and went off on three weeks summer leave.

I had devised a 'cunning plan' to extract the most out of my Travel Warrant, which was made out to Dunlaoghaire in Eire, my grandmother's home town and my ultimate destination. First, after a few days at home in Portsmouth with my family, I went up to London for two days. On Day 3 I met Jessie my platonic Torpoint girl friend off the overnight train from Plymouth at 5am to escort her to Euston for the train to Scotland where she was going to spend a holiday with her cousins. We had breakfast at Lyons Corner House and travelled together as far as Rugby where I was met by my brother George. Whilst the train was at Rugby there was just enough time for me to introduce him to Jessie and bid her farewell before her train left for Scotland. That brief encounter on the platform at Rugby was destined to prove fateful for George and Jessie. George was an Apprentice at Humber Motor Manufacturers, Coventry and I stayed at his 'Digs' for the weekend and had a grand time for we were great buddies and he knew Coventry well. On the Monday I went to the 'Centre of England'. There, visibly carrying my naval cap, but otherwise in civilian clothes and carrying a suitcase, I managed to 'thumb a lift' with an RAF Flight-Lieutenant who was returning to his air base from the Olympic Games in London after having been eliminated in the heats. He regaled me with first-hand accounts of the 'games' all the way to Manchester where I thanked him and made my way to my Uncle's home. I spent a few entertaining days there with my favourite cousin Patricia and then 'hitch-hiked' to Chester where I joined the 'Irish Mail' train to Holyhead and thence to Dunlaoghaire on my railway warrant. I spent ten enjoyable days in Ireland, mostly in Dublin which I then knew better than my own home-town, several of the days with my Godmother's daughter Norah Parsons. I returned home with no more stop-overs, to spend the last night of a memorable summer leave in Portsmouth.

Back in the real world I found Collingwood a bit of a culture shock after Fisgard. Although we were now Leading Hands and lived in centrally-heated huts with Corticene-covered floors, we were expected to clean the huts, polish the floors and keep the grounds around them tidy ourselves. Paradoxically this was the only time in our whole naval career that we cosseted Tiffies were ever required to 'look after ourselves'. At Collingwood as young EAs Qualifying we also had to wear boots and gaiters and march everywhere in that gigantic establishment. We were no longer a schoolboy elite but just another group of ratings under training in a pretty disciplined establishment. On the credit side however, we were reasonably well off, had all-night leave when not duty and, most importantly, I was a 'native' and could sleep at home most nights.

Our first four weeks course was dedicated to Direct Current and Alternating Current theory. AC was not then in use for Power and Distribution in ships, but solely for radio and radar supplies. We were told that after this course, much of which was 'old hat' to us, we would be divided into two, half becoming Radio EAs and the other half EAs with the implication that those who did best in the AC exams would have first chance of becoming REAs. In the event the class of 28 separated amicably into two by choice. Those who couldn't face the thought of an extra year, ie a total of 21 months, in Collingwood, after 4 years at Fisgard and wanted to go to sea, chose to remain EAs. This included Phillip Snell our genius, Bill Haddon, Eric Lemmon and Barry Partridge. The other 14 included several who had fallen in love with girls at the local Teachers' Training College, and others who were enjoying playing Soccer for Collingwood's crack First XI. These and others prepared to put up with 'Collingrad', were willing or eager to delay their sea-water baptism for best part of two years, perhaps to put themselves in line for future accompanied drafts to Shore Wireless Stations? Paradoxically having chosen to remain an EA, I spent most of my subsequent naval career in Electronics albeit in Sonar and Gunnery Fire-Control Systems. In fact the most interesting courses I ever took were the Long Radio and Radar Course and Pre-Commissioning Training Courses in 901, 903, 965, 995 Radar and JYA Tables, responsibility for and in the maintenance of which, I became actively involved.

The food at Collingwood was marginally better than at Fisgard. We ate in a Dining Hall that had a grass bank outside bearing the crests of Fisgard and Caledonia, created by Acting EA4 Woolnough of the 1943 entry. This proud proclamation of our origins was close to our huts. There was quite a lot of social and cultural activity going on in the camp and I particularly enjoyed attending the near-professional-standard Gilbert and Sullivan Operas and plays put on by the Collingwood societies. There was a lot of thespian talent available and the participants enjoyed entertaining the rest of us, as did the very high standard ship's Soccer and Rugby teams.

Back Row: Philip (John) Snell, George Butler, Fred Pointer, Bill Haddon.
2nd Row: Don Murdoch, Harry Taylor, John Cross, Eric Lemmon, John Dolley,
Fred Hall.
Front: Paddy McQuaid, Roy Palmer ,Frank Lyons, CEO C. Wager, CEA .T
Pook, Barry Partridge, Barry Elliott.

Our class of EAs Q was made up of ten ex Fisgard and four ex-Caledonia 5th Class plus one Direct-Entry Acting 4th Class EA who, being a Petty Officer, was naturally made Class Leader. We ex-Boys were happy with this arrangement, since he, Frank Lyons, nicknamed 'Nippy', was a good sort and happy to take all the flak. He had been an apprentice with an engineering company, was six years older than us, was married and had a child and lived locally. Our Divisional CPO was Chief EA Tom Pook, a genial ex-Boy who was like a father to us. Our Course Officer and Divisional Officer was a Commissioned Electrical Officer (L) Mr Wager, known as Charlie, who had our best interests at heart. He persuaded the whole class to take at least five of the RN Higher Educational Tests in order to qualify educationally for promotion for commissioned rank, while we might still remember our earlier academic studies. A subject pass in HET was declared by the Admiralty to be equivalent to 'O' Level, and a 'Distinction' (over 75%) a first class pass. Four years earlier we had all passed the apprentices' entry exam. whose standard in Maths, Science and English was accepted to be of School Certificate standard and, during our first two years as apprentices, we had studied Maths, Mechanics, Magnetism and Electricity to A level and English to above O level. During the last two years of our apprenticeship, we had studied Electrical Engineering to Ordinary National Certificate standard. However we had not sat the A level or ONC exams and thus had no proof of our academic and technical qualifications. We had no revision before the HET exams, which were conducted one after the other, but it is not surprising that all of us passed in at least 5 subjects. At that time the educational qualification for Sub-Lieutenant Pilot or Observer was 5 'O' levels and thus all of us were so qualified. One of our REAs Colin Moorcraft, and Charlie Poole, an OA classmate of ours at Fisgard, took advantage of this chance and became Pilots. I am grateful to Charlie Wager for putting us in for HET as I managed to get 5 Distinctions and 2 passes which gave me my first certified evidence of having achieved a nationally recognised, albeit modest set of academic qualifications.

Just before Christmas leave I received a letter from Jessie in Torpoint saying she would like to take me up on my invite to come down to Portsmouth for the festive season , I had quite forgotten my disingenuous suggestion when we parted at Rugby in August. This posed a problem for I was then going out regularly with a girl from Drayton named Shelia who shared my love of music and was in fact a good pianist and singer. Fortunately for me and for history, my brother George, who was spending Christmas at home from Coventry, volunteered to 'look after' Jessie during the holiday period. The four of us went out and about together and had a great time and George and Jessie 'clicked'. Shortly afterwards, Shelia and I parted amicably and, in another stroke of fate little more than a week later, I met the first and only love of my life. I had previously enjoyed the companionship, nothing more than that - honest, of three successive girls on different Leaves in Ireland but, as with Jessie and Shelia, we had been only 'just good friends'. However this girl was for real, my future wife Eileen.

My eldest sister Peggy's engagement to her fiancé Frank had ended at roughly the same time as Shelia and I broke up but she was considerably more upset than me and moped about the house. To cheer her up, and for the first and only time, I took her to a dance. It was held in the 'Angerstein Hall' in North End and was run by a Catholic girls organisation. After a couple of dances with Peggy I spotted Eileen 'across the crowded floor' a pretty girl who was petite, nice, fashionably-dressed and a good dancer. I asked her for the next dance and the next and the next and, as they say, the rest is history. From that day we became inseparable. Eileen and I shared a love of the theatre, in particular music and especially opera and ballet. We regularly sat 'in the gods' at the King's Theatre Southsea, along with the other cash-strapped lovers of music and drama. We were also very fond of ballroom dancing and often won a pair of tickets at a dance, for a future dance at the same or a different venue. A weekly visit to the Tivoli cinema near Eileen's home was de rigeur and we enjoyed many of that era's great films together in the back stalls.

Back at Collingwood we grew used to the daily grind of morning Divisions on the massive parade ground with PT from enthusiastic PTIs, drills by fanatical GI s and marching off to school. We would go to demonstration areas such as the 'Ring-Main' Building, or to the Gyro-Compass, Generator, Starter, Motor or Remote Control Servo equipment Strip and Assembly rooms in the 'White City'. We had instruction all day from Monday to Friday and on Saturday endured an hour being drilled by a bunch of trainee

GIs who had chosen Collingwood because it had such a huge parade ground and lots of 'cannon-fodder' like us to bellow at. After this tiresome period we went to the cinema where we were lectured, generally on current affairs, by a prominent local Civilian Speaker In those days, we had all voluntarily forsaken the '2 in I' Rum Issue and opted to be 'T', ie Temperance, not for the 3d per day but because 'grog' was not popular with 5$^{th}$ class Tiffies who knew they would very soon be able to draw a neat Tot. Notwithstanding our commendable abstinence from the Navy's most effective sedative, we still found it hard to keep awake during afternoon lectures in stuffy, pokey little airless classrooms. This was particularly difficult while some poor Instructor was trying to teach us how to work our way round the circuit diagram of a servo, rotary or audio amplifier, an electronic AC Voltage regulator or how to find the correct route "back to negative" on a 'Ward Leonard' Crane or Aircraft Lift..

In the Spring of 1949, my mother and ex RAF stepfather, having five grown-up children between them, of which I was the middle, were allocated a new four bedroom house on the embryo Leigh Park estate North of Havant. Earlier I had bought a new sports bicycle and thereafter used to ride from home to Collingwood in the morning then, after a busy day's instruction to Copnor where Eileen lived, go to the cinema or a dance with her somewhere in the Portsmouth area and then cycle home late in the evening, a round trip of more than thirty miles. However, I was fit in those days and in any case I felt no pain, for I was on 'Cloud Nine'. One evening, cycling along the A27 in uniform and in single file with Bill Haddon, a crowd of young female workers from 'Smith's Potato-Crisp' factory surrounded our bikes and pulled us off them and 'roughed us up' out of devilment. Our shouts of "Get Away", or words to that effect, made no impression on this man-mad mob and we were only saved from a fate worse than death by the approach of their bus. To explain my dishevelled state on arrival at Copnor, I told Eileen the half-truth that I had 'come off my bike'. In those days I was a fanatical supporter of Portsmouth football team and they were then top of the English League. On home match days I used to cycle to Eileen's home, leave my bike there and walk to Fratton Park and after the match walk back, pick up Eileen and go out to a dance with her. When Pompey were playing away I cycled from Collingwood to Southampton to watch them play and from there to Copnor to Eileen's. She tells me that the main topic of my conversation every Saturday night was football. I was among the well-behaved all-time record crowd at Fratton Park during the FA Cup Sixth Round match that year. Two weeks later, when I returned from a double-decker bus trip to London having seen Pompey beaten most unexpectedly by Leicester in the Cup Semi-Final, I found a black-draped 'coffin' on my bed with a Pompey RIP label and all of my EA and REA hut mates standing in mock grief as I entered the hut.

The Qualifying course pretty comprehensively covered all of the sea borne electrical and electronic equipment for which we were likely to become responsible, ranging from main generators through servo amplifiers to Typex Coding machines, the repair of the latter being taught us at HMS Mercury. We also visited HMS Excellent for an acquaint course in Gunnery Fire-control equipment following weeks of theory on the subject at Collingwood. One evening a week we attended the Drawing Office for instruction in 'Electrical' Drawing. Having been well taught Mechanical drawing at Fisgard, we found the drawing of cables and junction boxes simple and deadly boring.

Early one hot afternoon we were lying down near the classroom sunbathing before the class began. I had my head close to a high pile of bricks when my classmate John ('Tracer') Dolley on the other side of the pile saw a brick protruding. Being a tidy-minded Tiffy he pushed it into line. Unfortunately this displaced a brick on my side which I saw at the last moment, hurtling down. I tried to avoid it but it struck me on the head causing profuse bleeding. Feeling groggy and with a hanky on the wound and my cap on I staggered to the Sick Bay, which I found unmanned. I had to wait about ten minutes, stemming the flow of blood until a SBA appeared. He said he would have to call a doctor. Thirty minutes later a Doctor put in 8 stitches and I was sent back to the stuffy classroom. It was a good thing I wasn't seriously hurt. My classmates thought the whole incident was hilarious.

On 1st July 1949, just before the end of our course we were marched down to the Quarter Deck where, after all of our names were read out in alphabetical order, the Captain pronounced in the manner of a 'General Absolution':

"All Rated Acting Electrical Artificers 4th Class back
dated to date to be decided"
The Master at Arms then bellowed
"Right-turn Quick March"

Thus, with minimum fuss, in fact somewhat anti-climactically, we became Petty Officers and straight away requested to change from 'T' to 'G' so that we could draw a daily Tot of neat Rum. However, in Collingwood we were considered to be Acting POs as well as Acting EA4s so we had to continue to wear a red cap badge and black horn buttons. Furthermore all of the Acting 4th Class EAs, (and, for another year the REAs) still on course in Collingwood remained in the 'Tiffies' mess and did not move into the Establishment PO's Mess. When the course ended a few days later I learnt that I had earned six weeks advancement during the Qualifying Course. This was exactly the same amount of advancement that I had lost at Fisgard as a result of my Captain's Warning for Conduct. A couple of weeks later I was drafted to the Home fleet Light Fleet Carrier HMS Theseus then at Portsmouth. We knew that at sea there was no such rig as a PO in 'Fore and aft' rig wearing black buttons and a red cap badge. So I wore a raincoat over a gilt-buttoned gold-badged jacket leaving Collingwood and on the train to Portsmouth took off my red cap badge and replaced it with a bright new gold POs badge. I was now a qualified (albeit Acting) EA 4 on my way to earning my keep after 5 years training.

The weekend before I joined HMS Theseus turned out to be the most important in my life. On that very warm Saturday evening Eileen and I went to a dance on South Parade Pier. Since Eileen's 20th Birthday on the 9th of July, our 'romance' had really blossomed and I knew that I was in love with her. It was extremely hot on the dance floor and so at around ten o'clock on that moonlit night we decided to leave and stroll along the sea front towards Eastney. When we reached the steps opposite the pathway between the cricket ground and the miniature golf course we descended on to the shingle beach and sat with our backs against the wall facing the sea. A few minutes later five or six young Royal Marines came down the steps in high spirits. They didn't notice us in the shadow of the wall and stripped to their underpants and boisterously dashed into the sea and frolicked around noisily for about ten minutes. Whilst the Marines were having 'High Jinks', I seized the moment and plucked up the courage to propose to Eileen. Fortunately for me she accepted my proposal, and we were busy 'plighting our troth' when the Royals decided they were cool enough, began dressing and made their way to the promenade steps. Then they saw us for the first time and were terribly apologetic, although their behaviour and language during the 'skinny-dip' had been beyond reasonable reproach. Eileen and I accepted their apologies and after they had left for Eastney Barracks we, realising it was time to go to catch the last bus to Eileen's home, ran up the steps and along the promenade to the Canoe Lake to the bus stop. On the bus we decided not to tell Eileen's Mum of our intentions until the next day, but the die was cast. I cycled home happily to Havant that night full of joy and certain I had made the right choice of a partner for life.

# Chapter 7

## HMS Theseus July 1949 – July 1951

I joined my first ship proper, the 17,720 ton, 695 feet long Light-Fleet Carrier HMS Theseus at North Corner Jetty in Portsmouth Dockyard on 22nd July 1949, as an Acting Electrical Artificer 4th Class having just completed my five years training ashore at HMS Fisgard and Collingwood. Although Theseus was smaller than both Vanguard and Implacable, on which I had undergone 'Afloat Training' as an apprentice, she still looked pretty big to me as I went up the gangway with my kit and toolbox. I was directed to Petty Officers' Mess No 39 on the starboard side forward of the hangar which was occupied by 4th Class EAs, REAs OAs, Shipwrights, PO Electricians, PO Radio Electricians, PO Telegraphists, (PO) Yeomen of Signals, a PO Plumber, Painter and Blacksmith. After unpacking my kit and stowing my hammock I was taken to the EA's workshop where I met the Chief EA and the other 4 EAs. I then learnt that I would be taking over the maintenance of a section previously looked after by an ERA Fitter & Turner (E). This responsibility, for a young 'wet behind the ears' EA comprised the Crane, Aircraft & Bomb Lifts, Ammunition and Boat Hoists, Capstans, Conversion Machinery, Heavy Motors and Engine Room Electrics. I then met my predecessor, an ERA3 and my staff, which comprised an Acting PO Electrician, 2 Leading Electrical Mechanics and 4 Electrical

Mechanics. After being given a turnover including the complex drill for lowering and hoisting the Sea Otter flying Boat, the ERA (E) handed me the key of the Bomb Lift Machinery Space. This compartment was the unofficial 'cabin' of the 'Head of Section'. Thus, although I had a locker in the mess and ate there, for the next two years I slept on my late father-in-law's raised camp bed in a well-ventilated and private 'caboosh', rather than in a hammock in the very overcrowded mess. Most of the Electrical Department senior rates enjoyed similar perks as they had compartments scattered around the ship. I very soon realised what a great privilege and advantage this was for a young EA4.

My marriage proposal to Eileen having been accepted two weeks earlier, my Mother hosted an Engagement Party that weekend for us at her new house at Havant. I invited several of my old friends from Fisgard and  Collingwood but didn't know any of my new shipmates well enough to ask them. We had a great party but on the Monday afterwards I quickly learnt what being in the navy was really all about when the ship sailed for flying training in the Channel and Atlantic and Eileen and I were separated for the first of many times, albeit on this occasion for only a few weeks.

When two squadrons of Seafurys and Fireflies flew aboard from Lee-on the Solent shortly after we left harbour, I was given the low-down on how to 'goof' safely from the Flag Deck by 'Soapy' Hudson one of my new messmates a Yeoman of Signals. As the first Firefly made its approach, 'Soapy' said "This one is an early model and has a wooden prop so if it misses all 9 of the Arrester wires, dive below the parapet because the prop will break into a thousand pieces when it hits the crash barrier". I duly counted down as the arrester hook missed each successive wire and 'hit the deck' just before the aircraft went straight into the barrier and the prop disintegrated, spraying the 'Island' with splinters. Mercifully no one was hurt although the Firefly was pretty badly damaged and this crash-landing brought home to me how hazardous naval aviation could be. Later that morning I learnt that I was to be a member of the 'Crash on Deck Casualty team' tasked with closing up at the normally unmanned Sick Bay level of the Bomb Lift to call it down when it was carrying a casualty and to organise the carrying of the casualty(ies) through the nearby mess deck to the Sick Bay. During the next two years I was called upon to carry out, this job 'at the rush', after a number of fatal and serious incidents on the flight deck and saw some pretty horrendous sights as I reached into the unlit lift to pull out the stretcher borne victim(s).

During this flying training cruise of about six weeks the ship visited Penzance and anchored several times at night off the coasts of Cornwall and Devon but did not visit any foreign or significant places. For me the highlight of this deployment was my first really responsible job since qualifying as an EA, a somewhat apprehensive part in the repeated launch and recovery at sea of the ship's Sea Otter single-engined 'Flying Boat'

My maintenance responsibilities in HMS Theseus included the aircraft crane and I was required to certify to the Flight-Deck Officer (FDO), that the crane and all the special equipment necessary for the launch or recovery of the Sea Otter was fully operational before driving the crane when it was used to lift the aircraft. This special gear comprised a two-part 'Thomas Grab', a beautifully machined 'Quick-Release' hook and the crane hoist drum's compensating-barrel. When not rigged, I kept the Thomas Grab well greased and the QR Hook immersed in a drum of lubricating oil, inside the crane-house. The Sea Otter itself was crewed and maintained by the ship's own flight and was not part of the embarked Carrier Air Group. It carried a Pilot, an Aircrewman and generally one or two passengers. I think it is worth recording here the uniquely 'Harry-Tate' drill employed in the launch and recovery of this aircraft at sea.

Immediately before a water take-off at sea, I removed the crane's Ponder ball and hook, and fitted the mated Thomas Grab and the QR hook; cocked, proved and re-cocked the QR hook in front of the FDO and signed the A700 Log. At the same time the Sea Otter, having been brought up from the hangar and had its wings spread by the flight personnel, was positioned inboard of the crane facing forward. Although not used during the launch, the Thomas Grab was rigged, mated, in case of a launch mishap.

After the crew embarked, the Aircrewman climbed out of the cabin hatch and up a wire ladder through a narrow hole in the engine nacelle and sat on its after edge facing the propeller about three feet in front him. I was then ordered by the FDO to position the jib head above the aircraft and lowered the QR hook to the Aircrewman who attached it to the aircraft hoist ring. The engine was then primed, the starting handle engaged and two strong Naval Airmen began to turn the starting flywheel. After several minutes of strenuous effort this had gained enough momentum for the inertial starter to be engaged, through its reduction gearing, with the 850 HP 9-cylinder engine. The prop turned, the engine gave a loud cough and splutter and, after one revolution, generally died and the weary lads were ordered to try again. It was difficult to achieve a satisfactory prime and, more often than not, took at least three time-consuming attempts to start the engine, by which time the two lads were knackered. There was all round relief when, at last, the continuous roar of the engine was heard. With the prop rotating I was then ordered to hoist the aircraft, clear of the deck and to slew it outboard facing forward before lowering and then inching it close to the sea surface, until the FDO signalled the Pilot to "Slip when ready". When happy the Pilot told the Aircrewman to pull the QR toggle and the aircraft was launched in the same way as a sea-boat. The crewman then descended to the cabin, closed the hatch and the aircraft taxied away to starboard. When clear of the ship, the pilot revved up and took off. Apart from starting the engine, launching a Sea Otter, whilst underway at sea, was pretty straightforward. The Sea Otter occasionally took off from the flight deck but, except on the occasion of its 'swan song' in April 1951, always landed in the sea, recovery from which was a hairy 'Heath-Robinson' nautical /aviation affair.

The ship turned into wind at about 10 knots and the Sea Otter taxied to a position abreast of the crane, the upper. female, part of the unmated Thomas Grab was attached to the crane hoist wire and the lower part, and QR hook, were supported by two long 'tricing' wires, the ends of each of which were held by a team of 6 of the FD crew. Their job was to keep the lower male section as close to the upper section as possible until the aircraft's prop had passed under it. Then the 'Snatch Squad' went into action. On the FDOs verbal command, the FD team rapidly lowered. practically dropped, the QR hook to the Aircrewman whilst I lowered the upper part of the grab. As soon as the QR Hook was connected, the FD crew pulled hard on the tricing wires until the Grab mated. The pilot then shut down the engine. I took up the slack on the hoist wire and slowly hoisted the aircraft while the compensating barrel maintained the highest point of successive waves until the Otter was 'high and dry'. I then hoisted it safely on to the Flight Deck facing forward. The recovery evolution certainly caused a lot of Adrenalin to flow, not least on the part of the Aircrewman who had nano-seconds to avoid being hit by, but to catch and engage, a heavy QR hook as the aircraft tried to match the ship's speed. Protected only by a Biggles' leather helmet and a cumbersome flying jacket, this brave soul had earlier climbed up through a hot engine to sit precariously on the lip of a hole in the slipstream of a huge prop. I had a lot of respect for this intrepid aviator.

During those first few weeks at sea I worked hard and for long hours, learnt a lot, gained plenty of 'hands-on' experience and realised that life on an operational carrier was never dull, there was always something exciting happening and I found my ship-wide responsibilities very rewarding in terms of job satisfaction.

In October the ship returned to Portsmouth and began a three-month refit. Soon after settling down in dry dock we all 'fell-in on' the flight deck to greet HM King George V1 as he passed our bows on his way through the dockyard Although I had plenty of maintenance work to do on my own equipment I, and the other EAs, were soon press-ganged into overhauling the Supply, Ring Main and important Breakers, dressing their contacts and carrying out their 'milli-volt' contact tests, tasks that could only be readily carried out during a refit. After having completed a number of them I was glad to be able to get back to overhauling all of my own equipment. It was a very happy time for me, I was living at Eileen's Aunt and Uncle's house opposite her home, was ashore four nights out of five, when not duty EA, and we were able to go dancing or to the cinema and blissfully enjoyed our betrothal.

Whilst in dock, we occasionally had an afternoon off nicknamed a 'Shilling Make and Mend'. If you bought a ticket to watch a Navy, Command or ship's team football match you were allowed ashore for the afternoon and rest of the day. Needless to say the number who actually watched these games was somewhat less than the tickets sold and next morning, those who hadn't seen the match could be seen asking their mates for the score in case they were interrogated. Other memories I have of this period include seeing the painful transport of the enormous and brim-full buckets used on the ship as 'night-heads'. Duty-watch junior ratings heaved them across the gangway and up the dock steps to empty them safely down a drain, but inevitably, spilt much of the contents on the way. This leads me to my first clash with authority since my Fisgard days. As inferred earlier, in dock the ships 'Heads' (lavatories) and bathrooms were kept locked to protect personnel working on the dock bottom or lower ship's sides from being drenched by unwelcome fluid, or worse, discharges. One Saturday morning, just before we undocked and with the prospect of a happy short weekend ashore, I packed up work a little early. I repaired to my 'caboosh' where I had heated up a bucket of water, rather illegally on top of a portable electric fire, so that I didn't have to wait until after Captain's Rounds had finished before being allowed to use the shore bathrooms. My back was to the compartment door when suddenly it opened and, in my shaving mirror I saw with horror a short figure who, stepping over the high 'dwarf bulkhead', seemed to be all gold, four rings and a scrambled-egg peak in juxtaposition. It was our new and illustrious Captain 'Ben' Bolt who remarked, on seeing my uniforms hanging up neatly and me busy shaving, "What's this then, Montague Burtons?" The skipper had strayed off the official Mess Deck Rounds route to my disadvantage. The Master at Arms stepped forward and barked, "Outside my Office". At noon I was charged with 'washing in an improper place namely the Bomb Lift Machinery Space' and put in the Captain's Report. When I met Eileen, (rather later that afternoon than I had planned), I had to warn her I was likely to lose my liberty from the following Monday. Sure enough I was given seven days 'leave stopped' by the

Skipper and my happy time with Eileen was put on hold. However I made the best of it building up some 'duty credit' with my fellow EAs by assuming the role of Duty EA every day and, in my spare time by making a hearth rug as a present for my brother George and his new fiancée Jessie, my friend from Torpoint, who had just announced their engagement.

Shortly after Christmas leave, which Eileen and I enjoyed at Portsmouth, the ship returned to tidal waters and in mid January, after trials off Portsmouth, set off for Scottish waters (so beloved by Aircraft Carriers). While the ship was carrying out flying exercises I came out in a rash and with it a severe back ache. I had developed Shingles and, with the ship anchored for the weekend off Ardrossan I was confined to a sick bay cot and unable to visit my late Grandfather's nearby home-town, Kilwinning. It was to be 40 years before I had another chance to visit my father's roots. After 10 days of discomfort I resumed my duties and though it was pretty cold on the flight deck off Northern Ireland and Scotland I was glad to be back in harness.

Theseus carried 82,000 gallons of 100 Octane Aviation spirit so, to prevent the build-up of highly explosive vapour in the ship's tanks as her aircraft used it, the tanks were vented for 20 minutes every hour and were frequently topped up from a tanker. Whilst venting Avgas one could smell petrol vapour on the port weather decks and smoking was prohibited. During that Spring cruise the Sea Otter was deployed many times and I became quite experienced in my role in its launch and recovery at sea. I noticed that the Otter often carried a senior officer as a passenger. I believe that it enabled aviators who had non-flying posts onboard to continue to earn 'flying pay'. The time sped by and soon the ship was on its way south again. Eileen and I had decided to get married on 10th April 1950 and she made the arrangements while I was away at sea. After the wedding reception we intended going to Ireland for our honeymoon. However the ship's post-Easter programme was advanced by two weeks because we were now planned to carry out the first RN Jet Aircraft landing exercises in the channel followed by Home Fleet exercises and the Flag Officer Submarines' Summer War off the north of Scotland and Ireland before preparing to deploy to the Far East in September. As a result we had only six days

available for our honeymoon so we decided to go to Boscombe instead as the ship was sailing nine days later. Theseus returned to Portsmouth in mid March for seasonal leave. I went on 'Second' leave on 31st March. We were married at 9.15 on Easter Monday at St Joseph's Church in Copnor and after the Nuptial Mass we had a traditional wedding breakfast in the church hall followed by a dance. Early in the afternoon we were escorted to the railway station by Eileen's friends from her Drawing Office and by the EAs, Chief EA and Electrical Officer of Theseus, who gave us a noisy send off on our honeymoon. We thought that by getting my sister Eileen to apply for a temporary ration book in her name that, as my bride now had the same name, we would fool the hotel into thinking we had been married some time. That cunning ploy failed for we soon realised that we had 'newly-wed' written all over our faces. We were virtually indistinguishable from the scores of similarly dressed young couples strolling around Bournemouth and taking to the floor at the Tea Dances at the Winter Gardens. All too soon those halcyon days ended and it was time to return to Portsmouth where we set up our first home in rooms with Eileen's Uncle and Aunt before saying our fond farewells at the Copnor Bridge bus stop as I set off to rejoin Theseus for the 'Summer Cruise' and Eileen caught the bus to Havant to her job at the Admiralty Mining Establishment at Leigh Park House near Rowlands Castle.

We commenced deck-landing trials with Sea Vampire Jet Fighters of 702 Squadron soon after leaving harbour. As the pilot sat well forward of the two wing-mounted  engines he would have taken the full impact of the normal steel barriers if the aircraft missed all of the arrester wires on landing. We had therefore been fitted with canvas looped barriers designed to slip around the cockpit nose on impact and to catch the two wings inboard of the jets. It looked pretty hairy and the pilots seemed very vulnerable however they were very good and brave and, only once did any of the jet aircraft miss all of the arrester wires. On this occasion the Vampire was brought safely to rest by the canvas 'snare' which caught the jet squarely without harming the pilot or damaging the engines although the canvas cut deeply into the leading edge of the wings. I witnessed the first ever night landings of a jet aircraft on an RN carrier during that period, the historic event being covered by a renowned Air correspondent, whose hyperbole during that broadcast damaged my faith in the BBC. After two weeks the trials were declared a success and 702 Squadron departed. The two steel barriers were re-fitted and as, the ship sailed west, piston-engined Seafuries of 807 and Fireflies of 810 Squadrons embarked for the Home Fleet summer exercises. Government fuel economies imposed on the navy during 1949, limiting steaming to essential exercises, continued until June 1950 and, in consequence the few Home Fleet ships permitted to go to sea generally anchored at night. During the exercises in the channel, being a carrier, Theseus and its 'plane-guard' destroyer anchored off several 'run-ashore-worthy' places like Weymouth, Torquay, Plymouth, Mevagissey and Falmouth, but were too far off for leave to be granted, although I do recall an insensitive broadcast being made after we anchored one evening in Bigbury Bay – "There will be no leave tonight – Officers' boat leaves in 5 minutes". However we did get a run ashore in Penzance and the Scilly Isles before going up the Irish Sea to Portrush, my mother-in-law's childhood hometown, for a short visit before the start of FOSM's Summer War.

This was a pretty intense exercise involving a number of submarines and the whole of the active Home Fleet including cruisers, destroyers, frigates and corvettes with the fleet carrier Implacable and Theseus providing air support. In late May/early June up there it doesn't really get dark at night and so flying lasted non-stop for up to 18 hours a day. All of the flight deck personnel were in two watches except the Naval Airman who stood close to the aircraft revving-up on the catapult and showed the pilot the check board and pointed in turn to Engine, Airframe, Equipment and Crew and, if given the thumbs up for each, signalled the 'clear for launch' to the catapult crew and off went the aircraft. This chap had been on duty for several days when, having 'released' one Seafury he turned and, near exhaustion walked into

the whirling prop of the next aircraft in line. I heard the broadcast "Casualty on the Flight Deck – Emergency Team Close Up at the Rush" and dashed to the Bomb lift's Sick Bay level and when instructed, called the lift down and opened the doors. The young NA's face was missing and his yellow cloth helmet had turned bright orange with the spurting blood. I helped carry the poor lad into the sick bay where the doctors did their best for him as the ship made a dash for Bangor in County Down. Alas their efforts were in vain and this keen and overworked young man expired. A couple of days later while waiting on the crane to launch the Sea Otter I witnessed another tragic accident when the wings folded on the fifth of six Sea Hornets as it was taking off 'Implacable' and the aircraft fell into the sea. Despite evasive action by the ship, the aircraft was run down by the Fleet Flagship and the crew were lost. The official report said that an indicator 'flag' warning that the wings were not fully spread and locked, had been pushed in by one of the flight deck crew.

One day the C-in C Home Fleet, Admiral Sir Philip Vian (of WW2 Cossack/Altmark fame) flew from 'Implacable' in one of their Barracuda Torpedo bombers and afterwards landed onboard 'Theseus', temporarily transferring his flag. The Barracuda had a bad name for safety and there was some trepidation among the naval guard and Royal Marine band drawn up behind the second barrier as the aircraft came in to land. Fortunately it all went well; the Barracuda made a perfect landing and, as the 'C in C' stepped on to the deck the band played. and the guard saluted After spending the night onboard in the Admiral's sea cabin where he breakfasted, the admiral was coming out of the outward-opening door of his private heads when I, at the rush answering a call to fix a wind instrument on the bridge and dashing along the narrow passage, clumsily struck the door with my toolbag causing it to slam shut on him and smacking the distinguished Admiral in the face. Needless to say he was not best pleased but fortunately was unharmed and accepted my abject apology. I wonder if he thought that landing in a Barracuda was no sweat compared with bumping in to an over enthusiastic but clumsy clot of an EA.

Mail sent via GPO London from Eileen was very good when the ship was in home waters. We both wrote daily, a habit we maintained throughout our many and often long naval separations during the next 29 years. At the end of FOSM's Summer War the ship anchored alone in Loch Ewe as programmed. In WW2 this had been a busy base but the shore facilities and canteen were now closed and apart from a few crofter's huts and lots of sheep it was deserted. Eileen was not on the telephone at home so, having by then been separated from my bride for over two months I had arranged by letter to phone the nearest Telephone Box to her house on that Saturday at 5pm. The only liberty boat ashore, on which I was the sole passenger, left the ship at 1300 and I soon realised why no one else was interested in visiting this 'ghost town' on a wet and windy Saturday afternoon in June - it was the world's worst 'run ashore'. After booking my call in the only telephone box I wandered aimlessly all afternoon looking for non-existent things of interest, wishing and whiling away the time until 1700. At long last the time arrived for my 600 mile trunk call assignation and I eagerly dialled the Portsmouth number. To my joy Eileen almost immediately answered but sounded very anxious. I asked her what was wrong and she cried "There's a spider in the phone box and it's coming nearer". The whole of our long awaited and precious three minutes together on the phone was then taken up by her increasing alarm as this damned arachnid crept menacingly nearer until, as the pips started, she gasped loving greetings to me and ran out of the kiosk to escape his grasp. After another two hours wait in that god-forsaken place for the boat back I returned aboard somewhat peeved and frustrated. However 'true love knows no bounds' and so I resolved to go ashore a week later for a brief trip home by train whilst we were at anchor off Bournemouth overnight before paying a visit to Boulogne. The ship duly anchored off Bournemouth on the Sunday but even though this resort held recent very happy memories for me, I and hundreds of other Pompey natives, went ashore and nipped home by train for a few hours. Eileen and I enjoyed a brief reunion before I had to return. By the time I reached Bournemouth the last boat of the evening had gone and I, and many of the crew, had to sleep in deck chairs on the beach and caught the boat back next morning before the ship sailed for some more flying exercises before setting off for Boulogne. I found the town very interesting but run down and rather poorer than I expected. As none of the locals spoke English and in order to get the most out of my very first foreign run ashore I was happy to practise my schoolboy French for the first time with, I hasten to admit, some embarrassing misunderstandings, which fortunately were taken in good spirit by the natives. The ship left Boulogne on the 29th of June 1950 and as we crossed the channel the Seafuries and Fireflies flew off to Lee on the Solent and Yeovilton and I helped the Sea Otter take off from the sea for Lee before the ship entered Portsmouth next morning.

Just four days earlier Communist North Korea invaded South Korea and this act of war was swiftly followed by a United Nations decision to oppose this act of aggression. Our planned deployment to the Far East to relieve HMS Triumph, and to possibly visit Australia and New Zealand, was thus advanced one month and plans were put in place to prepare the ship for war service. The crew strength was increased by about 250 to the 'war complement' of 1400, including the 17th Carrier Air Group with Seafuries of 807 and Fireflies of 810 squadron; a total of 36 combat aircraft and the ship's own Sea Otter Flying Boat. Some urgent modifications were considered necessary to the flying facilities and the ship was docked for a final hull inspection in the only dock available, the large floating dock moored between Fountain Lake Jetty and Whale Island where the continental Ferry Port is now sited.

One early evening whilst we were high and dry in dock and I was duty EA, an explosion occurred in the armament depot on the opposite side of the harbour at the RN Armament depot at

Bedenham while ammunition was being transported. Fortunately for us the main blast was directed northwards and not eastwards for we were in a vulnerable position and closer to the explosion than any other ship. I was down below at the time and didn't hear the bang but was alerted by the subsequent broadcast. I checked the electrical supplies and they were unaffected, but the duty shipwright, aided by the duty hands had to go around and ensure that all the shores supporting the ship were still firmly in place by hammering each of them with sledge-hammers. He had only just finished this strenuous task and returned to the mess for supper when there was a second explosion and he had to do it all again. Mercifully no one was injured and the subsequent inquiry established that the cause was the incorrect filling of munitions.

I was rather more closely involved in a lesser 'cock-up' shortly afterwards. One of the modifications deemed necessary was the replacement of the flight deck landing lights. The wiring of some of these terminated in the Captain's cabin and the cabins of the Commander and Commander (Air). Because of the secret nature of documents kept in the Captains cabin, he insisted that the internal connections of the new lights were made by a responsible skilled naval rating, rather than a dockyard matey. Although the job itself was relatively simple I was specially selected for this task. (that's what I was told anyway}.The task involved receiving the cable fed through a hole in the deck of each fitting in turn, packing the gland and tightening it and, when all were in place connecting them to a junction box. I had to work from the top of a tall step-ladder because the deckhead was more than 8 feet up and had agreed a tapping code with the dockyard mateys on the deck above to ensure we all knew what we were doing. The whole task took one long day and I was busy doing it while the Captain worked at his desk below. He clearly remembered my recent misdemeanour but seemed to have forgiven me. At about 5pm he gave me the key to his cabin and said "Make sure it's all safely secured and return the key to the Duty CO when you have finished. A couple of hours later I was up the ladder close to an attractive mahogany display cabinet with a latticed glass front containing his prize silverware, when I completed the last connection. As I happily and over hastily descended the ladder my heel struck the cabinet breaking one of the thin panes of glass and splitting its delicate wood lattice frame. I cursed my clumsiness and decided I must seek the urgent help of a 'chippy'. After locking the cabin I set off at the rush forward along the gallery deck carrying the long step ladder in one hand and my tool bag in the other. In my blind panic I accidentally crashed into the wooden door of the Commander's office bursting it open and breaking its lock. What a shambles! I pulled the door closed and after putting the ladder and tools in my caboosh, I went to the mess and begged the duty Shipwright to come to my aid, offering him my Tot for a month if he would rectify my trail of destruction before the Captain and Commander came aboard the next morning. The Chippy, bless him, rose to the occasion cutting a new rhombus shaped piece of glass and very skilfully rebuilding the splintered lattice woodwork and re-polishing it. He did a similar 'invisible repair' job on the door of the Commander's Office while I acted as his mate and cleaned up. By the time he had finished it was well past midnight, and no one, not even the Captain or Commander would ever have known of the damage. Needless to say I never reported the incidents and profusely thanked my mess-mate for saving 'my bacon', my professional reputation and possibly my career.

During that docking we had to use the dockyard's lavatories which employed a 'tidal-wave flushing system'. A line of simple closets sat over an open sewer pipe at one end of which was a large automatic cistern which, every 5 minutes or so operated, causing a tidal wave to flush all of the closets. If they were all occupied at the time, the men waiting saw the occupants quickly and successively leap to their feet to avoid the communal down wash. One morning we all had to leap up particularly smartly because some joker in the closet containing the cistern, had made a paper boat filled with smoke making material and set it alight before launching it on its merry way down the line next time the cistern flushed!

I took early summer leave and Eileen and I enjoyed a 'Second Honeymoon' in Ireland. On return I found that Barry Elliott, my chum from Collingwood, had joined Theseus from the destroyer Scorpion, together with his classmate from Caledonia, Sammy Snell. The three of us EA 4s, who had all joined the navy on the same day six years earlier, became close buddies. The ship undocked in late July and moved to North Corner Jetty to complete storing, then to a buoy to 'ammunition ship' and on to South Railway jetty. When carrying out navigational checks whilst at NCJ, Barry found that the cables to the 'Steering Tape' in the wheelhouse below the bridge had been severed. He reported this and soon an investigation began which quickly escalated up to MI5 level. Sabotage by a communist sympathiser onboard was suspected. However after a couple of days it was concluded that the perpetrator was a non-technical rating who wanted to delay our departure for personal reasons. When given the OK by MI5 it only took Barry a few minutes to rectify the problem and the ship's programme continued to schedule. By now we were fully manned and on 14th August the ship left the harbour to anchor at Spithead. Having been advised that I, and many others, was due for a foreign commission and was likely to be transferred to a ship in the Far East before Theseus returned to the UK in the following summer, Eileen and I prepared to face a 2 ½ years separation by making the most of the few hours of liberty available during those last few days. Luckily I was able to go ashore on the night before we sailed and said an emotional farewell to Eileen at the bus stop at 6am on Friday 18th August, fully expecting not to see her again until the spring of 1953. I caught the MFV from King's Stairs and remember how silently thoughtful we all were on

the way out to the ship. After 'weighing', we embarked our aircraft and set off for Korea.

The non-stop passage to Malta was one of intensive flying activity during which there were a number of prangs the worst of which resulted in the destruction of several aircraft and the loss of a naval airman who was working in the cockpit of a Seafury hit by an incoming Firefly that had missed all of the arrester wires, and hopped over both barriers before crashing among the aircraft parked forward. The Firefly's crew was uninjured but the young lad was lost over the side with the aircraft.

Before we reached Malta our aircraft, which wore the letter 'T' on their tail planes, had black and white stripes painted on their wings to identify them as 'friendly' to the UN Forces they would be fighting alongside when we arrived in Korean waters.

We had a couple of days at Malta where Barry, Sam and I enjoyed our first visit and were shown the 'sights' of the island, including the notorious Valetta and Floriana night-club areas known as 'the Gut', and the 'Floriana Gut respectively, by some of our older EAs. While making an educational visit to the latter, infamous for homosexual  shows, we were taken aback to see our new Divisional Officer ashore in uniform, without shoulder pads and cap, drinking with and chatting-up a couple of young sailors. We young Tiffies, unused to this odd sort of behaviour, suddenly realised why our older EAs called him 'Trixie'. Next day Theseus set off for Port Said, continuing intense flying exercises all the way. One morning there was a 'Flight Deck Casualty and Fuel Leak on deck' call and a total ban on smoking. When I called the bomb lift to the sick bay level, two naked young stokers staggered out looking like cooked lobsters and reeking of aviation fuel. They had been fuelling an aircraft when the hose split and they had bravely tried to stop the leak and been drenched in 100 octane fuel. The doctor had removed their soaked overalls before joining them in the lift, which stunk of petrol. All three had their hands over their eyes to protect them. The Sick Bay staff immersed the two lads in baths filled with olive oil to soothe their 'spirit-burned' skin and happily they made a complete recovery.

It was getting quite warm as we steamed through the Eastern Mediterranean but the flying programme continued apace. The ship can seen here with an aircraft being worked on, as it steams southwards through the Suez Canal. As we passed Ismalia a number of soldiers lined the bank and gave us

their traditional greetings, shouting remarks like: "Get your knees brown Jack", and"You silly B's are going the wrong way" We looked forward to the day when we would get our own back.

It was very hot onboard as we made our way down the Red Sea and I had a particularly torrid time mending a defective Salinometer which, mounted above the Evaporating plant in an uncooled part of the For'd Machinery Space, had an environment temperature of over 140 degrees F. Fortunately most of the equipment for which I was responsible was sited in less unfriendly places. We stopped for two days at Aden where the three of us young EA4s went ashore. The conditions aboard Theseus were not terribly good. We were already living with weevil-infested bread, a colony of rats, and millions of cockroaches as well as high temperatures, and many of us suffered from tropical heat rash Furthermore the food was pretty awful. With a war complement aboard in the tropics the Evaporators could not produce enough water so it had to be rationed. The bathrooms were only opened daily for three half hours. In those pre-air-conditioning days the only cold drinks, we had onboard were the daily Tot of rum and glass of lime juice. It is small wonder we took every chance of a run ashore where we could cool off with a swim, a shower and have a few cold beers and a half- decent meal of SEAC (Steak, Egg and Chips) in the company of our chums.

After this brief break the ship sailed on the ten day non-stop passage to Singapore. Flying training continued throughout this passage and it was noticeable how very experienced the aircrews had become, the number of deck-landing mishaps falling away to zero despite the ever increasing tempo of the exercises as we drew nearer to the war zone. It was still very hot and many of the ship's company and officers slept at night in camp beds on the gun sponsons and boat decks. Our PO's mess only had 26 'slinging billets', which took up the whole of the deckhead space, but had 46 occupants. The 'en-suite' bathroom had two showers and four wash basins and very restricted opening times. I thanked my lucky stars that I had my own, relatively cool caboosh and outboard of it was a watertight workshop where I could while away my spare time making a set of rugs for home. I had linked into a little-used telephone line so that I could be called direct at my 'cabin' at any time, if any of my equipment became defective. This proved particularly helpful later on but had also been useful in home waters. We had a very good and large laundry onboard operated by a team of 'unofficial Chinese' and if any of their machines broke down I would receive a panic-stricken call from the 'No 1 Dhobey Man' to come and fix it. For my prompt attention to his problems I enjoyed free laundry services, including the replacement of buttons and repairs – no small saving in cash. If I was called out during the night to repair a laundry defect I was rewarded with a tin of peaches or something similar. I never asked how the Chinese managed to lay their hands on such luxuries while we were at sea. We had an excellent RN Photographic Section onboard who had first class cameras and developing and printing facilities. However they were making so much money on the side printing copies of official photos they had taken, some of which are reproduced in this Chapter, that they lost interest in developing and printing the ship's company's snaps. Sam and I decided we would fill this gap in the market and, with a set of gear we bought ashore in Malta we set up a private photographic firm. Every night Sam and I toiled away in my workshop developing and printing rolls of films taken by our messmates, ourselves and others, on box cameras. We had great problems in getting and keeping the temperature of the developer and fixer down to a satisfactory level and as the quality of the photography was pretty amateurish and we lacked the professional expertise and equipment of the RN Photographic Section, our end product was less impressive than we had hoped and we had to drop our price to stay in business. By the time we reached the Orient we were steadily losing money and with the prospect of being continually in 'Defence Watches' at sea and watch-keeping at night and thus having no spare time, we wound up our enterprise leaving the field clear for the professionals. In the absence of any other photos, some of the rather poor fruits of our tropical labours are shown, with apologies.

We arrived at Singapore on 16th September, 4 weeks after leaving Spithead and, during our brief stop for fuel and stores, there was just time for a few hours ashore in this interesting cosmopolitan city. In those days it was, as I expected from the films I had seen and the books I had read, a somewhat smelly colonial port with some grand buildings. We were soon on our way to the real Far East – Hong Kong and arrived on 24th September during a violent tropical

rainstorm. This photograph, taken that morning as we approached Victoria, gives a very different picture of the 'Pearl of the Orient' than one sees now, almost 60 years later.

Nonetheless I found Hong Kong a most fascinating place which I was destined to visit many times during the next 23 years. Back in 1950 the harbour was as busy if not busier than nowadays but the ships were all steam-driven and all the junks were powered by the wind. We spent a week there at anchor and most of us spent as much time ashore as possible in the best 'run-ashore' in the world, at that time. Our currency onboard became Hong Kong Dollars with an exchange-rate of 16 to the pound. We found that we could buy as much in HK with their dollar as we could in Singapore with theirs, at an exchange rate of only 8 to the pound, so we were quite well off in Hong Kong. I bought nylon stockings and sent them to

Eileen by airmail. They were prohibitively expensive at home and proved most welcome. I planned to save as much as possible during our time in Korean waters and to really go shopping mad next time we visited this 'shoppers paradise'. During our visit the ship's side was painted by a small team of Chinese girls operating from a sampan. In exchange for the gash food from all of the messes onboard, that would otherwise be ditched, these cheerful hard-working and petite young ladies, under the protective eyes of their leader Mary Ah Choy, endeared themselves to us all.

After 'taking over' from HMS Triumph and bidding farewell for a while to our side-party, (who gave us a tearful send-off), we sailed north to our new base at Sasebo on Japan's southern-most island Kyushu. On the way, we rehearsed typical flying programmes for the war situation facing us. Because of the continuous use of the flight deck by warplanes, our Sea Otter had not been deployed since we left the UK. As it took so long to start, launch and recover it became obvious that it was unsuited for air-sea rescue in a war zone and her role was taken over by a USN S51 helicopter loaned to us by the cruiser USS Worcester, complete with its air and ground crew. Our Sea Otter was therefore flown off the flight deck to HMS Unicorn off Japan and the helicopter flew aboard. As my services were not required with the 'Chopper', my potential work load was reduced. This was just as well since I was about to have a rather busy time.

Going into my caboosh one day as we passed through the Formosa Straits, I heard an ominous rumble coming from the large motor-alternator next door. This was the For'd of two DC/AC Conversion machines which supplied the 230volt 50 Hz power to all of the ship's Radar, Radio and Audio equipment. Each of the two machines ran for a week at a time and I changed them over every Saturday morning. On investigation I found that the alternator end motor bearing was overheating and was the source of the noise. I went aft and ran-up the after machine and changed over the AC supplies to it and then shut down the For'd machine and, after assessing the time necessary to take down the cooling system over the machine and strip the DC motor, remove the large armature, change the defective bearing and reassemble the lot. I reported this major defect to the Chief EA and asked for a couple of EAs to help me and my team for eight hours to rectify it. The news of this defect was rapidly passed 'upwards' via Commander (L) to the Captain who naturally asked how long it would take to repair. Concerned that if the after machine failed we would lose all radar, radio and internal communications including the 'Tannoy', the Skipper gave us 4 hours to get it working again and in the meanwhile ordered the ship to 'Action Stations', because of the proximity of unfriendly Communist China. The official reason broadcast to the ship's company for this first call to Action stations was because of "an unidentified aircraft shadowing the ship". After 4½ hours of toil and sweat in that hot and cramped compartment, with sound advice and leadership from the Commissioned Electrical Officer and the Chief EA, we completed the job and the ship's company returned to the more relaxed conditions of 'Defence Stations'.

We arrived at Sasebo on Thursday 5th October and after two days of preparations, sailed for our first operational period in the Yellow Sea, as flagship of the Commonwealth Carrier Task Group attached to the US Navy's 9th Fleet. Our aircraft were in action against the North Korean army within a few hours. The Communists were already retreating northwards at the time and we actively harassed them and blockaded the shrinking enemy held western coastline of Korea for a month, with four days to re-ammunition in Sasebo halfway through. By the end of our second patrol the North Koreans had been beaten and thrown back to the Chinese border and, no longer required, together with the other Commonwealth ships, we withdrew to Hong Kong, the war seemingly over. After carrying out exercises off Hong Kong, rather curtailed by a Typhoon in which our Canadian Destroyer escorts suffered severe and us superficial damage, we repaired to Junk Bay to tidy ourselves up before triumphantly entering Hong Kong harbour for a nice long visit. I was working on the crane with the Blacksmith trying to straighten the jib head pulley which had been bent during the storm, when I witnessed a piece of history. The Chief Yeoman of Signals came dashing out of the after door of the Island and ran diagonally across the flight deck where he was met by the Captain running to meet him. The CYS handed him a signal which he read excitedly and then the two of them ran past us into the island. Shortly afterwards, the Commander broadcast that "A Million-strong Chinese army has crossed into North Korea and are attacking the UN armies and forcing them to retreat. We are

therefore returning immediately to the Yellow Sea".

Then followed our most intensive period in the 'Korean Theatre of Operations', as the UN's Supreme Commander General Douglas McArthur called it, and it was later officially reported that we "played a major part in delaying the Chinese advance and stabilising the front. Flying only stopped to replenish stocks of bombs, rockets, cannon shells, aviation spirit and fuel". One very cold dark night while filling-up with Aviation Fuel alongside a tanker anchored in Inchon harbour, small-arms fire was heard and tracer bullets seen ashore. The RM bugler sounded Action Stations and the Commander broadcast "We have to get out of this harbour pretty dam quick because the Chinese have entered the town". Luckily for us the enemy's artillery was way behind their infantry, and we, the tanker and our escort were able to escape out to sea unscathed. In December 1950, despite the worse winter weather conditions many of us had ever experienced, 630 sorties were flown against the enemy. When working in exposed positions we wore duffel coats and other warm clothing but it was still dam cold. One Yeomen of Signals wrote a letter saying he was sustained by Mars Bars while on watch in the arctic conditions he faced, hoping to receive a parcel of Mars bars. All he got was a pen letter from one of the female staff.

During this long intensive period at sea our morale was kept up by the incredibly good mail service we received from home by air via New York, San Francisco, Tokyo, Iwakuni (the air base in the Inland Sea) and the next ship coming out to our operational area. We often received mail within a week of posting and I usually received several letters at a time from Eileen but, as they were numbered in sequence, I was able to open and read them in the right order. The Americans knew the value of good mail to us and our families and pulled out the stops to ensure a good service both ways. Notwithstanding this tremendous 'tonic', as this particular period of intense activity went into its sixth week, it was noticeable how tetchy we all became. There was a distinct 'Sense of humour failure' and tiny incidents in the queue for the Tot and Lime Juice sometimes led to angry confrontations among normally friendly messmates. We were on 'Opps' on 25$^{th}$ December 1950 and during the last sortie of the day before, several Time-Delay bombs were dropped on the enemy troop concentrations. The RM Bandsmen who brought them up from the Bomb Room marked them in chalk: "To Uncle Joe with Love, Do not Open until Christmas". The food on Christmas Day was the usual unimaginative fare we had every day. The Daily Orders declared that the routine was 'Daily Sea Routine (War)' and that Christmas Day was postponed until 31$^{st}$ December when we were expected to be in Kure on Honshu Island, in the Inland Sea. However we were all soon snapped out of our mood of self pity at missing the Yule festive season, by the Captain whose rallying broadcast drew attention to the relative comfort we enjoyed most of the time compared with the severe weather conditions our soldiers were facing ashore all the time and that they also had to continuously brave a vastly numerically superior and fanatical army. We got on with our jobs and at Tot time toasted our troops ashore. Besides the 24/7 maintenance responsibilities for our equipment, four of us EAs in turn kept night watches in charge of the Main Switchboard. It was my turn to have 'all night in' (bed) but found myself doing the ship's disciplinary duty of PO of the Day. 'Blow me down', not content with lumbering me with this duty on the real Christmas Day, I found myself doing the same duty on Theseus' own Christmas day held on New Year's Eve in Kure, our first run ashore for 6 weeks and the first time we had been alongside since leaving Pompey. I remember all of the ships in the harbour ringing in the New Year of 1951 and sounding their horns at midnight and handing 'Station Cards' back to hundreds of ratings returning aboard stone cold sober but nevertheless happy. Most of our many 'unofficial Chinese' went ashore that night and as they came up the gangway I wondered how I would be able to hand their cards back to the right man. I needn't have worried for the Laundry crew and Tailors Firm were known, with typical Chinese logic, as Dhobey 1,2,3 etc and the tailoring firm as Jackson 1,2,3 etc, the name the latter used when they set up in business in Portsmouth after our return home. On arrival several elderly Japanese Engineers visited the ship and one of them offered to take away and rewind the armatures of defective electric motors for which we had no spares, promising to return them repaired before we sailed a week later. It transpired that 'our' elderly Japanese had been the Electrical Engineering Manager when Kure was the biggest Japanese Naval Base during WW2 and he and his immediate subordinates actually repaired the defective machines themselves. They did this without drawings by cutting and measuring the gauge of the coils and counting the number of turns. All 14 jobs they undertook were completed on time by their skeletal workforce and all worked perfectly. Needless to say we were very impressed by this demonstration of Japanese know-how and industry.

We enjoyed a week's rest period berthed on a floating jetty, formerly a Japanese battleship, within walking distance of what was left of the town after the WW2 bombing, which had practically destroyed the dockyard. Kure was in the Australian Sector of Occupied Japan and incredibly, was dry. The only place to eat and drink ashore was in a sort of YMCA known as the 'Cheeroh' club staffed by kindly middle-aged and motherly Australian ladies who dispensed cakes, tea and sympathy. Here on the first night of night leave, 'Robbie' one of our senior PO Electricians came to grief. Back in September this lugubrious veteran, who had survived a WW2 torpedoing, consulted a fortune-teller in Hong Kong and had been warned of impending tragedy. He was convinced the ship would be sunk and throughout the following months of operations against the enemy, when not on duty below or snatching a meal in the mess, he occupied a position at the guard-rail on the boat deck, above my caboosh, in all weathers, day and night, wearing his lifejacket half-inflated. When his messmates, especially we 4th Class Tiffies, pulled his leg about his behaviour or asked him to "cheer us up" Robbie would reply in a melancholy way "You may laugh but I've had to swim for it before and I know we are all doomed". His doleful manner became even worse after our close shave at Inchon when the Chinese Army entered the town. Despite the very cold weather, and the ridicule he suffered, Robbie kept vigil at his own 'Emergency station'. Anyhow, coming out of the tee-total club at Kure in the dark after nothing stronger than a cup of tea, Robbie lost his footing on a narrow unguarded bridge and fell into a deep dry monsoon ditch and broke his back. After a difficult rescue operation Robbie was evacuated to a hospital ship where he was found to be very seriously injured. He was subsequently sent back to the UK and invalided from the service. The disaster he had feared turned out to be of a more personal nature than he imagined

and gave us, his former messmates and tormentors, something of which we thereafter felt less than proud.

Whilst at Kure we changed our 16 HK $ (1 £ Sterling) into Australian £s and were dismayed to get only I Aussie £ instead of 25 A shillings. We never did find out who was making a packet out of that exchange. Barry, Sam and I visited the sacred Shinto Island of Myajima where all of the natives wore traditional costume. I met up with my buddy from Fisgard, Martin Field who was serving in HMS Unicorn, and we visited Hiroshima together. Little rebuilding had taken place since the city was obliterated 5 years earlier and the scene was devastatingly awesome and moving. In a long road tunnel on the way back to Kure the engine of the ancient taxi in which we were travelling caught fire and, sitting in the back of the two door vehicle, we had some difficulty in getting out safely. On another organised trip we visited the cultured pearl farm at Takashima and the world famous porcelain factory at Arita. On 5th January 1951 we left Kure and after re-embarking our aircraft from Iwakuni, we passed through the narrow Straits of Shiminoseki and made our way to the Yellow Sea for our first operational tour of 1951. This and all of our subsequent tours were of a similar length, ten days operations preceded and followed by 2 days passage including a 'turn-over' at sea with our Task Group 'opposite number' the carrier USS Bataan, and each separated by six days in Sasebo, (3 days de-ammunitioning the spent cartridges and empty boxes and 3 days re-ammunitioning). The crane, ammunition hoists and boat hoists were used to lower the empty boxes over the side into lighters and to hoist the boxes containing thousands of rounds of 20mm armour-piercing and high explosive cannon shells, hundreds of rockets, 500 and 1000lb bombs and depth charges. The boat hoists were not continuously rated so I had to spend every passage out to the Operational Area time redressing all of the boat hoist controllers' contacts (which had become badly burnt), to ensure the hoists were ready when required for their proper purpose.

The weather off Korea and ashore in Japan during January and February was still very cold but operations continued apace in the Yellow Sea. However, just as the  extraordinary overwork of personnel during our last long spell of operations in 1950 had led to some fraying at the edges, the same happened to normally reliable equipment. The catapult failed and required spares which had to be flown out from the UK. Air operations continued with the aircraft flying off or, if carrying a 1000 lb bomb under each wing, with rocket assistance.

This RATOG was spectacularly effective although one day a Seafury's port rocket fired just before the starboard rocket and caused the aircraft to veer right as it left the deck and to lose its port wing tip on a forward D/F aerial. A somewhat apprehensive Naval Airman was photographed crouching only a couple of feet below the point of contact. The pilot was ordered to jettison his two 1000lb bombs and made a safe landing back onboard. Not long after the catapult was back in action, one of the bombs slung under another aircraft fell off as it was launched and 'hit' the flight deck above the CPO's mess. The aircraft quickly ditched the other bomb and made a safe return to the ship and, after examination; the bomb on deck was pushed over the side. On another occasion a live 60lb war-headed rocket hang-up came off when the aircraft arrested and hurtled up the flight deck at 100 knots. One of a gun's crew in its flight path jumped overboard and was rescued from the icy waters by HMS Constance's doctor. The rocket fell harmlessly into the sea. One Sunday morning we anchored in a bay south of Inchon, close to the heavy cruiser USS St. Paul who invited our Catholics to attend church onboard. As we were escorted through the ship the 'Tannoy' declared "Away all Card Games, Quit all Crap Schools, Holy Mass is about to be celebrated in the Sea Plane hangar". Sadly, during a Bombardment in the following week, one of their 8 inch Turrets exploded killing all 32 of the turret's crew.

One morning at 8am after coming off watch in the Switchboard, I was called to the After Lift by the operator because the Ward-Leonard Motor/Generator set was "sparking like mad". Fortunately the lift was up in the flight deck position and as it was the practice of starting every day off with as many aircraft as possible giving the enemy a dawn thumping, most of the aircraft were airborne on their respective Army ground support / Combat Air Patrol (CAP) and reconnaissance missions. The lift operator had shut down the machine but I soon found that the piano wire binder holding the generator armature coils in place had come undone and was hitting the pole faces in a shower of sparks as it rotated. The lift machinery space was very cramped and close under the flight deck but clearly the generator would have to be stripped and the armature taken below to put a new binder on under tension. The Lift would be out of action until the M/G set was operational again and the importance of this defect necessitated a maximum non-stop effort. In the meantime, with the brakes on the lift driving motor firmly locked in place, because most aircraft first touched down with a bang on top of this lift, the aircraft handlers had their work cut out moving 36 aircraft up and down to the hangar with only the forward lift. The Chief EA organised teams of EAs and mechanics to work day and night on this job but as the lift was my responsibility, I was left in (working) charge of the operation. However, I welcomed the guidance and moral support given me throughout the job by the very experienced Chief EA and by Horace Bunting our Senior Commissioned Electrical Officer,. The large armature had to be taken out of its small compartment, along the gallery deck, down four decks to the Engineers' workshop and set up on a lathe. After the new binder was fitted and the bearings changed the armature was tested and then heaved all the way back up again and meanwhile, the pole shoe damage repaired in situ. The M/G set was reassembled, tested and declared OK 35 hours after it became defective. Having already been on watch for the 4 hours before the defect occurred, I had been on my feet working for 39 hours non-stop, (a feat destined to be the longest spell in my whole career), I was ordered to turn in and I slept like a log for 9 hours.

Another evening, on my way to the Switchboard for the 'First' watch and passing the Air Chiefs' Mess the door flew open and several Chiefs came running out looking for a fire extinguisher and shouting "Fire". I looked in and saw that the five large 7-core MF Degaussing cables were on fire. I knew that they were powered direct from the Switchboard so I ran there and telephoned the Bridge and told the OOW that I would have to cut the supply to the De-Gaussing as the cables were on fire. He said "OK". So I opened the DG breaker. A few seconds later the OOW rang and anxiously asked if that meant we had no protection against magnetic mines. When I replied "Yes" he ordered 'Action stations'. The enemy was certainly laying contact mines and our aircraft had already sunk several ML Junks with depth-charges .The mooring gear of their mines was pretty poor and they often broke loose and floated. Indeed, only a few days earlier, while we were on a flying course and unable to manoeuvre, a floating mine had passed close down our port side and had been destroyed by marksmen on our chaser HMS Constance. We had no knowledge that they had magnetic mines. I joined the repair team after finishing my watch at midnight and helped complete splicing the 70 lead-cased cores to repair the fire damage and restore the De-Gaussing. The fire was caused by a dart holing one of the DG cables, in front of which the Airy-Fairy Chiefs had hung their dart board. This was the second time I had instigated the ship going to 'Action Stations' and again it had lasted for over four hours. Fortunately the ship's company were unaware that I had triggered this 'panic'.

I was up in the Island when one of our Canadian Tribal Class

Destroyers reported a submarine contact. The Chinese had four subs but seemed to be having trouble with them so every day, we sent an aircraft to their base Wei Hai Weh, to see if they were all still there. The absence of one that morning, may have sharpened the fleet sonar alertness. There is nothing quite like the emotive sound of the bugle call to 'Action Stations' and the sight of a huge 'Battle Ensign' flying at our masthead to focus one's attention and as I quickly made my way below to my Action Station, the Main Switchboard, I had a good flow of Adrenalin running.

After the escort had dropped a number of depth charges the sonar echo disappeared but was later attributed to a whale. There certainly were whales about for I had earlier seen a 40 foot whale swimming just off our starboard side, its size being similar to the ship's Motor launch I was standing alongside. A Seafury landing-on accidentally discharged a stream of 20 mm cannon shells as it was 'arrested', the alternative incendiary and Armour-piercing shells narrowly missing the open wing of the 'Flyco' position on which stood Commander (Air). Luckily the tail down attitude of the aircraft directed the lethal fusillade upwards so that it missed the ship and fell safely into the sea ahead of the ship. Later the same day, a Firefly suffered the same defect to one of its cannons but discharged one round only. Tragically, this was an AP shell and as the aircraft was horizontal when arrested, the round hit PO Airman Wigley in the stomach, passing through him before exploding in the tail of a parked aircraft. When I pulled the stretcher out of the bomb lift his eyes were glazed and the entry wound was small but I was told the exit wound was horrendous and in the sick bay the poor chap was pronounced dead. He was buried at sea with full naval honours the next day. An urgent modification was quickly designed and incorporated in all the Hispano Suiza cannons on our aircraft and we never had a repeat of this fatal defect.

Sasebo had a huge natural harbour which could accommodate the whole USN Fleet at anchor. We changed our HK $s in to US

Script $s at the rate of 4$ to the £ for spending in the large SSK Canteen ashore or the well-stocked PX Store, or into Japanese money at 1000 Yen to the £ if buying anything we fancied and could afford in the small shanty-town Japanese shops. I commissioned an elderly Japanese artist to paint a picture on silk of Eileen from a snap I lent him. After our next patrol I made my way ashore in the boat and trudged in a snow-storm to his wooden shack and paid (2000 Yen) for, and eagerly picked up, the result of his labours. His atelier was poorly lit by an oil lamp and it wasn't until I was back aboard in my caboosh that I had a proper chance to look at it and to realise that it was absolutely terrible. He had got the whole scaling-up from the snap out of all proportion and Eileen looked like a Russian Olympic female Shot-putter. I didn't show it to anyone onboard, when I later showed it to Eileen at home she laughed, and then agreed I should burn it. By odd coincidence Eileen had sat for an oil portrait by one of her artist friends at home and sent it out to me. I received this surprise a few weeks after I collected the awful Japanese painting and was thrilled with it. It still hangs in pride of place in my study at home, a very good likeness of the girl I married. During our inter-patrol visits there were sporting activities. I remember watching Barry taking part in the Fleet Cross-Country Championship race in the snow, which started at the bottom of a steep hill. I found it hard enough just walking up that slippery slope. The Japanese guides along the route held up arrows pointing out the direction and the children shouted "Hubba-hubba", hurry up or words to that effect, as the runners passed. Barry did very well in that race. During later visits, as the weather improved, the Americans, who were very generous and well organised, threw all-ranks 'Smoker Parties' and invited us 'Limeys' to them for free beer, hot dogs, a top notch boxing match and a first class stage show with top film stars like Bob Hope, Bing Crosby and Dorothy Lamour.

After setting off for our final operational tour we steamed North instead of West and in the Sunday evening twilight, met and passed the majority of the mighty USN 9th Fleet heading in the opposite direction. General MacArthur had ordered them to the Straits of Formosa to confront the Chinese, a move which soon resulted in him being sacked by President Truman. The sight of 2 Battleships, 11 Carriers, 13 Cruisers and hordes of Destroyers at sea in 'Defence Stations' and darkened, with just the twinkling of visual signal greetings between them and us, was to prove the most impressive show of naval might at sea that I ever saw. We then realised why we had been diverted to the East coast of Korea, where we helped the rump of the 9th Fleet maintain their presence and in particular kept up the bombardment of the Chinese supply route through Wonsan.

The weather improved in April and during the next 14 days a record number of sorties was flown against the enemy. Wonsan was the hub of a narrow coastal strip with the rail and road links between China and the front line backed on three sides by mountains. While we were there Wonsan was daily subjected to a bombardment by Frigates and Destroyers, often at anchor close to shore, and by Cruisers steaming further out at sea and the Battleship Missouri ('Mighty Mo') steaming even further off the coast and sending her 16 inch shells screaming over the others to land, together with their smaller shells , on that  narrow strip of territory.

Besides providing air cover and supporting the UN Armies to the south, our aircraft successfully attacked with rockets, troops and

road and rail transport hiding in the tunnels at the North and South ends of the strip. On the 20th April we were relieved by the USS Bataan, and our mission over, we made our way back to Sasebo for the last time.

Naval aviation is a hazardous enough activity in peacetime but in a war involving close-support of the Army, where aircraft are vulnerable to ground fire, it can be very dangerous. In the 86 days of operational flying off Korea, Theseus lost ten aircraft through enemy action and four aviators. A fifth pilot, a Petty Officer, was reported as 'missing presumed killed' when there was no sign of life from his Seafury, downed in snow-bound territory behind the lines in December 1950. I attended his Requiem Mass held later in Sasebo. A month later the enemy announced that he had been captured, was wounded and was the first RN POW of the Korean war. During the 3½ years he was in enemy hands the RN commissioned all NCO pilots and when he was released at the end of the war he was a Lieutenant. Sadly he died soon afterwards having been severely ill-treated by his captors. The intense flying training carried out en route to Korea from the UK, paid dividends for our aircraft flew a total of 3,446 sorties against the enemy with scarcely a landing prang. Several aircraft returned safely from sorties despite having been severely damaged by enemy fire, and 5 aviators were rescued from behind the lines or from the sea after being shot down. These air crews owe their lives to the heroic efforts of our American Helicopter crew and the crews of other USN choppers. The skill of the aircrews and the overall efficiency of the Air Group under war conditions during the winter of 1950/51 was later recognised by the award of the highest Fleet Air Arm distinction, the Boyd Trophy.

Throughout our war operations we had carried three or four renowned WW2 British War Correspondents. Their often wildly-exaggerated stories of our activities caused much mirth onboard when copies of their reports, sent to us from loved-ones at home, were put up on our notice boards. However they wrote so much 'bull' about the ship and her 'heroic' crew, we basked in the reflected glory of our gallant and intrepid Aviators and the authorities dropped any plans they may have had to transfer personnel from Theseus to other ships in the Far East. To my relief and delight and to that of many others, we were assured that we would all come home from Korea in the ship.

On the 23/24th of April 1951 Theseus handed over her role to the newly-arrived HMS Glory and after a last visit by most of our crew to the PX Store for goodies to take home and a 'Beer Up' in the SSK canteen with the lads from Unicorn and Glory, we left Sasebo for the UK, to a rousing farewell from all of the RN ships at anchor. After clearing the harbour we welcomed back aboard our Sea Otter from HMS Unicorn, our USN helicopter having already transferred to HMS Glory. To the delight of all of us who had a soft spot for the 'old girl' our Sea Otter made a perfect deck landing at sea without an arrester hook – she too just wanted to go home. We had two days at Hong Kong, most of it spent shopping for presents to take home, and were off again in warm weather for Singapore for a brief overnight refuelling stop before setting off for Aden. During this long passage we spent most of our spare time on deck playing games or just lying in the sun getting 'bronzy-bronzy for leave'. Many of us, unused to sunbathing, rather overdid this and suffered from blisters as a result. The Royal Marine Band gave frequent al fresco concerts and a 'Sods Opera' compered by 'Soapy' Hudson and performed by a talented bunch of junior rates, senior rates and officers, was a real 'hoot'. Some of the fleet recreational pursuits such as weight-lifting and 'circuit training' were resumed and I welcomed the re-opening of the Music Club, held for lovers of classical music, in the cool of the Air Briefing Room. I mentioned earlier that we were plagued with rats. Well, one of the Chief Aircrewmen, bored with no longer being required to fly on two or three 2 ½ hour sorties a day against the enemy in the back seat of a Firefly, volunteered to act as the ship's 'Official Ratcatcher'. He obviously knew what he was doing for he caught and displayed 15 of these unpopular intruders and almost certainly caused the unseen death of many more. One morning I was called to fix the Dough-Kneader. This was a stream-lined civilian machine mounted in the corner of the Bakery and to gain access to it my mate and I had to undo umpteen bolts to remove an access plate on the bulkhead to even get access to the machine's covers. The Chief Baker begged me to give top priority to the job as it was too hot for his staff to knead the dough by hand for the daily bake. As soon as I managed to gain access to the motor and gearing I could see the cause of the trouble. One of the 'Rat- Catcher's' poisoned victims had crawled inside the machine's carcase to die and had become stuck in the gearing. I handed the dead rat to one of the junior bakers for disposal and, as the motor was so difficult to get to I took it out, stripped, completely overhauled and tested it, cleaned up the gearing and reassembled the machine before testing its kneading ability and replacing the covers. When, after a full morning's work I went to the Chief Baker to report the machine "ready for use", I saw to my horror that the dead rat was still lying in a waste bin under the work surface being used to hand-knead the dough! I have also earlier referred to the poor standard of cuisine we had in Theseus but in truth, as I later learned, it was no worse than in any other RN ship at that time. Not uncommonly, despite the lax standards of the time, we never had any outbreaks of food poisoning, yet this does seem to happen occasionally nowadays in luxury cruise liners!

Theseus stopped to refuel at Aden and a few hours later was off up the Red Sea to Suez and through the canal 'in the right direction' as we delighted in telling the Pongos on the west bank. We entered Grand harbour Malta on the 21st May and manoeuvred the ship to a buoy without tugs by using 5 Sea Furys parked across the flight deck to pull the ship with their props revving at full speed in what was called 'Operation Pinwheel'. The seamen were highly delighted but it didn't do the aero engines much good for, without the cooling provided by an air stream, they overheated. We only had one night in Malta so I sought out my cousin Jean Murdoch, a L/Wren Writer who had recently arrived there and took her out to dinner and on a 'sanitised' run ashore which we both enjoyed. Sadly this was to be the last time I ever saw Jean for she died after an operation in Malta to remove her appendix went wrong. She was a lovely girl and great fun.

We anchored off Falmouth for our Customs inspection and then set off overnight for Portsmouth. At 0815 on the 29th May 1951, having flown off all of her aircraft to Lee-on-the-Solent, Theseus entered harbour, gun salutes were exchanged with HMS Dolphin, the ship's RM band played 'Iolanthe' to salute FOSM and soon afterwards we were alongside at South Railway Jetty and our families were pouring aboard. I find it impossible to express the joy and happiness I felt at being home and the thrill of first catching sight again of Eileen, so very much earlier than either of us expected. After this joyful reunion I had to fall-in again for 'Divisions' on the flight deck for the official 'welcome home' from the 'top brass' and after all the speeches, we fell-out and I was able to go home with Eileen.

The following six weeks were like a blissful dream. We spent a 'Third Honeymoon' at Hawkeshead in the Lake District at a hotel that had been Beatrix Potter's home, where all of the other guests naturally assumed we were newlyweds. At the splendid Ship's Company Homecoming Ball, held at the Savoy Ballroom in Southsea, Eileen lost a brooch I had brought home from Hong Kong. Luckily someone found it and handed it in to the bandleader, the famous Joe Loss, who formally presented it back to her. Barry and his girl friend Pat, later to become his wife, and Eileen and I spent a memorable day at the 'Festival of Britain' in London. It was really wonderful to be home again and to enjoy the best things in life.

Looking back on those two years, I was very lucky to have had

Theseus as my first sea job. She had a great Captain in Ben Bolt, and an outstanding Commander (Air) in Frank Hopkins; I was also blessed by serving under Horace Bunting and later Edward Ingani, two inspirational Commissioned Electrical Officers and their two experienced Chief EAs, all of whom let me have my rein but willingly stepped in to help when necessary. These four 'role models' for a young 'Tiffy' ensured that the department ran smoothly despite being nominally headed by two 'first- class passengers', who were conspicuous by their absence whenever there was a major programme-threatening defect. At a tender age I was given lots of responsibility but, with the help of a keen junior staff who never let me down, I, learnt a lot about practical electrical engineering and man-management whilst working under trying conditions. The ship was given and met a very tough programme and, if only in helping to prevent South Korea ending up like its northern neighbours, can be said to have done a good job.

Most of the ship's success during the Korean War is rightly attributed to the 17th Carrier Air Group, whose aviators flew two or three missions a day against a formidable enemy and whose maintenance crews often worked all night to replace the engines and wings of aircraft damaged by enemy fire. However they needed, and were provided with, a safe and secure mobile airstrip from which to operate and this required the combined efforts of almost a thousand men. I am proud to have been one of those 'Fishheads', as the CAG called us.

During my time abroad in Theseus, I missed my sister Peggy's wedding to John Strickland Scott. Later, I also missed the wedding of my step-brother George to Jessie Orr, my sister Eileen's wedding to James Lewis and the nuptials of my younger step-brother Fred. In fact, the only family weddings I was able to attend were my widowed mother's to Charles Helbrow, and my own!

My last memory of Theseus is hearing the broadcast "Attention on the flight and weather decks, face to port, HM X craft" and seeing a wet plate passing by, carrying a saluting Lieutenant and flying a White Ensign.

# Chapter 8

## Home Based   August 1951 – March 1954

When I left HMS Theseus on 28<sup>th</sup> July 1951, I went off on Summer Leave with Eileen, spending part of it with her paternal Grandparents at Darlington, before I joined HMS Collingwood, the 'depot' for Portsmouth Electrical ratings. I was accommodated in the Petty Officers' Mess on the North side of the massive parade ground but, being a 'native' I went home every night that I wasn't duty, i.e. nine nights out of ten, so I was able to enjoy 'normal' married life for the first time since Eileen and I wed in April 1950.

Being a member of the Collingwood staff, albeit temporarily, I didn't have to wear boots and gaiters or go on daily parade but 'strolled' to the maintenance workshop in which I was employed. My colleagues there were a number of EAs of various seniorities who were awaiting their next draft to a complement billet afloat or ashore, some of whom I knew from Fisgard. We were managed by a senior Chief EA whose official job was to maintain the electrical training equipment. In practice, the staff EAs of most of the training sections were quite happy to maintain their own equipment and the workshop staff was generally occupied in making 'presentos' ('rabbits') for departing senior members of Collingwood's staff and in the repair and maintenance of domestic items of an electrical nature belonging to the Wardroom, the Chiefs' and POs' messes or the residences of the Captain or Commander.

One of my earlier tasks was to fit a new element to the Captain's rather posh silver coffee percolator. Eileen and I had been given 3 coffee percolators as wedding presents, one electric, chromium-plated and nothing like as grand as the Captain's, and two to use on a hob, but we had not yet used any of them because, on the odd occasions we drank coffee, we used liquid 'Camp' Coffee and made it with hot milk, as was not uncommon in those 'tea-drinking days'. When I had finished replacing and electrically-testing the element and proving the gland was watertight, I gave it to the Chief EA and he said "Fill it up and we'll have a nice cup of coffee to prove it before we send it back to 'Nissen Hall'", the Captain's residence. I asked "Where's the milk to fill it"? He looked incredulous and, in the hearing of all of the EAs present said "You idiot, you can't fill a percolator with milk, it will boil all over the place". I came in for a lot of ribbing from my colleagues. After their laughter subsided, I filled the percolator with water, was shown how to add the coffee beans and made my first 'proper' coffee, and have to admit it tasted great. On the way home I bought some real coffee and demonstrated my new found knowledge to Eileen by 'christening' our electric percolator and giving us habitual tea-drinkers a tasty new experience.

Perhaps because of my recently demonstrated naivety, the Chief EA chose me to undertake a big job that the EA3s, 2s and 1s had avoided like the plague, the manufacture of a brass key-ring tally for every single room and building in Collingwood, a boring job requiring little skill. To relieve the boredom I spent alternate days cutting, filing drilling and polishing a number of tallies and the next day engraving them. This endless repetitive task kept me busy for weeks until I was assigned to do a 13 week course in the latest gunnery fire-control system. Twenty-five years after my engraving marathon, while carrying out rounds of Collingwood, I was delighted to find that the key tallies I had made in 1951 were still in use. I bet the Captain's percolator wasn't, or any of the other 'rabbits' we made.

The Flyplane Predictor System (FPS) was a new Gunnery Fire-control System being installed in the latest large RN destroyers, the Daring Class. Each of these ships carried a specially trained EA dedicated to the maintenance of the FPS. I was one of the eight EA3s and 4s who joined this 'back-up' course intended to build up a pool of 'Flyplane EAs' who, in due course, would relieve the first of the FPS EAs in the 'Darings'. Our course was conducted by three very good Instructors, Lieutenants Field and Butcher and EA3 Alf Eveleigh, who had been six months my senior at Fisgard. They used FPS2 equipment to teach us the maintenance of Mark 3 of this (then) 'state of the art' gunnery analogue computer. Although there was little to choose between them as far as Surface or Bombardment gunnery was concerned, the revolutionary British Flyplane system was superior in AA accuracy to its predecessor, the US Mk 37 mechanical fire-control system fitted in HMS Vanguard and in some 'Battle' Class Destroyers, whose gunnery computers used imported high-precision gears that were prohibitively expensive. On the other hand Flyplane was mainly electronic and its mechanical components were not expensive to manufacture. FPS3 was based on automatically, or manually, tracking the target aircraft and in so doing, measuring the vertical and lateral rates required to keep the axis of a gyro, sited below decks adjacent to the computer, aligned with the aloft Director's 'Line of Sight'. This data, referenced to a nearby vertical gyro and modified by other inputs, was then computed into the necessary gun elevation and training to point the gun at the target's future position. It was a far cry from the WW2 HACS fire-control system I had been taught in 1949 and I found the course very interesting and the three instructors put over what was a completely new subject to us, very well. Besides classroom study we had plenty of practical work on the system and I enjoyed this immensely. Unfortunately in those days of thermionic electronics, the amplifiers and their servos, tended to drift with changes of temperature even ashore in Fareham. The system required continuous tweaking to keep it in tune and this drawback indicated it would be a devil to keep it up to scratch at sea, particularly in the tropics in ships without air-conditioning, Nevertheless I had become 'hooked' on fire-control and thought "this is the job I would like to do at sea in future instead of heavy electrics and engine-room equipment". During this period I enrolled for a one evening a week course in advanced Maths carried out in Collingwood in which I revised the Calculus I learnt at Fisgard and then went on to study Boolean Algebra and Spherical Trigonometry. This was the start of the evening class habit I kept up, in Engineering-related subjects, and later in the Humanities, for the rest of my working life. By the time I completed the Flyplane course there was no billet available in a Daring, as most of them were still building, and their EAs had not yet been to sea in them, so all 8 of us new Flyplane EAs, trained for three months at enormous expense, were made available for drafting elsewhere. The submarine service was expanding and, in the absence of enough volunteers, two of the FPS class were given drafts to 'boats', much to their dismay. Next day I received a draft to the Anti-Submarine School HMS Osprey at Portland. I considered myself very lucky in the circumstances and telephoned Eileen from a telephone box close to the Quarter deck with the news. She asked me whether I had heard that the King had died. I looked at the flag pole and, seeing the ensign was close-up, ie not at half-mast, I assured her it was not true. It was February 6th 1952 and she was of course quite right. The biggest naval establishment in the UK was just not on the ball! The following day two more members of the Flyplane class learnt they too would be going into 'subs'. At the time I thought "what a waste of time the Flyplane course has been". However it was later to prove invaluable to me.

In 1951 the Admiralty decided that all non-seamen Petty Officers in the navy, traditionally considered to be 'non-combatants', would henceforth become 'trained killers'. So before I joined Osprey I had to undergo a 'Land –Fighting' Course at Tipner, with about 11 other 4th Class Artificers. We were put through a pretty tough course by RM instructors who taught us the fundamentals of military combat and how to use a .38 revolver, a Lanchester, (an RN Sten Gun with a wooden butt), a Bren Gun and hand grenades. At the end of the week I had demonstrated to the staff and myself that I was not the best of marksmen. During the final demonstrations of our military skills I failed to hit a door-size target from 12 feet with any of the six rounds from my revolver, my bursts while running with the Lanchester sprayed all over the place, except on the target and the first of my six hand grenades, that I had made a meal of priming, only just cleared the parapet from behind which I had lobbed it, and exploded with a deafening bang a few feet away in front of me and nowhere near the target. The only weapon I was able to use with any accuracy was the Bren Gun, which I could hardly lift, and only then when it was supported on a bipod and I was lying down. Although I was one of the least competent with small arms on that course I was later issued with a Lanchester 'for real' when on duty in unfriendly situations ashore in Egypt in 1954 and with a rifle in Malaya in 1958.

Eileen made enquiries and established that she could transfer from the AME at Havant to HMUDE, the Underwater Detection Establishment at the bottom of the Hill below HMS Osprey, in her grade as a Drawing Office Assistant so we were happy with my draft. I joined Osprey on 11th March. The Electrical Workshop was situated on the seaward side close to the main gate and had a staff of about 15 including 4 EAs. For the first month or so I had no specific responsibility; but was given a variety of tasks including the odd 'rabbit', while the boss was assessing me I guess, and then was given the maintenance of some of the Asdic, ie Sonar Training equipment. Although this was often in use by classes of 'makee-learnee' sonar operators it was, compared with Flyplane, pretty basic electronics and no sweat to keep going. Until I was allocated a married quarter 'hiring' in Weymouth during April, I travelled home each weekend in a coach organised by a Chief in Osprey, which carried love-sick sailors like me. home on Friday evening and back on Sunday evening and was known as the 'Passion Bus' During Easter weekend Eileen and I went up from Portsmouth to London to attend my old chum Jack Palmer's wedding to Audrey, whom he had met while she was training to be a Teacher at Portsmouth and he was qualifying as an REA at Collingwood. We also visited my Scottish Grandmother with whom I had lived at

Eastney until I was nine years old and for another year during the blitzes of 1940/41.Nana kindly offered me, as the sole surviving male Murdoch, several pieces of gold Orange Lodge regalia belonging to my grandfather, who had died in 1903. I told her that as a Catholic I could never join the Lodge and wear the regalia and if she gave them to me I would probably sell them. After a short pause she said "So be it" and handed me the only remaining material links with my late Granddad. Sadly that was to be the last time I saw her for she died two months later. To my shame I had already sold the regalia by then for a few pounds and have regretted this mercenary act ever since. Fortunately I did inherit several household keepsakes of Nana and together with many happy memories I have of her, I still treasure them. After Easter leave 1952 Eileen transferred to UDE and we happily set up home, independently from the family for the first time in, for those days, a pleasant well equipped, upstairs flat in Abbotsbury Road.

My hours at Osprey were from 8 to 4 but Eileen worked from 9 to 5 at UDE. Although this prevented us travelling to work in the same bus, which conveniently ran from Weymouth through Portland Dockyard, stopping at UDE and on up the hill to Osprey, it allowed Eileen to wash-up and make the bed before going to work and for me to do any urgent shopping and prepare our evening meal before she arrived home. We may have come late to drinking coffee but we were in the advance guard as far as liking curry for the great Indian Food craze in Britain was still some years away when we began to eat it regularly. One day Eileen asked me to buy some more curry powder on the way home so I called at the Grocers near to the flat but they didn't have any and I was told "try the Chemist next door". I was amazed at this suggestion but bowed to local customs and, sure enough they did stock curry powder and duly poured out 4 ounces of a green powder from a large blue glass bottle, into a paper cone. Unaware this was a mixture of neat curry spices I added the same quantity of curry powder as normal. When Eileen and I sat down to supper that night the curry nearly blew our heads off; it was the strongest curry we have ever tasted. My fellow EAs at Osprey also lived in hired MQs with their wives and we joined them in their low key but enjoyable social life. Canasta was all the rage then and each of us in turn hosted a weekly Canasta Party, the hosts providing the tea and sandwiches; this was before alcoholic drinks became the normal beverage in 'at homes'. The summer of 1952 at Weymouth was pretty hot and Eileen and I spent a lot of time on the sandy beach. In July, a few months before her 90th birthday, my dear Scottish Grandmother died and we travelled to Portsmouth on the evening before the funeral, after having rather overdone the sunbathing. The journey was agonising, particularly after a boisterous youngster crashed into my badly burnt shins when the train jolted. Next morning, after we both had lain on top of a bed all night, covered in calamine lotion, in Eileen's mother's house, we paid our last respects to my Nana.

Eileen and I joined a small private library from which we could borrow new best-sellers for sixpence a time. In those days Weymouth was a rather genteel resort with a charming sea-
front. Eileen became a close friend of her fellow DOA at UDE, Rachel Wing and her boy friend Dick Bellingham, a Draughtsman in the same office. During the filming of 'The Cruel Sea', Rachel, a pretty girl who regularly completed the Telegraph Xword in under 15 minutes, was 'spotted' by Donald Sinden who took her to dinner. In the face of such opposition Dick proposed to Rachel and soon afterwards they married. They are still among our closest Weymouth friends.

HMUDE was rocked about this time by two other employees known to Eileen, the traitors Ethel Gee and Harry Haughton who were found guilty of selling UK Sonar secrets to the USSR in what became known as the Portland Spy case. Notwithstanding this unwelcome notoriety, Eileen enjoyed working at UDE. At lunchtime she walked part of the way up the hill to meet me coming down from Osprey and we spent the lunch break together every day sharing the picnic lunch she brought. This ritual was seen by the Captain, 'Black Jack' JB. Frewin, as he passed us on his way to 'The Castle' for lunch. He remarked on this at a Chief's mess Ball and many years later at Admiralty House Portsmouth when he was C-in-C and Eileen and I were guests. UDE's Social Committee arranged visits to several theatres and I cherish the memory of a performance of Tosca by the company of La Scala Milan at Bournemouth with Renata Tebaldi and Tito Gobbi in the lead. On another occasion we saw the musical Carousel with the West End cast and I recall all of us men blowing our noses to hide unmanly tears as we stood up to applaud the sad finale of that great show. In those 'stiff-upper-lip' days it was infra dig for men to be seen crying!

Just before the six-month contract ran out on our flat, we had a surprise visit at 10 pm from Jack Palmer who arrived clutching a crate of beer, much to the consternation of our landlady who hitherto seemed to think we were teetotallers. A few days later he came again around 6pm and invited us to come down to the sea front. It was quite a chilly October evening, indeed Eileen had every excuse to wear her new fur coat, and we wore our great coats. Once on the beach, Jack persuaded me to strip to my underpants and to run down the speed-boat pier with him, dive off the end, and swim back - "Last one in the water is a sissy" sort of dare. Eileen said we were mad - she was right!

The water was 'freezing', well damn cold anyway and when we got back up the beach to where Eileen was guarding our clothes, our teeth were chattering and we had to dry ourselves with handkerchiefs and our coats, and dress still wearing wet underpants. Ugh! We decided we needed some alcohol so instead of drinking a warming tot we quickly downed 4 pints each of Bass in the bar of the Gloucester Hotel, the first time I had ever had Bass. Needless to say Eileen was not best pleased at being 'escorted' back to our flat by a couple of very tipsy Petty Officers. Shortly after this madcap incident, Eileen and I we were offered and enthusiastically accepted the tenancy of a super maisonette on the 4$^{th}$ and 5$^{th}$ floors of a building in Royal Terrace on Weymouth Sea front close to the 'Royal Hotel'. This 'MQ hiring' was very tastefully decorated and fitted out, had three bedrooms, a magnificent view of Weymouth bay and the beach and only cost me 17 shillings a week in rent. This enabled us to save and to buy our first house in Cosham in which we spent at least one weekend a month working on it to prepare it for our eventual use.

Our first rung on the property ladder was a terraced three-bedroom house in Highbury Grove that cost us £1800. We paid a deposit of £200 and our 20 year mortgage cost me £2.14s.6p a week. At that time this was 25% of my income, the statutory limit on mortgage payments. Eileen's income was not allowed to count so, with no car or other large expenses, we were able to live quite comfortably. Although our MQ was considered to be of a very high standard, like most homes in 1952 including our own house in Portsmouth, it had no refrigerator, freezer, washing machine, dryer, telephone, television or garage. Notwithstanding the absence of these modern 'essentials', we lived a life of luxury in this gem of an apartment for the next 9 months. We still have nostalgic memories of the Winter, Spring, and Summer scenes viewed from our lounge and bedroom windows – the winter beachcombers picking up driftwood from the cold wind-swept and otherwise deserted beach- the pedalo owners painting their boats ready for the season- the sandcastle builder producing his superb sculptures and the whole beach gradually coming to life. We often had our Tea on the sands, whoever lost the toss would cross the road, climb the stairs to our apartment, make the tea and carry it back on a tray with some cakes. We often put up members of our family or friends for the weekend and they all enjoyed their visit and thought we were very lucky to have such a great flat. On 20<sup>th</sup> May1953 I was advanced to EA3 by Captain Frewin and became a Chief Petty Officer. Rachel and Dick took us out to the Moonfleet Hotel on 2<sup>nd</sup> of June 1953 to watch the Coronation ceremony on television and we all had a great time.

Back at Osprey, the Electrical Officer Lt.Cdr. Fairfax had designed a Sonar teaching aid called the 'Student Response Analyser' and gave me the job of converting his brainwave into a practical reality. This was a very interesting challenge which I relished as it included employing all of the latest components and techniques and the skills I had learnt as an apprentice. Besides, it was a welcome change from repairing old sonar equipment, making 'presentos', making and rigging animated signs for wardroom parties or repairing the 'delayed-steering', remote-controlled model ships used on a 'buoyed channel' to test the after-dinner navigational skills of officers. In June, Eileen and I attended the CPOs' Mess Coronation Ball with our friends.

Later in June, Eileen and I travelled to Stokes Bay at Gosport with Rachel and Dick, to see the Coronation Naval Review at Spithead. A few days later I was transferred to the Portland based 2<sup>nd</sup> Training Squadron as 'Squadron EA' in place of a senior EA2 who had asked to stay in the post until then so that he could take part in the Review, before leaving the service. In my new job I was responsible for the maintenance of the 1005 Gyro compasses, navigational Instruments and 'Typex' coding machines in all 5 of the 'Castle' Class Corvettes and for the repair of defective Sonar and electrical equipment in the 'Castles', the 3 coal-burning A/S Trawlers 'Bern', 'Tiree' and 'Fetlar' and 3 Motor A/S boats (MASBs). I had a small workshop in the dockyard but spent most of my time working on the various ships of the squadron alongside or, on two or three days a week, at sea from 0800 to 1630.

Having been happily married for more than three years with no sign of a family, we decided to adopt a baby. In early July we were thrilled to learn that we would receive a baby girl for adoption on the 1st of August. Our maisonette was a no-children's tenancy and, being up five flights of stairs with no lift and having little drying facilities and nowhere to keep a pram, it was quite an unsuitable home for a baby. I therefore applied for a more 'baby-friendly' hiring. Eileen gave in her notice but had to work until Friday 31st July. We spent the rest of the month buying the layette, pram and cot and necessary linen and went home in the 'Passion bus' every weekend to prepare the nursery in our house at Cosham. Only one let became available during that

hectic period and I had to view it on my own only 15 days before the baby was due. The bungalow was pretty grotty compared with our beautiful maisonette, and to our own house, but time was fast running out, so I accepted it and gave vague answers to Eileen's questions on what it was like. We moved out of our immaculate maisonette on the mid July Sunday lunch-time with Eileen polishing the floor as we left to make our way to Wyke Regis where we found the previous tenants eating lunch and the tiny bungalow in a dreadful state. I tried to console Eileen as she fought back her tears at the awful comparison of this new MQ with the last one. After the other family had left we set to work to clean up the place and spent the evenings of the next 13 days doing it up. I saw that the light switch alongside the bath had a brass cover and when I tested it, I found it was live – a real death trap. Several other switches were also dodgy so I bought new plastic switches to replace them. We popped home to pick up some of our rugs and other items to make it more homely and by the morning of 1st August the Dolls house bungalow wasn't looking too bad as we excitedly set off to pick up our new baby girl, whom we had already decided to call Sally, with Elizabeth, after the Queen, as her second name.

We arrived at the Adoption Centre at noon and very soon saw Sally for the first time and were delighted with her. She was eleven weeks old, but quite small and very beautiful and had fair hair and blue eyes. After completing the formalities we set off by taxi and train back to Wyke Regis. If Sally was bewildered by our handling of her during the first few days and nights she didn't show it, but seemed to like her new parents. On the morning of Day 2, Sunday 2nd August we took her to Mass which was held in the skittle alley of the local pub. We were able to wheel her pram into 'church' and 'parked' next to a Shipwright from Osprey and his wife and their baby son David. Joe and Marianne Zammitt became our great friends and David, our Godson is still Sally's close friend. We walked Sally in her pram to Weymouth every Saturday and, after doing the shopping and showing the baby the beach attractions, Eileen went home by bus to prepare Sally's bath and feed while I walked Sally home in the pram.

My Summer leave coincided with our first two weeks with Sally and by the time I had to go back to work she had completely settled down. On the days that I was not required to go to sea but worked ashore, I cycled home at noon had a play with Sally, who was generally in her pram in the front garden when I arrived, had lunch with Eileen and then cycled back to Portland. I was home with them most weekends and every night, unless there was a big 'programme-threatening' defect in one of the ships. Whenever the whole squadron took part in a fleet or NATO exercise like 'Mariner' in the North Atlantic in October 1953, I was required to

go in the 'Half- Leader' HMS Tintagel Castle, being transferred when necessary, to other ships with defects. However such absences from Portland were few and far between and the three of us lived a happy and fairly stable family life. I invited the LREM from Tintagel Castle to share our 1953 Christmas dinner with us and all four of us thoroughly enjoyed the seasonal celebrations. We remained at Wyke until well into the New Year before taking Sally for the first time to our home in Portsmouth for the weekend. We travelled in the 'Passion Bus' on the Friday evening but had to get out at Fareham because Sally was sick in the coach, much to our horror, and that of the sailors on their way home for the weekend. We cleaned her up at the bus station and went on to Cosham by bus. When we put Sally to bed that night in the brand new nursery we had lovingly prepared for her she screamed her head off. It seems that, having been used to sleeping in a rather large and ugly bedroom, she didn't like the acoustics of this attractive little nursery. Back at Wyke after the weekend, she happily went straight to sleep in that awful room!

During my nine months with TS2, I went to sea in each of the ships and boats in the squadron that did not have their own EA, and while onboard I was in charge of the electrical department. In those days small ships had 'Canteen Messing' where each mess was self-catering and was issued with a daily allowance. In the ships where

they had a good cook and members used the money for its proper purpose, the food was great and we ate well, but in others, where the mess members tried to cater on less than the daily allowance so that they could share the pretty small 'mess savings', the meals were sparse, generally only two one-course meals per day, of an abysmal standard and were, in fact far worse than the 'General Mess' meals provided in the bigger ships. Nonetheless, I thoroughly enjoyed my first 'Charge Job' and the technical responsibilities that went with it. I learnt a lot from it and at the same time enjoyed a happy home life with Eileen and Sally. In fact this period was one of the happiest in our lives and we still remember our time in the grotty Dolls House with fond affection.

All good things have to come to an end eventually and, just before Easter leave in 1954, I received notice of a draft to join the 'Battle' Class destroyer HMS Saintes on 3rd May, for unaccompanied service in the Mediterranean. Eileen and I decided we would move back to Portsmouth during Easter leave to allow us the maximum time to set up our home together in our own house, before I went abroad. On the evening we arrived home at Cosham, I dropped and smashed the only baby-feeding bottle we had. We had heard that next door a young couple with a baby had recently moved in so I knocked them up. I was delighted to see that our new neighbours were Don Fraser and his wife Joan and daughter Janet, for whom they had a spare bottle. Don was an old friend of mine and my only Fisgard classmate in the 2<sup>nd</sup> Training Squadron at Portland during my time there. I reminded him of the day I spent at sea with him in his Seaward Defence Boat SDB3050 when it was so rough and the smell of petrol so strong that both of us spent most of the time sharing his bucket and looking forward to getting back into harbour. The two wives and baby girls became firm friends and this was a blessing with me about to go away to sea.

# Chapter 9

## HMS Saintes May 1954 – August 1955

After completing a five day course at Collingwood in MRS 7 Mod 0 and STAAG, the Medium and Close Range gunnery systems fitted in HMS Saintes, I joined the 2325 tons 'Battle' Class destroyer in Portsmouth dockyard where she had just returned from a 2½ year 'Foreign Commission' based on Malta. Many of her crew had been accompanied by their families but as we were to be the first of the new style 'General Service Commissions' lasting only 18 months, we would be unaccompanied during the 'foreign leg', the 12 months spent in the Mediterranean, before we returned to the UK to operate in the Atlantic and North European waters. Except for the Captain and a few officers and senior ratings who had joined the ship towards the end of the previous commission, the ship's company of Saintes was changed in one go on 13th May 1954, the old crew giving a brief 'turn-over' to their successors before marching off on leave. The new crew had just two days to become acquainted with their duties before sailing for a 'self-conducted

Work – Up at Portland, aided by the local staff.

Although, at thetime we thought it was pretty hectic, in those pre-Flag Officer Sea Training days, it was rather less exacting and very much shorter in duration than newly commissioned ships faced in later years After just five days of exercises we were considered. ready to join the fleet, having had a go at all of the drills expected of the leader of a destroyer squadron, including fairly accurate surface, and bombardment gunnery firings and satisfactory anti-aircraft 'shoots' with our two twin 4.5 inch turrets and two twin 40mm auto- tracking STAAG mountings, and of course, Sonar, Torpedo and Damage-Control exercises. Our Gunnery maintenance team comprised five OAs, an REA 4 and me as the Fire-control EA, and though MRS 7 was a poor cousin of Flyplane, it still required a lot of 'midnight-oil' to get and keep the system tuned up and ready for a 'shoot'. We left Portland for the Mediterranean on 22nd May, in company with our Devonport sister ship and fellow member of the 3$^{rd}$ Destroyer Squadron 'Barfleur' and the cruiser Glasgow, on the first of the Royal Navy's new General Service Commissions.

The Chief Artificers and all of the EAs , OAs, REAs and Shipwrights shared a 'Tiffies' mess on 2 Deck aft, but it was very crowded, as was the whole ship. I ate with and enjoyed the company of my messmates until it was time to 'turn-in' but then came up a deck and went forward to my tiny 'Fire-control workshop' opposite the gunnery Transmitting Station (TS) and slept on a camp bed set up on the work bench. My private 'sleeping cabin' even had its own scuttle (porthole), a luxury godsend in a non air-conditioned ship during the hot Mediterranean summer.

Our Captain was Desmond Dreyer a renowned WW2 Gunnery Officer, and son of Admiral Sir Frederick Dreyer, the inventor of the Dreyer Fire-Control Table. We carried the Squadron GO, a Destroyer GO and a Gunner onboard so gunnery featured heavily in our daily routine and exercises. The Electrical Officer was a Commander (L), who had never served at sea before, having come straight from the Dockyard into the RN as a Commander, and appeared to us to be little more than a First Class passenger. His Deputy was a 'thin stripe' Commissioned Electrical Officer called Mr (Tom) Finney. Tom who was my Divisional Officer and boss but, effectively being the ship's Electrical Officer and having his work cut out with the rest of the ship's electrics, radio and radar, he seemed pleased to be able to leave the Gunnery side to me. Our venerable Chief EA, Sam Brand was very experienced in all things electrical but not in electronics, so he too was happy to leave fire-control to me. I was very seldom called upon to help with problems affecting the rest of the Electrical department. This was just as well because throughout the commission, thermal drift of the electronics in the MRS 7's analogue system, necessitated frequent tuning. During the night before every morning 'shoot', the Fire-Control OA, John Fielder and I had to carry out a complete setting up of the TS and turret servos and electronics, to achieve the best possible performance from the gunnery system.

After a passage during which the three ships carried out exercises every day, we arrived at Malta, Glasgow going into Grand Harbour and Saintes and Barfleur into Sliema creek. In a display of skilled ship handling, Captain Dreyer turned the ship around in the mouth of the creek and then steamed astern at 14 knots up the creek to berth quickly and neatly between the two buoys marking Captain D3's billet between Manoel Island and Sliema front. Within seconds of securing, the cables were painted white and the fo'c'sle and quarter-deck awnings were spread and Captain D3 was back in Malta. A few days later we left for gunnery and torpedo exercises before returning for a long overdue 'maintenance period' alongside a Depot ship in Lazaretto Creek, the last such break having been back in February during the previous commission. We had Maltese cooks and Stewards onboard and they were looking forward to two weeks at home. Unfortunately one of our lads had become very ill and, in the absence of a doctor, the Leading Sick Berth Attendant had warned the Captain of his diagnosis of the illness. When we berthed alongside HMS Ranpura a team of Doctors and nurses came aboard and no one else was allowed on or off the ship.

Shortly afterwards we were told that we had an outbreak of Polio onboard and would have to be isolated for 14 days. We were cast off and proceeded into quarantine in St Paul's Bay. Whilst there

the number of suspected cases of polio rose to five and most of us privately and nervously tested our reflexes for the symptoms of this dreaded disease. It was mid June and very hot at anchor and, because of the danger from the ship's own discharged effluence, we were not allowed to swim from the ship but instead went by ship's boats to the uninhabited St Paul's Island. Louis Mountbatten, the CinC Med endeared himself to the ship's company by granting us two bottles of beer a day during this quarantine period, the first RN ship to enjoy this privilege, which was later extended to all ships at sea.

Immediately after our 14 days in 'purdah', by which time I had grown a fairly sparse beard, we resumed our original plan and took part in 'Medflex Baker', the fleet summer exercise in the Eastern Med, without having had any shore leave in Malta. After the CinC's

'hairy' finale- 'Exercise 'Gridiron', in which two columns of destroyers and cruisers, only a cable apart, passed each other at 28 knots), we proceeded straight to Port Said for active service in the Suez Canal Zone.

We berthed stern-to the jetty of 'Navy House' at Port Said, a small naval depot on the west bank of the canal, only walking distance from the city. It was early July and very hot and the political situation there at that time was a bit tense. The Canal Zone was still occupied by our Army, and the British were not very popular with the Egyptians, indeed, it was dangerous for British Servicemen to venture anywhere in small groups without an armed escort. Several soldiers had just been found in the Sweetwater Canal, murdered and mutilated and we mounted armed guards in the Navy compound and provided armed escorts to all parties going outside the fence. I found myself in charge of the guard on several occasions, armed with a Lanchester with instructions to shout "Stanna" (Halt in Arabic) if any intruder was seen inside the compound. The biggest threat was from thieves but we were told to be also on the alert against sabotage. My 'terms of engagement' were: if the intruder did not stop, to shout "Stanna" again and, if he still didn't stop, to shoot. Bearing in mind my proven inability to shoot with any accuracy, it was fortunate for all concerned that I saw no trespassers during my watches. I did visit Port Tewfik on the East Side of the canal and Port Said itself for escorted shopping visits and went armed to Mass every Sunday we were in the Canal Zone.

One 'Tot Time' in the Tiffies' Mess we decided to enter a whaler's crew in the Med Fleet Pulling Regatta scheduled to take place in Sardinia in late September and although I was the archetypal '10 stone weakling' and had no rowing experience, I volunteered to join the crew. We took part in early morning practice every day we could, in the placid waters of the canal, where the going was easy. After a few days at Port Said, Saintes was ordered to escort a convoy of ships down the canal to the Great Bitter Lake where we anchored and waited for the next northbound convoy to assemble before leading them back up to Port Said. We carried out this routine for a couple of weeks and while passing through the canal were at defence stations but never encountered any problems. Another few days alongside in Port Said was followed by leading a convoy down to Abu Sultan in the GB Lake. This time we anchored there for several days and assisted in the loading-up of an RFA with ammunition from the nearby army base which was preparing to close down. Whilst there we enjoyed the hospitality of the army

messes, carried out our daily practice for the pulling regatta, played games with the soldiers and swam in the very warm and salty lake. When the RFA Fort Rosalie was fully loaded we took her and the next convoy north and after a few more days guarding' Navy House we were relieved by another destroyer and were delighted to set off for Famagusta in Cyprus for a week long break.

After the scorching heat of the Canal Zone in August, Cyprus was a paradise. My memories of this 'Rand R' (Rest and Recreation) period are entirely pleasant. The golden sandy beach was beautiful and nearby was a submerged lost city that was fascinating to dive on, the locals were friendly, the booze cheap and it was pleasantly warm but without the harsh heat of Egypt. I remember watching with great amusement a western at an open-air cinema in which Gary Cooper opened his mouth to drawl and out poured a torrent of unsynchronisable Greek. Cyprus was the ideal place for our first proper run ashore for three months and we all thoroughly enjoyed ourselves. As we were due to visit Rome next, and my beard was still pretty sparse I decided it would have to come off and my 'Oppo' John Fielder, duly obliged revealing a terribly pale face that only just tanned in time for Rome. I had not told Eileen that I was sporting a beard and when she saw the photo of me wearing it she said "Why didn't you keep it on, I quite liked it".

We arrived at Civita Veccia the port of Rome on 22nd September 1954 where we spent a week, most of us making the relatively short, comfortable and inexpensive train journey to the Eternal City every day. Travelling with messmates I found

*Don, Ron, Christie, Lou, Monk and Archie at St Peter's*

Rome to be a fairly compact city and we enjoyed walking around it visiting all of the famous landmarks. The iconic Audrey Hepburn film Roman Holiday had just been shown onboard and we had a taste for the place before we got there. Tom Finney was the Senior Catholic onboard and he arranged for all of us 'left-footers' onboard to visit Castel Gondalfo one day where we had a public audience with the Pope. The essentials for a most successful run ashore were all there in Rome, inexpensive food, drink, souvenirs and travel, pretty girls (for the single guys) and great places to visit and I think that although we had to wear buttoned long white suits, (to quote the ship's own hymn) all of the "Saintes who from their labours rest"-ed during that week, thoroughly enjoyed the visit.

After leaving Rome we joined up with the rest of the Med fleet for exercises and then anchored in formation with them in Palmas Bay on the South coast of Sardinia. There were two columns of ships a Depot ship heading each of the two columns and the cruisers next in line and then the destroyers and frigates. The hot summer had ended and there was a strong wind blowing as the day of the fleet regatta dawned. Betting was not only officially allowed but encouraged among the ships and our mess boat's crew, representing the Chief POs of Saintes, had a number of bets riding on them. After dissipating our energy somewhat in Cyprus and Rome we were a well out of practice and more than apprehensive when we saw the size and obvious fitness of the CPOs crews of the other ships going out to the starting line. The strong cool wind was blowing down the course and we would have to row against it. In fact in the minutes before our race began we had our work cut out just keeping our bows to the starting line. At last the starting gun fired and we were off. It was soon obvious that we were out of our league as far as contenders were concerned and, despite pulling our guts out we fell further and further behind the leaders. When we heard the 'first over the line' gun we had only reached the half-way mark and eventually finished second to last and shame-facedly and absolutely knackered, slunk back to the ship where we were treated with some derision. Perhaps if the regatta had taken place in the kind of calm waters in which we had trained, our light-weight crew might have stood some chance but on that day and in those conditions, we were hopeless and deserved all the scorn heaped on us.

Next day Lord Louis the CinC Med ordered all ships to "Abandon Ship". This was a programmed exercise and in preparation, all ships had arranged for their 'non-swimmers' to remain on watch (we were all 'flashed-up' of course and someone had to look after the ships).We had 15 onboard Saintes who were excused the exercise and when the signal came the rest of our 200 odd crew jumped or dived over the side from our 'abandon-ship' stations. I had to wait on the starboard STAAG deck before jumping overboard because the guys tasked with releasing the 'Carley floats' couldn't get them away because they were stuck fast by layers of paint. In the end we were told to leap and make for the nearest 'Flotta Net' all of which were down in the water. I remember looking up the line of ships before I leapt and seeing lads diving off the Depot ship and thinking "I'm glad I only have to go off our gun decks". When I surfaced I swam to the nearest FN and grabbed hold of a pair of handles at the same time as about 20 of my shipmates did and found the whole float sinking fast. So I and all the others abandoned it and swam clear and enjoyed 'hands to bathe' as we generally did every day at sea in the Med. None of the ship's Flotta Nets supported the number of guys they were designed for and almost all of the Carley Floats remained 'glued' to their stowage positions. Needless to say there was considerable embarrassment for the First Lieutenant at the abject failure of the ship's life-saving rafts. Obviously too much attention had been made to looking 'Tiddly' and not enough to safety.

The last night of the fleet gathering in Palmas Bay was devoted to socialising and merriment at all levels and I remember St Kitts steaming up and down the lines with an illuminated and animated crocodile shedding tears at leaving the Med to go home at the end of her 2½ year commission; as she passed us she bombarded her leader with spuds. Next morning we left for a 12 week refit, not in Malta as expected by our Maltese crewmen but in Gibraltar.

After docking down in Gibraltar the crew of Saintes moved into the shore accommodation in HMS Rooke. The Chief and POs in spartan corrugated iron roofed dormitories marginally more comfortable than onboard the ship.

Unfortunately General Franco had closed the border with Spain and we were thus confined to the colony. Gibraltar is fine for a short visit but after you have seen all the sights, climbed the Rock, visited St Michael's Caves and tried all of the watering holes in the Main Street, it becomes a bit boring. One Sunday afternoon my chum OA4 Archie Furmidge, who had been a notable runner at Fisgard, persuaded me to join him in a run around the Rock. This proved to be somewhat harder than I anticipated for though it did not involve any climbing, we used the tunnels through the rock, I found it particularly exhausting and could hardly walk for two days after the event. We played a lot of sport and though not of a particularly high standard, we often had a crowd of local spectators. On the Feast of 'Christ the King' in late October the Garrison RC Army Padre organised an Inter-Service mass at the Catholic Cathedral and ensured that all of the ships' RC Church Parties, and those of the Army and RAF detachments', assembled outside the Dockyard Gates to march to church behind the Royal Marine Band. When we fell in I met Bernard Cleall, who was 6 months ahead of me at Fisgard, and we contrived to be in the last rank of the 3 columns. Unfortunately the army parade commander, following the biblical precedent, decided that the last would be first and put the band immediately behind us and then reversed the whole column. Bernard and I thus found we were leading the parade. As we passed down the Main Street we were surprised and not a little embarrassed to be warmly cheered by the locals from the pavements and from the balconies of the Flats. On arrival at the Cathedral, the Army Padre, a rather forceful Major, arbitrarily picked Bernard and me to represent the RN as servers and two Sergeants from the Army and RAF to represent them. In those days although attendance at church on Sundays was not compulsory a high percentage of Catholic servicemen did attend and on this occasion the large cathedral was packed. Before the first hymn the martinet of a chaplain declared he wanted to see the roof lifted off by the volume of singing and during each of the hymns he walked up and down the aisles prodding the servicemen with a swagger stick ordering them to sing louder. As one of the six altar servers I was out of his range but was able to wryly enjoy his extraordinary performance. The mass was very moving and well conducted and every year since, on that feast day, I have looked back with fond memories of that stirring service. Normally I went to mass on Sundays at Rosea high above the eastern end of the Dockyard. The congregation sat in high-backed chairs and I was intrigued by the local custom that girls and young women hooked their skirts over the back of the chair, so that their dress or skirt did not get creased, and sat in their knickers. In all the time I spent in Gibraltar I never heard of a Gibraltarian girl going out with a servicemen without being chaperoned by one of her family. Another of my abiding memories of Gib at that time was the Saturday lunchtime broadcast of the winning numbers of the Spanish Lottery in Spanish.

Like most ships at that time Saintes was infested with cockroaches. Towards the end of our refit the ship by then alongside, was evacuated and sealed and fumigated with a lethal gas for 24 hours. After this we never saw another live cockroach (although I found several dead ones six months later in one of the boxes containing spare thermionic valves in my workshop cupboard). Indeed from the end of 1954 I never saw a live cockroach at sea in any ship. We painted our mess and marvelled at how white the deckhead had become as we covered the yellow nicotine-stained surface. Soon afterwards I went ashore one Saturday night with several of my classmates from Collingwood to celebrate the birth of twins to the wife of one of them and we finished up drinking Malaga. Next morning onboard Saintes we changed into 'Blues' for the short Med winter and had ceremonial divisions. I had a terrific hangover, my No 1 Blue suit last worn six months ago was hanging off me and everything I ate drank or smoked had the sickly-sweet taste of Malaga. Sunday Divisions onboard always ended with 'For all the saints who from their labours rest ..." and as the ship's company lustily sang it I felt dreadful. I thought I really must pull myself together, do something drastic so, instead of tackling the direct cause of my discomfort, I illogically decided to give up smoking. The first few days weren't too difficult but the following three weeks were hell. However, I stuck to it and after going without my 30 cigarettes a day for four weeks, I had 'kicked the habit'.

In early December, as the refit neared completion we heard the great news that the ship would return to Portsmouth for Christmas leave, coming back to the Mediterranean in January for another three months. To prove the repairs made in the Dockyard to one of our shafts, we went to Tangier for a weekend. This was a welcome break after our long sojourn in Gibraltar and on the 18th December 1954, in high spirits, we left for home. Three days later we were met at Spithead by an MFV carrying families out to meet the ship and I was very happily reunited with Eileen and 18 months old Sally, who took an immediate shine to my bearded messmate Archie and informed my boss that "This is my Daddy's ship". It took all of the presents I had brought home for her to win her over to me. We had a wonderful Christmas and New Year together in our sparsely furnished home in Cosham made a little more homely by the TV set we bought with the money I had saved whilst away. All too soon I was bidding farewell to Eileen and Sally again and Saintes was off back to the Mediterranean to escape the British winter.

After a rough passage, we arrived at Gibraltar in company with the cruiser Bermuda and the destroyers Barfleur and St Kitts. Saintes and the other two destroyers of the 3rd DS left Gibraltar ahead of the cruiser and sped eastward towards Malta where they met up with three daring Class Destroyers, Daring, Delight and Defender and prepared to launch a WW2-like gunnery and torpedo attack on Bermuda as she approached from the west at dawn the next morning. The six destroyers formed a crescent with Saintes leading the attack, the two other 'Battle' class on her left and the three Darings on her right. As dawn broke, Bermuda approaching from the west at 28 knots, opened fire at maximum range with her

'A' turret, firing 6 inch practice (sand-filled) rounds with a 6 degree 'throw-off' to the left of the nearest destroyer, St Kitts. All six destroyers were steaming west at 28 knots and as soon as St Kitts had closed to 18,000 yards she opened fire first with the left gun of her 'A' turret, and then the right gun, firing two practice 4.5 inch rounds with a throw-off of 6 degrees to Bermuda's right. She then fired two rounds from 'B' turret. By then Barfleur had closed to maximum firing range and let loose her four rounds and then it was Saintes' turn, and we duly fired our four shots. A few minutes later came a 'flash' signal from Bermuda demanding an "Emergency Cease Fire". This was followed by: "All Gunnery settings to be left as set and Transmitting Stations evacuated and their doors locked". As we left the TS, Jack Limburn our Gunner asked me to confirm that he had applied the 'throw-off' correctly which, of course I was happy to do. We came up on deck and witnessed a most extraordinary 'Gung-Ho' torpedo attack. It was a fine sunny morning and ahead of us, but closing rapidly was Bermuda with most of her ship's company on deck to witness the grand finale. As soon as the nearest destroyer closed to 5000 yards all six of the destroyers began making smoke and when St Kitts was within 3000 yards she wheeled hard to port and fired all 8 of her torpedoes. This impressive 'death or glory' display was closely followed by a similar manoeuvre by Barfleur, Saintes and the three Darings as each destroyer fired her full outfit of 'tin-fish' set to pass under the cruiser; a total of seven of the fifty-four torpedoes fired actually being seen so to do. Then came more fun and games as all of the ships stopped while boats from the 6 destroyers rounded up and towed back their torpedoes which were bobbing about on the surface with their pennant numbers painted in 'day-glow' on their flotation heads. After this protracted evolution in which arguments arose over the ownership of some of the bobbing torpedoes, 53 of them were successfully recovered and we all set off for Gibraltar where the inevitable enquiry was held. It transpired that the 13th 4.5 inch round from the destroyers' 'throw-off' shoot, landed in the sea close to Bermuda's ship side, abreast 'A' Turret and the next round hit the top of 'B' turret just as an OA was leaving it. At that time on the open bridge of Bermuda, just aft of 'B' turret, were the CinC Med and the Flag Officers Flotillas of both the Med and Home Fleets. The Duke of Edinburgh had also intended to be there but had overslept. As the two shells whizzed down, the CinC 'Wee Jock' McGregor shouted "Everyone down, signal Emergency Cease-Fire" and when all was quiet he stood up, turned to the two Rear Admirals and said "Find the culprit" and stormed of the Bridge. I don't know what happened to 'the culprit', the Gunner of HMS Daring, who forgot to put on the 'throw-off,' but he must have gained some consolation for his very accurate opening burst at maximum gun range and at 28 knots.

I will never forget the sight of all those torpedoes leaping out of their tubes one after another, plunging into the sea and setting off at speed towards the target. However, although the torpedo shoot was most impressive we all knew that the cruiser would have sunk the lot of us with her longer range and heavier calibre guns long before we got anywhere near enough to torpedo her, witness HMS Glasgow's encounter with six German destroyers during WW2. Nevertheless it was spectacularly 'Yo-Ho' and stirring 'Boys Own' stuff, the like of which none of us was ever likely to see again. By now, despite the inevitable periods of being away from home, I had grown to enjoy life in the navy and, having been assessed as a 'Superior' EA3 at the end of 1954, I thought of making the RN my long term career. During Christmas leave Eileen and I had spoken at length on the matter and after leave I discussed my prospects with Tom Finney my Divisional Officer. He advised that I begin studying first for advancement to Chief EA and once I had achieved this aim and shown I could take charge, to go on to work and study for promotion to Electrical Officer. He then kindly recommended me for the next 'Fleet Board' for Acting Chief EA. Luckily, whenever an RN fleet gathers together abroad a sporting competition is held and 'Fleet Boards' are convened for advancement to a higher rating. While the combined Home and

Med fleets were in Gibraltar, my chum Fred Pointer, who was the 'Flyplane EA' in HMS Delight at the time, and I took advantage of this early opportunity to take the Provisional Professional Exam (PPE) for Chief EA and both passed. Ashore that night, we celebrated our next step on the ladder.

Shortly afterwards we left for a brief visit to Majorca and then on to Malta where we took up our billet in Sliema Creek. We occasionally left to bombard Filfla or to fire a live torpedo at that island and visited Tripoli from which our mess was taken by the 14th/20th King's Hussars westward along the Libyan coast to Sabratha, a well restored ancient Roman city complete with a splendid Ampitheatre and sea-flushed lavatories. After this cultural visit the Hussars took us out on the desert tank range in their tanks. We were wearing our No 1 Blue suits and after half an hour's bumping around in a 'battened-down' Centurion we emerged covered in sand and wondered how the devil they managed to keep their tanks running under such conditions. After a convivial evening in their Sergeants Mess they delivered us back to the ship in high spirits. Our next port of call was Palermo in Sicily where we had a run ashore on a Sunday morning before embarking the new Governor of Malta to transport him with due ceremony overnight to Malta. Our leave expired at 1300 as the Governor was due to arrive with his wife and family at 1500. Just before we went ashore at 0900, John Fielder received a telegram announcing that his wife had given birth. John  was naturally delighted and celebrated rather heavily ashore and we had to carry him back and put him to bed. Just as the Governor was coming down the jetty, and the Guard and Captain and Officers waited to welcome him aboard, a somewhat dishevelled John appeared in a deliriously happy mood on the STAAG deck loudly playing his cornet. John always led the music at Sunday divisions but, at that moment, his musical talents were not appreciated and he was chased out of sight down below by the Coxswain and duty watch. Mercifully John's personal tribute did not spoil the pomp and circumstance of the occasion and he was not only forgiven after being punished, but two years later was commissioned and later transferred to the South African Navy where he rose to the rank of Captain.

That Spring in Malta the weather was very pleasant and we enjoyed the routine. When not at sea doing exercises with the Squadron or Fleet we finished work at 1300 every day, went ashore by dghaisa to play games on Manoel Island followed by a bottle or two of Simmonds, Farson and Cisk's 'Blues' beer or a 'John Collins'. If we were making an evening of it, we would have a meal in one of the small restaurants on Sliema front (enticed by the billboard promising 'Big Eats HMS'), washed down by a 3d glass of Marsovin and rounded off with a bed in a 'Doss House' whose drab dormitory walls were decorated with pictures of the Edwardian RN fleet circa 1907.

In the 'Tiffies' mess at sea we played Mah Jong a lot and to a lesser extent 'Uckers' (the naval version of Ludo) and, as one of our members was the ship's film projector's maintainer, we had private showings of each film loaned to the ship. It is strange that we played Mah Jong so much in the Med for in the three ships I served in the Far East we never played the popular Chinese game of 'Four Winds'. We had a good library onboard which was supplied with a few new books every month and I read them as soon as they were available. Besides writing to each other every day, Eileen used to send me the Portsmouth 'Football Mail' every week for I was a supporter of Portsmouth FC. In our mess we had a fanatical Geordie OA who spent half the week crowing about how

Newcastle had tanned the backside off their opponents or, moaning about the eyesight of the referee if they had lost, and the rest of the week boasting that they would demolish their opponents on the coming Saturday. He was a forceful character and his one-track conversation was irksome to say the least. One day I received the FM from Eileen and read the account of a match played between Portsmouth and Sunderland and then read the account of the same match but in the Sunderland newspaper, printed by the same firm, (The Portsmouth and Sunderland Newspapers Ltd). It was like reading of two completely different matches, both reports were so prejudiced and were mostly hype. What with this and our domineering Geordie I became completely disillusioned with professional football, told Eileen not to send me the paper anymore and have never attended a league soccer match or read an account of one since.

During Med Fleet exercises held in the Tyrrhenian Sea, a storm blew up which was so severe that an Italian Liner foundered, a Type 15 Frigate was driven ashore and one of the Darings had its for'd boiler shut down by a deluge of sea water down the funnel. One normally associates the Med with calm waters but this was really rough and quite the worst weather we met in the whole commission. We took shelter off Golfe Juan on the French Riviera and after the storm had subsided, visited this small quiet resort before catching a train to Cannes for a memorable run ashore.

Our next visit was to Marseille where we berthed stern – to in the Vieux Port, at the bottom of the main street the Cannabiere, with Barfleur, St Kitts and a submarine similarly berthed but not alongside us. All we had to do was walk down the gangway and we were right in the centre of this great city. Just across the road from our stern were a number of cafes and bars and up the main street were all the shops and clubs. On board the ship was the famous BBC correspondent Wynford Vaughan-Thomas, whom we had entertained in a modest way in our mess during the recent exercise and storm. On the first night he took the whole mess 'Up the Cannabiere' for a truly great run ashore, details of which are rather hazy. Apparently I returned onboard in the small hours carrying the Chief OA and pretty sloshed, and lowered him down the ladder to the mess before staggering forward to my 'cabin'. The rest of our visit was given over to sight-seeing, shopping and more moderate drinking. I remember travelling to the hill top church of 'Notre Dame de la Garde' on the Napolonic water-driven 'Ascenseur', and observing that 'Le Chateau d'If' was an uninteresting looking low lying island, nothing like I imagined from Victor Hugo's Count of Monte Christo.

In April 1955 we made our last visit in the Mediterranean, to the small port of Sete half-way between Marseilles and the Spanish border. It was a pleasant friendly place where I made the mistake of greeting the elderly local Parish priest in my school-boy French and was then subjected to a friendly 'tete a tete' during which he breathed garlic over me for an interminable five minutes.

A brief call at Gibraltar and we bade farewell to the Med and set off home to Portsmouth for a short spell of leave before beginning the 'home leg' of the commission .with a visit to Bremen in Germany which we reached after a trip up the river Weser from Bremerhaven. The city was in the day and night throes of being rebuilt after the RAF's bombing during WW2 but, during our week long visit I never encountered any animosity from our former enemies, quite the opposite in fact. We were convivially entertained by the German equivalent of the RNA, visited the local car factory, brewery, Radio station and surviving museums and enjoyed the local beer halls where we drank many foaming steins of beer.

After this 'jolly' we made our way northwestward to Reykjavik, the capital of Iceland. This was before the 'Cod War' began, but Britain was not enjoying the friendliest of relations with Iceland and we anchored in the harbour rather than went alongside. On the first night a group of we 'Tiffies' went ashore. There didn't seem to be any bars as such but beer was sold in Milk Bars. As soon as we entered one of these, all the indigenous natives ostentatiously walked out. When we asked the 'barmaid' why the locals had left she replied in perfect English "We hate you English, you steal our fish". One of our OAs said "I'm not English I'm Scottish" the girl snapped back "You are all the same to us". We drank up our expensive beer and left and, after a stroll around the town we caught the next boat back to the ship. Other liberty men reported similarly cold responses from the locals and for the rest of the time we were there, apart from the RC church party on the Sunday, who received a distinctly tepid reception, none of the Saintes went ashore there. However what almost all of the crew did do was to live up to our reputation and steal their fish, from under their noses. During the week we were there at anchor, literally hundreds of fish were landed from the harbour. I was no great angler but during a one hour long fishing contest with a hand line 'fishing off the bottom' I landed seven large Plaice, three of them with one piece of bait, it was that easy. The 'iron deck' was aflap with fish and a team of volunteers gutted them before they were put below on ice. We lived very well on fish for days afterwards, and ever since, I for one have always been partial to Plaice.

We slipped out of Reykjavik, "Unwept, unhonoured and unsung" and steamed to Londonderry to operate with the local squadron for a few weeks. The routine was that all ships sailed down the River Foyle on a Monday morning, made for the Atlantic NW of Ireland and carried out Anti-Submarine Exercises every day returning to the mouth of the Foyle to anchor overnight and then 'weighed' next morning and proceeded to do the same again. On Friday afternoons we came up the river to Lisahallee to refuel and then, after doing a three-point turn in the river off the city of Londonderry, berthed facing to seaward for the weekend. The first time we carried out this manoeuvre under the command of our new Captain, Arthur Fitzroy-Talbot, the ships bows became impaled in the wooden 'Queens Jetty' causing the shore berthing party to scatter. George Brewer the GO, standing in the bows calmly turned and faced the Bridge and reported "Captain Sir, we have hit the jetty". We enjoyed our runs ashore in Londonderry and across the border in Buncrana in those 'Pre-Troubles' times and were well received by the locals. However I was dismayed when after mass on a Holy Day, the Parish priest of the church just inside the Bogside and his flock deliberately ignored the friendly greetings of our uniformed church party. They seemed to think we were some kind of traitors. That was the only sign of bigotry I recall on either side of the Northern Ireland border at that time.

Eileen's mother had been brought up in Portrush and had friends who owned the Londonderry Hotel in the main street of that delightful little holiday resort. They invited me to spend a weekend with them and I travelled by train and bus on the Friday evening and enjoyed a wonderful break with the charming family. On the Saturday, their three single daughters, who were members took me as their guest to play golf with them on the 'sacred' Royal Portrush Golf course. Although I had played before in Dun Laoghaire, I was really a novice, but they insisted I play, provided me with a set of clubs and quietly gave me advice during the round. I thoroughly enjoyed that game, made even more memorable by the party thrown afterwards in the club house by a player just in front of our 'foursome' hitting a 'hole in one' and being presented by the club with a handsome Table Lighter. The Public Bar of the hotel was only open until 9pm and for two hours at Sunday lunchtime so I offered to serve in the bar. The McNally family were delighted with this and as I left on Sunday evening, after a really nice and comfortable weekend, they invited me to come again the following weekend and to bring a chum too. The following Friday Archie Furmidge and I set off for Portrush. This was the weekend of the 'North-West 200' motor-cycle race and the town was really throbbing. All of the great exponents were there and the weather was perfect. Archie and I ran the Public Bar during the lunchtime and from 1900 to closing time at 2100. In between we had time for lunch in the hotel and to watch the race live, just up the road. In the bar during the evening there was a crowd of Chief and POs from a visiting frigate and as we wore our uniforms without jackets they assumed we were local bartenders. As we served them each of many successive rounds at their tables, they generously invited us to "have one on us Paddy". We played along and thanked them in pseudo Irish accents and naturally accepted their kind offer. After closing time we went to the 'NW 200 Ball', attended by all of the sporting celebrities and had a ring-side table with our hosts the McNally family. By now we were wearing our full smart No1 uniforms and during the festivities saw several of the senior rates we had been 'treated' by earlier, wearing that befuddled drunken expression of "where have we seen those guys before". The McNallys were very nice people and Archie and I were very grateful to them for giving us a fantastic weekend.

In the absence of a submarine 'mother ship', on our last Friday evening in Londonderry, Saintes offered the submarines returning from exercises, 'hotel' (showers etc) and repair facilities. A newly arrived 'S' Class submarine reported having trouble with her 1005 Gyro Compass with which our Gyro EA had no experience. So as I had looked after five of these 'hunting compasses' at Portland I was sent over to fix it. The sub's EA was in the small stuffy CPO's mess drinking with his messmates and broke off to show me the compass before going back to his mess. I could see that the Gyro had been neglected and so, after giving it a thorough clean up, a long overdue maintenance routine and setting it up, the old compass was as right as rain. This job took about 90 minutes and when I went to tell the Submarine's EA that his compass was OK, he and his mess mates were still 'knocking them back' in the squalid mess instead of going over to Saintes for a shower. I could not understand why, having been without a shower for a week, they were so reluctant to get out of that hot diesel-stinking boat and ashore in fresh air.

We then steamed around the top of Scotland to Rosyth where I saw how palatial HMS Caledonia was compared with its sister establishment HMS Fisgard, where I had trained, enjoyed a swim in its swimming pool and was persuaded by one of our EAs Johnny Wiseman to give my first pint of blood. Recorded on a Scottish Blood Donors card I now had official 'proof' of my Scottish blood.

From Rosyth we went to Oslo where we berthed close to the Rat Haus and paid an official visit to the Norwegian capital. The weather was fine and warm and I enjoyed the many sights. Among some amusing local events I recall seeing the Film 'Bread Love and Jealousy' in Italian with Norwegian sub-titles. It was slightly easier to try to follow the story in Italian than to try to make any sense of the written Norwegian. We were made very welcome by the locals and together with a visiting cruiser we put on a parade with a march past led by the cruiser's Royal Marine band containing several naval musicians, dressed as Marines, including our messmate OA2 John Fielder.

Before we left Oslo we embarked Admiral of the Fleet Sir John Cunningham and hoisted his Union Flag at our masthead for the long and picturesque journey to Tromso where he was to present the ship's bell of the cruiser in which he had rescued King Haakon and his family from the Nazis in 1940. The passage north up the length of the Norwegian coast and through Tromso Fjord was quite beautiful with its surrounding mountains snow-covered. Tromso itself, was a friendly little town which was enjoying its six months continuous daylight and the locals made a big fuss of us. We were taken by boat to see the partially submerged battleship Tirpitz and marvelled at how incredibly quiet was the whole fjord, you could hear the slightest sound from miles away. I bought a pair of sealskin slippers and a bright multi-coloured traditional Norwegian 'jellybag' hat for Sally in a shop there. Coming back aboard at 0030 one morning after attending a party put on for us by the local council I remember being amused by the gangway sentry cheerily saying "Goodnight Chief" with the 'Midnight sun' beaming down from an elevation of about 40 degrees We were all awarded 'Blue-Nose Certificates' for having crossed the Arctic circle but this was a bit of a cheat since we has only crossed it in high summer and continuous daylight. After this relatively low key but nonetheless enjoyable visit to the 'Far North' we returned to Invergordon before going south to anchor for a few fine summer's days off Great Yarmouth. This lively resort, was full of holidaymakers who seemed to love the ship, which was illuminated at night. The ship's company, all ashore in uniform in those days, and some of whom were also lit up at night, were very popular with the 'wakes weekers', well the girls anyway, and everyone enjoyed the visit. At one of the theatres a young Petula Clark topped the Bill and after the matinee one afternoon, she invited several of my messmates into her dressing room where they found her enchanting.

The final visit of our commission was to Hastings in August 1955 where we anchored for a few days. On the last night there we had a Gunnery run ashore, organised by George Brewer and attended by the Squadron GO Geoff Foggo and Gunner Jack Limburn, the OAs, GI and other Gunnery Senior rates. It was an end of commission hair-letting down evening and most enjoyable and I vaguely remember having double-vision on the ship's riding lights during the long boat trip back to the ship, which was anchored well off shore.

Next morning we made our way back to Portsmouth where we were happily reunited with our families. In addition to the presents from Germany and Norway, I remember bringing Sally home a two-storey dolls house and a Scotty Dog table lamp I had made for her. She loved the smelly sealskin slippers and insisted on wearing them in bed, and the first time I saw her playing with the doll's house she had removed all of the furniture and was using it as a cooker. I left Saintes on 15th August at Portsmouth for leave.

Looking back on my time in Saintes it proved to be a watershed in my career. Before I joined her I felt sure I would come out of the navy at the age of 30. However, aboard this happy ship, I was very lucky to have an enjoyable and responsible job, the periods away from home were not unbearably long and we visited a number of quite interesting places. Furthermore, I had friendly colleagues and messmates and a supportive boss who encouraged me and set me in the right direction towards a long and rewarding career in the service. I owe a lot to Bernard Finney and he and his wife Jeanne and family became and remain good friends of Eileen and me.

# Chapter 10

## HMS Cleopatra October 1955 – February 1956
## and
## Chief EAs Qualifying Course – March 1956

On 8th October 1955 I joined the light cruiser HMS Cleopatra, flagship of the Portsmouth Reserve Fleet. The ship was berthed at North Corner Jetty, her electrical supplies provided by shore connections and her auxiliary steam by a mobile 'Donkey Boiler'.  The ship's complement of about 200 including a small detachment of Royal Marines, as befits a Flagship, was made up entirely of personnel who had just returned from sea service abroad. Only the electrical equipment necessary to provide 'hotel' services was kept operational, the WW2 standard weapon systems were cocooned. This proud warship, which had served with distinction in the Mediterranean and survived a bomb hit which destroyed her C turret and a torpedo hit in the forward engine – room in 1943, was now a pale shadow of its former self. Flagship of a paper fleet and kept within a refits length of being operational standard by a skeleton crew, most of whom, including me, went home nearly every night.

I shared a commodious Tiffies mess with about 10 Chief Artificers and 1st – 4th Class Artificers of the different specialisations (except ERAs), almost all of whom were 'natives' and, as at most only one or two of us were required onboard at night, the mess was very quiet. When not duty, I went ashore at 1600, got on my bike parked by the forward gangway and cycled home to 41, Highbury Grove Cosham, returning onboard at 0755 next morning.

The Electrical Officer was Reg Tunnicliffe a Commissioned Electrical Officer (R) who had been in charge of the ship's Radio department during its last commission at sea. We also had a Chief EA, a couple of EAs and PO Electricians, REAs and PO REls and junior rates. I was put in charge of 'Low Power' but, divested of Gunnery, this was a laugh for all that was left was AC conversion machinery, the 24 volt DC system, Automatic Emergency Lighting, Teleprinters and Motor Boat Electrics – the least demanding job I ever had in the service and I had an LEM and two EMs to help me do it. During my 5 months in Cleopatra, I was never called back from shore to deal with a problem, there just weren't any because the equipment left running to provide the necessary accommodation and security services was pretty robust, uncomplicated and reliable, except the teleprinters.

The Admiral, Captain and Officers of Cleopatra insisted on maintaining the ship's appearance so that it looked, from a distance at least, as 'tiddly' as an operational sea-going Flagship. We played our part in inter ship sports matches, although we had fewer sportsmen to call upon than other cruisers and some destroyers and threw the occasional party on board. I recall Sally thoroughly enjoying the Christmas 1955 Children's Party.

Whether or not it was to earn a 'Duty-Free' entitlement, the ship left her alongside berth in the New Year and moved out into the middle of the harbour and secured to an Ammunitioning Buoy, although of course with no operational weapons we did not 'Ammunition ship'. However we were 'flashed-up', generating our own electrical power and auxiliary steam and looked like a real flagship with our 'riding lights' burning and quarter deck manned, ladders out and boats smartly secured to the booms. The Captain's boat was manned by Royal Marines with a Corporal as Coxswain. He and his crew had collected two fully charged motor boat batteries from me before the ship left the jetty and whilst lowering one of them into the boat his un-seaman-like granny knot had come undone and the very heavy battery had fallen, and glanced off the newly painted canopy and the side of the Skipper's boat causing superficial damage, before disappearing over the side and sinking into the mud of Portsmouth harbour. The RM Corporal was duly arraigned before the Captain and I was called to declare the age, condition and thus value of the lost battery. The battery being brand new the coxswain was charged full 'rate book' value and had his leave stopped for a week. A few days later, now an Acting Chief EA and bearing the grandiose, but empty title of Low Power Chief EA, I was called to go by ship's boat to another ship to fix our Captain's Motor Boat which was stranded there because it wouldn't start, reportedly because the starter was defective. It was a dry clear but very cold January morning and I went across the harbour wearing overalls, cap and a jacket and carrying a replacement starter in my tool bag. After replacing the starter and starting the boat I took passage back to Cleopatra in the boat carrying the defective starter in my tool bag. The RM Corporal told me he had to be inshore at King's Stairs soon to pick up the Captain so I told him to pass the QD Companion Ladder as close as he could so that I could step across and he could then continue down the harbour. As I stepped across, the boat moved away from the bottom of the ladder and I fell straight into the 'oggin'. I was still clutching my toolbag in my right hand and immediately found it difficult to tread water without being dragged down by the weight of the heavy starter motor. However, as a fairly hard-up married man of Scottish descent, with a mortgage and a family. I could not bear the thought of being charged for a motor boat starter and the tools if I let the bag go, so I shouted "Help" as loudly as I could and trod water like mad. The QD staff saw me clearly in some distress, only my capped head and wildly flailing left arm visible and my right arm straight down like an Irish dancer's, and hailed the boat and told them to go round again and carefully pick me up. After an interminable minute or so it came abreast me, one of the Royals relieved me of my burden by taking the toolbag from me and another helped me out of the water and on to the ladder. Very fortunately I had fallen into the only warm patch of water in the middle of the harbour, warmed by the outflow from the engine room and I didn't feel cold at all until the chilly wind hit me as I staggered up the ladder soaking wet but still wearing my rather battered 'Tiffies' cap. Following a hot shower and change I was fine and after I had given the starter a thorough wash in distilled water, overhauled it and changed the bearings, it too was fully operational again.

I had passed provisionally for Chief EA at Gibraltar in February 1955, and on leaving Saintes in August, I was recommended to sit the annual professional examination for promotion to Commissioned Electrical Officer at my first possible opportunity, in March 1956. The 'cushy number' I had in Cleopatra allowed me to put in a certain amount of private study at home for this all-important competitive examination, concentrating on those areas of naval electrical engineering in which I had little or no experience. I also studied electrical engineering theory one night a week at school. The waiting time (roster) for advancement to Chief Artificer varied from one specialisation to another and between the three port divisions but generally, artificers who had passed provisionally were 1$^{st}$ Class (ie had been CPOs for at least 8 years) or 2$^{nd}$ Class ( at least 4 years as a CPO), before being rated Acting Chief Artificer. This was particularly so with ERAs. I was very lucky to reach the top of the Portsmouth Chief EAs roster after only 3½ years as an EA3rd Class and when rated Acting Chief EA in January 1955, two weeks before my 26$^{th}$ birthday, I was, for six months, the youngest Chief Artificer in the RN. On top of this stroke of luck, in February 1956 I was surprised to be drafted to Collingwood to do the 3-week course for Chief EA. This course would clearly give me the best possible preparation for the exacting examination for a commission being held a week afterwards.

There were eight acting Chief EAs on the course, one of them having held the rank for over 4 years and three more having carried out the role at sea. On the first day we learnt that at the end of the course we would face five exams:

Electrical Power, Gyro Compasses and Sonar
Electronics, Servos and Weapon Control
Damage control
Instructional Technique
Oral Examination, by a Board of Electrical Officers.

We were then told to arrange our own individual instructional course with the appropriate training section in the subjects in which we thought we most needed training, and were told to "get on with it". As I had knowledge and experience of Gunnery Fire-Control, the older Sonar systems, Gyro Compasses and 'General Electrics' I chose to concentrate

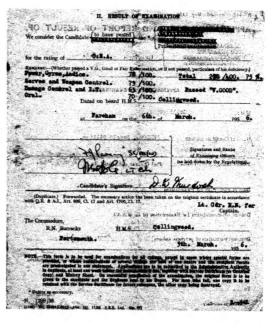

my 15 days worth of invaluable instruction on the new Gyro and Gyro-Magnetic Compasses, the new Sonar weapons and equipment and AC ships electrics. On the Monday morning of the 4th week we took the first 3 hour long paper and the rest of the exams followed in close succession, the individual IT lectures being given to EAs on the staff who had been briefed to be awkward, inattentive and to ask difficult questions. On the Thursday morning we had our individual searching oral examination by a Board of Electrical Officers and that afternoon were assembled to hear the results. I was delighted to hear I had passed but shocked to learn that only three of the eight had done so. It was clear that the older candidates who had held the Acting Chief EA rate for years, but who had little experience in electronics, Gunnery Fire-Control or Sonar, had no real chance of passing and, in an act of insensitivity, they were disrated that very day to EA1. I felt very sorry for the poor chaps who failed for they had held down the job of Chief EA in older ships and now faced embarrassment and a pay cut. Paradoxically, as there was an acute shortage of qualified personnel, some of them were soon back at sea in Chief EA's billets and picked up the acting rate again. On the following Monday, 9th March, I received a draft chit to join the brand new Type 14 frigate HMS Dundas after Easter leave as Chief EA. A few days later, my memory still crammed full of useful data, I sat the 3-paper highly-competitive examination for a commission.

Looking back, I think that my brief period in Cleopatra, which gave me the time to swot up at home, followed by the short but self-tailored Chief EAs course and a difficult comprehensive examination, gave me the best possible chance of securing a commission in competition with my contemporaries, some of whom had proved during five years of training together at Fisgard and Collingwood that they were cleverer than me.

"There is a tide in the affairs of men, which, taken at the flood, leads on to fortune - - ". I thank my lucky stars that I had the good sense to recognise that this was the tide for me and was able to seize the opportunity.

# Chapter 11

## HMS Dundas April 1956 – August 1957
## and
## Electrical Sub-Lieutenants' pre Commission Course September 1957

I joined HMS Dundas as her first Chief EA, at Portsmouth on 27th April 1956, two months after she was first commissioned at Cowes where she had been built at Samuel White's shipyard. The ship sailed next day to work-up at Portland before becoming part of the local 2nd Training Squadron.

Dundas was the first of the 1180 Ton 'Blackwood' Class of Anti-submarine Frigates to join the 2nd Training Squadron and, at that time was the first post WW2 ship to be based at Portland. As the only ship there with the latest Sonar and A/S weapons and the most junior Captain in the 2nd TS, Dundas naturally attracted a lot of attention and interest. Dundas was also the first ship with AC electrical power and distribution to be based at Portland and we very soon found that the small Portland Dockyard and the tiny local naval Maintenance facility were unfamiliar with AC and were quite incapable of rewinding an AC motor stator, or indeed of providing any meaningful assistance with any of our many electrical 'teething'

problems. The ship had no handbooks on the maintenance or handling of the supply and distribution system, in fact they didn't arrive until August 1957, just before I left the ship. All we had were some makers' drawings and notes made by the installation contractors at the shipyard and their oral instructions to the ship's Chief Electrician, who had never had a formal course on AC electrics in his life, poor chap. I was horrified to see that when synchronizing two main generators while preparing for sea, he made no adjustment to keep the power factor steady at 0.8 and the result was a noisy and unprofessional operation. When I looked askance, he told me "That's how the makers showed me how to do it". As diplomatically as I could, I took over the loading-up and transferring of load between generators and instructed all of my staff in how to do this properly, as I had recently been told at Collingwood.

The ship was commanded by Lt Cdr. Hugo Hollins who was previously Captain of HMS Petard but had been discharged from the service for failing a colour-blind test but was quickly reinstated after receiving glowing recommendations from several Admirals. He was an outstanding CO and ship-handler and later went on to become Vice-Admiral Sir Hugo Hollins. The First Lieutenant was Lt Peter Beeson another fine officer who later became Commodore RN Barracks Portsmouth. The (Marine) Engineer Officer was a jovial Lt. Cdr named Sullivan and the Navigating Officer was a young Lt. Chatterton - Dickson.

The Electrical Division of Dundas comprised Lieutenant 'Dougie' Hammacott, a former Torpedo Officer and ex-WW2 Swordfish Telegraphist/Air Gunner, a Chief EA (me), Chief Electrician 'Tubby' Masterson, a Direct Entry EA3 Gerry Beale (a term mate of mine at school), REA 3 Stewart, a National Service EA4, 2 PO Electricians and 15 junior rates. Besides heading the 'Electrical' members of the division I also worked closely with the

Chief OA Dick Goble who was 6 months ahead of me at Fisgard and became my 'run-ashore Oppo' in Dundas.

There were no habitable electrical 'cabooshes' in Dundas so I had to sleep in the Chief's Mess which had eight occupants, the Coxswain, Chief EA, OA and Chief Electrician, an EA3, REA3, Shipwright 3 and Chief Stoker sharing six hammock slinging billets and two berths on the ship's side settee, on one of which I slept. The mess was right up forward and felt the worst of the ship's movement in any sort of sea. The ship's bows pitched up and down heavily and the bows described a strange hesitant circular pattern, often hovering at the crest before suddenly crashing down into the trough of a wave. This jarring motion threw all of us in the mess around a bit and we often sustained bruises in heavy weather.

Dundas, had a single screw, a high-freeboard fo'csle with a deep break to a destroyer-like 'iron deck' and a narrow beam, which resulted in her rolling and pitching heavily in most sea states found in the Portland area and caused many of the young sonar trainees we took to sea every day to have a wretched time. The ship was fitted with A/S 170, the latest attack Sonar and with two three-barrelled Mk 10 mortars, A/S 147 and A/S 162, a sea-bottom object detection sonar. I was delighted and proud of Eileen, to find on opening the handbook for the latter, that a number of the drawings of the equipment had been 'Drawn by EMM' when she worked in the Drawing Office of HMUDE at Portland in 1952. The ship was fitted for, but not with, the long range Sonar A/S 177 and the Torpedo Control System for firing Mark 20 A/S torpedoes. It is just as well we didn't have these as well in the first commission, for we had more than enough problems to cope with.

Before I joined Dundas I rather fancied my chance as a good sailor for although I had experienced a typhoon off China in 1950, a near hurricane in the Atlantic during Exercise Mainbrace in 1953 and a ship sinking storm in the Med in 1955, I had never been sea-sick except for once during a day in the 'Portland Races' in 1953, bobbing up and down like a cork in a MASB doing 4 knots. In Dundas I was actually sea-sick at least four times and felt queasy on many occasions. However, Dundas really gave me my sea legs for I was never sick at sea in any of my subsequent ships. In Force 6 and above, life lines were rigged along the 'iron deck' of Dundas and were really necessary. During one storm we lost a young newly married Leading Hand over the side, His body was later recovered and we buried him at Gosport. Before we left Portland for a NATO exercise in the Bay of Biscay in early 1957, we embarked a Doctor who intended to study 'Mal de Mer' and to try out different cures. This keen young Medic was flat on his back within an hour of leaving harbour and spent the next ten days occupying one of the two swinging cots in the Sick Bay. Throughout that exercise the wind was never less than Force 8 and, on the Sunday it reached Hurricane Force 12, I was called to the Bridge to sort out the Pelorus and found everyone there being sick. I very soon joined them. It was later established that on that day every man jack onboard from the Captain down was sea-sick. The trainee OOW was a young Lieutenant Pilot who was trying to gain his watch-keeping ticket but had been sick all the time since we left Portland and he looked dreadful. On return to Portland, the poor chap resigned his commission That particular storm also caused the coaming of the midship hatch to the Officers' cabin flat to split away from the deck causing concern that this split, at the 'break of the fo'c'sle', (the most vulnerable part of the ship's hull), might spread right across the ship. HMS Hardy, the first of the class, had to withdraw from the exercise and limp back to Plymouth for urgent repairs to a similar defect. Devonport dockyard confirmed she was splitting apart at the same position and carried out a major strengthening of the decks in that area. Shortly after our return to Portland at the end of the exercise, we were ordered to proceed to Portsmouth for similar urgent remedial action.

We had two vital but very unreliable pieces of domestic electrical equipment in Dundas, both of which were civilian hotel models that were not sufficiently robust to stand up to being 'thrown about' at sea in a Type 14 frigate. They were respectively the galley cooking and domestic hot water services. I was often called at unsocial hours to sort them out, the latter, known as the 'Donkey Boiler' being prone to failure.

During one particularly rough period at sea, the 5005 Gyro Compass 'follow-up' amplifier failed and the compass toppled. I replaced it with the spare, kept un-powered in the amplifier console, only to find it too was defective. I managed to find the fault on the original amplifier, rectify and replace it and to right the compass and precess it to the ship's head. This highlighted to me a requirement to have a 'warm' working spare amplifier which could be tested in the console before being fitted to fulfil its vital role. So I designed a circuit to do this, fitted it to the console and produced the necessary drawings. The Navigating Officer suggested I submit it as an official modification and I was subsequently given a 'Herbert Lott' award for this simple modification which was later incorporated in the equipment. This was of course a case of 'necessity is the mother of invention' but I cannot claim the same of the illuminated and animated display I made for the ship's company dance held at the Royal Hotel in Weymouth. It comprised a ten  foot long floodlit aluminium sheet metal silhouette of Dundas, with a five foot long submarine, positioned ahead and below the ship.

The submarine was illuminated after 30 seconds, 10 seconds later the A/S mortars on the ship 'fired' and then in rapid succession a mortar bomb 'travelled' over the ship's mast and 'exploded' on the submarine whose lighting was immediately extinguished leaving only the 'victorious' Dundas illuminated. This whole sequence, actuated by relays was repeated all evening. The display was later put up on the fo'c'sle when the ship gave a party whilst alongside the Coaling Pier at Portland and gave us, as 'Canteen' ship of the Squadron, some kudos with the more 'senior' ships.

One day early in the commission, the Engineer Officer anxiously asked me if I could cut a screw thread on the ship's lathe. This was a brand new Harrison lathe exactly the same as I had done my 'passing-out' test job on at the end of my apprenticeship at Fisgard eight years earlier so I said "Of course". He told me that the adaptor for his boiler igniter was broken, there was no spare at Portland, and he needed one to 'flash-up' overnight before we went to sea next morning and neither his Chief Mechanician nor any of his staff felt able to make a new adaptor. As there was no drawing I measured the defective unit and, enjoying the challenge, got stuck into it straight away. Fortunately the job went to plan and the ship sailed on time.

Later the EO experienced difficulty in getting the ship's steam sirens to sound properly. He wrote to the Admiralty Design department at Bath to seek advice and in his letter succinctly described the problem as:
" . . . .and, despite all of our efforts, the sirens still emit a wet, spluttering 'fart-like' sound".

Back in April 1956 when Dundas joined the 2nd TS at Portland, I thought she would have the relaxed 'family-friendly' daily routine I had enjoyed in the same squadron two years earlier, sailing every weekday morning at 0800 with a class of would-be Sonar Operators from HMS Osprey and returning about 1600, alongside every weekend and only absent from the Portland area for major fleet exercises. I therefore quickly arranged to rent a ground-floor MQ hiring with a garden overlooking Portland harbour. Dundas' distinctive shape made her easy to recognise among the older ships of the squadron and when the family moved into the flat Eileen was able to see the ship enter harbour and berth and could gauge when I would be home. For three reasons this plan proved hopelessly optimistic and naïve.

1. The ship's brand new equipment and weapon systems suffered from more than their fair share of problems, the ship was invariably due to sail next morning and no help was forthcoming overnight from ashore so the ship's staff had to sort out the problems themselves. As Chief EA I was responsible for directing the effort to remedy any electrical defects affecting the ship's programme, and clearing them before I went ashore. This not only delayed my arrival home for several hours after we berthed but sometimes kept me onboard for the whole night.

2. Dundas was the 'Junior Ship' of the squadron so we were often 'browned-off' to do the out of hours tasks at sea and didn't return to harbour until hours after the rest of the squadron were snugly tied up alongside and on shore supplies of steam and electricity. This particular extra duty did occasionally have a bright side, for example we took part in the 'rescue' of the castaways at the end of the film 'The Little Hut' shot at Church Ope Cove in Portland one fine evening with everyone on deck wearing tropical rig. Although we never saw Ava Gardner or David Niven, the ship's welfare fund benefited handsomely.

3. Our Captain was a bachelor with a roving eye so, whenever Dundas was not Duty ship, he took the ship away for a weekend jolly at an English, French or Channel Island port. This move was of course very popular with the ship's company, most of whom did not have their families at Portland. As a result Eileen and I spent

most of the time separated and, since we had no telephone, she often did not know when I would be home, if at all.

*HMS Dundas Ship's Company 1957 – (Don 4<sup>th</sup> from left in 3<sup>rd</sup> row)*

The uncertainty of the ship's programme and my frequent inability to get home to Wyke, even when the ship was alongside at Portland, made Dundas Eileen's' favourite 'hate'

ship, a distinction it retained for the rest of my naval career. In April 1957, after a year of frustrating, sporadic and uncertain domesticity, we decided to give up the MQ and Eileen took Sally home to our house at Cosham and, for

the next four months I remained onboard the ship, travelling home as best I could whenever I had a free weekend.

I remember several of the ship's channel visits for different reasons. The day we arrived at Guernsey in July 1956 I learnt I had passed the examination for a commission and had been put on the 'waiting' list, so I went ashore with my 'Oppo' and had a slap-up meal at a smart restaurant to celebrate. In March 1957, to commemorate the first anniversary of the ship's commissioning, Dundas visited Cowes and besides attending the official reception at the shipyard I visited my long lost IOW cousin together with the Chief OA and had rather too much to drink. Dick Goble, bless him proved to be my saviour for he steered me safely back to the ship without anyone witnessing my return. The ship's trip to Le Havre facilitated a splendid weekend visit to Paris where we were billeted free at the French Foreign Legion barracks at Vincennes and, at minimal cost were able to see and enjoy the sights of the French capital. During one visit to Brest we accidentally strayed into a wedding reception and were invited by the Bride and Groom to join the all day party. During our next visit to Brest a group of we Chiefs missed the boat back to the ship after a great run ashore and were subsequently docked a day's pay by the Captain. "C'est la vie". I remember too some other incidents that occurred in Dundas. On 23rd December 1956, the ship was at Portsmouth for the Christmas leave period and was detailed, as duty ship, to bury an Admiral at sea off St Helens. I had met the deceased Admiral, Sir Frederick Dreyer, father of my Captain in Saintes, and also coincidentally, the grandfather of my later Captain in Falmouth, and as a mark of respect to the 'father of naval gunnery fire-control', I attended the funeral held on the Fo'c'sle because the Quarter deck was too small for the guard and mourners. During Captain (D)'s inspection at Portland, the readiness and reporting for rounds of the 'Spirit Room' was entrusted to a Leading Seaman and the 'three-badge' Able Seaman 'Rum Bosun', (Tanky). This was a big mistake for when Captain (D) and his entourage arrived at the Rum Store, the two Trustees were as 'smashed as rats'. The Leading rate lost his hook and tanky his job and badges. On 1st January 1957 I became a confirmed Chief EA and, for six months at least, the youngest confirmed Chief Artificer in the navy. While the ship was in dock at Portsmouth for a propeller change in July 1957, I was visited by a Naval Tailor's rep who told me I had been selected for promotion to Sub Lt. This news was confirmed by a 'Fleet Order' a few days later. On the evening of the 30th August, back at Portland, I was invited into the wardroom where I was given a traditional 'send off' by the Captain and officers.

Although Dundas holds few happy memories for Eileen, I have to say that despite the inherent drawbacks of a Type 14 frigate, it was quite a happy ship. During my 16 months aboard her I enjoyed the camaraderie of a well led small ship's crew, memorable visits to Torquay, Plymouth, Brixham, Guernsey, Cowes, St. Malo and Brest (twice), Cherbourg and Le Havre and am proud to say that throughout that period the ship never failed to meet its operational programme.

During the year I spent 'on the waiting list', after passing the professional exam for a commission, a fundamental change took place in the officer structure of the RN. All Officers holding permanent commissions were thenceforth assigned to either the 'General List' or the 'Special Duties List' and those with a (non-pensionable) Short Service Commission to a Supplementary List. The General List contained all ranks from Midshipman to Admiral and included 'Upper Yardmen' commissioned from the Lower Deck before the age of 25 and the few 'Branch Officers' given 'Direct Promotion' to Lieutenant from Commissioned Officer, at any age. The new SD List contained all of the previous 'Branch Officers', that is to say all officers commissioned from the Lower Deck between the ages of 26 and 33 years and their successors. The old 'Branch' Officer ranks of 'Commissioned' and 'Senior Commissioned' Officer (who wore a 'thin' or 'thick' stripe respectively and were addressed as 'Mister') were abolished, the former becoming Sub-Lieutenants and the latter Lieutenants. The promotion zones for officers on the SD List were set at 4 to 8 years for Lieutenant and 5 to 9 years for Lt. Commander. The avenue for a 'Branch' (i.e. SD) officer to transfer to the General List was closed and thus their promotion ceiling was firmly set at Lieutenant-Commander (until the rank of Commander (SD) was introduced ten years later in 1966. At the same time the old 'Direct Promotion' route to the upper ranks via the General List was reinstated for SD Officers selected for early promotion to Lieutenant. *(Alas, too late for those promoted to Lieutenant before 1966)*.

On 31st August 1957, seven Chief EAs, two Electrical Mechanicians and one PO Electrician assembled at HMS Collingwood for the three-week Pre-Commissioning Course for Electrical Sub- Lieutenants (L).The 'spread' of places on this course, vis a vis the age and technical status of the members, followed the well established pattern from previous years. My chum Fred Pointer and I, the two successful but youngest artificer candidates in the 1956 examination, who had been 'stood over' for one year, were still among the youngest in the class of 1957. On the first day, we were addressed by the Officers' 'Appointer' Lieut. Commander Hamilton-Bate, who outlined the purpose of the course. He told us that as the post-graduate technical course would be devoted to Radio and Radar Engineering, so the next three weeks would concentrate on bringing us up to date on the latest ships' electrics. After going through the changes in the officer structure, and reminding us that our behaviour would be closely monitored and we would be assessed for 'Officer-like qualities', he ended with the thinly disguised threat, or sobering remark:

"Remember, you are not there yet".

The electrical update was largely devoted to AC ships and, since I had only just left one, I found it a bit of a 'doddle'. We were accommodated in the CPO's mess and enjoyed the company of our old friends and colleagues, heard again and ignored the old 'chestnut': "I know an officer who wishes he had remained a Chief" and, heeding the 'Appointer's' warning, managed to avoid over indulgence in the bar at lunch-time, We had no establishment duties so I went home every evening, thus avoiding any further temptation. The course was pleasantly interrupted by organised visits to 'Gieves' for measurement of our uniforms and the free issue of our complete kit from 'Officers' Slops and the steel black trunk in which to pack it. On the morning of the last Friday the 'Appointer' again addressed us and this time congratulated us on passing the final hurdle, wished us luck in the future and told us that, statistically speaking, nine of the ten of us could expect to eventually become Lieutenants and three of us Lieutenant-Commanders. This forecast proved accurate and, I never once wished, or met any other officer who wished, he had remained a Chief.

That afternoon our packed and locked steel trunks were collected and shipped to the storeroom of the wardroom of RN Barracks Portsmouth, HMS Victory, (later renamed Nelson), and the ten of us were handed our Service Certificates and told we were officially discharged from the service but ordered to report to the wardroom Hall Porter of HMS Victory on the Sunday evening in plain clothes and the next morning at 0800 to be fully dressed as Sub Lieutenants and ready to begin instruction as junior officers.

# Chapter 12

## Commission and Post-Graduate Course September 1957 - March 1958

On the evening of Sunday 27<sup>th</sup> September 1957, I travelled to HMS Victory by bus in plain clothes and as instructed, reported to the Wardroom Hall Porter, completed a joining card and was allocated a 'Mess Number'. Whilst there I met a number of my contemporaries including Ivan Sallows who lived fairly near me at Cosham. After our brief preparatory visit, he kindly gave me a lift home, during which we agreed to share the costs of daily travel in his car to and from HMS Victory and later HMS Collingwood for the duration of our Post Commission courses. At 0715 next morning, the day our commissions appeared in the 'London Gazette', Ivan picked me up at the end of my road and wearing our brand new and rather smart Sub Lieutenant's uniforms, but having to bow our heads as the canvas 'hood' of his old Morris Minor rested on our caps, we drove to the Wardroom with a mixture of excitement and trepidation. After parking the car in the car park behind the Wardroom and tidying ourselves up, we joined the rest of our promotion L and R classes respectively and other newly commissioned classes milling around in the foyer of the wardroom. Just before 0800 we were marched across to the RN Barracks, to the former Warrant Officers' Mess at the North End of the Parade Ground, where we moved into a large classroom. There were about 50 of us very smartly dressed 'mature' Sub-Lieutenants sitting there and, strangely, one chap in plain clothes.

Just as every pub in Wales has a barman who had a trial for the Welsh Rugby team, every Chief's mess in the RN has a member who claims to have been offered a commission but refused it. Anyone who has been through the process knows that what the claimant means is that one of his Captains was prepared to recommend him to take the competitive professional exam. As less than 25 % of the candidates pass and are selected for promotion, the claim is well wide of the truth. However, that morning we witnessed the only recorded refusal of a commission. The chap in plain clothes was an ERA 2nd Class who took advantage of the fact he had been legally discharged from the service three days earlier and refused to accept the commission awarded him that morning. Needless to say there was quite a kerfuffle and the officer in charge of the course took the chap away and, after consulting with the RN 'Legal Eagles', returned alone and our four week long 'Induction and Junior Officers' War Course' began. We never saw the 'refusnik' again and the incident was not officially mentioned although we gathered that he achieved his aim.

The officer in charge, Lt-Commander Charles Kavanagh RN, a former Frigate Captain, soon recovered from the unscheduled delay to the start of the course by introducing his team of lecturers and outlining the aims and syllabus of the two courses. We were then separated into four 'Syndicates', each comprising members of the branches and sub-specialisations represented on the course This was to foster 'team spirit' and an appreciation of the roles of the different officers with whom we would serve in ships and would, at the same time avoid branch 'tribalism'. The Syndicate I was assigned to was made up of three Acting Electrical Sub-Lieutenants, one Marine Engineer, one Shipwright, one Supply, and four Seamen (1 Communications, 2 Gunnery, and a TAS officer), in short a microcosm of the service. For the next two weeks we would study, drill, debate, act role plays and play games as members of our Syndicates. Copies of the programme were handed out and we then began what proved to be a well thought out course designed to smooth our transition from 'afore the mast' to the Wardroom.

*Acting Sub-Lieutenants Syndicate 28<sup>th</sup> September 1957 at HMS Victory*

The three brand new, but rather mature Electrical officers, Acting Sub-Lieutenants Murdoch, Noakes and Renson are the first three from the left in the front row, looking a little apprehensive.

Naturally, with our first meal in the most elegant officers' mess in the RN only a few hours away, it dealt first with wardroom etiquette, humourously referred to as the 'knife and fork drill'. This sensitive subject was dealt with in a common sense and un-patronising manner We had already each been given a 'Mess Number' to be used when eating and ordering drinks and were surprised to learn that there was a strict 'no treating' rule in the wardroom. If an officer wishes to join a 'round' he automatically tells whoever is writing the bar chit which drink he wants and adds his mess number. This eminently sensible rule enables an officer to take a drink with his friends without feeling obliged to reciprocate and risk drinking more than he intends or running up a huge bill, or both. We were also advised that pints were infra dig and that a half-pint of beer or a single measure of spirits with a mixer, e.g. a G&T, (Gin and Tonic), 'Horse's Neck' (Brandy and Ginger Ale) or Whisky and Soda was a more appropriate drink in the Wardroom. With our heads reeling from the advice crammed into them during that forenoon's lectures, we entered the Wardroom Ante-Room shortly after the sun went over the yardarm to find it packed with officers of all ranks engrossed in enjoying a pre-prandial drink with their friends and colleagues. It didn't take us long to master the bar chit routine and soon we were joining them for 'just the one', scarcely enough 'Dutch courage' to face taking our first lunch in that august environment in the company of officers of all ranks. After nervously queuing at the door to enter I gave my mess number to the Steward, picked up a clean linen napkin from the

rack and looked around to find a spare seat. I found one at a polished oak table between one of my friends and a friendly young seaman Lieutenant, facing the famous artist Wylie's superb illuminated mural of the 'Glorious First of June'.

This friendly officer, realising that this was our wardroom debut, soon put both of us at ease with his cheery manner and, looking round the splendid dining room I saw that all of us rookies were being similarly welcomed by the other members of the mess. Suddenly one hapless Acting Sub-Lt, attempting to cut his crusty roll with a knife instead of breaking it, caused it to slip from his grasp and he and his classmates watched in horror, and everyone else with amusement, as it rolled along the carpet between two tables. This minor social gaffe broke the ice for the whole class and we never looked back. During that first meal in the mess I admired the murals, the silverware, the service but not least the superb standard of the food.

The culinary revolution in the standard of 'General Mess' food, which occurred during the 1960s was still some way off but the standard in the wardroom was already very high and all of us newcomers really enjoyed the quantum leap to haute cuisine. In the Coffee room afterwards, my chum Fred Pointer, kindly offered 'to be Mum' by pouring the coffee for some of us from a handsome silver samovar. However he was unable to turn the tap off and, in an unrehearsed display of teamwork we had to rally round forming a chain to supply him with a steady stream of empty cups until a steward arrived to turn the blessed thing off. The more senior officers present thought this was hugely funny as we strove and thankfully managed to avoid spillage but though embarrassing for Fred at the time, he now recalls the incident as a cherished memory of that first lunch in the 'Flagship' of naval wardrooms. As we made our way in small groups back to the classrooms that afternoon, we were embarrassed in a different way at being saluted for the first time by the ratings we passed and self-consciously returned their salute.

During the rest of the two-week 'Divisional Course' we were taught a Divisional Officer's responsibilities for the welfare of his men including being a friend of the 'accused', engaging in role play with members of the staff playing the Captain and the 'accused'. We learnt how to carry out an audit of public funds, how to compile S264 reports on a rating, how to write a formal report on an incident and were tested in our ability to do these tasks concisely and legibly. We were taught the duties of Officer of the Day and practiced these in disciplinary role play with the staff, playing drunken sailors returning onboard and other incidents we would meet in the future. We were also taught sword drill on the parade ground.

Apart from the drills on the Parade Ground, which were conducted by a Chief Gunnery Instructor in the only way GIs know, bless them, all of our instruction was given in a friendly manner with us being treated as mature students by officers dedicated to putting over their message. We had no evening classes or duties so I went home with Ivan every night, but those living in enjoyed dinner in the mess preceded and followed perhaps by a convivial drink in the best bar in Portsmouth. They also enjoyed the sheer luxury of an old-fashioned cabin with a coal-fire attended by an elderly orderly, who wakened them in the morning with a nice cup of tea. They really appreciated the comfort of a contemporaneous Five Star Hotel.

A Ladies Night on the eve of the end of our stay in RN Barracks was advertised in the mess and was heavily booked by members. Lt. Cdr. Kavanagh made a block booking for all of the 'near natives' on the course to attend this event, which was very popular with members of the mess of all ranks, and told us we would be silly to miss this golden opportunity to give our wives a treat they would remember for the rest of their lives. He also told us that the Commodore and his wife would be attending and that there would be dancing and roulette after dinner. Needless to say, with or without pressure from our 'better halves', we all jumped at the chance to attend this jewel in the wardroom's social calendar and our wives rushed out to buy evening dresses, money being no object.

The last piece of advice I remember from the 'Divisional Course' was on how to introduce our wives to a senior officer, doubtless prompted by our impending attendance at the Ladies Guest Night, we were told to say:

"My Dear, may I introduce the Commodore"

The two-week long Junior Officers' War Course (JOWC) was designed to make us look at the broader picture of the navy's role in peace and war and to learn how to play our part in its management. It contained a number of lectures on every aspect of life in Britain including the nation's economy, law, industrial relations, politics and foreign relations. All of these illuminating talks were extremely well delivered by renowned experts in their fields. These enlightening lectures were followed by lively question and answer sessions with the speakers. In between this advanced course in Current Affairs, we were lectured by the staff on the necessity of keeping up to date with world affairs by reading a 'good' daily newspaper. In our Syndicates, we tackled hypothetical political, strategic and tactical situations, produced the appropriate reports, and recommended the necessary actions. Naturally at the subsequent whole-class 'wash-up' of these exercises we found that each syndicate had made many mistakes but we all learnt from them and went away much better prepared for our future as naval officers.

On the last evening of our course in HMS Victory, I changed at home into my brand new 'Mess Undress' complete with stiff white shirt, wing collar and bow-tie and helped Eileen get into her expensive new gown. She looked terrific. We had just been given admiring approval by her mother, who was baby-sitting, and by Sally to whom we gave a goodnight kiss, when the doorbell rang. It was my chum Ivan who had kindly offered to collect us in his car and take us to the mess with his wife. Ivan's wife, Audrey came in looking stunning in a new long dress followed by a distraught Ivan with his white shirt front terribly buckled and his bow-tie in one hand exclaiming: "Can you help me tie this damn thing Don"? With the help of Eileen and Audrey we managed to make him look reasonably presentable and then set off in his Jalopy for the barracks. The ladies climbed into the back seats trying to keep their dresses from getting creased and at the same time to look dignified and Ivan and I got in the front, I knew the nearside door handle did not work and duly locked the door with the hut door type hook and eye catch

Ivan had fitted inside the car. Ivan was well built and six feet tall and with a full car he was rather squashed in the driver's seat. As the bottom of his shirt was anchored by his cummerbund, his stiff and already crumpled 'Dickie' front billowed forward like a spinnaker in a force eight gale, reducing his visibility. This was further impaired by his peak being depressed by the canvas hood bearing on the top of his cap. As a result I had to guide him as we made our way through the town to Queen Street. As we entered the Wardroom 'In' gate the two ladies proudly clutched our formal invitations declaring:

"The Commodore and Officers of HMS Victory Request the Pleasure of the Company of Sub Lieutenant and Mrs Sallows/Murdoch to Dinner in the Wardroom on - - - - -"

When we reached the head of the queue of generally rather smart cars, Ivan pulled up at the foot of the red carpeted stairs leading up to the Mess and two smartly dressed sailors wearing white gloves stepped forward on either side of the car to open the doors. The one on the nearside wrestled, seemingly for ages, in vain with the useless door handle making it impossible for me to unhook the hook and eye and there was an embarrassing standoff until he relaxed his pull and I was able to unlatch and push the door open. I staggered out, folded up the front seat and, with as much dignity as they could muster, Eileen and Audrey, smoothing out their bouffant gowns, followed suit. As Ivan made to park the car behind the mess, as he had every morning, he was curtly informed that "Junior Officers have to park over the road on the barracks Parade Ground". I escorted the two ladies up the steps and into the Hall where we studied the dining Seating Plan while we waited until a very grumpy, flustered, and somewhat dishevelled Ivan joined us. Collectively gathering our composure we entered the Ante Room which was packed with Officers and their Wives enjoying a lively pre-dinner drink and chat with friends. We joined this happy throng and were soon doing the same with fellow members of the course and officers we knew.

At Eight o'clock the gong was struck and we made our way into the mess and to a round table we were to share with three members of our course and their wives. To say that our wives were impressed by the splendour of the scene was a gross understatement. (In modern parlance they would have probably said they were 'Gobsmacked').

The polished oak tables were candlelit, the murals floodlit, all the diners were splendidly arrayed, and up in the 'Minstrels Gallery' a Royal Marine orchestra was playing in the guests with 'The Roast Beef of old England'. None of us had ever before been part of such a grand social occasion and have cherished the memory of that first Ladies Guest Night ever since.

The whole of that evening proved a huge success. The haute-cuisine dinner was superb, the service extraordinary, the wines excellent and the company convivial and everyone on our table thoroughly enjoyed themselves, not least our wives who had earlier put up with a lot of loneliness as a result of our pre-occupation with study for the examination which led to us being commissioned in the first place. Now they too could enjoy the fruits of our labours. On the following morning we had a course 'wash-up' and after a farewell drink and lunch with our syndicate friends, returned to our own branches, the Electrical (L and R) Sub Lieutenants setting off for HMS Collingwood and our technical conversion course.

We joined HMS Collingwood on the Sunday afternoon and completed the 'Joining Routine' in the wardroom. Built at the outbreak of WW2 this consisted of a collection of wooden huts with several brick two-berth cabin blocks and their associated communal ablution rooms. The Wardroom Ante-Room was comfortably furnished with extraordinarily long leather settees, and with leather arm chairs and the bar was extensive, well fitted out and amply stocked. The Dining Room contained five very long polished oak tables and chairs for 200 officers but had no pictures except for a portrait of the Queen. Notwithstanding its poor comparison with the splendour of our first officers' mess there was something about

*Electrical Sub-Lieutenants (L) Qualifying Course October1957* Front
Row: Austin Edbrooke, Bill Mc Nabb, Brian Callus, Freddy Plowman,
Harold Timberlake Back Row: Duncan Bell, Brian Wallett, Brian Noakes, Don Murdoch, Fred Pointer

Collingwood's Wardroom that attracted us 'mature' Sub-Lieutenants, perhaps because we felt more at home there amongst old friends and in less historic accommodation. I had travelled to Collingwood with Ivan Sallows and, as we were 'natives' of the Portsmouth area, we were not allocated a cabin because when duty Officer we would have to sleep in the designated cabin close to Main Gate. The non-natives in our class were allocated to permanent two-berth cabins. Brian Callus, looking forward to being awoken with a cup of tea on the first Monday morning by a beautiful Wren Steward, unlike the elderly male retainers at RNB, was somewhat deflated by being served his morning 'cuppa' by a pimply adolescent male Steward.

Shortly before 8 o'clock on that Monday morning the class, dressed in our still very smart No 5 uniforms but thankfully excused wearing gaiters and boots, made its way independently to the eastern edge of the huge Main Parade Ground until we were summoned to fall in with the hundreds of other classes under instruction. We were marched from morning divisions by the designated class leader, our oldest member Freddie Plowman, to the 'Radar Parade Ground' in the NE quarter of the establishment where we 'fell-out' and went to the relevant classroom or demonstration area. After the morning's instruction we made our way independently back to the wardroom for lunch. Most of us had a 'quick half' of beer or a small 'VC' (Vintage Cider-an inexpensive drink popular at the time), followed by a first-class 3-course lunch and coffee, before leisurely returning to our studies.

At the end of the afternoon, if not required for duty, I met Ivan back in the wardroom and we went home to our families. The pattern of this daily routine persisted, more or less throughout the six months technical course aimed at giving us Electrical specialists a good 'cross-training' in Radio and Radar and our R specialist opposite numbers a training in ships' electrics, so that all of us could take charge of all aspects of the branch's responsibility at sea.

We were required to carry out an overnight duty every ninth day, the task alternating between Assistant Officer of the Day, at the Main Gate, and Assistant Security Officer with responsibility for carrying out perimeter and other security Rounds. Each of us in turn was also required to act as 'Officer of the Guard' at morning Divisions for one week. This entailed wearing boots, shiny black leather gaiters, carrying a sword and marching the guard from the Armoury to the Parade ground, behind the Collingwood Band, and looking every inch a 'Gunner' My turn for this 'un-tiffy' like duty came during a particularly cold spell in January 1958 and although everyone else on the parade ground was dressed in Greatcoats or Burberrys, the band, guard and I were not permitted that comfort. I wore leather kid gloves so my hands were warm but when not on the march I had a job concealing my shivers as I stood out in front of the guard holding my drawn sword. One particularly cold morning, having reported the guard 'present and correct' to the Commander on the dais, and full of 'Pomp and Importance' I returned to my position in front of the guard, I was mortified to feel a 'dew-drop' starting to run from my nose. Standing alone in a rather prominent position I could hardly lower my sword and get out my handkerchief, so I had to resort to a juvenile remedy by surreptitiously and repeatedly sniffing until I fell-out the guard at the Armoury some 20 minutes later. Another memory of that week is that for four mornings I had to order the Guard to "Eyes Right" whilst I carried out the traditional and somewhat flamboyant sword salute to the Commander as we led the 2000 odd trainees in an anti-clockwise direction around the parade ground and past the dais at the end of Divisions. On Friday the Commander i/c of Apprentices took the salute but instead of standing on the dais he stood on the south side of the parade ground and the march past was carried out in a clockwise direction. This cunning ploy by the Gunnery Officer to exercise my co-ordination forced me into ordering the guard to "Eyes Left" (including me) whilst giving the Commander (Apps) a sword salute to my right. Being rather cack-handed, I found this manoeuvre very difficult.

Since we already had a sound knowledge and years of experience of thermionic electronics through audio and servo amplifiers, and gunnery and sonar computers, our 'cross-training' began with four weeks radio theory. This proved enlightening and invaluable and was followed by two months detailed instruction in contemporaneous MF, HF, VHF and UHF equipments, their power and aerial systems, test equipments and testing and tuning procedures. We then moved on to Radar Principles including those governing Wave guides, Magnetrons, Klystrons and Aerials. After receiving a good foundation in this new (to us) subject, we underwent practical instruction in the maintenance of the equipment we were likely to meet at sea, viz: Radar 974 (Navigational), 293 (Warning), 275 (Medium range Gunnery) and 262 (Close Range Gunnery). The final two weeks of the course were devoted to Navigation Aids (Decca and Loran), D/F (FH4 and FM12) and Crypto equipment The whole course was well structured, delivered and made interesting by the instructional skills of dedicated Officers and Senior ratings and I thoroughly enjoyed it.

When we were commissioned in 1957, the standard of living in Britain was very different to what it became in the 1960s. Only two of our class had passed the driving test and owned a car, few owned a mortgaged house or had a bank account, had been abroad for a holiday or flown in an aircraft. Although Eileen and I had our own home, we couldn't afford to furnish the front room, to buy a refrigerator, washing machine or even a telephone, considered to be expensive luxuries in those days when mothers of young children did not go out to work. The pay of a Sub Lieutenant on first promotion was less than that received by the six of us who had been Chief EAs and though we didn't get a drop in pay, we 'marked time' after being commissioned and it was six years before, as a Lieutenant of 2 years seniority, that I overtook the pay I would have received if I had remained a Chief EA. We accepted this state of affairs because we knew that there would then be a substantial and ever increasing pay differential. However back in 1957, my classmates and I were not very well off and had to be pretty economical.

Having said that, I enjoyed the monthly Mess Dinners, except one where the pheasant I ate on the night before I took my driving test made me distinctly queasy but thankfully didn't cause me to fail it. Fred Pointer and I were coerced into decorating one of the rooms in the mess as a restaurant for the Christmas Dance. As we had visited the first Chinese Restaurant in Portsmouth, which had only just opened, we chose to turn our room into a Chinese Restaurant with banners, lanterns and menus we made at our house, copying from library books. Fred and Jean and Eileen and I had a great time at the ball and our restaurant received plaudits from the diners. I still couldn't afford to buy even a 'Jalopy' but celebrated my driving licence by hiring an old car for the weekend from a 'dodgy' garage and drove Eileen, Sally and my mother-in-law all the way to Southampton for the day. In the spring of 1958 our class was treated to its first flight. We were taken to Lee-on-the-Solent where we were given a flight over Gosport Portsmouth, the Isle of Wight and Fareham at about 2000 feet in an RN De-Havilland Domine. Sitting in comfortable individual seats, we had a splendid view of the landscape and thoroughly enjoyed the experience.

One Friday in February 1958, near the end of our cross-training courses, the L and R classes were assembled in one classroom to learn our immediate fate from the 'Appointer'. In alphabetical order he read out the first sea appointments of the 20 of us. I don't remember what I expected or even hoped for but found that I was to join HMS Cheviot, leader of the 8th Destroyer Squadron in the Far East as Deputy Electrical Officer for an 18 month foreign commission, flying out to Singapore on 14th April to join her. Ivan Sallows learnt that he too was going out to the Far East to join HMS Cardigan Bay as Squadron Radio Officer of the 3rd Frigate Squadron. At lunchtime Ivan and I, wondering how best to tell our wives that we were about to leave them for 18 months, imbibed rather longer and more heavily than usual and when we arrived home full of 'Dutch Courage' we were met by Ivan's wife Audrey, who had come to collect their young son from Eileen's temporary care. Ivan and I were in a 'Silly Tipsy' mood and made a big joke of our news which went down like a concrete parachute with our wives. It took several hours of grovelling on our parts to rectify our terribly mistimed light-heartedness.

The following week Eileen and I learnt that our long wait for a brother for Sally was about to end and in mid March, barely 3 weeks before I was due to leave the UK for 18 months, we took Sally to collect her new baby brother whom we decided to call Paul. Before then Sally was always 'accompanied' by an imaginary brother and sister 'Mickey and Jackie' but as soon as she met Paul they completely disappeared and she, Eileen and I returned home with Sally and Paul as a complete and happy family. Sally, then almost five years old had already moved into the newly decorated middle bedroom and excitedly assisted in the preparation of the small nursery for the new baby and now helped Eileen to bath and put him to bed that night. From that day on they have been as close as any sister and brother could possibly be. Paul was a very good and contented baby and settled down with us straight away without any problem. As I would be abroad at the end of the three months probationary period before we could officially adopt Paul, the three of us had to go to Court where all of us were questioned by a Judge, who was enchanted by Sally, and declared that he was satisfied that we would be as good as parents for Paul as we had proved to be for Sally. I then had to swear an affidavit that as I would be "on the High Seas on the date of the formal adoption hearing, it was my intention to adopt the infant ....".

We had less than four weeks of family bliss in our own home before I had to bid them a sad farewell and set off for Stansted Airport and Singapore, leaving Eileen on her own to bring up a baby and a little girl about to start school, while I gallivanted around the far flung Eastern outposts of our diminishing empire.

# Chapter 13

## HMS Cheviot April 1958 – February 1960

I travelled to Hendon Air Trooping Centre in plain clothes on Monday 14th April 1958 where I met the First Lieutenant (Designate) Lt. Cdr Alex MacDonald, who was the officer in Charge of the Trooping flight, and the twelve Senior Ratings who formed the Advance Party for the re-commissioning of HMS Cheviot, Leader of the 8th Destroyer Squadron in the Far East.

We left Stansted at 1700 in a 'Skyways of London' Handley-Page Hermes aircraft with 76 passengers, most of whom were Army and RAF wives and children. Shortly after take-off the pilot told us that our flight would be in seven stages, stopping to refuel at Brindisi, Basra,, Karachi, Delhi, Calcutta and Bangkok and that we were due at Singapore at 1800 local time on Thursday. We sat backward-facing and I had a window seat abreast the starboard wing and was glad I had read the leaflet advising passengers that the red glow around the engines was quite normal.

During our brief stop at Brindisi we were given a midnight Italian meal of tinned spaghetti on toast. Having already enjoyed pasta at home for several years this was a real let-down. Next morning I had a spectacular geography lesson as we flew down the Rivers Tigris and Euphrates at about 20,000 feet to Basra. I recall the terminal building there was festooned with huge photographs of young King Feisal of Iraq. Months later the poor chap was assassinated and the country became a republic. We had a 24 hour stopover at Karachi where we were accommodated in Minwalla's pretentiously named Grand Hotel, on the city's outskirts where we were warned not to drink the local water or any beverage made from it and even advised to clean our teeth with Coca Cola or a well known beer. The RN group toured this huge, teeming, rather dirty but interesting city on the day of our arrival. When the next day we arrived at Delhi no one was allowed out of the plane until the interior, including all of the passengers and crew, had been hand-sprayed with disinfectant, presumably because we had come from Pakistan. Shortly after we left Delhi there was a run on the only two lavatories on the aircraft as a considerable number of the passengers went down with Delhi-belly, or its Karachi equivalent. The flight between Delhi and Calcutta became a bit of a nightmare particularly for the wives and children who were most affected. I felt pretty 'iffy' myself and recall somewhat anxiously queuing for the loo. The Air Stewardesses did a great job dealing with the situation, nursing the worst affected and bringing relief to the rest of us by doling us out 'concrete' tablets. I was glad of the breather on the tarmac at Dum-Dum Airport while the aircraft was sorted out. When we arrived at Bangkok, a bevy of beautiful Siamese Ground Hostesses boarded the aircraft and made a fuss of the children, women and the RN contingent, in that order. After this encouraging welcome to the Far East, we flew fairly low over the dark green Malayan rubber plantations and suffered severe turbulence all the way to Singapore. We were all pretty relieved when, as forecast three days earlier, we touched down at Paya Lebar airport at exactly 1800 local time on the Thursday. Several passengers, mostly women and children and my future Fire-Control EA, Mick Bowden, were stretchered away to hospital ill with some kind of dysentery. The rest of the Cheviot draft was soon on its way to HMS Terror to await the arrival of the ship due on the following Monday. After sending Eileen a Safe Arrival telegram I was shown to a large, comfortable first-floor cabin with jalousied windows and overhead fans, unpacked and enjoyed a shower. Having been told that non-duty officers may wear plain clothes in the mess after 1800 I changed into 'Planters' rig, long-sleeved shirt and tie, long trousers and shoes, as worn by English plantation managers in Malaya after sunset. I then went down for a drink and dinner and afterwards wrote to Eileen, before retiring to bed feeling dead tired after the journey For the next three days I was effectively on leave and spent the daytime exploring HMS Terror's facilities, swimming in the pool and visiting the local shops and

 spending the evenings after dinner in the nearby popular Officers` Club. There were a number of ships in the base and the club was full of visiting officers; I met several I knew including Gus Simpson my classmate from Fisgard, who was `R` officer of HMS Belfast. He had been out there a year and knew the routine in the Far East fleet and gave me much invaluable advice during those first few days which helped me settle down quickly.

When HMS Cheviot berthed in the Naval Base basin on Monday 21st April 1958 all of the Advance Party, dressed in tropical rig, met her, looking unhealthily pale in comparison with the bronzed Cheviots of the Old Commission. I spotted my former Fire-Control instructor, Lt. Ron Butcher, the Deputy 'L' Officer who was highly delighted to see that his relief had safely arrived for, having completed his 18 months away from the UK, he was very keen to go home and had already booked his flight for the Friday. Ron began his turnover to me straight away and suggested that I move onboard into his cabin and he took over my cabin in HMS Terror until he left for home. When I saw the cabin I was to share with the Senior Engineer and TAS Gunner for the next 18 months I understood why! I met his boss Commander (L) Jock Morrison a short, jolly Scot with an Air Radio background who had joined the

ship three months earlier. I was delighted to be assured that he would leave the day-to day running of the ship's L and R department to me, as he had done to Ron, whilst he concentrated on Squadron matters. Since I had already served abroad in a WW2 destroyer with very similar equipment, there was nothing technical in Cheviot which held any fears for me and so the turnover was completed quickly and Ron departed. By the 1st May when the main body of the new commission arrived and the old crew departed in high spirits, I had already become acclimatised to the heat and cramped conditions aboard and had lost the deathly pallor with which I had joined. On 5th May the ship was ceremonially re-commissioned, under the command of Captain WD (Bill) O'Brien DSC RN and a few days later sailed for a Shake-down and a short Work-Up at Pulau Tioman with the Dutch Destroyer Groningen, carrying out a full gambit of exercises off the east coast of Malaya for ten days before sailing with her to Hong Kong.

Captain O'Brien had served in eight destroyers before joining Cheviot, had commanded a Hunt Class at Normandy on 'D' day as a Lieutenant and another destroyer as a Lt Cdr and was one of the very rare breed of Seaman Officers who was not a Gunnery, Torpedo, Communications, Navigating or Air Direction specialist, known as Salt Horses. He was, de facto, a Seamanship specialist and demonstrated this to all of us and to the ships' companies of the fleet already alongside when we first arrived at Hong Kong. The carrier HMS Bulwark was berthed on the outer arm of the Dockyard tidal basin completely obscuring the view of the inner basin in which Cheviot was told to berth alongside HMAS Voyager. The berthing signal failed to mention that Voyager was herself berthed outboard of the cruiser HMNZS Royalist and that the survey vessel HMS Dalrymple was secured across their bows. There were several merchant ships in the approach to the entrance to the basin and it wasn't until the ship turned to port around them and Bulwark, that the limited manoeuvring space between Voyager and the ships berthed on the landward side of the basin became apparent. The ship was stemming the ebbing tide at 10 knots, when her bows entered the still water of the jam-packed Dockyard tidal basin. The Captain immediately ordered 'full astern both engines', went hard to port around the large destroyer's stern and, with a flourish brought Cheviot neatly alongside HMAS Voyager without touching her or HMS Dalrymple. Commander (E) Colin Reynolds was rewarded with a stiff gin for the engine-room's very prompt response to this daring, skilful and, in the circumstances, absolutely essential manoeuvre.

The 8th Destroyer Squadron comprised Cheviot, Cossack, Cavalier and, temporarily attached, the Australian Daring Class destroyer HMAS Voyager. This was the first time Captain (D) or we had met the rest of the squadron and during our five day visit, most friendly relations were established and oiled with Horses' Necks and G&Ts. In 1958, Hong Kong was undoubtedly the navy's favourite run ashore and, as the squadron was very handily berthed, the 8$^{th}$ DS enjoyed many of the reasonably priced amenities available. Around this time I heard that, as there was then no path for transfer from the Special Duties list to the General list of officers, the avenue was to be opened again to Electrical SD Officers who gained certificates of competence as Bridge and Engine Room Watchkeepers and in Naval Storekeeping. In my short time aboard Cheviot I realised that, as I had a first class Division and the equipment was fairly simple, I was hardly likely to be worked to death by my proper job. I was already in charge of `F` stores onboard, half of all the ship`s stores, and as we were in the most friendly seas for keeping watch on an open bridge, I volunteered to join the two Seaman Sub-Lieutenants, Tremayne Rodd, (Scotland`s Scrum-half), and the ship's Gunner 'Oscar' Wild and the Captain's Secretary Lt. (S) Peter Jackson. in their compulsory quest for a Bridge Watchkeeping certificate under 'Sea Daddy' Lt Cdr Jerome Benson, the Squadron Navigator. I kept watch 1 in 4 on the way to Singapore and from then on and found I was able to deal with L and R problems just as well whilst on watch as in the office and enjoyed the experience and additional responsibility. Most of the Far East was not then covered by Radio Navigational Aids so, in the open sea we had to 'shoot' the stars at dawn and dusk every day to work out our position, a task I found very satisfying, particularly whilst on passage in the great open expanses of the Pacific and Indian Oceans. In coastal waters, well lit by buoys and lighthouses, position finding was simple. In fact I had more inquiries whilst on watch regarding the evening's film, (I was the Cinema Officer), than I ever had about equipment failures. In harbour, I also had to carry out the duty of Officer of the Day (OOD) which was often eventful, especially when at anchor.

In 1958 Malaya was preparing for independence from Britain but Chinese Communist insurgents, hiding in the jungle were attempting to seize power and already had active guerrilla units as far south as a few miles from Johore Bahru, just across the causeway from Singapore. Large numbers of British troops, mostly National Servicemen, were actively engaged in jungle warfare with this covert enemy and though this was largely a land war, the navy was sometimes requested to bombard areas close to the coast or the Johore river, believed to be harbouring the enemy. Eventually the army triumphed, mainly by protecting each of the thousands of Kampongs (villages) and guarding their food supplies and so starved the insurgents into surrender. It was widely reported that some guerrillas had even tried to sneak into the 'All Night Café' at Johore Bahru in plain clothes, under cover of darkness, for a Chinese meal.

The 8th Destroyer Squadron took part in an exercise off the coast of Malaya with the New Zealand cruiser HMNZS Royalist and the fixed- wing Carrier HMS Bulwark to demonstrate the Commonwealth's firm commitment, to a free Malaya. This was followed by a PR exercise called 'Show Boat' in which civic officials from Malaya and Singapore and their families were treated to a day at sea in an  operational Carrier Task Force. During this exercise I received a telegram from Eileen giving me the great news that our adoption of Paul was now official. My letter home that evening showed my delight.

After landing our fairly impressed visitors at Singapore we sailed for the annual Commonwealth-bonding exercise known as JET (Joint Exersise Trincomalee), involving the navies of India, Pakistan, Ceylon and units of the RN`s East Indies and Far East Fleets. By this time the ship's company of Cheviot and the Electrical

Division in particular had bonded together into a team that worked and played well together. For a ship with a total complement of less than 200 we were blessed with a wealth of sporting talent. Besides Tremayne Rodd, our Rugby XV contained three other RN players and together they inspired the rest of the team, including several 'Greenies' (members of the Electrical division), to beat the Kiwis of HMNZ Ships Rotoiti and Pukaki. The 8th Destroyer Squadron XV, largely made up of Cheviots, later went on to win the Far East Fleet Championship beating the cruiser HMS Newfoundland in the final at Hong Kong's Happy Valley. We also had an excellent Soccer team and punched well above our weight at athletics, aquatics including Water Polo and, of course at boxing, with the 'Greenies' well represented in all of the ship's teams.

The officers of Cheviot were accommodated in two cabin flats, the one forward comprising single cabins for the Squadron Staff Officers and 'heads of departments' and the other aft, with 2 or 3-berth cabins. The only cool places onboard were the Main Wireless Office and Gunnery Transmitting Station which were air-conditioned. The ship's Gunnery Officer, Vic Sheather and Captain's Secretary, Peter Jackson shared one cabin. Sub Lts. Tremayne Rodd and the Gunner 'Oscar' Wild another and the 'Senior Engineer' Lt. Eric Roberts, the TAS Officer Lt Ed Garnett and myself the 3 berth cabin on the port side. I had the lower bunk below Ed and had a scuttle level with my midriff which was left open in harbour and whilst on passage in calm seas affording some cooling. All of the cabins aft were extremely well-looked after by Tshum Yeng a very pleasant and efficient Chinese steward in his 20s who shook us awake each morning with a cup of tea, provided us with a jug of hot water for shaving, we had no running hot water, made up our bunks and laid out on them clean clothes of the 'rig of the day' complete with shoulder bars and clean white shoes. By the time we arrived in the Wardroom Tshum Yeng and the other Stewards were busy serving a breakfast of choice to the officers. The standard of cuisine in the wardroom of Cheviot was very high and the service first rate. We had a Cheviot Ram's head on the mess bulkhead which the stewards solemnly covered with a napkin whenever we had lamb! For all of their keen attention to their duties, the 10 Hong Kong-entered RN Chinese cooks and Stewards and the four strong 'Unofficial' Chinese laundry staff showed they had Work Study off to a fine art for, although they did a great job over many hours every day looking after us, they still managed to spend every afternoon fishing and were easily the best anglers onboard. In fact, if they weren't having any luck fishing, we soon realised there were no fish around.

By a strange coincidence, seven of Cheviot's officers were Catholics, including the Captain, his Secretary, the Squadron Navigating and Supply Officers, the Doctor and two of the Sub-Lieutenants, including myself. Early in the commission, the First Lieutenant, an Anglican, declared that he was "nailing St George's flag firmly to the mast". The traditional naval C of E service was held onboard every Sunday at sea throughout the commission and, twelve years later, Admiral Sir William O'Brien hoisted his own St George's flag as CinC Western Fleet and later as CinC Fleet.

On the advice of my predecessor, I took my duties as Cinema Officer very seriously. In those days the 3 films we collected from the RN Film Corporation every week, either from the Film Library or from another ship, were the only onboard entertainment we had. So the standard of films and their presentation was important to the morale of the whole ship's company. If the film was not up to expectations due to a poor story, acting or direction it was considered to be the Cinema Officer's fault, not the film makers. Since I was going to 'carry the can' anyhow, I made it a point of principle that I would personally select each film shown onboard. I trained up a team of operators, all members of my department and ensured that the projectors were always in good order. Many of the latest films shown were in Cinemascope and as most films were shown on the Quarter Deck I had a large curved screen frame made in the Dockyard at Singapore and our Sailmaker made a huge canvas screen for it. Films shown in the Wardroom were critically judged by the officers and I was often ribbed, especially by my boss, who unfavourably compared all films I put on with Hitchcock's 'Rear Window'. He often rose from his front row seat within a few minutes of the start of the Sunday night film to denounce it as "Rubbish, Donald" and to storm out to cheers from the assembled officers. My messmates named the ship`s cinema The Bijou, after a rundown flea-pit featured in a Peter Sellars comedy which was one of my first shows and proved popular with all onboard, including Cdr (L).

'JET 1958' began with two weeks of Anti-Submarine, Anti Aircraft and surface gunnery and torpedo day and night actions in the Indian Ocean between two fleets, each comprising ships from all four participating countries. At the end of this WW2 style fleet exercise we anchored in the huge natural harbour at Trincomallee where much socialising took place ashore and in the ships. We had to anchor because the Ceylon government was so hard up it had sold the buoys for scrap. It was sad to see how run-down the place had become since they had gained their independence:: most of the former RN Hospital had been taken over by the spreading jungle and the roads were in a poor state but I suppose the locals preferred to be free and poor to being a colony, at least that is what they said.

A week long mini Commonwealth Games was held ashore, in which Cheviot did well. This friendly sporting competition culminated in a Hockey Final, ostensibly between the Indian and Pakistani navies but reportedly between the two countries. Most of their players had been temporarily conscripted into their respective navies and, while the rest of us were at sea, the two national hockey teams had been ashore, training hard for this annual 'Grudge match.' The ground was packed and the standard of hockey displayed was terrific with India narrowly winning. The real purpose of JET had been successfully achieved for the sub-continent's two great antagonists had worked well and played happily together for three weeks without coming to blows. Next morning the various fleets departed, the Far East Fleet ships eastward to Singapore where Cheviot was scheduled for a long overdue 3-month refit.

The ship arrived at Singapore Naval Base on 5th July and after de-fuelling and de-storing the ammunition and stores, the ship's company moved into the relative luxury of the shore base HMS Terror. Cheviot docked down in the huge graving dock, in which RMS Queen Elizabeth had docked in 1940, where our masthead scarcely showed above the dockside and the ship looked tiny. Every morning after breakfast a Land Rover took the First Lieutenant, the Senior Engineer and me to the ship where we worked with the Dockyard Maties, some of the Seamen and all of the ship's Electrical and Marine Engineering departments. We returned to Terror for lunch, back to the ship for the afternoon and back to Terror for tea, invariably cucumber sandwiches, followed by a swim in the pool, a game of Squash, a pint of fresh lime juice in the officers' Club, a shower and change for dinner. I followed this routine for the next three months broken only by a regular Saturday evening visit to Singapore and, on Sundays afternoons a sailing lesson from Jerome Benson in the ship's RNSA dinghy. All of the Staff Officers set up their offices in Terror and worked from ashore, or joined another ship of the 8th Destroyer Squadron, especially if it just happened to be going somewhere desirable like Australia, New Zealand, Hong Kong or Japan. The ship's Seaman Officers also found it necessary for them to remain ashore and not to return to the hot and noisy ship until just before the refit ended. To remind these 'Dabtoes' what the ship looked like, some wag posted in the Wardroom ashore a photo of the ship lost in that gigantic dock, having large sections of its corroded hull replaced. During those torrid months we all took advantage of a break in the shape of a week's Station Leave. Our adventurous Chief Electrician Kelbrick led a party of seven lads up into the jungle in central Malaya for a week's service with the New Zealand Army, which was actively engaged in fighting the Communist Insurgents. The Cheviots only carried enough anti-malarial Paladrine tablets for the journey to and from Singapore and were told the Army would take care of their welfare in the jungle. Unfortunately, the tough as nails Kiwis were so acclimatised by then, they were biting the mosquitoes and had long given up taking tablets. Consequently, several of our lads contracted malaria and returned from their break feeling pretty poorly and went off to hospital for a while. In a somewhat less heroic vein the Chief EA Jim Trainor and I spent our leave at the Cheshire Home in Changi where we helped build a new ward.

The awful conditions in which we worked onboard during the 90 days we spent in Singapore were made tolerable in my case by the great professionalism and co-operation of our dockyard electrical staff led by a splendid Sikh, Mr Singh. We also enjoyed the camaraderie and comfort of our evenings in the Mess and Club at Terror and the weekly run ashore into Singapore with our messmates. Each officer in a ship undergoing refit was allowed one trip a month into Singapore and back by RN Land Rover so, in groups of four, we could all legally enjoy a trip to town every Saturday night. We took advantage of this privilege and enjoyed visits to the Tanglin Club, of which we became Associate Members and where we ran a mess bill, and to various renowned 'watering holes' in that cosmopolitan city of which we gradually grew fond. The ship's great sporting potential, already exercised at Trincomalee, came to fruition during this period with success in the Commonwealth Combined Services Swimming competition. This was held in the Services 50 metre Swimming Pool, handily sited next to the NAAFI Club and opposite the 'Raffles Hotel' in Singapore and Tremayne Rodd won the 100 metres free style final. The same sporting legend was the 'Victor Ludorum' of the Commonwealth Combined Services Athletics championships held at Terror where he famously won the, Long Jump, Hop, Step & Jump and, after winning the High Jump final, walked across the field to the track where the finals of the 120 yards hurdles were held awaiting his arrival and he then won that race and went on to win the 100 yards Sprint final. The Captain appointed each officer to look after one of the ship's teams and during the refit all of our sports teams performed frequently and well against other ships, Army and RAF teams. I was given the job of managing the Water Polo team, as four of the crack team just happened to be in the Electrical division, including its Captain, PO Electrician Jack Frost. I arranged the transport, travelled with them, enjoyed the post match socialising and even got to play in goal for them several times when our goalkeeper AB Slingsby, who was a bit of a lad, was under punishment for some misdemeanour. Fortunately we had an excellent set of backs and forwards including Chief Electrician Ron Kelbrick, REA Hugh Johnson and PO Rel. John Petrie, who swam by instinct for, without his glasses he could hardly see, and they protected me from the opposing forwards.

Later in the refit the Captain decided that 15 of the most 'restless' members of a ship's company becoming fed up with being stuck at the north end of Singapore Island, miles away from the bright lights, would benefit from an 'Exped', (Expedition training). He decreed that the two Acting Subbys, the Gunner as CO and me as Navigator together with a Stoker PO as Engineer, should take these 'likely lads' away for six days on a Motor Fishing Vessel (MFV) to explore the upper Johore river and Trusan Tiris and to carry out a hydrographic study. We completed our mission successfully and had a lot of fun but the lads pined for female company so, on the way back to the Naval Base on the last day, when we spotted some nubile ladies on the beach of Pulau Tekong near Changi, the lads persuaded Oscar to close the beach and anchor for a while. When they returned onboard, somewhat disappointed to have found themselves heavily out-numbered by RAF guys, we weighed anchor and, without checking the chart, I picked up our original leading mark and we set off home. Three minutes after getting underway  we went hard aground on a sand bank and two hours later at low water we lay ignominiously over on our side like a beached whale, with our White Ensign fluttering forlornly in the slight breeze. I went over the side and ascertained that the screw was not fouled or even slightly damaged but then we espied a large motor boat flying a White Ensign coming down the channel. The boat, which appeared to be on a 'Jolly', anchored in the fairway and when we scanned it with binoculars we were horrified to see that among the passengers enjoying a jolly boating Sunday afternoon, were the famous 'Baldy' Hezlett and Frank Twiss, two WW2 heroes destined for Flag rank and then in command of the cruisers Newfoundland and Ceylon. In trepidation Oscar and I rowed across to them in the dinghy and received a severe 'rollicking'. We assured them the MFV was undamaged and we did not require assistance and, after suffering a a few more unkind remarks about the standard of "today's Acting Sub Lieutenants", we returned to the sad looking MFV with our tails o between our legs to await the rising tide. Six hours later, we safely floated off and set off in the dark for the Naval Base. As we neared Loyang we were hailed by a passing tug who asked if we were the MFV that had been reported aground. "Oh Lor, that`s torn it" said I, or words to that effect. An hour later as we tied up in the dockyard basin and disembarked, a messenger informed Oscar and me that we would have to give our reasons in writing to the Captain by 0900 tomorrow for grounding the MFV. For our sins we were both 'logged' by the Captain and later on I was singled out for further punishment by King Neptune in the Line-Crossing ceremony on the way to Australia. I received special treatment, "to right the dreadful wrong of bringing shame on the ship by making a navigational error".

Oscar and I had more than a little chuckle two weeks after our 'grounding' to learn that the same 46 foot MFV, under the command of an experienced Seaman Lieutenant from HMS Newfoundland and manned by personnel from her, had run on to a reef off Singapore and the HMS Newfoundland-crewed tug sent to pull them off also went aground and both vessels were damaged. I suspect Bill O'Brien also enjoyed a little smile as doubtless he had been ribbed by his senior fellow Captains over our earlier mishap.

Not long afterwards, I received another salutary lesson in humility. As a rookie officer I took my Divisional Officer duties very seriously and whenever any of my division got into trouble I did my best for them, but always prefaced my interview by telling them that I was on their side but unless they told me the truth I would be unable to give them the best advice. One morning I was called to the huge Army base at Nee Soon to where two of my lads had been held overnight in custody awaiting a civil charge of stealing a prostitute's handbag. I interviewed them separately and though both were very hung-over they gave similar versions of the previous evening's events and adamantly denied the charge. As hitherto they had unblemished records, I believed them.

During the subsequent investigation by a young Singapore-Chinese Inspector, I put their case as strongly as I could, casting doubt on the young woman's testimony. In view of the lack of evidence, and, after some deliberation, the Inspector decided to drop the charge and released the two guys in my custody and I took them back to HMS Terror. When I was debriefed by the Captain he asked me whether I was sure they were innocent and I stoutly declared my belief in them. The Captain did not appear to share my confidence. On the following Sunday afternoon, after the two lads had downed their tot and a few beers in the canteen, and were full of alcoholic remorse, they interrupted my siesta to confess that they had lied to me and had in fact taken the handbag, stolen the money in it and ditched the bag out of the window of a taxi somewhere in Singapore. Needless to say I was not best pleased with this news and gave them one hell of a rollicking. After tea, cap in hand, I called on the Captain to admit I had been duped by my lads. Bill O`Brien gave me the benefit of his years of experience in dealing with wayward sailors and told me to "put this case down to experience and not to be so naïve in the future". The young woman was traced through her evidence given at Nee Soon and the lads were made to apologise profusely for their drunken misbehaviour and to reimburse her for the handbag and its contents. So justice was done.

By the end of September Cheviot was looking more shipshape, all of the electrics were working again, and we began tuning up the weapon systems, and radio & radar equipments. In mid October we moved out of our luxurious cabins ashore and back aboard ready for going back to sea. We had a short shakedown off Pulau Tioman, which included firing all of our weapons, an evolution that was filmed by the Squadron TAS Officer John Bailey. Some weeks later when he showed the film during a Sunday Night Cinema in the wardroom, the three Gunnery Officers were very embarrassed to see the crew of Y Gun, who were not visible to them or the Captain during a Shoot, performing in a terribly undisciplined manner. Out of sight down aft, this motley gang of Scallywags, hitherto considered to be the best of our three guns crews because they achieved the highest rate of fire, were seen to be throwing the 4.5 inch cartridges and shells around light-heartedly, wearing scruffy undone No 8 working dress and no protective clothing or headgear.The GO, Vic Sheather and Squadron GO, Bill Melly almost had apoplexy and the Captain wasn't happy! During shoots the Gunner and I were in the TS so we escaped any culpability. Fortunately the Torpedo and Squid firings went off OK, but then, the Squadron TASO was filming his own men!

After this mini Work-Up the ship steamed north to South Vietnam to represent the RN at the third anniversary celebrations of their independence from France. The Saigon River winds through the 'rice-bowl' of South-East Asia to reach the picturesque old colonial capital of Saigon. I found the city and its people possessed a charming blend of the cultures of France and Indo-China and, since French was still widely spoken I enjoyed exercising my schoolboy French, which somehow seemed to me to improve with each successive drink. An RAF Vulcan bomber flew to Saigon to join in the national celebrations and her crew were looked after by Cheviot to the mutual advantage of both parties. On the 'big day' the Vulcan put on an impressive air show and we entertained local children and gave a cocktail party onboard. The locals seemed to be pretty impressed by the UK effort. However, all this good PR activity almost came to nothing next day when our First Soccer X1 had the temerity to defeat the South Vietnam team 3 - 1 in their national stadium in a match watched by everyone who was anyone in Saigon. As if that wasn't a big enough loss of face for our friendly hosts, our 'tanked-up' Chief GI almost caused an international incident when he excitedly grabbed the Chief of Police's 'brass' hat` from his head and threw it up in the air when the final whistle blew. Immediately, every policeman in the stadium drew his revolver and rushed to defend his boss from this great indignity. All of our CPOs were sitting together in the front row with the officers immediately behind them and the Captain ordered those sitting around the Chief GI to arrest him and get him back to the ship pdq whilst he placated the angry VIP and defused a potential diplomatic disaster. During the night before we left Saigon our Chinese uniformed personnel and the civilian laundry crew were seen bringing sack after sack of rice aboard from boats running from the opposite side of the river and stowing the sacks anywhere they could for the short passage to Hong Kong, where they were landed in sampans to feed their families during the coming winter.

Everyone onboard was pleased to be back in Hong Kong, the natural home and by far the most popular base of the Far East fleet. Cheviot was destined to remain there for over two months as Garrison Destroyer and was only expected to go to sea about once a week to carry out a patrol of the Pearl River and its islands (code-named Patrol Indigo), to 'show the flag' and to discourage illegal immigrants from entering the colony. Jenny and her Side Party greeted us on arrival and we settled down to a pleasant life alongside the dockyard wall with easy access to Wanchai, the China Fleet Club, the tram to Shaukiwan and Kennedy Town and the Star Ferry to Kowloon.

As a former CO of the Petty Officers' school, at the time when one of his Lieutenants, Prince Phillip, became engaged to the future Queen Elizabeth, Captain O'Brien was keen on leadership and adventure training and being aware of the possible effect on the ship's company's discipline and morale of a prolonged period of self-indulgence in the fleshpots of Hong Kong, he encouraged all forms of sport and expedition training. He appointed John Bailey the Squadron TASO as Exped Officer and me as his Assistant. When 18 volunteers were called for to take part in the first land-based Exped – to climb Ma on Shan, the highest peak in the New Territories, the list was heavily oversubscribed. Loaded like pack-asses the Exped Team was put ashore in Tolo Harbour and set off, with great enthusiasm and little experience, losing various items of inadequately secured kit and food, to climb the mountain from the most difficult south side. After inching up the last 200 feet of sheer rock the eastern peak was reached and gave an impressive view of the mountains of China to the north, Hong Kong to the south and below us the tiny Cheviot. After a brief rest, the team walked along the ridge of the mountain to Ma on Shan itself before making an easy descent of the other side of the mountain. However, this took rather longer than expected and, with the sun fast going down, we were forced to camp overnight. At dawn we realised the camp was 600 feet above sea level with a difficult descent ahead. So two fit and lightly laden men were sent on ahead to meet the ship, while the remainder, resigned to having missed it, proceeded at a less demanding pace to cover the many remaining miles. With no

*Ma on Shan*

portable radio, we hoped that the two guys we had sent on ahead reached the ship in time. Fortunately they did. The rest of the Exped made their way to Sha Tin where the Army provided a good meal and transport to Kowloon and we crossed to Hong Kong on the Star Ferry just as Cheviot came up harbour. Despite our missed rendezvous the Exped was counted a success and was thoroughly enjoyed by all who took part.

We spent Christmas alongside in Hong Kong with the carrier HMS Albion. This was before it became easy to phone home and I missed being with Eileen, Sally and Paul and being able to speak to them. However our daily letters to and from home kept us closely in touch. My presents for the family, purchased in HK eight weeks earlier, arrived home by Air Mail in good time and I received theirs' promptly too. Each of the officers drew the name of another for whom he had to buy an appropriate 'humorous' Xmas present. I drew John Walters the Squadron Supply Officer and, as he 'wore two hats' SO of the 8ᵗʰ Destroyer and 3ʳᵈ Frigate Squadrons, I bought him a sailor's cap and the cap ribbons of Cheviot and Cardigan Bay, (the two 'leaders') and made a cap ribbon reading HMS Cheviot Bay. John, a most jovial chap, was very pleased to wear it on Christmas day. Our Doctor Roger Doherty drew me and gave me a cinema commissionaire's uniform cleverly made from a bus conductor's outfit, with the cap bearing the insignia 'Bijou', the name by which the ship's cinema was known. On Christmas Eve I attended Midnight mass onboard HMS Albion and after the service, a party in their wardroom. Next morning after breakfast the Captain led all of the officers on a 'rounds' of the messes to wish all of the Cheviots a Merry Christmas before everyone, except the Officer of the Day and the duty watch, went ashore and walked to the nearby China Fleet Club where we all sat down together to a splendid Christmas Lunch. On return to the ship that afternoon I was handed a telegram which had just arrived for my Duty Leading Electrical Mechanic reporting the sudden death of his young daughter. I went to the Electrical mess deck and called him out and told him the very sad news and consoled him and called upon his chums to comfort him while I made arrangements for him to be flown home on Compassionate Leave. Although it was Christmas Day, all of the personnel in the chain involved, pulled out the stops in a quite magnificent way and the LEM was soon on his way to Kai Tak airport for the evening flight home to his distraught wife.

A few days later the Far East Fleet Boxing Championships were held at HMS Tamar and, after a hard fought three round bout against an AB from HMS Cardigan Bay, one of our lads, young Lynch, collapsed and was found to have suffered a brain injury. His ex RN father was flown out from Glasgow and was at his bedside when he began his recovery. At the same tournament our 'Super sportsman' Tremayne Rodd, standing in for the injured EA Mick Bowden, won the Light Heavy-weight title by a technical knock-out. In a later Inter-service competition held in an Army barracks, close to the Dockyard, Tremayne met the Army favourite, a Corporal known as 'Killer' and, during a ferocious first round onslaught by the young Lieutenant, 'Killer' was knocked-out to the cheers of the Cheviots and the utter devastation of the crowd of 'Pongos' present.

On New Year's Eve the Electrical Officers of all of the ships visiting Hong Kong were kindly invited to a New Year's party held in the Base Electrical Officer's Married Quarter on the Peak and we all saw 1959 in with style and had a great time. Two days later, while John Bailey was busy training a crew to row around Hong Kong island, I found myself leading the next Exped, this time to climb Lantao Peak (3067 feet), the highest mountain in the colony. In those days Lantao was a sparsely populated island with no roads, two small villages Lan Tao and Shek Pik and, halfway up the mountain, a Buddhist monastery at Ngong Ping The many lessons learnt during the first Exped eased the progress of this venture and after setting up a base near the monastery, the unburdened climbers hauled themselves to the summit to enjoy the best view in the colony before returning to the base camp to enjoy a good meal, with fresh fruit

*Don is 2nd from left in back row*

purchased from the kindly monks. That night we again enjoyed a celestial panoply of stars and despite the hourly clang of monastery's cracked bell, had a good night's sleep

Whilst descending a narrow goat track next morning, the path suddenly crumbled away under Chief Electrician Kelbrick, who was bringing up the rear causing him to disappear over the edge. He was carrying a 60 pound pack on his back but managed to grab a shrub 10 feet below and some 50 feet above a flat shelf. With the aid of ropes lowered by his team mates, he was hauled to safety and, despite a painful ankle, gamely continued the Exped without assistance. The party made its way to Shek Pik and on along the coastal path to Silvermine Bay, the ferry to HK and the ship, having had a memorable time.

On 6th January Cheviot's ten week spell at Hong Kong ended and we sailed into a typhoon on our way to flying exercises with HMS Albion. These were followed by a short self-maintenance period at Singapore before, in the Malacca Straits, and together with the cruiser Ceylon, our fellow 8th DS destroyer Cavalier, two Aussie destroyers and the frigate Chichester, we made a ceremonial steam past the Royal Yacht carrying the Duke of Edinburgh. Later Cheviot closed Britannia to receive the Royal Mail by line transfer, with all of us manning the side and smartly turned out in white. My division standing to attention on the 'iron deck' were watched with wry amusement by a crowd of off-watch, hat-less stokers wearing scruffy, undone overalls who were standing on the yacht's lower deck level with, but only a few feet away, from us, and out of sight of their own officers.

During our ten days at Singapore I was entrusted with command of MFV 742, and an Exped to establish which of the two optional recommended routes to Kota Tingi, indicated, but not shown on the chart, was in fact the best one. As several Cheviots had earlier contracted malaria whilst serving with the New Zealand

Army I was ordered by the Captain to ensure that all onboard took a Paladrine tablet every day. To ensure no one missed his dose I personally issued them with the daily 'tot' of rum. We flew the White Ensign and, as South Johore was 'Black' (ie infiltrated by Chinese Communist guerrillas), we were armed. That is to say that I carried a rifle and 50 rounds which had to be kept locked up separately and, in accordance with my briefing by the Malay Police, was not to be used unless we were fired on. It was just as well I didn't have to unite the weapon with its ammo as I am the world's worst shot! I made my choice of the two routes and we set off northwards. About 3 miles up the river it became narrower and less deep and I suspected I had made the wrong choice. On the eastern bank stood a rubber plantation and we came to a jetty with a track

leading away. We berthed alongside and, leaving EA Bowden i/c of the MFV and rifle I walked down the track with one of the lads to the plantation bungalow to find a lone Englishman wearing a smart white shirt and shorts, socks and sandals who was simultaneously smoking, typing and giving orders to someone on the phone and apparently terribly busy. It was just like a scene from a Somerset Maugham story. Putting down the phone he said cheerily, "Hello chaps, how the devil did you get here?" When he learned we had come in a 46 foot fishing vessel which drew 5 feet, he offered us a drink and said "I'm afraid you'd better leave here pretty dam quickly as the river dries up at low water!" After thanking him profusely, we ran all the way back to the MFV, cast-off and went astern until the river was wide enough to turn. During this difficult passage we took frequent depth soundings and came very close to bottoming. This caused me considerable anxiety as I recalled my earlier MFV grounding. However we made it back to the point where the two optional routes met and I took the alternative route. This proved to be the correct one and after an uneventful 20 mile passage, we berthed close to where the town bridge barred further passage. We spent two days there and everyone had a chance to explore the town and its environs but we all slept onboard and maintained a watch. Having noted the hydrographical details and taken lots of photos we were later able to prove that the Admiralty chart required amendment to show only one "recommended route to Kota Tingi". On the east bank of a river near Changi, we passed a large plantation and I anchored close to a small jetty and rowed over hoping to buy some fresh fruit. Although there were thousands and thousands of ripe pineapples there, the Overseer could not sell me any "because they all belong to the local canning company". I politely declined his offer to sell me tins of the stuff and we spent the last couple of days alongside at Changi where we enjoyed the RAF's extensive leisure and social facilities, before safely making our way to the naval base.

At the end of February, Cheviot sailed for Australia in company with Chichester and Olna an RFA tanker and, two days later Crossed the Line. This was my first crossing of the Equator and I was duly arraigned before King Neptune, and charged with bringing shame on the ship by grounding an MFV. After the reading of the charge, I was robustly 'punished' for my sins in the traditional manner, much to the amusement of the ship's company.

During the morning watch on the day we approached the coast north of Fremantle from the NNW, I was Officer of the Watch on the Bridge. The weather was fine, I had just sighted the 'loom' of the lighthouse the Navigator's notes had warned me to expect at that time, we were steaming at 14 knots with Chichester astern of us and the tanker behind her. There were no other ships in sight but the coast of Western Australia was visible on the radar displays. At around 5am there was a loud bang from the small watertight radar display on the open bridge. Realising that the power pack had blown up and knowing we had no spare and would have to signal UK for a new sub-unit, I told the Ops room to keep a sharp look-out on their radar displays and to give me frequent updates. The lack of radar on the Bridge constituted a hazard so I thought I had better tell the Captain, who was in his Sleeping Cabin. Using the voice-pipe I said, "Captain, Sir, the radar display on the bridge has blown up but the displays in the Ops room are working OK and I am receiving frequent reports of the navigation situation" and, as a footnote, I cheerily added, "in any case there is no need to worry Sir, I have a good pair of eyes". The Captain acknowledged my message with a grunted "Thank you Donald" and gave the impression he was happy and was going back to sleep. I suspect that as he lay down he realised that the safety of his ship, and possibly his future, lay in the hands of an Electrical Sub-Lieutenant of limited experience whom he had already had to 'log' for a navigational error, because he suddenly appeared on the bridge in his dressing gown. After quizzing me and taking a good look around, he returned below.

After the ship rounded Cape Leeuwin on the SE corner of Australia, I tuned my radio to the local station and, while I was shaving in my cabin on the morning of our landfall at Albany, I enjoyed my first example of Aussie humour. It was a spoof sketch on the musical 'My Fair Lady'. A frightfully well spoken young lady from South Kensington emigrated to Sydney but was unable to find employment in a Florist's shop because she spoke too 'posh'. She went to a Professor of 'Strine' to be taught how to speak like an Aussie. After many lessons she finally managed to say "The rine in Orrstrylia lies minely in Sinny" at which the Professor and his 'cobber' broke into, "By George she's got it Blue". Albany was a small port and former whaling station nestling in the picturesque King George sound. We berthed alongside and were immediately overwhelmed with visitors from the town and the surrounding farm areas who invited the Cheviots home in their cars to enjoy their generous hospitality. After nearly a year away from fresh milk we surprised our hosts by our taste for the white stuff and we gorged ourselves on salads and put away many schooners of Aussie beer during this memorable visit. I spent a wonderful day with the Mayor of Albany and his family and visited the wood mill he owned some 90 miles north of the town. Once away from the lush agricultural area around Albany, the roads were rough and the countryside barren, being largely covered in trees ring-barked by their ex-servicemen owners, who could not afford to fell them to clear the land they had been sold cheaply by the government. On our last night in Albany we threw a cocktail party, seemingly attended by every adult in the town and many from the environs. Our normally imperturbable and very efficient Chinese Stewards were nonplussed by having the distribution of the drinks and canapés taken away from them by our enthusiastic guests in what proved to be a hell of a party Next morning we bade farewell to that friendly town and sailed East to the Great Bight for exercises with the Australian Carrier Melbourne and her destroyer escorts; and RFA Olna HMS Albion and HMS Chichester. This ended up in Fremantle where we berthed alongside, just astern of HMS Ceylon and HMAS Sydney. Again we were overwhelmed with offers of hospitality. Cheviot's wardroom accepted all invitations, however unpopular and operated a 'Lurk List' so that if someone had enjoyed a particularly entertaining party he went to the top of the list and had to accept the least popular invitation next time. Having been guests of the Mayor of Albany, Jerome Benson and I found ourselves at the top of the Lurk List and were allocated to an 'Away Day' with two elderly spinsters. Biting the bullet we met the two sweet old ladies and, watched with amusement by the many Cheviots being picked up by virile young Australians in smart cars, we climbed into the back of the ladies' ancient 2-door Ford Popular and set off for a Sunday treat.

The two dear ladies of the Primrose League gave us a detailed tour first of Fremantle then along the Swan River and all over the beautiful city of Perth. They were charming and we probably saw and learnt more of the city than any of our shipmates before, at around 11am, they pulled up outside a smart modern house in the suburbs, in the garden of which a large number of 20 to 30 year olds was enjoying a party and barbeque around a huge pool. The two ladies then asked us to alight, and introduced us to the host and hostess of the party. They then explained they were only the couriers and said our hosts would see we got back to the ship OK that night, wished us a happy party and bade us farewell. We were lent bathing trunks and enjoyed a fabulous all day party with superb food and charming company and were taken safely back to the ship late that night and unseen by any Cheviots except the gangway staff. Next day, when asked by our messmates how we had fared with the 'old dears' we replied with eyes upturned, "Don't even ask".

While we were at Fremantle, I developed a severe toothache and, as the RN dentist in HMS Ceylon was away visiting a vineyard, I was referred to HMAS Sydney. I went to their dental surgery and during the fifteen minutes the anaesthetic was taking hold I walked around the ship and marvelled at how clean the interior of the ship was being kept and how smart the crew were dressed in tropical conditions, compared with her sister, my first ship HMS Theseus. The dentist painlessly removed the tooth and I went on to enjoy the rest of the visit. On a pay night I visited the Perth 'Returned Servicemens' Club' where I witnessed the playing of 'Two-Up' in which two coins placed on a flat stick were thrown up in the air and either came down as odds or evens. The members, who were downing copious schooners of beer in the '5 o'clock swill', seemed to be gambling up to half of their week's pay on a very short time thrill. Many more of them staggered home about 6.30 pm very short of cash than were left flush for the rest of the week. I had thought the Chinese were the world's biggest gamblers but concluded that the Australians had them licked. We found the people of Western Australia to be most friendly and hospitable and our visit proved to be one of the great highlights of the commission.

The fleet sailed from Fremantle on 18th March and, with a cyclone threatening, was ordered to top up with fuel. Whilst embarking fuel at sea from Olna in the gathering storm, a huge wave struck the ship engulfing the men tending the fuelling gear and carried Ordinary Seaman Galliford over the side. Supported by his yellow inflated life jacket he bobbed to the surface and was picked up unconscious by HMS Chichester and luckily soon recovered. The whole fleet continuously exercised together for the next two months, the centre of operations moving north to Singapore, then Manilla with the US Navy and finally to Hong Kong.

*HMS Cheviot 18th March 1959 off Fremantle Australia*

My boss, Jock Morrison, was quite a lively, friendly character given to joking and winding-up his messmates. One day in the mess he publicly questioned my organisational skills using a well known naval saying. A little miffed at this, I decided to organise a divisional visit to the 'Tiger' Brewery in Singapore, to prove him wrong. At that time the Far East Fleet was evenly divided between those who drank 'Tiger' beer and those who preferred the other local brew 'Anchor'. The aficionados of the two beers sometimes even came to blows in the Fleet Canteen over which was the better. One afternoon all of the Electrical Department, less the duty watch, and including Jock and me, went by coach to Singapore and were given a detailed and interesting tour of the brewery culminating, at the end of the production line, with the golden liquid being bottled by two distinct plants, one putting it in one pint bottles of Tiger and the other in half pint bottles of Anchor. After this revelation we were taken to the Tiger hospitality bar where they were used to providing free beer for up to 100 visitors at a time. The 30 odd Cheviots thus did rather well that afternoon and by the time the free beer had run out, most of the division had imbibed a goodly measure, not least Commander (L). The Chief Electrician and I managed to get everyone on the bus OK and apart from the lively singing of rugby songs, there was no trouble getting them all back to the ship and quietly onboard. However, after merrily leading many of the ribald songs, Jock fell asleep and was out like a light when we arrived. I stayed with him in the coach until my chum the Gunner arrived and together we were able to secrete my boss aboard the ship, down to his cabin and into his bunk. He didn't appear for dinner that night so I visited his cabin regularly to check he was OK. He just slept like a log and next morning breezed into the mess with his customary greeting "Good Morning Lo Yan and what is Messyman titillating our palettes with this morning" at which the PO Steward smiled and recited the menu. Jock completed his pre-breakfast ritual with, "Cho Si Char, Moy flied bled" his pidgin Cantonese for full breakfast and tea and toast, less fried bread, at which the Mess man dutifully and politely guffawed. Jock was a good boss to have; he let me have my reins but was there if I needed him and we got on very well together. When he left the ship he called me into his cabin, said I had done a good job in Cheviot, thanked me for being a loyal deputy and wished me luck in my career. Then he gave me a piece of advice: "You take things much too seriously Donald, you should lighten-up a bit". His relief, Commander Mike Antrobus was an ex-torpedo Officer who, as a Lieutenant had survived the sinking of HMS Hotspur off Tobruk, had swum ashore and fought with the Army defending the besieged garrison against Rommel's Afrika Corps. He too seemed a nice chap and I was pleased when he told me he was happy for me to continue the day to day running of the department.

Whilst moored for the weekend at Singapore naval base we had a USN destroyer tied up alongside us and we entertained them and vice-versa. The Cheviot CPOs' Mess invited their Chiefs to a party onboard which, as alcohol is unavailable on USN ships, was very popular. Next morning, because the Americans could not reciprocate, they presented the RN Chiefs with a box of USN issue toilet rolls because they were horrified at the shiny, durable and non-absorbent toilet paper issued to the RN. I was Officer of the Day and that afternoon their OOD, a young Lieutenant came to see me and asked if I could send our motor boat to pick-up his Captain from ashore, his boat being away on a trip. I noticed that there was a hoisted boat on their outboard side so I said, "Why don't you lower your boat?" and he replied, "Only the Captain or Executive Officer has that authority and both are ashore". It transpired that his ship only had two regular officers, all the others were National Service and were not given the authority enjoyed by RN OODs, even junior Electrical Sub-Lieutenants. I sent in our Captain's Motor Boat straight away with a very smart crew to pick up his CO.

Our Captain met a Chinese Film magnate at one of the parties in Singapore and persuaded him to loan Cheviot a 16mm copy of one of the latest and highly praised Chinese sagas, to enable us to show it to the patients of the local Cheshire Home. I took our projector and my best operator and the 3-reel film out to Changi one evening in the visiting ship's Landrover and set up the gear in the largest ward where a really excited audience of incurably-ill patients were gathered. The first reel, easily identified by the title graphics, was received with great pleasure by the viewers but I chose the wrong one of the two equally long unmarked reels remaining, to put on next. The audience rolled in the aisles with laughter and excitedly told me we had the wrong reel on. The 2<sup>nd</sup> reel was substituted and our severely handicapped patrons settled down happily to enjoy the rest of the film. It was a truly moving evening for EM Whittingham and me and obviously a real treat for them.

During the subsequent SEATO exercises off the Philippines, involving some 30 warships, HMS Cossack became the 1000<sup>th</sup> ship to refuel at sea from USS Yorktown and the carrier passed over a large quantity of ice-cream to the destroyer whose Captain, Commander the Hon David Seeley, (later Lord Mottistone), promptly went over on the jackstay clutching a bottle of Champagne for the carrier's CO. Because of the strict no-alcohol rules in the USN, and as the incident was witnessed by hundreds of USN personnel, the gift was politely but firmly refused and a pantomime resulted in which the bottle went to and fro between the two COs. In the end the American Captain agreed to take the gift below and have it put in bond until they returned to San Diego.

A group of our officers was invited aboard the USS Sirago at sea and were impressed by its performance and amazed at how spacious and clean this 13 year old WW2 submarine was kept. With the USN nuclear submarine programme already well under way, we were given a book of matches inscribed,
"If you can't go Sirago, go nuclear".

The high esteem in which I had held the USN ever since working with them in the Korean War, was furthered by their enthusiasm and professionalism above, below and on the sea during those two months of joint RN, RAN, RNZN and USN exercises. Regrettably my opinion is not shared by some chauvinist armchair critics at home with little or no experience of working with our American cousins.

I spent most of the short time we spent at Manila in overalls refitting the bearings of one of our Steering Motors and only managed to watch a professional game of Pelota, on which the locals gambled heavily, and have a quick tour of the city before we set sail to Hong Kong. The sea was calm and after dinner the Senior Engineer and I started work in the cabin on updating our maintenance records in preparation for the harbour and sea inspections by the Flag Officer 2$^{nd}$ in Command of the Far East Fleet (FO2), due to take place soon after our arrival. After several months of very intense sea exercises our paper work had piled up and time was short before it would be perused by Rear Admiral Varyl Begg and his staff. It was a particularly hot night and as the sea was flat calm we put a wind scoop out of the cabin scuttle to provide some cooling as we toiled at our desks. In the small hours the ship made a sudden change of course which sent a quantity of the South China Sea shooting through the scoop and all over the completed documentation we had piled temporarily on the deck of our crowded cabin. The vital remedial action added to the normal frenzy of preparations for an inspection and, except for the memorable first weekend, limited my free time during the ship's penultimate visit to the colony. On a previous visit to Hong Kong, we had entertained a Chinese Shipping Magnate Mr Mok and on arrival there was an invitation for John Bailey and me to spend the Saturday and Sunday aboard his luxury yacht. He had a mixed bag of very interesting guests including a charming former Gaiety Girl,

and the company and conversation was sparkling and the meals superb, just like an Agatha Christie scenario. We cruised around the waters surrounding the colony, during which I was professionally taught to water-ski. Our kind host brought us back to the ship in his motor boat just in time for 'Sunday Night Cinema'. After this super break I had to get down to the serious work of preparing for the inspection, in fact I was so busy in the run up to the 'big day' that

I was only able to snatch one brief trip to Kowloon, with Chief Electrician Ron Kelbrick, to choose the design and order a camphor-wood chest and to buy some silk dress material and jewellery for Eileen and toys for the children before the Admiral's harbour inspection began. Next day we sailed with the staff for a detailed sea inspection of our capabilities at the end of which the Admiral declared himself satisfied that we could handle any naval war or peace situation we might have to face.

On the day after FO2's Inspection we left Hong Kong in company with HMS Cossack and the cruisers HMS Ceylon and HMNZS Royalist and passed through the politically-sensitive Formosa Straits with our Ensigns illuminated, and anchored in the harbour of Inchon in Korea on 13th May. My mind went back to December 1950 when my first ship HMS Theseus had perforce. to beat a hasty retreat from this same harbour when the Chinese Army entered the town. On our arrival the US Army invited two officers from Cheviot and Cossack and six officers from each of the two cruisers, to a tour of Korea. The doctor Roger Doherty and I were lucky in the draw and at 0900 next day, we joined two officers from Cossack, similarly selected for this gem of a trip, and the Captains and five senior officers from the two cruisers, at an air strip near

Inchon. We were welcomed by an American Colonel and boarded a large US Army helicopter for a day long tour of the de-militarised zone (DMZ) between North and South Korea. Flying low over the former battlefields we saw the massed defences deployed to prevent

another incursion of Communist forces and appreciated what a difficult terrain the UN soldiers had to contend with when they faced the North Koreans and Chinese armies during the 1950-53 conflict. We landed six times and each time we were greeted ceremonially, shown over the defences, given refreshments and a detailed briefing. At the forward HQ of the UN Armistice Commission, we enjoyed a formal lunch attended by two US Senators, and saw through binoculars, gigantic graffiti painted on the hills to the north reading:

"Yankee Go Home – Don't Get Dysentry – Keep Korea Green"

We were even flown slowly over Gloucester Hill so that we could see where the Glorious Gloucesters repulsed wave after wave of Chinese infantry in April 1951. At 1600 we witnessed the daily meeting of the former combatants at the Panmunjom Conference Centre, in a hut straddling the armistice line, before flying back to Inchon at the end of a memorable day in which I saw infinitely more of Korea than I had in seven months, some eight years earlier.

I also enjoyed a long day visit to Seoul with other members of the mess in which we had, I cannot say enjoyed, a Korean meal and toured a city still trying to recover from the ravages caused in a number of exchanges of occupancy, during the war. On the eve of our departure the British Ambassador kindly hosted an All-Ranks party at the Embassy in the capital for Cheviot, after which he reported the loss of a silver cigarette box  presented to his grandfather by Queen Victoria. Next morning an appeal was broadcast onboard for its return and a few minutes later a shame-faced Stoker handed it in to his Divisional Officer and it was personally returned by the Captain to its owner, with apologies, before we sailed for Japan.

The four ships entered Tokyo bay, Cheviot and Cossack then steamed up the river to berth alongside in the city close to the Tokyo Tower with a civic welcome, while the cruisers Ceylon and Royalist berthed at Yokosuca. We enjoyed six hectic days in the Japanese capital, which was already fast recovering from WW2 and was bustling and self-confident. The view from the top of the tower was terrific and though prices in the shops were high compared with HK and the roads were very pot-holed, it was a great run ashore. One night after dinner in the wardroom someone suggested we have a 'mess-run' to the famous Imperial Baths. So after imbibing some 'flying speed', ten of us set off and soon found ourselves in the reception area where we paid our 2000 yen fee (about £2.00), were given a number and a coffee. After a while a beautiful, petite Japanese girl wearing a white kimono came in and sweetly called the Captain's Secretary's number and led him away to admiring, or perhaps envious, looks from the rest of us. I was the third in succession to be called by a similarly attractive young lady and was led away to the Bath suites. My hostess took me into a small room containing a steam bath, a pool and a massage couch and removed her kimono and, dressed only in a white bra and panties, passed me a towel and indicated I should undress and enter the steam box. During the time I spent in there she softly sang in Japanese and mopped the perspiration from my head. After about 30 minutes she opened the doors of the box and propelled me into the icy cold pool. Wow! I was then helped out of the pool and dried and asked to lie on the couch face upwards where she gave me a head, body leg and foot massage before turning me over to repeat the same on my back. The perfectly decent massage ended with her daintily running up and down my back on her toes. As I dressed after the one hour long rejuvenation I felt terrific, thanked the young lady and stepped out of the suite 'walking on air'. Outside in the corridor my messmates were emerging with similar satisfied looks until my new boss, Mike Antrobus, staggered out of his suite looking rather less than happy. Apparently he had been one of the last called and his hostess, unseen by those called earlier, had been an, "old hag who looked like a suomi wrestler, had grunted throughout the hour long session, thrown him in the pool and had nearly crushed him when she ran up and down his back at the end!" Our senior bather swore he would never go on a mess run with us again.

On 25th May we left Tokyo for Hong Kong on what was effectively the first leg of our 5 month long passage home. During the three days there we made our final purchases and a junk delivered all of the camphor wood chests ordered from the makers in Kowloon. We had a mess-run, not attended by Cdr (L), for a farewell 'Hong Kong haircut' where, for 8 HK dollars (50 pence) we had a haircut of our choice, a head and neck massage and manicure, all performed professionally by pretty Chinese girls. On our last night there, we threw a party onboard for service and civilian friends in the colony. Jenny and her side party dressed in new silk cheongsams and with new hairdos, radiantly, served our guests and the party was a huge success. Next morning, as Cheviot steamed towards the Lie-U-Mun pass we were given a Chinese Fireworks farewell by a tearful Jenny and her girls. As we passed Kai Tak I asked my division, as they stood 'manning ship', what part of Hong Kong they would miss most and almost to a man they replied "Wanchai". When I added "What did you think of Kowloon, Aberdeen, the Peak and Repulse Bay?", I was amazed at the number of junior ratings who had never strayed beyond Wanchai during the many days we had spent alongside in Hong Kong during the past 13 months. As we sailed south with Cossack, Ceylon and Royalist a rumour ran around the ship that one of the Chiefs, curious to look at his camphor wood chest, opened up the transport crate in which it had been delivered and found it contained only a cheap box and packing. All of us had purchased our chests from the same renowned maker and, at first, I dismissed the very idea that we had been conned but soon other Cheviots were reported to have found the same scam had been played on them. In the confines of my cabin, I secretly opened my outer crate to find under packing, a plywood case. Shocked I opened this with some difficulty and found more packing which when removed revealed the beautiful chest I had ordered. It was quite a job getting all the packaging back in the two boxes and stowing the crate safely for the long passage home. Needless to say I didn't let on to my shipmates that I had fallen for the hoax.

The three Commonwealth ships joined up with a US Marine Corps Helicopter Carrier and its brood of landing craft for an amphibious exercise which culminated in a landing on the coast of North Borneo. in which we hosted the HQ for the participating Green Howards and provided simulated bombardment support Afterwards, we had a run ashore in Jesselton where the Kiwis from Royalist put on a farewell Maori concert including a war dance and ended aptly with " Now is the hour for us to say Goodbye".

As I was pretty skint after my shopping spree in HK, and Singapore prices were relatively high, I spent most of the next three days at the naval base making use of the pool and Officers' Club. I did however enjoy a great Mess Dinner with the Captain and most of my messmates as guests of the Green Howards at their HQ at Kota Tingi. Wearing tropical Mess Undress, we travelled the 25 miles to their Jungle HQ in army transport, escorted by armoured cars. Their officers' mess was a large Attap hut and facing outwards in the open sides were armed soldiers protecting the diners from Communist guerrillas. Down the centre of the mess was a huge polished oak table groaning under the weight of numerous silver trophies won by the regiment in ancient campaigns and, with the Colonel and our Captain next to each other, the Cheviots sat with host officers on either side. It was a superb dinner and the speeches by the Colonel and Captain were witty and appropriate and, at about 0100, after some robust competitive Army/Navy mess games, led by the Colonel and Captain, we were driven back under escort to the ship extolling the special relationship existing between the Army and Navy.

I was duty OOD on our first day at Penang. We were anchored off the island and at 0545 next morning I had to see off one of our young sailors being escorted ashore to be taken back to the UK to be discharged from the service and to serve six months in jail. When the motor boat came alongside I called the prisoner and escort forward and noticed how 'cocky' the defaulter was but when he looked around and saw that none of his messmates had bothered to come up on deck 5 minutes before 'Reveille' to see him off, he was visibly shaken and before he went down the ladder to the boat he was in tears as I shook his hand and wished him Good Luck in his next career. I noticed that tattooed on his fingers was HATE NAVY. Many years later, at a reunion in Portsmouth, a well dressed middle-aged chap came up to me and offered his hand saying "You won't remember me, but you were the last naval officer I ever saw before I left the navy. I glanced at his hand, saw the tattoo and said "Oh yes I do". He told me that after completing his prison sentence he had turned over a new leaf, found a job that suited him and enjoyed life, but still had happy memories of his time in Cheviot.

On the second day at Penang we held a Cocktail party for local service and civic people and afterwards I was invited ashore by an RAF Dentist and his wife who lived on the hill and kindly asked me, after a splendid evening, to stay overnight. It was a very convivial party and next morning I didn't awake until about 0830 to find the house silent. I arose and noisily washed, shaved and dressed in my white Tuxedo. My host then appeared and apologised for oversleeping, dressed and kindly drove me down to the harbour where I found a boatman willing to row me, still dressed in evening suit, out to the ship. It was 1000 when I arrived, in full view of the Captain who, like many of the Ship's company, was enjoying a mid-morning breather on the upper deck, and I disappeared below to my cabin. Whilst I was rapidly changing into uniform, the Bosun's Mate arrived and told me I had to "Report Immediately to the First Lieutenant in the Wardroom". When I arrived all of the officers were enjoying a 'Stand easy' coffee and witnessed No 1 giving me a right rollicking for returning onboard late and, with the slightest twinkle in his eye, ended with " - - and the worst offence was that you arrived back onboard 10 minutes after Cdr (L) and me".

On the morning of our departure from Penang for JETEX 59, the ship's motor boat was missing from the boom and its Coxswain was absent. The lovesick Leading Seaman, concerned that we were about to depart the China Station for good, leaving his Chinese girl friend behind and, ignoring the limited range of a ship's boat and its fuel capacity, had set off before sunrise for Hong Kong. The old naval adage that, "It will drag you further than gunpowder can blow you" can seldom have been more appropriate than in this case. The missing boat was soon overhauled and the ship resumed its passage to Ceylon.

During the year since our last visit (for JETEX 58) the harbour and town of Trincomalee had become even more run down and the jungle had swallowed the last wards of the former RN Hospital, but the sea and harbour exercises were carried out with their traditional enthusiasm and national pride by the Ceylon, Indian and Pakistan navies and by units of the RN East Indies and Far East Fleets. On the final day of the exercises at sea, HMS Hogue collided at speed with the Indian cruiser Mysore holing her badly amidships and pushing the destroyer's bows back to 'A' turret. As OOD, I was on deck at dawn when the cruiser limped, and the destroyer was towed, forlornly into harbour. Unknown to us at the time, this accident was to alter the course of Cheviot's future. That evening HMS Andrew received a signal from the flagship of the East Indies fleet reading rather haughtily: "When in company, it is customary to follow the Senior Officer, and cover guns at sunset". The submarine replied: "My gun has been free-flooding since 1945". During the sporting activities I played on the wing in a rugby match against the Ceylon police which Cheviot won. In this game, Tremayne Rodd {later Lord Rennel), kindly popped the ball out to me to go over the line and score when, as the best player on the field, he could easily have touched it down himself. The social chit chat at the many gatherings held after the sea exercises was dominated by the arrest of the second in command of the Ceylon Navy for the murder of his wife and her lover whom he had caught 'in the act'. Most of the Commonwealth officers present seemed to fully support the wronged husband.

On the 3rd of September, on passage from Trinco to Cochin in SW India, Lt Cdr John Bailey compered a programme on the ship's radio in which he asked several Cheviots: "Where were you and what were you doing 20 years ago today when war broke out?"

Captain O'Brien replied: "I was OOW on the bridge of a destroyer in the Red Sea when a signal arrived from Whitehall. I leant over the parapet of the bridge and shouted to my Captain, who was reading a book on the flag deck, Captain Sir, we have just received a signal saying 'Commence hostilities with Germany'. The Captain let the monocle drop out of his eye on to his book as he replied, "Oh! Very good - Carry on". He then replaced his monocle and continued reading.

My office writer EM Savage was born on the 2nd September 1939 and he replied that he was in hospital and when asked what he was doing he gave a passable imitation of a baby crying.

Lieutenant Ed Garnett, The TAS officer and oldest man onboard, was the last Cheviot to be questioned and his interview went like this:

"What sort of ship were you serving in when war broke out?"
Ed replied "A V & W destroyer"
"What were you doing at the time?"
"Preparing a Mark 9 one star torpedo" replied Ed.
"Where was the ship at the time?"
"In the North Sea"

"What was the ship doing"
        "Looking for Zeppelins"
" Oh no Ed! not that war, let's start again –"

What were you doing when World War 2 started?"

Without hesitation, Ed's reply to the first two repeated questions were:
        "Serving in a V and W Destroyer"

        "Preparing a Mark 9 two star torpedo"

Cochin is known as the Indian Venice because of its network of canals, rather less grand than that of the Italian city. We anchored in a river, swollen by the recent monsoon and down which the bloated carcases of dead animals floated past the ship. Whilst there I went on an interesting organised trip up into the hills to a tea plantation. We then set sail for the sailors' paradise, the beautiful unspoilt Seychelles, then practically isolated from the world, 1000 miles east of Africa and south of India with no airfield, only one visiting ship per month and nine women for every man. We anchored off Victoria, capital of Mahé the largest island of the group and only a short boat trip from the Seychelles Club, a venerable wooden pavilion overlooking a cricket pitch and frequented by colonial characters straight out of fiction. Advance literature had warned that many of the nubile young women, who were rather free with their favours, were likely to give unwary sailors a 'present' they would rather not have and liberty men were offered protection before going ashore.

The scenery was quite stunning, the beaches of golden sand amazing and the fishing was fantastic. Food and drinks ashore were very cheap and the Seychellois were friendly and, though they normally spoke in a French patois, all could speak English. We were entertained in 'The Club', played cricket against the locals and put on a dance for them in the hotel ashore and generally had a good time. One day when I was duty OOD and the only officer onboard, I checked our cable to see if it was holding firmly and felt a slight movement. I checked the anchor bearings and thought there was a tiny change so I called out the duty watch and prepared to lay more cable. The ship's Tannoy calling for the cable party to close up on the fo'c'sle was heard by the Squadron Navigator who was sailing the dinghy nearby. He returned aboard and rushed up to the fo'c'sle and asked me what I was doing. I said "I fear we are dragging anchor" to which he replied "Rubbish". I invited him to stand on the cable. He did so, confirmed my suspicions and immediately took over and lowered more cable. In addition to the normal level of trouble ashore from drunken sailors, we had a nasty incident in which a Stoker attacked the Leading Hand of his mess with a knife. As the Senior Engineer was the Divisional officer for both the assailant and his victim I was asked to act for the attacker, a Scot well known to have a violent streak and almost incomprehensible to me. Whilst on passage to Mombasa, he smashed up the cell in which he was put and I had to have a sentry with me whenever I interviewed him. My first couple of days in Mombasa were taken up with the court martial of the stoker who was found guilty, and was sentenced to prison and discharge from the service and handed over to the Army to transport home. This was put on hold when a medical exam showed he had ignored the advice given before he went ashore in Mahé. During the trip to Mombasa, we happened to be in the ideal position to witness a total solar eclipse when at 1400 the bright equatorial afternoon sky gave way to total darkness. I was able to view the sun's corona safely through a lens provided to monitor the ship's searchlight's carbon arc. It was a sight I will never forget.

Mombasa was another good run ashore and whilst there I went with the Captain and several officers on a two-day safari to Tsavo National Park half-way to Nairobi. We stayed overnight at Voi Lodge and saw many different animals especially at the watering holes we visited just before dusk and at dawn. I also went deep-sea fishing with John Bailey, who caught a 22lb Yellow Fin Tunny. One day, after three hours of trying, I finally managed to get up on a surf board in the sea at Malindi, north of Mombasa and to ride it in-shore and right up the beach, and to repeat this feat several times!

Cheviot next moved south to the port of Tanga where I visited a massive sisal plantation before going to the, then independent, Arab Sultanate of Zanzibar. The Sultan's son had been at school with our Captain's Sec and, in those pre PC days, when they met again Peter called his royal schoolmate by his school nickname "Inky". The prince was obviously not offended for he invited the two of us on a tour of the island followed by tea at the palace. The front bumper of his car bore an intricate crown and every one of the locals salaamed as we passed. A few years later, by which time the Prince had become Sultan, Zanzibar was annexed by its large African neighbour Tanganyika and became part of the new independent state of Tanzania. The new Sultan was deposed and fled to the UK. The Zanzibar we saw was a quaint little feudal Arab state which, in East Africa, was out of place. My lasting memory of returning aboard at Zanzibar is of the all pervading smell of cloves coming from the biggest store of cloves in the world. Whilst at Zanzibar we visited a nearby island sanctuary for tortoises where each of them had the year of its birth painted on its shell and one dated back to 1815. I rode on a younger one - only 97 years old.

Our next port of call was Dar Es Salaam, capital of Tanganyika a former German colony acquired by Britain during WW1. Approaching the mouth of its perfect harbour we passed the ornate white palace built by the Germans in the Arab style. This splendid building was the official residence of the Governor. We held a cocktail party for local dignitaries on the first night and on the second night the Governor invited the Captain and Officers of Cheviot to an official Dinner attended by the Prime Minister, Julius Nyere, who later became the first President of independent Tanzania, and other civil, political and military dignitaries. I was astonished to find I was seated on Table No 1, next to Julius Nyere who was a charming neighbour. I still have my invitation card as a memento and proof of the equal opportunity given to junior officers in Cheviot to mix in the highest circles. Whilst at Dar we received the first of many invitations from Durban and Cape Town  and they were about to be allocated when we received a signal telling us to turn round and stay within easy steaming distance of the Persian Gulf until the destroyer sent to take over from the damaged HMS Hogue, arrived on station. We would then go home via the Suez Canal and Malta. We made the most of our remaining time in Dar and 'stooged' around off the Somali coast until relieved and then fuelled at Aden and made our way up the Red Sea to Suez. At short notice I had to 'jury-rig' a propeller direction indicator system with a receiver on the Bridge, for the benefit of the Canal Pilot. In true Heath-Robinson manner, I used an 'M' Type Transmitter driven by a cinema projector belt, and the engine revolution counter shaft in the engine room, to achieve this. The passage up the canal, recovered after the 1956 war, was uneventful and we were soon in the Eastern Mediterranean headed for Malta, our last stop before UK.

On the night before our arrival, the Captain spoke to the ship's company on the SRE, not from his cabin but from the small wire cage on 2 deck which passed for our 'broadcasting studio'. He explained many of the customs of the island, corrected a number of misunderstandings and demolished a few myths widely believed in the navy and ended his short talk with, "You may wonder how I know so much about Malta, well, both my mother and my wife are Maltese. Enjoy your visit." I am sure that the Cheviots' visit was enjoyed the more for that informative broadcast.

We didn't stop at Gibraltar on the way home and on 21st October held a Mess Dinner in the wardroom as we passed Cape

Trafalgar on the 154<sup>th</sup> anniversary of the battle. It was our final formal dinner and although the Captain and Navigating Officer had to leave the mess briefly whilst we passed through a large Spanish fishing fleet, the evening was a hugely successful and poignant occasion. Two days later we anchored in Falmouth Roads and embarked HM Customs and after they cleared us we weighed anchor and set sail for Portsmouth. I had the 'First Dog Watch' on the bridge as we steamed eastward up the channel and, just before 1800, I was told to go to the Captain's cabin when I came off watch. He welcomed me, gave me a drink and said I had done well in my first ship as an officer, handed me my 'flimsy', a chit summarising his assessment of me, and my Bridge Watchkeeping Certificate of Competence, wished me good luck in the future and ended with the advice that I should be less flippant at times when seriousness was more appropriate. I suspect that he was especially referring to that early morning call I made to him from the bridge, off the Australian coast.

I still have my rather tatty Watch keeping 'ticket', typed on an A5 sized piece of re-cycled paper, but signed by a future CinC Fleet. I fondly remember pitch dark early mornings as Officer of the Watch in charge of a destroyer at sea, greeting passing ships in the night and asking them their name and where bound and compiling and sending the regular four hourly signal to Whitehall giving the ship's position, wind speed and direction, cloud cover in eighths, and the sea and weather conditions. The experience I gained as OOW in Cheviot made me more aware and appreciative of whole ship matters and alerted me to easily remedied shortcomings in some of the electrical, radio and radar equipment that the non-technical watch keepers had accepted as normal

Next morning we hove-to at Spithead and a tug brought out our families to us. It is impossible to describe my feelings of joy and happiness as I was reunited with Eileen, Sally and Paul after over 18 months apart. The short trip into harbour and securing alongside to

a ceremonial reception with crowds on the jetty waving and cheering, passed like a dream. Very soon we were sitting in the wardroom having this happy photo taken by the local newspaper.

Although Eileen and I were 'old hands' at being sadly separated for long periods, and then happily reunited, this home coming was even more thrilling than its predecessors for Sally was now a bright six years old school girl who remembered me and though Paul didn't, he was almost two and had heard of me and we quickly bonded. As one of the two longest serving officers onboard, I was to go straight on leave so, the Murdoch family went home by taxi with all of the presents I had brought home with me, including the camphor-wood chest. When we arrived, I was delighted and proud of her to find that, during my absence, Eileen had not only brought up the children on her own but redecorated and furnished our front room and our home looked great, comfortable and homely.

I had been given 10 days of the 27 days Foreign Service leave I had earned and was determined to enjoy it to the full with the family and to take advantage of the closing days of Britain's 1959 Indian summer. First we all went to pick up our first car, bought with the money I had saved whilst abroad. This gave us mobility and we picnicked on successive days in the country and on the beach, wallowing in the unseasonably warm sea. Then it all went wrong. After returning from the beach I had a sudden attack of severe breathlessness and Eileen phoned the ship, who sent the Duty MO to our house. By the time he arrived I was gasping for breath. He gave me an injection and called an ambulance and I was rushed off to RNH Haslar. By the time we reached the hospital I was breathing normally and walked out of the ambulance unaided, to the surprise of the medical team, waiting with oxygen for me. It seems that I had been suspected of being struck down with some rare foreign bug picked up in the Far East or Africa. A private ward had been prepared for me and they put me to bed in it and there I stayed for five days in splendid isolation whilst I was subjected to a series of tests to identify the problem. As it was the Senior Officer's ward, the previous occupant had been the Commodore of RN Barracks, it was first on the route for distribution of all of the 'goodies' and food. The lady with the Book Trolley offered me the first read of a brand new Best Seller - Doctor Zhivago. As I had read and enjoyed the works of Tolstoy and Dostoevsky, I jumped at the chance and spent my time in that well appointed ward enjoying Pasternak's masterpiece and the detail in a large print of Canaletto's magnificent painting of Maria Therese's Palace and courtyard. In the end, the tests indicated that I had suffered my first Asthma attack, brought on by falling leaves during that particularly hot English October and I was allowed home for the last couple of days of my leave, during which the long hot spell of weather ended.

When I returned aboard, I found that Captain O'Brien and all but one of his Squadron's 'gilded staff' had left the ship and we had became a 'private ship' under the command of our former First

Lieutenant Alex MacDonald with Jerome Benson as First Lieutenant.. Eric Roberts was now the Engineer Officer and I the Electrical Officer and we both moved forward to the rather more commodious cabins of the Commanders (E) and (L) respectively. A few days later we sailed for the Clyde area to be the moving target for trials of a homing torpedo. I had the Middle watch on the Bridge and had turned in after dinner to be awakened in my spacious new cabin by the Bosun's mate with: "Its 20 to 12 Sir, and it's snowing". When I reached the bridge the ship was in Cardigan Bay and was steaming straight into a NNE snowfall. Being used to balmy nights on the Bridge in the Indian Ocean, Red Sea and Med, this was a culture shock and I was glad to spot the 'Calf of Man' light four hours later and to hand over the watch to my relief and to go below into the warmth.

We arrived at Greenock around noon and berthed alongside, embarked the trials equipment and then began the torpedo trials in Loch Long and off Arran. Each weekend we returned alongside in Greenock and during the weekdays had a total of 50 inert 'homers' fired at us as we steamed at different speeds and on various courses. All of them hit us, generally in the stern and after each hit Eric and I had to inspect the tiller flat for damage. The 50th shot struck our port screw and took a piece off the propeller blade which, on the way back to Portsmouth for Christmas, caused us to vibrate at what was known onboard as 'Honeymoon Revs'

HMS Cheviot berthed alongside at Portsmouth just before Christmas 1959 and, after seeing her safely connected to shore supplies, I went on leave and had a great time at home with the family. I had bought their Christmas presents in Glasgow and they were well received by Eileen, Sally and Paul. The present most popular with Paul was a hobby horse which he later rode every day when taking his big sister to school.

After leave we put the ship's equipment into 'moth balls' for its towed passage to Rosyth where it was to become a Harbour Training Ship and, on St Valentine's day 1960 I left the ship for leave made up of the balance of my Foreign Service Leave.

Looking back on almost two years in Cheviot, I consider myself to have been extremely lucky to have served under the command of quite the most outstanding man and ship handler, and the most compassionate and kind RN Captain. These qualities were known, recognised and rewarded by the Admiralty. I was also very fortunate to have been blessed with two very understanding and considerate Commanders (L), very friendly and helpful messmates, an excellent right-hand man in Chief Electrician Ron Kelbrick and a loyal and hard working division. Cheviot was a happy and efficient ship and, though far from our loved ones, we all enjoyed a great camaraderie in the Far East, during the long homeward passage and in the ship's Swansong in the Clyde areas. My subsequent happy and rewarding naval and civilian careers owe much to the good start I received in HMS Cheviot and I am eternally grateful to all who contributed to making my first sea appointment as an officer, so job-satisfying.

# Chapter 14

## HMS Vernon March 1960 – October 1961

On the Sunday before I was due to join HMS Vernon, I suffered a 'Chauffeur's fracture of the Scafoid bone in my right wrist whilst trying to start my car by handle to take the family to Mass. During that day, the pain became more intense and after visiting the RNB sickbay I was sent to Haslar where they set the broken bone and fitted me with a fibre-glass (light weight) 'plaster' from my fingers to elbow. I was therefore a trifle handicapped when I took up my second appointment and this became evident on 'Day One' when I had great difficulty in signing for all of the hundreds of pieces of training equipment for which I was to become responsible. They were all originally Naval Stores items and were collectively put on charge to their custodian.

In 1960, HMS Vernon was the home of the Navy's Torpedo, Mine, Diving and Anti-Submarine (TAS) School, and, before 1946, had been the Portsmouth alma mater of the embryo Electrical branch. Although run by Seamen Officers of the TAS specialisation, because of their earlier responsibilities for naval electrics, Vernon had an interest in and understanding of naval electrics and was sympathetic to members of the relatively new Electrical Branch and they were made very welcome.

As when I joined Cheviot two years earlier, I relieved another renowned Lieutenant, Bill Jewell, who was considered to be a Sonar expert. My new job was to keep all of the Anti-Submarine and Tactical Training equipment, which was in near constant use, fully operational. As most of it was new 'cutting-edge' material I could see that this post would prove a more technological challenge than Cheviot.

The small electrical department of HMS Vernon was headed by a genial Acting Commander (L) Arthur Bailey who had a staff of two officers, 12 Electrical/Radio Electrical Artificers/ Mechanicians and PO Electricians and 20 junior ratings. His deputy a Lieutenant, was responsible for the Electrical and Radio maintenance, (including the changing of the wire sweeps, of the Vernon Squadron of Coastal Minesweepers), normally berthed in Vernon Creek, who had half of the electrical work-force. As Training Equipment Electrical Officer, I had the remainder, including among the Artificers, a keen young EA4 John Stupples later the Secretary of the Fisgard Association and editor of the Fisgardian.

The basic training of Sonar Operators was carried out in Asdic Training Houses (ATHs) and these were little trouble to keep going, but the more advanced instruction was given in Mobile (in as much as they were transportable, but needed external power supplies) 'classrooms' called MASTUs, Mobile Anti-Submarine Training Units and in the more modern and sophisticated Anti-Submarine Universal Attack Teachers (ASUATs). All of the mobile units were parked on the parade ground near the Heliport. There was also a static Attack Teacher Unit capable of simultaneously training the command teams of several ships and A/S Helicopter crews in A/S warfare. This unit had a radar simulator which constantly gave the tactical position of each of the 'ships' to each of the Command teams and, to focus the minds, across the auditorium was writ large, the slogan:

"Thrice-armed is he who has his quarrel just, but nine times armed, he who gets his blow in first".

The Attack Teacher and both ASUATs were in constant use by ships' command teams and since they were tightly programmed, any defect affecting their operational capability was considered an emergency. All other repair and maintenance was carried out after the day's instruction ended and was worked on until completed, so that it was operational by the next morning. It soon became clear to me that the pressure for a 'quick fix' had led to the replacement of electronic units by 'universal' spares not properly set up for the job. So one weekend I went through all of the units with the Artificers concerned and together we set them all up correctly and then tuned up the whole systems. The result was a very much improved performance and reliability from then on.

One day, I had to collect a 'Secret' document from the Confidential Book Office. The Officer in charge was Commander Donald Cameron VC RN, who as a Lieutenant, had commanded a midget submarine which had disabled the German battleship Tirpitz in a well defended Norwegian fjord. He walked with a pronounced limp and it was understood that he had been wounded by the Germans after escaping from the X-craft and had spent the rest of the war in the Naval POW camp near Bremerhaven. I told him which book I needed and why, and had to sign for it. After studying my name and noting I spoke with a Southern English accent, he said, in a cultured Scottish accent, "You'll not leave here until ye can pronounce yerr name properly". He then had me repeating over and over:

"Dawnell-dde Marr dosh", until he was satisfied.

Not long afterwards, this modest WW2 hero was invited (as a serving VC) to take the salute at a passing-out parade of cadets at

Sandhurst and a few weeks later he collapsed coming through the Vernon gates one morning and sadly died. We later learnt that his wounds had actually been the result of 'friendly-fire' by an RAF Typhoon which, spotting a column of naval personnel marching away from the advancing British army, had thought they were Germans and tragically strafed a column of RN POWs, killing 35 and wounding many, including Donald Cameron.

Although Cdr (L) was my boss, for all practicable purposes, I was, in fact responsible to the Lt Cdr in charge of A/S Training since I had to meet his requirements. One day he asked me if it was possible to link the two ASUATs together so that the command teams of two ships could exercise together against one submarine target just as they would in a 'two-ship' action at sea. I studied the circuitry of the servos concerned and realised it was possible. I was then authorised to engineer the link, which was carried out over a weekend and proved to be successful. I then produced a full set of drawings of the modification, for the records, and to aid in future maintenance of the two ASUATs. The A/STO later submitted his invention for a Herbert Lott Award and he was awarded £120 and I received £60. The 'two-ship' attack facility was still in daily use by ships' command teams a year later when I left Vernon.

I enjoyed being the junior member of the three officers regularly tasked with giving a lecture to 'Commanding Officers Designate' on how to get the best out of their Sonar equipment and A/S weapons. Led by Lt Cdr, Joe Streatfield-James and including Lt. Harold Clapson, we gave a joint scripted and illustrated presentation which, judging by the number of questions fired at us individually and collectively, went down well with our students.

During my 18 months in HMS Vernon, the Murdochs settled down to a 'normal' happy family life in our own home at

Highbury, Cosham. Sally moved from the local Primary School to the Convent of the Cross at Waterlooville and Eileen and Paul saw her on to the school bus every morning and collected her every afternoon Early on we were given a Labrador/Collie puppy by a friend and called him Bruce. He was the ideal pet for a young family and the children, especially Paul, loved him. Bruce grew rapidly and became difficult for Eileen to handle. On his lead he would jump the front gate, leaving Eileen and the children in the front garden and unable to open the gate because he was pulling it closed. Although he was very gentle with Sally and Paul he would eat anything, including nylon stockings,

cockle shells, sun glasses, whole platoons of plastic toy soldiers and even a pedal off the piano, and of course any kind of food left unguarded for a second. He was however, a great playmate for the children and he took Eileen, Sally and Paul 'walkies' every day. Fortunately he was also a good traveller in the car and loved to go to the beach to swim.

Captain Morgan Giles, who commanded HMS Vernon for most of the time I was there, was a very generous host to his officers and their families. However, when he left, he caused most of them a momentary shock when they opened the envelope containing their 'flimsy'. The opening phrase of which normally said "- - - has conducted himself to my entire satisfaction". The flimsy envelopes were in the wardroom letter rack and the Captain's Secretary stood close by at lunch time to explain to officers taken aback at the omission of the word "entire", that Captain MG believed that his officers had conducted themselves to his satisfaction, or had not!

I was able to get tickets for Eileen, the children and me to

witness the launch of HMS Nubian on 6th September 1960. Lady Holland-Martin, wife of the famous Captain of her WW2 namesake, was looking away from the ship when it suddenly started to move slowly down the slip. The bottle, being attached to the ship, crashed against its bows, the Royal Marine Band struck up 'Rule Britannia' and the Lady calmly faced the disappearing ship and managed to say "I name you HMS Nubian and may God Bless You and all who sail in you" before the ship entered the waters of the harbour. Nubian's keenness to get to sea was laughed off as a good omen for its future. My family thoroughly enjoyed the whole spectacle, little knowing we would soon be closely associated with the ship we had seen almost launch herself.

HMS Vernon had a cinema with a proper civilian projection room and two 35mm projectors but it was rather run-down and the captive audience often complained to the ship's 'Welfare Committee' about it. So Commander (L) 'volunteered me' to take over as Cinema Officer and tasked me with giving it a 'make-over'. I persuaded the relevant authorities in Vernon to chip in and help give the auditorium a long overdue redecoration and the

Shipwrights to build a new kiosk and a ticket machine, ice-cream and pop-corn counter for the foyer. Noel Paulett, an old friend of mine since 1950, when he was my Chief EA in HMS Theseus, and now an Illustrator in Vernon's Drawing Office, kindly painted to Eileen's design, a cycloramic collage of iconic scenes from famous films, on a huge canvas screen which was hung in the foyer. I had the two projectors overhauled and the cinema was ceremonially opened and was well received by all of the patrons.

The wardroom of HMS Vernon was a particularly friendly mess and though largely populated by Seaman Officers of the TAS branch, those of us of the other branches were made to feel at home in a cosy environment which was vibrant with social activities both formal and informal. Having just spent almost two years separated from each other, Eileen and I took full advantage of all of these and had quite a social whirl throughout my time there.

On hearing that HMS Vanguard was about to relinquish her role as Flagship of the Portsmouth Reserve Fleet and be towed away to a ship-breakers, I rang up my Cheviot chum 'Oscar' Wild and asked whether I could bring my daughter, brother-in-law Jim and nephew Jimmy aboard so that I could show them around the last British battleship. Oscar sent in a ship's boat to pick us up on the Saturday morning and I took them all over the ship in which I had undergone 'afloat training' as an apprentice in 1947/8. After the tour, which included the 15 inch 'X' turret that had been kept fully operational, we were entertained in the wardroom. We all enjoyed this visit immensely and it is still a vivid memory. for the family.

The following week, on 4ᵗʰ August 1960, Eileen phoned me to tell me that the TV was reporting that HMS Vanguard had gone aground near HMS Vernon. We were all at work at the time and no

ship's broadcast reporting this historic and poignant event had been made, but I went out on to the parade ground and saw the great battleship's bows impaled in the sea wall close to the famous 'Still and West' pub. The old girl just wanted a last pint before she went to the 'Knackers' yard. It wasn't long before the tugs pulled her clear and, sadly, my first and most powerful ship, passed reluctantly into history.

I was required to carry out the 24 hour duty of OOD once every nine days and, out of working hours, to man and sleep in the office at the Main Gate. I recall several memorable incidents:

The first involved Peter Martin, a friend of mine, when he was OOD. One morning around 0745, a flustered AB came into the office and said: 'Dooks are owt in rood Sir'. Peter said "I beg your pardon" and in a broad Yorkshire accent the AB repeated his message. The OOD said "Who are you?" and he replied, "Dook pond sweeper".

During WW2, HMS Vernon's chapel had been destroyed by a bomb and the crater was turned into a duck pond in which lived a flock of ducks. This agitated sailor's first task every morning was to clean the pond and feed the ducks.

It transpired that the senior drake had decided to lead his flock over to the United Services Ground opposite the southern gate of Vernon and, waddling sedately and diagonally across the road, had brought the early morning rush of traffic to a halt and all the Able Seaman's efforts had failed to get them to move aside. The OOD called out the duty watch to direct the traffic around the obstinate canards and to gently push them on to the pavement and eventually the traffic started to move. At that time there was a TV programme called "What's my line?" in which people with unusual jobs mimed and the panel had to guess his or her occupation. No panel would have ever guessed, 'Duck-pond sweeper'!

One evening at 1800, Eileen called at the OOD's office to see me. It was raining heavily at the time and she was amused to see the changing of the guard. The two sentries, dressed in oilskins, reported to each other flapping their arms and saying "Quack - Quack"

On a more serious note, one evening about 2100, I received an urgent signal from HMS Hermes which, anchored out at Spithead, had been landing its libertymen at Vernon pier. The signal asked me to prevent anyone from Hermes going through the gates, and thus into the town, and to send them back to the ship. Quite a large number had already passed through the gates before I received the signal, which I immediately actioned. I later learnt that, whilst the ship's Supply Officer (Cash) was attending a mess dinner in the wardroom, wearing the then popular pocket-less trousers with his mess-undress jacket, someone took the keys of the safe from his desk drawer, where he left them because he couldn't carry them with him, opened the safe and stole the contents leaving the door open.

The Master at Arms interrupted the dinner to inform the hapless Sub-Lieutenant at the dining table, of the robbery. The culprit was never found and the Cash Officer was court-martialled and fined the several thousand pounds stolen.

While I was dining in the wardroom one duty Sunday night a newly arrived young Midshipman told me a moving story about one of the officers serving in the training cruiser in which he had just returned from an official visit to Germany. On the ship's arrival at Hamburg, a distinguished looking elderly German civilian waited patiently on the jetty until all of the ceremonies were complete and then came up the gangway, raised his hat to the Ensign, and asked him, the duty Midshipman, if he could speak to Lt Cdr Roope. When asked who he was, the German said "I was the Captain of the

Hipper in 1940". Lt Cdr Roope was found and the German took off his hat and shook his hand. He told the navigation specialist that his father was the bravest man he had ever encountered. He added that, after the action in which his father's fatally damaged destroyer, HMS Glowworm had rammed the heavy cruiser Hipper, severely damaging it before, ablaze from stem to stern, the destroyer sank, he, the Hipper's Captain, had signalled the First Lord of the Admiralty, Winston Churchill, extolling the heroism of Glowworm's Captain and recommended he be awarded the Victoria Cross, posthumously. When the few survivors of the Glowworm returned from captivity in 1945 and told their story, the award of the VC to Lt. Cdr Gerard Roope was confirmed and back-dated to May 1940. He thus became the first VC of WW2. The German Captain then told the hero's son that he had followed his progress through school and into the navy and had travelled to Hamburg from Bavaria to meet him.

After 18 very happy months in Vernon, the Appointer told me I would be going back to sea soon and asked if I had any preference. HMS Nubian, then fitting-out at Portsmouth, her future home base, was equipped with the latest gunnery and Anti-Submarine equipment and, I had seen her launch, I disregarded the old naval maxim and volunteered for her. A few weeks later I received my appointment to join HMS Nubian on Monday 4th October 1961. In wardrooms it is customary to give a VdH, ('Vin d'honneur') at lunchtime to leavers on their last day. On that Friday morning, having completed my turn-over to my relief, I made a brief visit to Nubian in the dockyard to meet my future boss Lt.Cdr. Jack Harris and while chatting to him he received a phone call from my boss, Commander (L) at Vernon who wished to speak to me urgently. Arthur Bailey congratulated me on my promotion, at the earliest possible date, to Lieutenant. I was delighted at the news and after ringing Eileen, telephoned the wardroom mess manager at Vernon to cancel my VdH and convert it to an RPC, the traditional response of a newly promoted officer, who bought his messmates a drink to celebrate his good fortune. I thus left Vernon on a high note.

# Chapter 15

## HMS Nubian
## October 1961 – July 1964

Thirteen months after watching her almost launch herself, I joined HMS Nubian on 4th October 1961, proudly wearing a new 'second stripe' added to my suit during the weekend by a Gieves' seamstress. The ship was alongside in a non-tidal basin and was already beginning to look like a warship although 'down below' there was much fitting-out work still to be done. A building on the jetty adjacent to the ship contained the offices of the officers 'standing-by' Nubian whilst she was building and I joined that small team. I had already met the Electrical Officer Lt Cdr Jack Harris and the Engineer Officer Lt Cdr Vic Jones who had been EO of HMS Chichester with my previous ship Cheviot in the Far East. In one of the several changes of nomenclature popular in the RN at the time, Jack Harris became the Weapons & Radio Engineer Officer and I became the Deputy W & R E Officer. Although we had lost the prefix Electrical in our temporary new titles, we were still responsible for all of the ship's electrics. However, Jack decided that I should look after all of the Weapons and Radio equipment and be the junior ratings Divisional Officer and, besides being in overall charge of the department and DO for the senior ratings, he would run the ship's electrics. This arrangement was just what I had hoped for as I preferred weapons and electronics to 'heavy electrics'.

Some of the ships Weapons and Radio equipment had been installed by that time but much of the associated wiring was incomplete so after a week of 'standing-by' the ship and getting the feel of it, I went to HMS Collingwood to learn about the new MRS 3 gunnery system, the successor to the Flyplane System, and its 903 radar, and Gun Direction System, the long range 965 Radar and the JYA Radar/plotting tables, being fitted to Nubian. I thoroughly enjoyed the course and returned to Nubian feeling fairly confident I could cope with these new systems and with her latest Sonar and A/S weapons with which I was already familiar.

HMS Nubian was the 6th of the 7 Type 81 frigates of the 'Tribal' Class to be laid down and it says something for the naval dockyards that she was second in the class to join the Fleet and, HMS Tartar' 7tth of these COSAG (Combined Steam and Gas) propelled, single – screw, 'General Purpose' frigates, built at Devonport, finished third. Almost all of the machinery and equipment fitted in Nubian, from the Gas turbine engine and generator to the 'clock-winder' radar aerial on top of the mainmast, used 'state of the art' (circa 1960) techniques. Furthermore she was fitted with stabilisers, was fully air-conditioned and quite the most comfortable class of ship ever built for the RN.

Nubian was chosen to be class subject for a so-called 'accurate' measurement of its weight. Every piece of equipment, cable, pipe, or any other material brought on board or landed was weighed and the details meticulously recorded. This onerous time, budget and manpower-hungry routine could surely have been done more scientifically using Archimedes' principle?

Standing-by a ship building gives officers, particularly engineers, the chance to really get to know the ship's equipment in detail and affords them the chance to incorporate some of their own ideas to help improve its efficiency. Jack Harris had earlier served as the Electrical Officer of the Frigate HMS Tenby and had first-hand experience of running a modern warship's Electrical department.
He and I hit it off well together straight away and with our two very different past experiences, we 'bounced ideas off each other' some of which we put into action to, I think, the greater benefit of the ship. We cooperated closely in writing the W & R Standing Orders, incorporating in them a routine at sea where the duty Electrical Mechanic of the watch would carry out rounds of all electrical

machinery and electronic equipment every hour using the fundamental maintenance maxims:

"Stop, Look, Listen, Smell and Feel"

In the event of a piece of an equipment arousing suspicion during this basic test, the duty EM would consult and act in accordance with the Instructions posted locally. We also wrote into the Standing Orders that all Weapons equipment would be tested and tuned every morning before 0900 and left running with the maintainers in attendance while Armament Quarters, and exercises involving the equipment were carried out by the users.

Jack persuaded the dockyard to make and fit an A5 size card-holder in each compartment containing electrical, electronic or weapons equipment. He then got me to compile each of the Instructions to the EM of the watch and to 'prove' them before they were typed and laminated and placed in the card-holders. In doing this I learnt a lot about the installations myself and the junior ratings` knowledge of the equipment and their sense of purpose improved. It also led to many potentially serious defects being nipped in the bud. Later when the ship worked-up at Portland, the Admiral's staff was impressed by our rounds and daily weapons testing routines, and they were eventually adopted by all ships.

The Murdoch family took full advantage of my long period of 'Standing-by' Nubian in Portsmouth Dockyard. While on courses at Collingwood Eileen and I attended the Christmas Ball and Sally and Paul enjoyed Christmas parties at Collingwood and HMS Nelson for, as a member of Nubian's ship's company, I was also a member of Nelson' wardroom. We also attended Ladies, Guest nights and the Summer Ball in 1962.

During this period we moved into a new bungalow at Purbrook to be near Sally's school. We had decided to send Paul to the same school in September 1962 before I went back to sea again and subsequently went to the Persian Gulf for a year. Besides leaving our first home in Cosham, we regretfully had to part company with Bruce, our now fully grown dog. Our new home was an 'Open Plan' bungalow and it proved quite impossible to keep him from going seriously 'walk about' in the surrounding countryside, causing Eileen to spend hours trying to find him. With great reluctance we had to find a new home for him which, with the help of the RSPCA, we did, and were told he had settled down happily with a family in Denmead. Fortunately Sally and Paul had made friends at school and with the neighbours' children and they accepted that Bruce was better off in a more secure environment. Eileen and I took the children on our first family holiday to Jersey for ten days in August. We travelled by ferry from Weymouth, having left our car there. The first and last of the ten days we spent on the island were the only really fine days and, as we were only staying at a boarding house for bed, breakfast

and the evening meal, we had to go out every day. However, we made the best of the

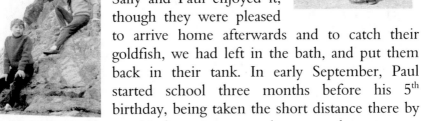

unseasonable weather and Sally and Paul enjoyed it, though they were pleased to arrive home afterwards and to catch their goldfish, we had left in the bath, and put them back in their tank. In early September, Paul started school three months before his 5<sup>th</sup> birthday, being taken the short distance there by his big sister, who was his favourite games playmate and mentor.

Throughout the twelve months before the ship was ceremonially commissioned on 9<sup>th</sup> October 1962, the number of Nubians grew. In the summer we moved onboard and took the ship to sea for Contractors Sea trials. These included trials of all of the main and auxiliary machinery, electrical machinery, and some of the weapons. The accommodation was not finished at the time but indicated that it would be of a high standard by the time the ship commissioned. The embryo ship's company moved back ashore to RNB, after the trials were successfully completed, to allow the dockyard to finish the ship's interior. The harbour trials of the weapons and radio equipment then began. Having enjoyed a 'family-friendly' routine up to then, Standing By Nubian suddenly ceased to be an '8 to 5' job and I often worked late into the evening and occasionally all night to meet the very tight harbour Weapons and Radio Acceptance Trials programme, due to be completed before the ship commissioned on 9th October 1962.

On Saturday 6th October, with all of these trials satisfactorily completed, I went home for the weekend. That afternoon Paul attended his pal next door's birthday party. Next morning we couldn't wake him to go to church and soon realised he was very ill and called our Doctor. He came very quickly and then swiftly followed a long nightmare of anxiety when Paul was rushed first to the local hospital for tests and then an overnight journey in thick fog to the Atkinson Morley Hospital at Wimbledon. We had left Sally with Eileen's mother and had travelled with Paul in the ambulance and on arrival a young brain surgeon declared Paul had a blood clot on his brain, was critically ill and needed a life-saving operation immediately. Eileen fainted and was put to bed and I helped the nurse to prepare Paul for the five-hour long operation. An hour after he emerged from the theatre, Eileen and I, dressed in gowns and masks were allowed in to see him and were so thrilled to see him awake and though pale and wearing a huge head bandage, answering in a deep voice, questions put to him by the doctor. The doctor told us that Paul was slightly paralysed down one side and that the next three days were critical. During the operation I had telephoned the ship and been given leave to remain at the hospital until he came off the critical list. The local Catholic priest, a famous

Jesuit, Joseph Corbishley, came to visit him and he was a great comfort to us and helped us and Paul to get through the next three days. By the Thursday, Paul's partial paralysis had worn off and his condition was downgraded to Serious, so I went home by train leaving Eileen at the 'digs' close to the hospital arranged for us on the previous Monday. I picked up my car from the Portsmouth hospital car park, went aboard the ship and was given the long weekend off and then took Sally and her grandma back to Wimbledon to see Paul. When asked by his Grandma what he would like as a homecoming present he replied, "A dog". When she said, showing him a toy dog donated to the children's ward by a grateful parent, "One like this?" Paul replied, "No a real one". I brought Sally and her grandma home on the Sunday evening, leaving Eileen there to spend every day with her now visibly-mending son and returned to the ship on the Monday morning before she sailed for the first of the Sea Acceptance Trials.

These were carried out in the English channel and went very well. First, we completed the radio communications sea trials, then the Radar trials and then moved on to the gunnery and Anti-Submarine Weapons and Sonar trials, all of them allowing the ship's company to become familiar with the ship at sea. Most evenings we anchored in the Solent or Spithead but every weekend we spent alongside in Portsmouth harbour. On the first Saturday in November I drove up to Wimbledon and collected Paul and Eileen and brought them home, where Paul was delighted that his grandma had a pedigree miniature poodle waiting for him. A few weeks later Paul returned to school where he was welcomed back as the miracle child they had all prayed for. During November and December we completed all of our trials and the ship's company and officers settled down and became familiar with their tasks. Our Captain Ian Jamieson DSC, RN, was a TAS specialist and Scottish international hockey player, First Lieutenant Lt. Cdr. Murray Johnstone led a lively and sociable wardroom of characters, all of whom got on very well together and who enjoyed the loyal support of their senior and junior ratings. We also had, for a small ship, the unusual bonus of a great Royal Marine detachment led by Lt. Frank Blackah RM. All of the officers had single cabins and mine was just below the Bridge, comfortable and handy for the Operations Room and radar offices. As Frank Blackah had a batman, the 1st Lt decreed that he should share the services of Marine Brian Carlson with one of the RN Officers and I was extremely lucky to win the draw and was very well-looked after for the whole commission. All of the officers also enjoyed the services of a very good team of Goan cooks and Stewards. Nubian's wardroom was large for a frigate. Its décor and furnishings were tastefully chosen by the 1st Lieutenant whilst the ship was building and his mother, the renowned artist Doris Zinkeisen, produced a splendid oil painting of a Nubian tribesman, which dominated the fireplace. The mess also boasted a sizeable sitting out area which bode well for the entertainment of guests. So, what with having a brand new air-conditioned ship with superior accommodation and victuals, it is not surprising that Nubian was destined to be a happy ship.

By mid December, this happy breed felt ready to face the rigours of a Work-Up at Portland, due to commence in early January 1963, and went off in two watches for 14 days Christmas leave. Having just survived a harrowing period with Paul's illness, our small family particularly enjoyed this festive season together. We almost had a White Christmas too, for on Boxing Day 1962, snow began to fall, heralding the most severe winter since 1947. Sally and the now-recovered Paul had a great time in the snow but it wasn't so much fun for adults trying to get to work. I set off in our Morris 1000 to drive to the dockyard at the end of my leave only to find the road blocked on Portsdown Hill. I nursed the car back home and garaged it and then walked all seven miles to the ship as there were no buses or taxis running. I stayed onboard then until we sailed two days later at 0830, in a snowstorm, for Portland. That afternoon we were assessed at sea off the Dorset coast by the staff of the Flag Officer Sea Training for our suitability as a ship's

company and material fitness as a ship, to undergo a rigorous regime of demanding warship exercises, beginning with harbour drills and ending, seven weeks later, with a full-blown war. Our major harbour Fire and Riot exercises and the Disaster Exercise, in which we had to come to the aid of a flooded Mediterranean town, were conducted in snowstorms. Meanwhile, we engineers had to work all hours demonstrating that all our equipment was tuned to the optimum standard and, of course, to clear defects arising in the unfavourable weather conditions. We then began six weeks of sea exercises in pretty awful weather. All of our guns and A/S weapons had open mountings so working on, or firing them was quite painful in the arctic conditions prevailing. The northerly winds whipped up the sea, making us thankful for our stabilisers but the heavy seas still caused our exposed decks to be covered in ice; there were even ice floes in the sea and in Portland harbour. Coming into harbour late at night to secure to a buoy in the freezing cold was a particularly hazardous operation especially for the 'buoy jumper'. I recall the 1st Lt. coming into the enclosed bridge from the fo'c'sle after supervising the mooring, with his face covered in ice. Cuy Liardet, in charge of the diving team, says he can still feel the effects in his knuckles today, forty-six years later.

The anti-submarine, surface gunnery and damage-control exercises ran to schedule, but the weather often caused the postponement of anti-aircraft tracking and firing exercises. These were all eventually and satisfactorily completed before the end of the work-up. A work-up at Portland, particularly that of a new ship with the latest equipment, is a pretty hectic affair but this one, carried out in such atrocious conditions, was a real 'humdinger' and we all were mighty relieved when we completed the gruelling and exhausting 'passing-out' sea examination by the whole staff and received a 'Good' pass from FOST himself. The ship happily left Portland next morning for Portsmouth, but as I had to attend the Magistrates court at Weymouth with one of my young lads, the Navigating Officer asked me to drive his car back to the ship at Portsmouth taking the lad to court and onward with me. The roads in South Dorset had huge snowdrifts on each side; it was like driving through tunnels in the snow.

After a great Long Weekend at home with the family, we began two weeks of trials to prove the capability of a modern frigate (ie a Tribal or Leander) to operate a Wasp helicopter at sea, starting with a week of harbour trials at Portsmouth. Although it was still very cold on deck, we then carried out successful sea trials in the channel in which numerous landings, refuelling and take-offs were carried out from our elevated and quite small flight deck by an RN test pilot. These proved successful and cleared the way for frigates to carry a Wasp helicopter. We then returned to Portsmouth to store and prepare for our passage to the Middle East. A team of officers and senior ratings, led by the First Lieutenant made a day long visit to Fawley oil refinery and to a super tanker to familiarise ourselves with the scenario should we be called by a tanker in distress in the Persian Gulf. We were all amazed at how big the tanker was and what a mammoth task fighting a fire and salvaging such a ship would be, with or without the help of her crew. The ship's company went on leave in two watches and during mine we had some great news. We had to take Paul to Wimbledon to be

examined by his brain surgeon who afterwards told us he had completely recovered and, turning to Eileen said, in Paul's hearing, "You must not mollycoddle him, you must let him live a normal active life and, when he is old enough, there is no reason why he shouldn't play Rugby".

On 5th April 1963, after a fond farewell from Eileen and the children, I returned aboard and the ship set sail for the Gulf.

Nubian made brief stops at Gibraltar and Malta where we were visited by various dignitaries including the husband of the lady who had (just) launched the ship, Admiral Sir Derek Holland-Martin, CinC. I visited my chum Don Fraser and his wife Joan and daughter Janet, who were living in a MQ. On passage to Port Said we diverted to Tobruk to land an AB by helicopter to the local RAF hospital. After passing through the Suez Canal in a sandstorm we emerged at Port Suez to a welcome from HMS Loch Fyne the frigate from which we were taking over on the station. Seeing their tanned torsos as we passed at a distance, and they began to steam happily north up the canal, a pallid and innocent Nubian asked, "Why are they wearing lifejackets?" as we set off southward down the Red Sea. At around 1930 on that Sunday evening, as we were passing a fully laden northbound tanker, we suddenly had a complete power failure. The main circulator pump stopped dead causing the steam propulsion and electrical generator to fail. The sudden automatic transfer of the electrical load to the Gas Turbine driven Generator caused it to trip leaving the ship powerless. Our 'cunning plan' hatched at Fawley a few weeks earlier, to rescue and salvage a nice fat tanker and earn lots of prize money, received a kick in the teeth when the passing tanker asked the blacked-out Nubian via a signalling lanp: "Can we help you?" We embarrassingly, but politely declined her kind offer, started up the Gas Turbine

Propulsion plant, the GT Generator and Diesel Generator and resumed our passage. Our steam plant, normally used on passage, ran on Furnace Fuel Oil whereas the GT plant ran on Diesel fuel and we had insufficient Dieso to get us to Aden so we had to stop at Massawa in Eritrea where from railway wagons we embarked, by hand pump, enough Dieso to get us to Aden. This took 24 hours and gave us time to meet a few real Nubians in their native habitat. We eventually arrived at

Aden to be met by the Flag Officer Middle East and, whilst the new circulating pump was being fitted, we had a chance to do some duty-free shopping. I bought a new camera and the photo, shown here, shows me, without a beard for the last time, writing home before we left Aden. A few days later we entered the gulf and enjoyed the first of many 'banyans' (picnics with beer) on an uninhabited desert island, before arriving at Bahrain and berthing on the Mina Sulman Jetty. The temperature was very high and we were all most grateful for air-conditioning and for the use of HMS Jufair's cool open-air swimming pools.

I was not required to carry out Bridge Watchkeeping duties in HMS Nubian but regularly carried out the duties of Officer of the Day at sea and at anchor or alongside and, on several occasions, Officer of the Patrol. I also once acted as Liaison Officer for the state visit of the flagship of the Ethiopian navy to Bahrain and had to make all the arrangements and collect their money from the local bank and deliver it to the ship on arrival together with the social programme I had to supervise, throughout their visit. Both the Captain and the Executive Officer of the ship were Norwegian Naval Officers and I thoroughly enjoyed this unusual 'Diplomatic' task in which I met the Ruler of Bahrain and all of the VIPs in the Sheikdom. I had to smile at the all-male cocktail party given in the ship's seaplane hangar, when the Sheik's younger nephews kept sliding away into a side compartment for a quick 'noggin' unseen by their elders, all of whom were strict Muslim teetotallers.

I remember my first duty as OOD. The first in the queue to draw his mess' rum issue was the Corporal i/c of the Royal Marine's Barracks, as the RM's mess was known. Later, with the issue almost complete, I saw him rejoin the queue and when it was his turn again, he saluted smartly and thrust forward the mess rum 'fanny' (billy can) and said: " One tot too many in my mess Sir!" Neither the Stores PO, nor the 'Rum Bosun', or I had ever heard of such an admission and were flabbergasted. After recovering my composure I thanked him and took the 'extra' tot of '2 in 1' and poured it back into the rum tub and invited the corporal to witness it being ditched. As the grandson of a Royal Marine I had always admired the discipline of the Royals and this incident seemed to demonstrate this quality. At lunch I told the OCRM and he said "Beware, this corporal is renowned throughout the Corps as an accomplished confidence-trickster who probably added enough water to the issue to make up that extra tot so that he could demonstrate his integrity and get you on his side". Later in the commission, he ran into big trouble, was disrated and was moved to another ship.

 I was the OOD when we visited Khasab and was involved in the official welcome given to the Wali and his sons as they came aboard. Even the youngest of these carried a long ancient rifle. But I noticed that several were clearly suffering from an eye disease common among the gulf Arabs. During our year on the station we visited many small states and were well received, particularly our doctor Mike Davies who, with his Leading Medical Assistant (LMA), provided the only medical care available to many of the poor male villagers along the

Batinah Coast. The men flocked to receive attention but would not allow him to look at, let alone treat their sick women.

Although Bahrain had oil, the only small really oil-rich state in the gulf in 1963 was Kuwait and our visit in high summer with its universal use of air-conditioning was a great success. Later, I noticed that most of the schools and hospitals in the less affluent states had been, "Donated by the Government of Kuwait". I once asked an American oil prospector at our cocktail party during our first visit to Muscat, "What's it like when you strike oil?" He replied, "Hell, do you know I've been drilling for the stuff for thirty years and never found any yet!" Within a year he struck oil in Abu Dubai and went on to find more in the neighbouring states, many of which are now oil-rich. In Muscat there was a hospital run by a husband and wife team of American Missionary Doctors. They also ran a Leper colony adjacent to the hospital. I have never met such a dedicated pair of doctors and after we were shown around their charges, Nubian's ship's company took them to heart. In Bahrain the local hospital paid donors for blood. However, no one from Nubian would sell theirs but instead, during each of the three visits we made to Muscat, every one of our many blood donors gave a free pint, taken personally by one of the two 'saintly' American doctors. The Nubians' blood was used on patients within 24 hours because the

blood-count of the local Arabs was too low for them to give blood and the hospital totally relied on visiting ships for blood. Muscat was a fascinating old Arab Sultanate with some fearful customs. Anyone out of doors after dark had to carry a lantern, or risk being thrown into the old Marani Fort, a medieval jail, and all convicted thieves had their right hand cut off. As the left-hand was only used for one purpose, and was sat on whilst eating, this punishment was 'a fate worse than death'. I took this photo of the Fort returning Nubian's salute on the day after our first arrival, on a Friday. The local shops preferred to be paid in Maria Theresa Thalers, large silver coins which the local Omanis and Bedouin had adopted as a trusted currency in the late 17$^{th}$ century, the story being they liked the look of Maria's bosoms. The present coins had of course been much more recently minted and were attractive, so I brought two in mint condition home and they are still often worn as silver pendants by Eileen and Sally.

Shortly after our first arrival at Bahrain, Mrs Kyrle-Pope the wife of the Senior Naval Officer Persian Gulf (SNOPG} invited the officers of Nubian to a tea party she was holding for the wives of several local Arab traders who would be appearing, for the first time, out of purdah. I wrote back a 'Much regret unable' letter to the good lady explaining that I had 14 days of beard growth at the time and was not really presentable. However she insisted that I come and so, just meeting the Captain's rule that leave was stopped until I looked as if I was growing a beard rather than needing a shave, I duly went, along with several of my messmates. The ladies concerned were all middle-aged and dressed accordingly, and terribly shy at this first venture to a 'mixed' gathering with western men in attendance. None of them spoke English but all of them could speak French. So diplomatically and somewhat haltingly, the Nubians made small talk with the Arab ladies for an hour. Apparently this pioneering venture into western society by ladies, previously restricted to female company and their husbands, was a success. During our subsequent visits to Bahrain the increasing liberalisation of the local womenfolk was noticeable with most of them abandoning the veil and, when shopping with their children, being accompanied by their husbands. The Souk (Arab market) in Manama was very popular with all of the Nubians for you could buy genuine Persian carpets, ornate brass Arab coffee pots and all sorts of other Middle Eastern mementoes quite cheaply.

We played a lot of sport during our one year foreign tour and most of it at Bahrain where the facilities were good although Soccer, Rugby Cricket and Hockey pitches were just marked out areas of desert. I made good use of the pools at Jufair playing water polo and swimming. Robin Rankin the ship's Gunnery officer and I had a party-piece diving stunt with which we always ended up our visit to the officers' pool. We stood together

*Don (centre) playing in goal at Jufairn*

on the edge of the high, about 12 feet, diving board, with our backs to the pool holding a palm branch and one of the mess would shout "Timber" and we would fall backwards letting go of the branch as we hit the water. One day, after many successful dives, something went badly wrong. The water was only about 6 feet deep and it was our practice to hit the bottom with our hands, push off and surface. Somehow, this time I grazed the bottom with my nose and when I surfaced I was bleeding profusely from a long cut right down the length of the bridge of my nose. Fortunately Mike, our doctor, was present, and put in a row of stitches that remain visible to this day. We sailed next morning and when we returned a few days later the diving boards of both pools had been removed so I was unwittingly responsible for the loss of this popular facility. Shame on me.

During a visit to Ras al Khaimah we were invited by the British-officered Trucial Oman Scouts to a 'Mutton-Grab' with

some of the local tribesmen. In fact, the meal comprised a whole cooked goat with saffron rice. We ate sitting on our left hand on the ground in a large tent with one of our Arab hosts on each side of us and the goat and bowls of rice before us. Following their lead, we tore with our right hand the delicious and tender meat from the goat, wrapped it in rice and ate it. Afterwards, and incongruously, we were offered a bowl of tinned peaches and, with our right hand still covered in rice and goat's meat, reached into the bowls of peaches. I have to admit they still tasted very nice. We then had small cups of very hot coffee and, having been briefed beforehand by Major Jock Wilson of the TOS, drank two cups each, one cup being taken by our hosts as indicating we didn't like it and three that we were greedy. After this men-only lunch, we were invited by our hosts to watch the mating of two camels as a form of entertainment. We were then taken under escort by the Scottish Major, who wore a red and white spotted headdress, was very sun tanned but had blue eyes, to a scene of dispute between two neighbouring tribes. Soon we heard rifle fire and became a bit concerned but 'Jock' said "Don't worry, they are the world's worst shots". He told us to get out of the land rover and sit on the sand on the lee side of the vehicle and then shouting loudly in Arabic to the two adversaries to stop firing, calmly walked forward and called the two sides together. We then joined them and witnessed him, more or less amicably. settling the dispute between the two heavily-armed sides. We Nubians were most impressed.

We made two visits to Karachi and during the first one in July 1963, seven officers took the opportunity of a free air travel warrant to go to Lahore 800 miles inland. We flew there in a Fokker Friendship airliner of PIA and thoroughly enjoyed our short visit to the Punjab. The 1st Lieutenant and Navigator went on to visit the NW kingdom of Swat but Guy Liardet, Mike Davies, Jack Harris and I toured Lahore marvelling at the Shalimar Gardens and the Great Mosque and, though it was very hot, we had a great time. Back in Karachi we enjoyed the luxury of the Karachi club.

*Guy, Mike & Jack, !6.07.63) Great Mosque, Lahore*

Four months later, after taking part in a Central Treaty Organisation Exercise with over 40 ships from five countries, including 3 Tribals and 3 Minesweepers from the Gulf, 3 Diesel-driven frigates and the carriers HMS Ark Royal and USS Franklin Roosevelt and 3 USN cruisers, we were back alongside in Karachi, but with the cruisers and carriers anchored outside, On arrival I was given the duty of Officer of the RN shore patrol for the first night and, together with sailors drawn pro rata from the RN ships alongside, was picked up by Pakistan naval transport and taken to their Naval HQ at 2000. After being briefed by the Pakistan Naval Provost Marshal and briefing our respective Petty Officers of the patrol, the duty USN Commander and Lt Cdr of their patrol and I were taken in the Provost Marshall's land rover on a tour of Karachi's likely problem areas that night with hundreds of sailors ashore after a busy spell at sea. Naturally the city's red light district featured prominently in our itinerary and our host really knew his city and showed the three of us the worst of it. We saw men of all of the visiting navies in some revolting places and situations and had to send a number of them back to their ships under escort, but no more than expected. At about 0100, things had quietened down and we returned to the HQ. The four of us were sitting together chatting and enjoying a coffee when an ashen-faced Petty Officer came in and agitatedly spoke in Urdu to the PM who jumped to his feet and told the USN Commander, "I have terrible news Sir, your President has been assassinated". All hell then broke loose; I offered my condolences before the American officers left with their large patrol and all of the transport to collect the US personnel still ashore. After briefing the RN patrol and warning them that we would have a long wait for transport, we sat in the PN HQ until about 0530 when we were taken back to our ships. As I came aboard, all was quiet and the Quartermaster and sentry had heard nothing, so I went to the Captain's cabin and woke him with the momentous news. Later that morning all of the USN ships weighed anchor and sailed. Shortly afterwards we too sailed back to Bahrain. Soon after our arrival we attended a solemn Requiem Mass at the Catholic Church in

Manama where they had a coffin draped in the Stars and Stripes with a large framed photograph of the late President Kennedy standing in front. We marched there wearing full white uniforms with swords and medals and I remember how very upset our Goans were at the 'funeral service'. Everyone seems to remember where they were when President Kennedy was assassinated. In truth, I was being given a conducted tour of the brothels of Karachi!

Except during the daily Armament Quarters our quite sophisticated weapon systems were rather underused due to a lack of targets in the Gulf. We seldom had a submarine and only one period with a Pilotless Target Aircraft (PTA] in the whole of our deployment. My recent experience with the Attack Teachers in HMS Vernon made me realise that, in the circumstances, and, in the absence of shore A/S Warfare units on the station, our Command and A/S Warfare teams were likely to become 'rusty'. What we needed was a computer capable of continuously producing the relative bearing and range of a synthetic submarine from the ship's and target's course and speed, in conjunction with an up to date plot showing own and submarine's position. My familiarity with Gunnery fire-control and radar plotting tables provided me with the solution.

We had a basic Operator Trainer that provided an 'echo' which marked the A/S 170 attack Sonar's Range and Bearing recorders and Display unit. However, although the relative range and bearing of the synthetic submarine was adjustable, it was nigh impossible to realistically simulate the changes in these which would occur in an A/S warfare situation. I realised that this Trainer Unit could be linked by sound-powered telephone headsets and earphones at the (surface) Gunnery Fire-control table and at the two JYA radar plotting tables. Synthetic own-ship's course and speed could be made available to the FC table, both JYA tables and the A/S 170. Together these simple modifications would provide the ship with its own A/S Warfare Attack Teacher for use in harbour, at sea on a steady course, or when free to manoeuvre. My plan was to use the Local Operations Plot (LOP) as the monitoring and controlling table run by the 'instructing' officer i/c of the exercise. The ship's Command Team would man the Action plot and the Sonar and Mortar Mk 10 crews would close up as normal. If my idea worked, it would allow the ship's own equipment to be used to carry out realistic Command and A/S warfare training, in the absence of submarines and shore training facilities.

I put the idea to my boss, Jack Harris, who was supportive, gave me a free-hand to develop and engineer it and, with the help of the Chief TASI and a young Control Mechanic, and the keen support of our outstanding TAS Officer (later Rear Admiral) Guy Liardet, it was put together and proved viable. Jack suggested that I call it by the acronym Syntax (Synthetic Tactical Anti-Submarine Exercise).

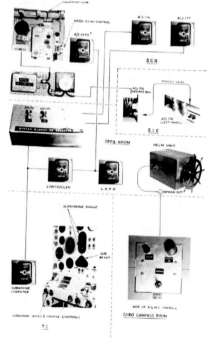

The prototype Syntax was demonstrated successfully to the Captain, whose enthusiastic approval led to an invitation to the Third Sea Lord, Vice-Admiral Sir Michael Le Fanu, who was visiting the Middle East Station at the time, to watch a full blown Command Team and A/S Warfare Training exercise. The Admiral showed a keen interest and asked me lots of pertinent questions afterwards, pronounced his support for Syntax and endorsed it. We used Syntax in harbour and at sea on passage in the Middle East and later in home waters and I produced the necessary drawings.

A year after its invention, while the ship was in dock after our return from Lisbon, I took my son and his chum camping in the New Forest for a weekend. One night in my tent I woke up with a very simple method of extending the scope of Syntax to include the passive sonar A/S 176, the medium range Sonar A/S 177 and the A/S Helicopter weapon system MATCH, ie the whole of a frigate's A/S warfare equipment. I amended the drawings to Mod 1, and updated the Nubian Syntax installation, also improving the 'Own ship's' steering, and proved the changes at sea and in harbour. This Mod 1 system was fitted in HM Ships Phoebe and Falmouth and other ships including an Indian frigate, at a material cost of less than £50 per ship and 2 man weeks for the manufacture of the small units and their connection to the existing system. Later, I was delighted to learn that Syntax had earned me a substantial award from the Herbert Lott Trust fund for inventions. A detailed description of Syntax Mod 1 and its scope and use was published in November 1967 in HMS Dryad's magazine the ND bulletin.

In October 1963 Nubian crossed the Equator and though I had been through the ceremony and punishments meted out by King Neptune once before, and there were plenty of first-timers, I still had to suffer his forfeits. We were on our way to the Seychelles, and the lush vegetation of Mahé and the delights of Victoria were very welcome after our months surrounded by desert sands. Mahe's skyline now sported a giant 'golf ball' aerial and the islands were beginning to open up to tourists but there was still no airfield and only one flying boat in and out a week. Prices seemed to be higher than during my last visit four years earlier and there seemed to be less blatant immorality, but it was still a great run-ashore, the fishing was magnificent and I particularly enjoyed a short trip in a three-masted schooner in full sail with Marine Carlson. After 5 days in Mahé, the 'Garden of Eden', we set sail for Mombasa, another place I had visited in 1959. This time I palled up with an Inspector in the Kenyan police at our first night cocktail party and he and his charming wife kindly took care of me for quite a lot of the three weeks we spent there, showing me many local sights I had missed before. I took them to Supper and Sunday night cinema onboard a couple of times, which they thoroughly enjoyed, and out to dinner to the Mombasa club on the last night there and they came aboard for a farewell 'nightcap' afterwards.

We went back into blue uniform at Bahrain on the 15th December and had Sunday divisions. A photograph of me, taken then appears on the right. A few days later we were back in tropical rig again on our way to Bombay for Christmas.

As during earlier separations, Eileen and I wrote to each other every day but this time, once a week, I enclosed a small audio tape for the children. It started with a few bars of 'Scherazade' and then I told them a story about where the ship had been - in which we always ran into Sinbad the Sailor. Sally tells me she still fondly remembers those stories of over 40 years ago. Eileen then recorded messages from her and the children's to me and sent the tape back in the next letter. We had three or four of these tapes in circulation and they proved a great morale booster during our year apart. At the start of Nubian's first commission, Jack Harris took the post of Cinema Officer and gave me responsibility for the Ship's Radio Entertainment (SRE) which I pretentiously decided to call the Nubian Broadcasting Corporation or NBC as it became known, I had the acronym NBC carved to clip on our 'outside microphone' to add a touch of class every time we were addressed by a VIP. Imagine my disappointment when I saw the photographs taken at the ship's commissioning, which I was unable to attend, to see that the letters NBC had been put on the wrong way round so that they faced the speaker and not the audience and the camera! The importance of NBC increased when we left the UK and once we were in the Gulf I think it is fair to say that it became vital to the ship's company's morale. I managed to persuade a number of Nubians to regularly act as Disc Jockeys, to compere 'chat shows', give live sports reports, a nightly epilogue, VIP interviews and a review of the English newspapers, taken from the daily signal from Whitehall, generally from the Sun or Daily Mirror. Apart from scheduling these programmes my only personal contribution was to write the daily ship's news which was broadcast every night at 1800 and began with the opening bars of Richard Rogers' stirring 'Song of the High Seas' and was introduced with the words "Good Evening Gentlemen, here is the news from NBC", delivered by our silver-tongued announcer REM Derek Kimber. I was often required to add items to the script while Derek was reading earlier parts of the news bulletin, which started with news of the ship's programme, the days events and programme for the next day and immediate future and went on to report personal items submitted by individual Nubians. One morning I had my hair cut by the ship's barber and when I paid him and booked him for the next cut he told me that he was leaving the ship to fly home that afternoon, I said how fortunate he was to be going home early and wished him luck. I wrote in the script for the evening news a short article about how sorry we were to lose the services of our popular barber and how we all wished him good luck in his next job. Within seconds of this item of news being broadcast, the First Lieutenant was at the door of the NBC studio beckoning me to accompany him and the Doctor to the Captain's cabin. The Captain asked me how I knew that the barber was leaving the ship so I told him that the Petty officer concerned had told me himself that morning. The 'old man' then asked me if I knew why the barber was leaving and I said "No". There was an awkward pause before the First Lieutenant told me that the PO had been caught in a compromising situation with a young sailor and was being sent off the ship. Naturally I had no idea of this and said so. The First Lt. said that in future I would have to pass the script of the news to him for censoring before every broadcast. I said that I could not do that as it would destroy the independence and integrity of the evening news bulletin. After some discussion, the Captain agreed with my point but expected me to check with the appropriate Divisional Officer if I received a similar item of news in the future. *While I was writing this chapter, Councillor Derek Kimber, a survivor of the sinking of HMS Covrntry during the Falklands conflict, was Mayor of Gosport.*

Naturally, I received a number of complaints regarding NBC programmes , particularly on the type of music played. One

such comment was: "There is too much classical music like 'The King and I'.

NBC's greatest success in terms of audience participation was the 'Nubians' Choice' Christmas programmes compéred by the Captain's wife at Portsmouth and by the wife and daughter of the Air Attache to India and another  young lady at Bombay. At home the families of the Nubians had listened to taped messages from us and the music we had chosen for them at a gathering at Portsmouth a week before Christmas. Their written responses were read by the lady of the appropriate generation at Bombay on Christmas morning before the choice of music was played for the Nubian concerned. The programme generated considerable emotion and was very well received by all.

HMS Nubian anchored off the 'Gateway to India' steps, only a short boat trip away from the centre of Bombay on the 21$^{st}$ of December. At lunchtime on the first day we entertained officers from the Indian ships present including some aviators from the carrier Vikrant. When asked what type of aircraft he flew, one of the Indian pilots said "a Grumman Martlet", (a WW2 fighter). We choked on our drinks when he added "They're pretty good kites for wog-bashing". It transpired that they had recently been engaged in strafing some bothersome Pathan tribesmen on the Indian frontier.

During that party the Captain was asked by the CO of the new Indian Navy Leander class frigate, the Tulwar, for help with his sonar. Next morning at 0800, I went over to assess the problem and was horrified to see that the wardroom wall light shades were burnt by having too large a lamp fitted and the carpet was already badly worn after barely a year's use. I waited there for 30 minutes before the Electrical Officer appeared and then there was an ominous delay in finding the keys to the Sonar Instrument Space hatch and opening it. I could tell that the compartment and the Directing Gear compartment below had not been ventilated for a long time. The panels were running with condensation and the heaters were off. I sent over to Nubian for my Sonar Maintenance Artificer and requested that the Indian ship's Sonar team be put at our disposal throughout the time we would be working on the system. First, we had to dry out all of the panels, restore the internal heaters and then gradually switch on each unit repairing those found defective. Finally we set up first the A/S 170, then the A/S176 and finally the A/S 177. After two days of hard graft in the humid atmosphere, my Chief and I, helped by the Indian ratings, but hardly ever visited by their officers, we had all of it working and had 'Phased and Scaled' the A/S 170 computer. I turned the system over to the ship's officers but stressed the need to keep electronic equipment working, especially in the tropics, and went back to Nubian. Our Captain received a nice VMT (Very Many Thanks) signal but I regretfully suggested to him that, as soon as we left the Indian frigate, the sonar equipment power and ventilation would probably have been switched off and the hatch closed.

The local British and Anglophile Indian Communities looked after us very well, advising us on where to buy the best presents to take home, (I bought very good table and bed linen) and entertaining us in their homes on Christmas day. Bombay was a dry city and liquor could only be purchased by visitors, including sailors, who had declared themselves to be Alcoholics. Despite the stigma of this epithet most of us signed the form in order to present our ration of spirits to our generous hosts ashore. After Midnight mass ashore in the Catholic cathedral, I was invited by an Indian Lt. Cdr. and his wife, daughter and son, to spend Christmas Day with them. He picked me up in his car at the Gateway to India after NBC's special Christmas programme, and took me to his delightful home where I enjoyed a very pleasant day with a charming Indian family. I gave my kind host my visiting alcoholic's ration of spirits and some chocolates and sweets, fresh from the NAAFI that morning, for his family. He drove me back in time to catch the 2200 boat and before going up to my cabin I decided to have a nightcap in the mess. When I opened the door I thought I was on the wrong ship. All of the lights were dimmed but, standing behind the well lit bar were four visions of loveliness, a dusky lass and three blondes. One of the blondes poured out a glass of champagne and beckoned me and, after pinching myself and rubbing my eyes to make sure I wasn't dreaming, I saw in the semi-darkness of our very spacious wardroom that half of my messmates and several other male and female guests were sitting chatting. I accepted the bubbly from Heidi, a German air stewardess and learnt that our surprise guests were from British Airways, Lufthansa, and Lebanese aircraft on a stop-over for the day and delighted to come to a party on a ship. I finally went to bed at 0100 feeling that I had enjoyed as good a Christmas Day away from home as I could possibly have. On Boxing Day, I was a dinner guest, with Captain Jamieson, of the Head of the Pakistan branch of Phillips, the Dutch Electrical Company, at his luxurious mansion and enjoyed a splendid evening. The Captain, a very generous host himself, made a habit of inviting each of his officers in turn to share his table at dinner onboard, an honour and pleasure I had enjoyed several times and knew him to be a great raconteur. During our five days in Bombay our Goan cooks and stewards were given the opportunity, and railway fare to go home to reassure themselves that their families were safe after the recent annexation by India of the former Portuguese colony.

We arrived at Cochin on 29th December and anchored in the river. Nothing had changed in the four years since my last visit but I did see and learn more about the local people and their customs. An umbrella, more often used as a parasol, was a sign of one's status and most statues of Christ had him holding aloft a golden umbrella. Kerala was politically communist yet it was the most Catholic in India and it also had the highest rate of literacy in the country. I found the locals, most of whom were terribly poor, to be very friendly. Going around the network of canals by ship's boats it was amusing to see neighbours chatting to each other whilst sitting in their 'thunder boxes' mounted on stilts over the canal, and waving cheerfully to us as we passed. On New Years Eve we went to a formal party held in the Indian Naval HQ at which Indian girls in beautiful traditional dress gracefully performed colourful dances. At midnight the New Year was welcomed in the traditional manner with, Auld Lang Syne. On January 3rd we set sail back to the Gulf and resumed our normal patrol routine but this time in 'blues' as it was unusually cold there that 'winter'.

Nubian was the only serviceable Tribal of the three on the station at this time so we had to remain in the Gulf. The high efficiency and availability of the ship's modern marine engineering equipment was largely due to the leadership, experience and hands – on efforts of our tireless MEO Vic Jones who was most deservedly promoted Commander. In mid January we received a distress call, not from an anticipated big fat laden tanker, but from a dredger which was adrift in a NE gale to the SW of Bahrain. We passed sustenance across to her and stayed with her all night in the storm until she was taken in tow by a salvage tug next morning. That was to be the closest we ever came to earning prize money! We then went north to Kharg Island in Iran for the official opening of the Naval Base there by the Shah of Persia. It was very cold on the 'big day' and we wore greatcoats. That day, 100 miles to the south in Bahrain, for the first time in decades, there was a frost.

We next took part in an exercise in the gulf together with the submarine HMS Anchorite and the newly repaired Eskimo and Gurkha. The three Tribals led by Nubian, carried out a live A/S Mortar firing at a synthetic submarine at a depth of 60 feet 500 yards ahead of us and around 750 yards slant range ahead and to port and starboard of Eskimo and Gurkha, so that all nine bombs exploded simultaneously around the 'target' position. Anchorite, carrying several observers including our Doctor, was steaming at periscope level on the same course and at the same speed as the frigates and was closed up at action stations and shut down for a depth charge attack, and was some 500 yards astern of us so that her crew, could experience a mortar firing. The bombs exploded with a spectacular plume of water and Mike Davies reported on return to Nubian that it was quite an event down below with various leaks and equipment failures and even the regular crew showed some concern.

There was little or no night life in the largely Muslim Middle East station so the Nubians looked for other ways to while away the long evenings. NBC did its best to fill the gap as did the ship's cinema and library, and fishing helped, but the most beneficial pastime was undoubtedly the pursuit of learning as the key to advancement. There was no shortage of candidates for the evening classes run by Jan Pole the Supply Officer, 'Sandy' Fiddes the Navigator, Jack Harris and me. I took the candidates seeking to qualify educationally for Leading Hand and RM Corporal and gained a lot of pleasure in getting lads who had failed to reach the 11 plus standard before they left school at15, to achieve this standard in English and Maths, through their own efforts. One of my students was particularly thrilled to pass for LH and at the same time to become able to write a letter to his daughter, who was at university.

On one of our regular patrols of the Batinah coast, the minesweeper with us encountered a small, heavily overloaded motor vessel found to be carrying 120 pilgrims who were clearly in great distress. A boarding party, including our Doctor, was put aboard and found that four of the passengers were dead. The Master and Mate were arrested and the small vessel was taken in tow to Dubai where it was learned that the poor pilgrims had been conned by the pair of rogues into paying to be landed near Mecca but were going to be landed on the gulf coast over a thousand miles of desert away from the holy shrine. The perpetrators of this crime received short shrift from the local Arab court in Dubai and, after treatment in the local hospital, the poor would-be pilgrims were repatriated to Pakistan.

In February 1964 we took part in a Middle East exercise in which, besides Anti-Submarine exercises, we had day and night surface and bombardment firings and, AA shoots against PTAs {Pilotless Target aircraft). These were 'flown' by an old school chum of mine, Lt. Eric Beats and although they had proved suitable practice targets for homing missiles, their erratic, model aircraft, flight paths made it difficult for fire-control systems designed to use the rates of change of movement of an attacking aircraft to predict its 'future' position. In consequence, the two Tribals, whose MRS3 gunnery systems were working well, failed to down any of them.

Early in our service in the Gulf we found that the ship's side grey gradually turned a dirty brown colour due to being bombarded with fine sand during the post dawn and dusk storm caused by the desert warming up and cooling down rapidly. Every month we had to give it a good wash down, but the aerials, whose performance was affected by the layers of fine sand, could not be washed in salt water from the fire-main. These were washed down with fresh water using an immersion pump lowered into one of our FW tanks. The chap cleaning the huge 965 Aerial on the masthead, wore a helmet because great clods of mud fell from it during this process.

Our last major event in the Gulf was the Admiral's Inspection, but first we had to give the ship's exterior and interior a good clean up and get all of our paperwork up to date. We suffered the usual intensive harbour drills and Ceremonial Divisions and a long sea day in which we demonstrated our warship capabilities. The whole inspection went well and we got a good report from the Flag Officer Middle East, Rear Admiral John Scotland, who stayed onboard for

*Don is 2nd from the right in front row*

the photo shown above, before taking passage with us as far as Aden, on our journey home. We made brief stops at Muscat and Aden and were soon emerging from the Suez canal at Port Said and steaming west through the Med. A brief stop in Grand harbour to land a sick sailor and on to Gibraltar for last minute shopping on 28th March, before the final leg to Portsmouth, where we arrived on a damp 1ˢᵗ April.

My reunion with Eileen, Sally and Paul, shown here coming aboard, was one of the happiest days in my life. They all looked terrific and this time Paul remembered me. Eileen had sold our Morris 1000 just after I left for the gulf and had banked the money. I had saved quite a bit and, after discussing the purchase of our next car in our daily letters, Eileen had chosen and arranged delivery of a fairly new and very smart Hillman Minx which was on the jetty waiting for me to drive the family home. By the time I returned from a blissfully happy two weeks leave at home with the family at Purbrook, our popular Captain Ian Jamieson had left the ship and been relieved by Captain Ed(ward) Brown an Observer, who proved to be equally friendly and proficient.

In early May HMS Nubian began the home leg of her commission with a plum visit to Lisbon for a week ending in the social activities  and safety duties of Guard Ship for the very first Tall Ships Race. I was given the role of Entertainment Officer and my task was to organise tours and co-ordinate the offers of hospitality for the ship's company received from the local residents. Henceforth I was to be very busy at the first night cocktail party, wherever we went, bent on encouraging local Brits or Anglophiles to invite our lads out We sailed alone to the Portuguese capital and carried out a Syntax and other exercises on route before arriving at  the mouth of the river Tagus. It was fine and sunny as we passed

Prince Henry the Navigator's monument and berthed alongside quite close to the city centre. Unsurprisingly, the guests at our cocktail party were more interested in the forthcoming race than in entertaining sailors from the Guard Ship so I drew a blank. I therefore had to resort to cadging as many tour guides, train timetables and other information as possible for the Nubians to enable them to take full advantage of our visit. We toured the city, admiring the mosaic pavements and some very impressive buildings, untouched by war, and enjoyed the night life, even growing to like the rather sad-sounding Fada music. I took a group of Nubians to Estoril by train for a day, noticing the beautiful wild red geraniums blooming all along the track. We all enjoyed the sights of this up-market resort, the doyen of whose society at the time was the ex-King of Italy. I also organised a coach trip to Fatima, in my capacity as Senior Catholic. This was very well supported, particularly by our Goan shipmates. We left Lisbon early in the morning and drove straight there. During this trip of about 100 miles we saw quite a bit of the beautiful countryside and its people. My lasting impression was that, in those days anyway, Portugal's natural beauty was saddened by the old tradition that all women wore black mourning dress for seven years after the loss of any male member of their a family. This resulted, particularly in the rural areas, in most of the females over 16 being perpetually dressed in black. We arrived at Fatima at 0900 and, being out of season for pilgrimages, had it to ourselves and were given a special mass and personal tour of the Basilica and shrine and were even introduced to the surviving sister of one of the children to whom Our Lady appeared in 1917. Several of our Portuguese speaking Goans were thrilled to talk to this old lady. The visit to Fatima was a moving experience for all of us. On the way back to Lisbon we stopped at the picturesque fishing village of Navarre and saw the fishermen and their brightly coloured pulling whalers launch into the Atlantic surf. Back aboard Nubian we hosted a series of parties for the race participants and officials, local VIPs, including Nubar Gulbenkian and the media, until we sailed and took up station off the mouth of the Tagus to supervise the start of the Tall Ships Race. The ships were a magnificent spectacle and, as they passed us in full sail, we had the best view. After the last of the Tall Ships disappeared over the horizon, we set off northwards

just off the Portuguese coast for our next programmed port of call, Londonderry. We had only travelled a few miles when suddenly something struck our propeller and we began vibrating and had to stop. We put the ship's divers down to find out what was wrong and they found that one of the tail shaft's fairing plates had come off and had struck the propeller damaging it. We were only able to steam at 4 knots which, with a fairly strong westerly wind pushing us sideways, placed us at risk of being driven on to the lee shore. The First Lieutenant suggested we hoist sails to supplement our motive power and all hands turned to and hoisted the fo'c'sle awning as a foresail and the quarterdeck awning as a mizzen sail. The result was an increase of 2 ½ knots in speed but it was found that the mizzen sail made

it difficult to steer so it was lowered and the ship made a forward speed of 6 knots with just the foresail and screw. This was just enough to keep us at a safe distance from the Iberian coast and helped us cross the Bay of Biscay, during which a passing French submarine, presumably unable to believe the periscope view of a modern British Frigate under sail, surfaced and photographed the phenomenon. We obviously couldn't go to Londonderry for an Atlantic A/S exercise as planned and instead were told to proceed to Portsmouth for a docking to replace the fairing plate and propeller.

During this unscheduled but, to us Pompey natives, very welcome visit, Sally celebrated her 11th birthday. Marine Brian Carlson, who had looked after me so very well for two years, offered to help run her birthday party and entertained Sally and all her friends and organised all of the party games. This good-looking young and friendly Action Man who was a trained parachutist and frogman, proved a huge success and made the party, so much so that Sally and her friends still remember, over 40 years later, "that nice Marine", shown behind them in the photo below with Sally in the centre.

Following more than three years with the ship, my boss, mentor and great friend, Jack Harris left and was relieved by Lt. Cdr Peter Lipscomb. Having missed the 'serious' part of the home leg we picked up the jolly part again with a visit to Amsterdam. After passing through the huge North Sea Lock, which we shared with a huge tanker and a magnetic influence causing our Gyro-Magnetic Compass to go awry, we berthed right in the middle of the city, close to the main railway station.

*The Murdoch family at 55, St John's Avenue, Purbrook in May 1964*

During the first night cocktail Party, the Dutch being the most anglophile people on earth, our guests bombarded me with offers to entertain our sailors. These kind invites included one from  the Burgomaster of Amsterdam to a Supper Dance for 100 of them with free beer, at one of the city's best hotels. I was also provided with lots of tourist information and complimentary tickets for museums and other places of interest, and guide books in English I was also strongly advised to recommend that our sailors took advantage of the good bicycle-hiring facility at the railway station where, for a £1 a day you could have your own wheels to get around the city. All of the Nubians thoroughly enjoyed the visit, most of them taking full advantage of the easy cycling and the generosity of our hosts. Needless to say the Civic Supper and Dance at the

Krasnapolski Hotel was heavily oversubscribed and so we had a public draw in the main dining hall. However, I have to say that with true naval prudence, I weeded the names put in the hat to avoid the evening being ruined by known trouble-makers. On the night of the event, I was Officer in charge of the patrol and was present at the entrance when our lucky lads arrived by coach and were met by 100 pretty Dutch girls, all of whom spoke English. They soon paired up and sat down together and started chatting. A good dance band began playing 1950 style 'Swing' music and a few of the keen dancers among the lads took girls up on the floor but most of them were happy to down as much free beer as they could first. So I went around each table side-whispering to them, "Come on lads, get up on the floor" which most did. All seemed to be going very well so I told the PO of the patrol that they could take off their armbands and join in the dance but to be prepared to act as a patrol if I called. I then returned to my seat at the Top table next to the Burgomaster and his wife. After a friendly supper I asked her for a dance and we went around the floor a few times enjoying a Foxtrot before going back to our seats facing the dance floor. Suddenly, one of our most notoriously badly behaved sailors, whom I knew had not been given a ticket to attend, but somehow had managed to get in, came lurching towards us in an aggressive manner and leaning over the table, demanded of Amsterdam's Leading Lady, "Give us a dance". I jumped to my feet and ordered him to "Get Away" and signalled the PO of the patrol. Then followed an embarrassing and difficult minute or so, as the PO and I restrained the rather large and very drunken sailor, until the patrol arrived on the scene. I sent him back to the ship under escort where it was found he had coerced one of his messmates into giving him his ticket for the dance. Friendly Anglo Dutch relations were very quickly restored, the Burgomaster and his wife accepted my apologies for the incident and the rest of the evening passed harmoniously, with all of the lads proving a credit to the ship and the country. After the band had played the two National Anthems and before the last waltz started, I thanked our charming and distinguished hosts and the City

Corporation for their generous party and then called the patrol to don their armbands and caps and stood with them at the door. As the lads walked to the door with their new Dutch girl friends, one of my EMs, who had been one of the first on the floor with a pretty Dutch lass and had spent the whole evening dancing with her and 'chatting her up', gave me a wink as if to say, "I'll be alright tonight". A few seconds later they were met by her big Dutch Daddy who said, "Thank you very much for looking after my daughter, Good Night" and, to the young lad's utter dismay, wheeled her away. All 100 of the well brought up young ladies were similarly chaperoned home by their devoted fathers. Notwithstanding the abrupt end to the expectations of several of Nubian's young sailors, the evening was considered by most to have been a huge success. Our visit to Amsterdam proved to be a fitting and memorable climax to this first commission after which we returned to Portsmouth in high spirits.

Before I was relieved by my former classmate and friend, Brian Green, I had one last social duty to perform, to organise the Ship's Dance at the Royal Sailors Home Club in Portsmouth. This proved to be a great and happy event. A few days later Sally boosted the family's already high morale, by skipping home waving a small piece of paper saying she had passed the '11 Plus Exam'. When I left HMS Nubian I had another pleasant surprise, my flimsy from Captain Brown said I had conducted myself to his, "special satisfaction".

I look back on my time in HMS Nubian with great affection. It was a happy ship, commanded successively, by two great Captains. I was very lucky to have in turn, two proficient, kind and considerate bosses, very professional fellow officers, all of whom were good friends and messmates, a great division of loyal and hard-working senior and junior ratings, and the services of a terrific Royal Marine steward. The wardroom, led by Murray Johnstone, was one of the two most comfortable and friendly of the many officers' messes I had the pleasure of membership.

# Chapter 16

## Portsmouth Fleet Maintenance Unit/Group

### September 1964 to June 1967

Two months of leave comprising the balance of leave owed me by my service in HMS Nubian, leave between appointments- a first for me, and 14 days summer leave, allowed me to enjoy a lot of prime time in high summer with the family. Eileen had done a grand job with the garden and bungalow during my absence and I had few outstanding jobs to do at home so we enjoyed a great time together.  Early in this holiday season, Sally was confirmed at Corpus Christi church by Bishop Thomas Holland. Interestingly, he appeared to have three doctorates but the first award listed wasn't a Doctor of Science but a DSC won on 'D Day', on the Normandy beaches.

 After the very best of summer breaks I joined the Fleet Maintenance Unit as the Electrical Officer. The FMU was based in a small workshop and office complex sited at the furthest point in Portsmouth dockyard from any of its gates, the NW wall. The officer in charge was a kindly Commander (E) Mervyn Lanyon, to whom I was responsible for assisting the ships' staffs in the repair and maintenance of their electrical, radar and radio equipment, in order to meet their operational programme. The Marine Engineering staff was led by a Lt Cdr, to whom an Ordnance Sub Lt and Shipwright Sub Lt reported. There were

about 120 in the unit altogether, 35 of whom, were mine: two Chief Artificers, 9 senior Artificers/ Mechanicians, a Chief Electrician, 6 POs, 8 Leading Hands and 9 EM/REMs, all of whom were experienced having recently come from ships. Some of the Artificers were weapons specialists in the latest gunnery, A/S and radar systems. I was also responsible for overseeing the refit of the local Squadron ships including the minelayer HMS Plover and an LCT, neither of which had an Electrical Officer, or posed much of a technical problem. I soon learnt that I had been blessed in the FMU with a top team of industrious and professional senior rates.

The bread and butter of our task was to help the ship's complete their Planned Maintenance within the prescribed time limit, during their Maintenance Period alongside. To facilitate this, most destroyers and frigates receiving our help were berthed on the NW wall or on nearby Fountain Lake jetty. This work was carried out during normal working hours 0800 to 1200 and 1300 to 1600. The FMU block was normally closed down by 1700 and as no one was required to do a duty, we all went home every evening. This was considered to be the reward for having been separated from our families in our previous job.

However, our most important and professionally satisfying role was to carry out the urgent repair of equipment affecting the operational capability of ships not necessarily undergoing a formal Maintenance Period. This work usually started on a Friday when, presaged by an Operational Defect signal (OPDEF), a ship required to be at sea the following Monday 'limped' into harbour with a major defect which civilian staff shortage, budgetary or other considerations, prevented the dockyard staff from tackling. When this happened I would receive a call from EEM (the Electrical Engineering Manager) asking me if my team could undertake the necessary work. I suppose that, on average during my 33 months with the FMU, elements of my staff worked every other weekend to meet this requirement and when they did I visited them on site each day and often had to don overalls and personally direct the work. I am proud to say that we always managed to remedy every electrical, weapons/ electronic, radar and radio task given us, before the ship's sailing deadline, even if it meant working for the whole weekend and all night to achieve this. Fortunately, I was able to give my willing and able staff, time-off in lieu, during the following week.

The officers of the FMU lunched in HMS Nelson's wardroom and I used to drive there and back but used my RN bike when visiting ships. One morning during the winter of 1964/5 I had a particularly irritating case of chilblains on my toes, a problem which had plagued me every winter since childhood. I was particularly busy so I sent my office EM to RNB Sickbay on my bike to get some of the black ointment they gave for it. The EM returned with two small tablets and said that was what the doctor prescribed, after looking at my medical records. I saw the MO in the wardroom bar at lunchtime and queried the prescription. He said, "Take one tablet after lunch and one going to bed tonight". I was incredulous. Those two tablets did the trick for I have never had a chilblain since. Apparently they increased my slightly slow heartbeat rate a little, and thus the blood supply vital to the toes and fingers.

At Easter 1965, Paul made his first Communion in the school chapel and is the centre boy in this photo with Mother Van Heems, the legendary football playing Head Mistress. Paul enjoyed games rather more than lessons.

Early one Monday I had to take one of my Leading Hands up to Stoke-on-Trent in my car as he had to appear at 1030 at the Magistrate's Court on a charge of Driving under the Influence. As his Divisional Officer I was required to attend. A policeman, consulting his notebook, reported at length, how he had seen the accused stagger out of a Pub searching his pockets for his car keys, had followed him to a nearby car park and waited until he put the keys in his ignition before arresting him. This was a Stipendiary Court and the kindly-looking Magistrate turned to me and asked if I had anything to say in support of the accused. I trotted out the standard: "He has been in the service for umpteen years and his conduct has always been Very Good" and then added " I thought the primary purpose of the Police was to prevent crime but the Policeman who arrested my Leading hand clearly waited until he had committed a crime, (that he could easily have prevented), before arresting him. A Police Superintendent sitting in the front of the court leapt to his feet with a livid face and bellowed, "You can't say that in court". The Magistrate half-smiled at me and said," I'm afraid you can't". I apologised. However, I'm glad I had said it, that it was recorded in the records and possibly in the local press and the Leading Hand received a slightly smaller fine. I hope the policeman received a ticking off for his lack of common sense. After leaving the court, realising that my journey back to Portsmouth would take me past my niece's boarding school at Stone in Staffordshire, I stopped in Stoke to buy a box of chocolates for her and set off with the sailor in the car. I drove into the grounds of the Convent school, parked and rang the doorbell on a heavy oak door. Eventually, a spy hole opened and a nun appeared and, rather surprised, (in the middle of England), to see a naval officer in uniform, asked me what I wanted. I said I was passing by and wondered if I could have a word with Mary Strickland-Scott. The little old Nun asked me who I was and I replied "Her Uncle". Then, following the unbolting of several locks and chains on a solid front door, I was ushered into a waiting room adorned with pictures of the Pope and various Saints, while the Nun went off to find Mary. I then realised I had left the box of chocolates in the car and went to get them only to find that I had been locked in the room. Eventually, the Nun reappeared with my sister's 15 year old daughter and together we went out to the car and collected the chocolates and had a brief chat. Mary was a talented pianist and her music teacher was a great-niece of Elgar and one of her classmates was a granddaughter of Tolkien. Henceforth I could claim to have been locked in a nunnery.

Paul was due to leave the Convent school, which only took boys to 8 years, and, when we found that the local junior school class he would join had 48 pupils, we decided to send him to a Prep School at Chichester. During the Easter holidays of 1966, before he joined Oakwood, I took Paul and Sally swimming every day and he took to the water like a fish. At Pitt Street Baths on the last Sunday of the holiday, he passed the RN Swimming Test. His new school had a swimming pool and by the end of his first term there he was Junior Swimming Champion.

Back at work in the FMU, I generally received the utmost help and co-operation from ships' Electrical Officers and their staff, with one or two notable exceptions. One of which I will always remember. One Monday morning I had a telephone call from the Electrical officer of a Tribal class Frigate berthed at Middle Slip Jetty some distance from the FMU. He said he had a bit of a problem and asked if I could help. I cycled over and a very smart young officer met me and told me there had been a flood overnight. We walked to the hatch down to the Gearing Room and he pointed down and said "The flood is down there". Unaccompanied by the ship's Electrical Officer I went down the ladder to find that due to a young ME, instructed to open the sea valve, pump out the bilges, and close the sea valve, forgetting the latter. Overnight the compartment had quietly flooded all equipment below sea level Fortunately, none of the nine motors affected had been running at the time but the supplies to their starters and several junction boxes had been interrupted by fuses blowing when shorted by the sea water. I had dealt with a number of flood situations before and after assessing the remedial work necessary I came up the ladder to find the ship's s officer had gone to the wardroom for a cup of coffee. When he told me the ship was due to sail on the Thursday morning. I asked him what his Captain had said about this major operational defect. He told me that the CO was at home at Wickham and didn't know. Astounded, I impressed on a reluctant listener, the necessity of telling the 'old man' that his lovely ship was non-operational and then outlined the task ahead for his and my staff.

It took 54 continuous hours of work for the combined FMU and ship's electrical team to strip and decontaminate all of the electrical motors and replace their bearings and to thoroughly wash all of the starters and JBs with warm fresh water and dry them in situ. After successfully testing the last motor at 1800 on the Wednesday I sought out the Electrical Officer who was getting into Mess Undress in his cabin. I told him all his equipment was now operational again and the ship could sail on time the next day. He replied: "Good. I would give you a drink but I have to go and pick up my guest for a Cocktail Party". Although I visited the flood scene first thing each morning and on both evenings until the 'night-watch' had taken over and were well under way with the job, the ship's Figure-Head of Department never appeared on site to give technical advice or even moral assistance or refreshments for any of his own men or mine during that mammoth task. I suspect that, as an isolated relic of pre- WW2 social attitudes, this young gentleman never wore overalls or ever got his hands dirty. To do so, would be beneath his dignity. This dereliction of responsibility, or was he just being 'laid back', (ie lazy, unsure or incompetent or a bit of each), was fortunately rare among Engineer Officers and non existent among those of the Mechanical specialisations.

Years later when Head of General Electrical Training in HMS Collingwood, I used this incident in a lecture I gave to all

Officers as an example of how not to meet the professional responsibilities of an Officer, defined by Drake when he executed one of his officers for not 'mucking in' during his circumnavigation of the world:

"I will have the gentlemen haul with the mariners".

I am not suggesting that the head of department should always breathe down the neck of his Chiefs but do think that when there is a defect threatening the ship's operational programme, he should keep himself in close touch with progress and provide technical support or seek technical advice, make the repair policy decisions and should always provide the repair team with moral support and overnight refreshments as necessary.

While I was in the FMU we had three more major sea water floods caused by firemain defects and affecting compartments containing Electronic units. In each case the ship's staff had no idea how to save the situation and restore the ship's operational capability. My team already had the de-contamination of electrical equipment weighed off and soon we had mastered the best way of doing the same with thermal and micro-electronic units, with the ship's staff standing in fresh water showers and thoroughly washing the units and printed cards, and my lads spraying clean the cabinet sockets and wiring using fire extinguishers filled with warm distilled water from the ship's evaporators before drying the units with warm air. In each case the decontamination of all of the equipment was completed and the systems concerned were tuned and tested and found correct before the sailing deadline and the three Captains were delighted. One of them, the CO of a brand new HMNZS Leander class frigate, even presented me with the first Waikato tie to be given to a 'Pom'. 'After- sales' checks by the Cin-C 's staff showed that the equipments concerned were still working correctly two years later. Meanwhile the Fleet Staff Electrical Officer asked me to write down my decontamination procedure and it was published under the title 'Apres le Deluge' in the Naval Electrical Review. *Several years later I submitted a copy of this as a thesis with my successful application for chartered engineer status.*

Besides the limelight jobs described, I was personally involved in the fiddly overnight assembly of the aerial pillar wave-guide run on an AD frigate one freezing cold January night; and in the weekend supervision of the renewal of the journal bearings of a steering motor on an old destroyer. Both of these tasks were completed just before the scheduled sailing time.

However, it wasn't all work in the FMU. I was home almost every night to spend prime time with the family and to watch Paul play games at school and to take him to mass on Sundays. One Saturday we went to see him play soccer but couldn't see him on the pitch and were told he was playing rugby. Eileen nearly had a fit and, at half-time railed at him. Paul replied, "The Doctor in London said I could play rugby when I was old enough". Paul went on to have a trial for England as a schoolboy and to play rugby for Havant, and Hampshire.

Eileen and I also enjoyed the elegant Christmas and Summer Balls at HMS Nelson, and Cocktail parties there, in the Dockyard Staff Officers' Mess and onboard a number of ships in the harbour.

We decided to build an extension on to our bungalow and I drew up the plans. When it was completed we threw a party to christen it and our lovely new parquet floor was irreparably ruined by the stiletto heels of the lady guests on its opening night.

On Sunday 9th March 1967 I was called to repair the electric capstan of a Leander due to sail on the Monday and found the motor was burnt out. Close by, and nearing completion was HMS Andromeda, so I sought permission to take hers and fit it to the frigate. I worked up the chain until the top man at Northwood told me I would have to wait, as he was dealing with a major problem - the tanker Torrey Canyon had run aground off Lands End and was spilling tons of oil. He gave me the go-ahead that afternoon and the ship sailed on time.

One day I had a phone call from the Appointer asking me if I would like to join the crew of the first RN Polaris Submarine which had just been laid down. He said it would entail training for about nine months in America and then being stationed at Faslane for five years and going on alternate 4½ month-long submerged patrols, but my family could live in a married quarter near the base. He said "You won`t be a submariner but will be a Nuclear Weapons Engineer and will almost certainly be promoted". I said "Half of every 18 months submerged sounds like being a submariner to me!" He gave me a week to think it over but I replied that I would let him know within 24 hours. Next morning, after several hours of weighing the pros and cons with Eileen, I declined the offer. A few months later I received an appointment to the staff of the Flag Officer Sea Training at Portland, as a Sea-Riding Weapons Electrical Officer.

I enjoyed my long spell as a head of department in the FMU and learnt and practised a number of new techniques and had a great deal of job satisfaction. I was fortunate to have a most pleasant and considerate boss in Mervyn Lanyon and a very good team. I was pleased to recommend four of my artificers and mechanicians to take the examination for a commission and later delighted to hear they had been promoted. My period in the FMU also gave Eileen,

Sally, Paul and me a nice long and happy period of family and social life and enabled us to face up to my next and more demanding job.

# Chapter 17

## Flag Officer Sea Training, Portland

### Assistant Staff Weapons Engineer Officer Sea-Rider (L)

### June 1967 – June 1969

I was no stranger to Portland having twice served in ships of the local Training Squadron, or even to Work-Ups having been through the process there in three ships. However, I was advised on joining the staff of FOST that the working hours of a Sea Rider would not fit in with family life and it would not be worthwhile moving my family to a local MQ. Having earlier suffered the disruptive vagaries of ship's movements at Portland, Eileen and I agreed that I would live in HMS Osprey from Sunday to Thursday, for what was left of the night after returning from sea, and travel home on Friday and back on Sunday evening except every sixth weekend when I would be Duty Staff Technical Officer for the whole weekend. Shortly after joining the staff, the prefix to my naval title was changed from Electrical to Engineer and so I became an Engineer Lieutenant (L).

My boss was Commander (WE} Don Fletcher and, for my first six weeks, FOST was Rear- Admiral Plillip Sharp. There were four WE Sea- Riders, a Lt Cdr who normally handled the Work-Up of Cruisers and County class Missile Destroyers, and an L, OE and RE specialist who handled the frigates and destroyers between them but were called to the other ships if there was a specific problem, As the L specialist, besides full responsibility for the ships allocated to me, I also had to participate in the Damage-control exercises in all of the ships, including the large vessels and in the Gunnery exercises in all of the frigates and destroyers. I was also allocated four of the Dutch and two of the German ships though I had a Dutch and German Liaison Officer with me for their work-up exercises. During my two years as a Sea Rider at Portland, I was responsible for the work-up of the Weapons Engineering departments of 26 RN and allied ships and the weekly and final reports on their efficiency and that of their officers and principal senior ratings. These were vetted by my boss before being sent to the MOD and Captain of the ship.

I had a one-week overlap with my predecessor, Lt Cdr Jim Cleal and he gave me a good 'turn-over' taking me through the gambit of tasks that would occupy about 80 – 90 hours of every week henceforth. This phase included my first jackstay and helicopter transfer between ships and the conduct of a damage control exercise from the electrical standpoint and instruction of the ship's staff in the necessary remedial action. I also took part in the supervision of the equipment preparations for, and conduct of, gunnery and A/S exercises including firings, during the first half of ships' seven-week long work up. I also monitored the progress made by the crew of another ship halfway through its work-up. By then the ship's staff was becoming experienced in the use of their equipment and a Sea Rider's role changed from instructing to reporting on progress. In practice I was responsible for two ships per week, one in the first half of its work-up and the other in the second half; so I was involved straight away in both of the major roles of the Sea Rider.

Every ship starting Work-Up, arrived off Portland on a Friday morning and was boarded by Commander Sea Training (CST) and a strong team of Sea Rider Officers and Senior Ratings dressed in navy 'foul-weather' coats and berets. They put the ship' s company and all of its equipment through a searching two-hour inspection involving every aspect of a warship's role, to assess their fitness to begin a rigorous work-up. On the way into harbour, the technical Sea Riders listed any defects shown up by the inspection and discussed their remedy, and the work-up programme, with the ship's officers. The first week of a work-up was then spent alongside in harbour during which Harbour exercises and equipment repairs were carried out and systems tuned with the skilled assistance of FOST's naval WE shore staff which included a Lt.Cdr, a Chief EA, Chief REA and Chief OA and specialist Artificers.

As part of its Social/hospitality training, the newly arrived ship usually held a cocktail party on the evening of its arrival which was attended by FOST himself, CST  and the shore staff and their wives and, by the odd Sea Rider who had finished his End of Week report by 1800. All of the Staff Officers appeared in plain clothes and the only CTP I was ever able to attend was during my first month there. I wore my Waikato tie and was buttonholed by the Admiral who was wearing the same tie given to him when the Kiwi ship worked up at Portland a few months earlier. He too had been been told that he was the first 'Pom' to be given one. A few weeks later when the new FOST Rear-Admiral John Roxburgh, attended his first CTP on a ship, in plainclothes, he asked Lt Ron Sherhod, similarly garbed, who he was, Ron cheerily replied " Your Staff Shipwright Officer Sir" at which FOST asked " And what do they call you?" He was not amused at the reply, "Chippy". Next morning there was a signal saying that all staff officers attending CTPs in ships must wear uniform.

One young Lieutenant, WEO of a CA class Destroyer told me on arrival that he thought he would take advantage of his ship's first week to go skiing in the Alps. I said "Who is going to take charge of the harbour drills and oversee the remedy of the defects we found during our inspection?" When he said, "FOST shore staff and my Chiefs" I told him he needn't bother to come back to his charge job if he went on holiday during work-up! He took the point, worked hard throughout the next seven weeks and went on in the service.

To add a sense of urgency to the ship's company's response,

during a ship's work up, the broadcast announcing an exercise attack or fire was never preceded by, "For Exercise". At the major harbour fire aboard my first German ship, I found it was not on shore supplies but already had a diesel generator running and providing electrical supplies. I was supposed to trip the shore supply on cue, as soon as I heard the ship's broadcast "Feuer, Feuer, Feuer in der Kesselraum", plunging the ship into darkness. I then had to observe how quickly the ship's staff restored power using their own ship's resources. I went to the running Diesel Generator compartment and stood close to its big, tough, leather-suited watchkeeper. I gave him a friendly smile and asked him if he spoke English. Just as he replied "Nein", the ship's Fire Alarm sounded and the pre-arranged broadcast was made. Grabbing hold of the supply breaker handle I said to the burly German: "Voor Oefening, Diesem machine ist kaput", Unfortunately, I had used the Dutch "For Exercise" (instead of the German "Fur Ubang") and he didn't understand me and, thinking his ship was on fire for real and this mad English officer was trying to stop him doing his bit to save it, he grabbed the other side of the handle to prevent me tripping it, and angrily shouted "Diesem machine ist nicht kaput" pointing to his perfectly sound running diesel. Fearing I was about to get "a bunch of funf" or perhaps even trigger the third war with Germany in half a century, I took my hands away and asked him to: " Telephonen Kapitan-Lieutenant Prochnow" (the German Staff Liaison Officer) whom I knew was at the ship's DCHQ and had made the initiating broadcast. When the situation was explained to him by my friend Jurgen, a grin came over the watchkeeper's face and he said, "OK" and tripped the generator.

During my early FOST staff sea time on the RN ships, I witnessed the change-over of AC generators and was horrified at the standard of drill exhibited by the switchboard operators and even quite senior electrical ratings. At the same time I noticed that junior mechanics were keeping solo watch in switchboards, and were carrying out rounds of running electrical equipment without the authority or training to take the necessary action in the event of a failure. This serious shortcoming was evident even in the County and Daring class destroyers commencing work-up. Change-over of generators in the older DC ships posed no problem. I began giving ad hoc lessons in the correct drill. My boss then told me to produce a Switchboard Drill Manual for each class of AC ship and to organise the carrying out of drills on all of them, before the relevant electrical ratings were certified by their WEO as competent to load and change-over AC generators and undertake meaningful rounds. Ship's WEOs were advised to adopt the Compartment Instructions to men doing rounds, introduced in HMS Nubian five years earlier.

In February 1968, the Staff Gunnery Officer Lt. Cdr Hugh Orme and I were sent to Den Helder for a 5 day course on the Digital Gunnery and Missile system fitted to the new Dutch Leanders. We flew to Amsterdam on a Sunday afternoon and landed in a snow storm. The Dutch naval transport taking us by road was unfazed by the weather and on the snow covered roads we passed huge barges following ice-breakers on a canal with the water feeezing behind the last in the string of barges. The course, my first on a digital computer, with which no RN ship was fitted in those days, was very well conducted in English, and most interesting. The barracks accommodation was very comfortable and we were picked up by car at the wardroom every evening after dinner and driven through the snow to a different home where we enjoyed the hospitality of Dutch Officers and their families. On our return, as our BA Trident landed at Heath Row, it was beginning to snow. We were the last aircraft allowed to land and we had the devil of a job getting to Waterloo and even more in getting to Havant by train. No taxis or buses were running so I had to walk to Purbrook in the snow thinking, why can`t we face up to the snow like the Dutch?

One of the three Dutch officers on the staff, Lt Cdr Jaap Innsinger, was an Electrical Officer, who not only spoke and wrote excellent English but also spoke German and French fluently. His wife also spoke English very well and, when I visited Jaap's married quarter I was intrigued by his 6 year old son, speaking English to me with a Dorset accent and to his parents in Dutch without any effort. I got on very well with Jaap and enjoyed his friendship. I spent a total of more than three months at sea in the Dutch ships working up at Portland and admired their professionalism and enjoyed their company. It was interesting to note that their new Leander class frigates, though of the same dimensions and fitted with similar propulsion and weapons systems, had much more space down below than their RN counterparts largely due to their neater arrangement of pipes and cables. All of their crews from the Captain down to the most junior rating, spoke good English and their navy was run along the same lines as ours with similar branch structures. Although their food was not entirely to my taste, I loved their Pea Soup, and their Indonesian curry Rice Tafel was superb, and I tried to arrange that I was aboard one of the Dutch ships on Wednesdays for this exquisite lunch. The Dutch have a good sense of humour and often sent witty signals to the staff and they knew how to play us well. One day a Sea Rider stopped a Repair party rushing to a 'damage incident' by drawing a large hole in the deck with a piece of chalk, and told them to build a bridge across it. Quick as a flash, the Dutch CPO took the chalk and drew two lines across the hole and, shouting "There's our bridge," he led his team g across it. In the wardroom of HNMS Isaac Sweers, there was a barsign in English, stating, "The 5 Kilometre rule is observed in this establishment." Whenever a lady guest asked, "What is the 5 Km rule" the sign was turned round and it then read, " When we are more than 5 Km from the Netherlands, we are all bachelors." The Dutch Officers nicknamed me Twee Knevels, (put at least Two clips on a bulkhead door), as that was the only Dutch I could pronounce properly.

We got on pretty well with the Germans as well, but we shared a communication problem. Very few of them spoke English and we spoke little German. Furthermore they ran their ships quite differently to the Dutch and British. In the late 1960s, their frigates and destroyers still operated as they had done during WW2. Only their submarines and battleships were equipped to operate away from base for longer than two or three days. In consequence some of their older destroyers, though well designed to resist damage to their hull and provided with back-up weapons systems, had little onboard skill to repair them if they became defective. They also had no proper galley and their crews lived on iron rations at sea. Their standard of cuisine was worse than anyone in the RN had faced in living memory so we Sea Riders tried to avoid a German ship at meal times, but often had to endure their awful fare.

Although I spent a lot of my time at sea and in harbour on electrics, with my Gunnery and Sonar history, my principal and favourite role was to help improve the efficiency of ships' weapon systems. It was very satisfying to see the improvement in the performance of the Flyplane 5 and MRS 3 auto-tracking systems and their guns as, after on board training, the ship's staffs became more expert at regularly setting up and tuning the equipment. During the AA shoots in the last two weeks of work-up, I 'rode shotgun' on the top of the director to assess the performance of the auto tracking through the camera eye-piece, in anticipation of the film record, and if this was satisfactory, I gave the nod to the Staff Gunnery Officer to allow the ship to open fire. It was always a great pleasure to see the target-triggered bursts (TTBs) appearing smack in the middle of the camera cross wires and conversely, very disappointing if there were none. Sea Cat firings against radio-controlled PTAs also proved successful if the director tracking was good and the aimer had a steady hand. Onc day, after locating and clearing a defect I found on the digital computer during pre-firing checks on the Dutch frigate Tjerk Hiddes' missile system, both Sea Cats launched downed their PTAs. The Dutch Captain was so thrilled that he gave me the wooden propeller of one of the two PTAs shot down and said "it isn't fair, the biggest boozer on my ship was the aimer who shot both PTAs down". Before I left FOST in May 1969, a brass plate listing all 26 of my work-up ships was fixed to that prop in the shore workshop and was re-presented to me as a farewell gift from the staff, together with a switch and drill mounted on a board as a memento of Switchboard Drills. The PTA prop still hangs in my summer house.

At the end of the first Damage Control Exercise I attended as a Staff Officer, I was shocked when the out going CST began the wash-up by telling the ship's company concerned that they were, "the worst 'effing' shower he had ever seen in his two years at FOST". This was the first time I had ever heard an officer publicly swearing at ratings, or anyone else for that matter, in the 23 years I had been in the service. So much so for the 'Swinging Sixties' or were they more like the Scandalous Sixties? The next CST did not find it necessary to use the Anglo-Saxon expletive to express his displeasure. A larger than life and tireless character, Commander John Cox was lucky to survive his tour as the hardest working officer in the RN, putting in more than 100 hours of work a week. Nevertheless he was a born leader who had a great sense of humour even in the most difficult circumstances. One day, as the Senior Officer, he was the first to cross over by jackstay between two ships early in the first week of their work-up. The staff thought it was a good idea to let our 16 stone boss go first, after the test weight, before we followed. The Captains of the two ships were relatively inexperienced and did not maintain a constant distance apart with the result that during the transfer, the jackstay parted and CST was thrown into the turbulent stream between the two ships and disappeared. Underwater, he delayed inflating his 'Mae West' until he had passed the screws of the two ships and then surfaced some distance astern of the two ships. Immediately a nearby frigate lowered its sea boat in lifeboat mode to pick him up. However, he was too heavy for the boat's crew to hoist aboard so he hung on to the gun whale and told them to tow him to the frigate. Still wearing his beret and soaking wet, CST climbed the ladder to be met by a 'piping party' and its Captain with a large brandy, which he promptly downed. He then turned and 'bollocked' the boat's crew for bad boat drill before walking for'd to shower and change.

Sea Riders seldom remained aboard the same ship all day for, after a specific exercise, eg an AA shoot, we had to transfer to another ship to cover theirs. If a large team of us was transferred, this was done by jackstay, but smaller numbers went by (SOOTAX), Staff Officer

*Don transferring from Grafton to Rhyl* Operations' Taxis, in helicopters of the Portland based Fleet Air Arm squadron. We usually flew in a Wessex Mk 1, having been winched up and down to it with our holdalls, often marked with a 'Fly Navy' label but, if only two or three of the staff were being transferred, we were flown off the flight deck in the ship's own Wasp. Transfers between ships had to be booked during the planning phase of the week's programme carried out in FOST's Operations Room in Portland Naval Base, at 0700 in the morning of the

Wednesday of the week before going off to sea. One such morning going down to breakfast at Osprey, I heard Reveille being played. What a paradox! As an apprentice at Fisgard I seldom heard Reveille and yet 23 years later, as a Lieutenant Commander I was up, dressed and going to breakfast, while all of the lads were still fast asleep. When they were completed, copies of the comprehensive weekly programme were distributed to each Sea Rider and to every ship working-up. This was before the age of sophisticated photo- copiers and it took all of the junior office staff including messengers and cleaners to correlate the 20 -30 pages, each of them walking round a long table laying a copy of their page on to the piles in sequence.

On 1ˢᵗ October 1967, at sea in HMS Naiad, whilst having a cup of coffee in the wardroom, I had a contretemps on a technical matter with the ship's genial Commander (L). He said he would go and look the matter up in his cabin. Fifteen minutes or so later I was ordered to go to the Captain's cabin. I thought, "Oh God, he was right and has taken the matter to his Captain." When I arrived Cdr. (L) was in the cabin and Captain Sir Peter Anson Bart, with a smile, congratulated me, not for winning the argument with his Cdr (L)) but, showing me a signal he had just received, saying I had been promoted Lt. Cdr. He then poured out three glasses and we drank to my good fortune. Back in Osprey that night I phoned the good news to Eileen. About a year later I was at sea in another ship when the WEO showed me the latest issue DCI, (Defence Council Instruction), which said that I had been awarded £600 for Syntax, the shipborne Attack Teacher I had invented. My boss in Nubian, who had suggested the name, and the Chief TASI and a young Electrical Mechanic who had helped put it together, had also been rewarded. Naturally, I telephoned that piece of good news home.

One weekend during the school holidays, Eileen brought Sally and Paul down to Weymouth and all four of us stayed at the Naval Hotel. On the Saturday while Eileen took Sally shopping, I went out with Paul on one of the organised fishing boat trips which guaranteed a successful catch. I sat next to him and after half an hour without a bite, the boat deployed to another area by which time Paul was bored with fishing and gave me his line. Shortly afterwards I had a tickle and gave Paul his line back and told him that we should soon be landing some fish. He was so excited when he felt the fish wriggling and in the next half hour he landed four macarel and I caught two. We took them back to the hotel and I asked could we have them as a fish course with dinner that evening. When they were served, Paul was horrified to see a complete fish served to him, with a slice of lemon. He imagined it would be in batter like fish and chips and couldn't face it, and has never been fishing since. Sally ate his fish and Eileen and I enjoyed our two each. On the Sunday night, Paul and I saw Eileen and Sally off home on the train and I took him up to Osprey where he stayed overnight on a camp bed in my cabin and, next morning after early breakfast, he came down to the Operations Room with me. Then, having previously arranged it with my boss and the Captain of HMS Mohawk, I took Paul aboard the ship, then nearing completion of her work-up, for a day at sea. As I was tied up with my duties, the ship's WEO kindly nominated one of his lads to show Paul around the ship and I asked the young mechanic to show Paul everything. During the day he witnessed an AA shoot wearing full Anti-flash

gear and, took part in a 4.5 inch gun's crew, sat in the ship's helicopter with its rotors running and, after dusk landed on a Dorset beach with the ship's Royal Marines from an assault craft, with his face blackened and wearing a helmet. After dinner onboard, Paul and I landed by boat and, on the way up to HMS Osprey I asked him had he enjoyed his day. Paul said he liked everything except going below. Apparently he was terrified by the noise and heat when he was taken below into the boiler room. That single incident in an otherwise fantastic experience for a young boy, completely ruined my plan of encouraging him to make a career in the navy by giving him a perfect Boy's Own adventurous day at sea. Although he subsequently enjoyed many sporting and social contacts with the RN, he never expressed a desire to join.

*FOST Staff Officers April 1968 - Don is 3rd from right in middle row*

Sea Riders had their own flying kit: 'Bone-dome' Mae West and overalls for the summer months and immersion suit, aka 'Goon-suit', from October to May. All of us had to undergo a survival course and were advised to have our life insurance policy endorsed to specifically cover us, "when required to fly as a passenger in military aircraft". During my time at FOST I often flew from ship to ship and shore and had only one scare. Aboard a Wessex , flying inshore at 400 feet in thick fog from 20 miles south of Portland Bill, the shore radar directing us lost contact. As usual, we were all listening in to the radio and became somewhat concerned when after flying northward blind for some time we were urgently told to, "Climb, Climb, Climb" after we suddenly showed up on the radar approaching high ground near Dorchester. We were all mighty relived when we later safely made a blind landing in the fog at Portland Air Station.

In accordance with tradition, the Captain or Senior officer is always the last to join, and first to leave a boat and this also applies to joining or leaving a helicopter, even by winch. One rough day at sea a group of us had been winched up from the tiny bucking quarter deck of a destroyer and sat in the hovering 'chopper' waiting for the Admiral to be winched up. As the hoist began to lift, the rating holding him let go and FOST's legs smashed against the QD winch on his way up. When he reached the aircraft he was clearly in great pain, nursing his shins, and was not a happy Admiral.

On 18th January 1969, I was at sea in my old ship HMS Nubian and, as my last task ended at 1730, and the ship was remaining at sea all night, I had booked a lift ashore in her Wasp with the mail at 1800 so that I could host a drinks party in Osprey wardroom from 1830 to 1900, to celebrate my 40th birthday. I landed at the air station and ran to a small telephone box to phone for transport to take me up to Osprey, I was still wearing my Goon-suit and Mae West but had removed my bone-dome and left it outside the door with my hold all. Suddenly the door opened and our waggish Staff Air Engineer reached in and pulled the toggle of my Mae West which inflated immediately, slamming and blocking the hinged door and filling the small box completely. Painfully-slowly, I had to bleed the lifejacket until I could get the door open and join my waiting transport. By the time I reached Osprey and had peeled off my flying kit and cleaned up, it was 1859. I had to extend the party to get a drink with my, by then well-oiled, mess mates.

The saddest day for aviation at Portland was 11th November 1968. The 5th of 6, Wessex helicopters, flying at 90 feet over the ships making their way south after leaving harbour, and each carrying 3 crew and 5 passengers out to join ships south of Portland Bill, had a catastrophic engine failure. Being too low for the main rotor to 'auto-rotate', the aircraft plunged straight into the sea, tearing off its flotation bags, and sank. Despite heroic efforts by the aircrewman and pilots, all of whom were injured, the five passengers, all American journalists, were killed. I was travelling in the 3rd of the 6 helicopters and was quite unaware of the disaster going on behind us until after I was lowered by winch on to a ship. Apparently the victims were all experienced ex-Vietnam war correspondents and photographers well used to travelling by helicopter and were not strapped in when the aircraft fell. They were killed by its impact with the sea. The Taranto Night Dinner, the Fleet-Air-Arm's annual Trafalgar-like Dinner, arranged for that evening in HMS Osprey's wardroom was immediately cancelled as a mark of respect.

The South African Navy invited several of FOST's Staff to a meeting at SA House in London and my chum, Alex Barnet, and I were given a railway warrant and the day off to go. We were met by a Captain and Commander and given an illustrated talk clearly aimed at getting us to transfer to the SAN, followed by pre-lunch drinks and then lunch at a London hotel after which we were taken to Waterloo for the train back to Weymouth. Our hosts, particularly Captain Dieter Gerhardt were charming and, in the case of Alex, most persuasive, for he later transferred and emigrated to the Cape. I remember one of the stories Dieter Gerhardt told us. As a young Lieutenant on course at Greenwich he returned pretty tipsy and late from a visit to the West End to find he was locked out of the cabin block. He climbed up a drain pipe to gain access via an open first-floor window but fell and broke his arm. Next evening there was a banquet in the Painted Hall. Although he was then under report, as the only South African student at the college, he was seated next to his country's Ambassador's wife. Seeing his arm in a sling she asked him how he had broken it. Dieter received sympathy and respect from her when he replied, "in a climbing accident M'am".

*Four years later, when he was Captain of Simons Town Dockyard, he hosted a great party at his residence where he played the piano, sang and told jokes to his guests and then came back aboard HMS Falmouth with me for a protracted night cap. All of us thought he was a great character. A few years*

*later as a Rear Admiral, he and his wife were arrested and charged with spying for Soviet Russia for over 15 years, were found guilty and sentenced to long spells in jail. Dieter's Swiss wife was released after 15 years but Dieter died in prison. I was questioned about my knowledge of the man, which of course, was entirely social, and no help to the security authorities.*

I had a day off on Trafalgar Day in 1968 to move house. Eileen and I had long admired a unique detached cottage-style house on the main London Road at Widley and when we heard the dentist who owned it was migrating to South Africa, we stepped in and bought it. I travelled home to the bungalow at Purbrook the night before and spent most of the night packing up for the move and, by

*Sally and Eileen 1967*

prior agreement with the owner, I arrived with the first load at the house at 0800. Tommy the dentist and his wife Phylis were having breakfast and asked me to join them. I explained I had already eaten so he asked me to join him in a whisky which I politely declined. For some reason, they was taking the chandeliers and several other electrical fittings with them to Johannesburg so I had to get cracking and put up light pendants. While I was up a ladder doing this, he once more tried to ply me with Scotch. When I again declined he said he had never heard of a naval officer refusing a drink. I pointed out that I had only 9 hours to settle my family in before I returned to Portland and, reluctantly accepting my excuse, this friendly mad Irishman retired to the kitchen with his bottle. Eileen arrived with the removal van about 1030 and together we had our new home looking comfortable by tea time. Tommy asked us whether we would like to keep the lady who 'did for them' three days a week. Eileen, who wished to go back to work now that the children were growing up, jumped at the chance and so, Molly began her four years with us until she retired and moved to Southsea to join her son. We knew straight away that this was our ultimate home and changed its name from 'The Rise' to 'le dix avril' (the French version of our wedding date), and have lived happily in it for over 40 years.

On Fridays, the work-up exercises ended by 1400 and we all returned to harbour. After finding out if my ships were free of defects or arranging for the base staff to assist in the repair of any defects likely to hazard Monday's programme, I then repaired to the WE Sea Riders' office and wrote the End of Week Report on the three ships for which I was responsible, plus the final report on the ship that finished work-up the day before. These reports were compiled from the notes taken during the five days at sea and dealt with the performance of the WE equipment and its maintainers comprehensively, and included confidential personal reports on the officers and senior ratings. The completed EOW reports had then to be discussed with the Staff WEO, the fearsome Don Fletcher and amended as he saw fit, before I could go up the hill to Osprey and change to go home with Alex Barnet. It was at least 1900 and sometimes as late as 2100 before we were released by SWEO. and occasionally nearly midnight before I arrived home. On arrival, after the welcome home kiss, I was usually given a list of jobs that needed doing to Eileen's car, the house or garden. After a hectic but great family weekend, I left home again on Sunday evenings at 2100 to travel back by car with Alex listening to 'Your 100 Best Tunes' on the radio and was abed at Osprey by 2300, ready for an 0700 visit to the Ops Room on Monday morning.

During the summer holidays of 1967, Sally, Paul and I had a week's camping holiday in the New Forest, being joined for the weekend by Eileen, who was not keen on life under canvas. Sally and Paul had already taken up riding at Denmead as a hobby and Sally was quite proficient, so I joined them in a couple of lessons at a riding school at Brockenhurst and a pony trek through the forest and became hooked. A year later, we all went to Dartmoor for a week's holiday which incorporated a riding holiday for Sally,

*Dartmoor 1968*

Paul and me and a restful country holiday for Eileen. Details of this very successful family holiday are given in the next chapter.

Back at Portland, going out to HMS Intrepid at 0745 in one of her landing craft with most of the of Sea Riders including CST, for a Damage-Control exercise, we were literally 'crapped-on from a great height'. The ship was in ballast, ie not docked down and, as the boat, (also carrying uncovered trays of bread rolls for the wardroom), came under the davits to be hoisted up, the outflow of effluent from the ship's Heads (lavatories), normally below sea level but then, well above the craft's gunwale, suddenly discharged a spray of 'you know what', all over the staff and the bread rolls. Fortunately and appropriately, we were all wearing foul weather coats and, naturally avoided the rolls at lunch, like the plague. A simple modification, the fitting of lead-weighted canvas extensions to the sewage outflows, prevented this happening again.

FOST's unofficial flagship was the RFA Engadine, a specially built helicopter carrier which was permanently based at Portland. I was given responsibility for working-up her electrical, radio and radar staff and spent three days at sea in her. All of her own civilian crew and the two RN PO Radio Electricians were accommodated in spacious single cabins but the RN embarked staff, including the Lt Cdr CO of the permanently embarked squadron of 4 helicopters, and FOST staff Officers like me on temporary secondment, shared communal cabins with 3 other RN officers. However, we all ate in the very spacious officers' mess and enjoyed first rate meals. I noticed that the ship always seemed to carry out refuelling at sea and personnel transfers by air or jackstay, during unsocial hours. I soon found out why, their civilian crew, unlike the RN, was paid extra for working outside of normal working hours.

When covering AA and Surface Gunnery preparation and shoots I was usually paired with Frank Trickey the renowned 18 stone Gunnery Officer with whom I had served in the 8th Destroyer Squadron in 1958/9. He was a great character and we worked well together on many ships. One day, after a particularly ill-disciplined first AA shoot by a German destroyer, when his order to cease-fire was ignored, he addressed the Captain, a former U-boat survivor and POW, who spoke English, and the ship's gunnery staff who did not. He told them in his loud and outspoken way, "That was the most disgraceful exhibition of gunnery I have ever seen in my 25 years service, I don't know how the hell it took us so long to beat you in the war!" Incredibly the Germans loved it, seemed to appreciate his authoritative tone and thereafter always did what he ordered them.

Frank was big-hearted and, if I told him the standard of tracking was good he would let the ship fire to help the crew's self confidence when other less experienced GOs would not have taken the chance without photographic evidence. Frank was too big for a normal size flying suit so he had a special one made in Dayglow Red. It had big horizontal rolls and when he was dressed in it he looked like a giant red Michelin Man. I hated travelling by Wasp with him for, though it always flew without doors, because he was 6 months senior to me, he got to sit in the front with the pilot while I was in the back seat wondering how I would ever get out if we ditched. Frank occupied three-quarters of the cockpit space, making it difficult for the pilot to operate the controls and nigh impossible for Frank to get out without outside help.

During the 1968 Christmas leave I played Totopoly with the family and realised I could devise an after dinner game on the same lines for FOST staff. I called it 'Refit and Work- up'. Players were the Captains of ships of either the new Leander Class or aged Type 15 class Frigates. Players first had to go round a board of shipyard building delays or dockyard refit defect hazards respectively, and then go around a Work-up- board and pass a different set of criteria. The winner was the first ship to complete both boards. Sally helped to make all of the cards and it was played by the staff with great interest and gusto after Mess Dinners.

Perhaps because the staff worked so hard, some developed a rather weird sense of humour. One of them enrolled CST, arguably the busiest officer in the navy, as an agent for a Mail Order firm which promised him he could earn a few shillings a week commission in his spare time. He also had an unsolicited piano delivered to his house, ordered by some joker. One Friday afternoon after a week at sea, I opened my desk drawer to find it 'booby-trapped' with a thunder flash which blew up and nearly gave me a heart attack.

I suspected my chum Alex was the culprit but he denied culpability.
I only had one dunking during the countless jackstay transfers I did

at Portland. It was on the first 'Sea day' of the two ships concerned and having been told they were too far apart they closed in and the jackstay sagged and I went completely under for a few seconds until the slack was taken up. I was wearing a goon-suit and only my face got wet and my hold all remained watertight. On surfacing I heard the lads on both ships giving a cheer at the sight of one of the staff officers, getting a dousing.

One day I was invited to lunch at Portland Castle, the official residence of the CO of HMS Osprey, by the new Captain, Ed Brown who had commanded HMS Nubian during my last six months aboard her. They had one other guest that day, the Admiral, FOST himself, who was not renowned for his sense of humour. Luckily for me, Ed Brown and his charming wife were in good form and the occasion was memorably lighthearted.

Sea Riders were pretty unpopular with most of the crews early on in their work-up; many of them thought of us as a kind of Gestapo for highlighting their deficiencies and working them hard. However as ships' companies realised that their own performance was steadily improving, they came to appreciate that FOST's staff Sea Riders were not the 'bastards' they first thought, but were on their side and working very hard themselves to help each ship to reach its full potential as a warship. In fact all Sea Riders were devoted to their ships and always considered the ships' successes to be due to the crew's efforts but their failures to be the fault of the Sea Rider concerned.

Except for a charge-job at sea, this was quite the most professionally satisfying post in the navy for a technical officer. It was also the most physically demanding job I ever had. During my time with FOST, two technical Sea Riders left their appointments prematurely and two ship's technical officers were also replaced. I am proud to have been a Sea Rider and to have lasted the pace. I am very appreciative of the dedicated professionalism of my fellow Sea

Rider Officers and Senior ratings of all branches, and in particular, the WE Chief Artificers, Mechanicians and Electricians, for the loyal support they gave me. Besides helping to train the WE departments of many ships being put through a rigorous regime of exercises, I learnt a lot myself and this stood me in good stead in the three work-ups I would later face in my own ships.

# Chapter 18

*Head of General Electrical Training Group*
*HMS Collingwood*
*June 1969 to May 1970*

On the 2$^{nd}$ of June 1969, I joined the biggest electrical training group in HMS Collingwood as its Head. Although I had never before taught in a classroom, I had been given the top training job ashore for an L specialist, almost certainly because of my recent introduction of Switchboard Drills and experience of damage-Control on FOST's staff at Portland. However, since most of my career had been spent in looking after Weapon Systems I felt a little like a fish out of water. With my recent association with some of the best Instructors in the navy, I decided to spend the whole of my first week in the White City, a large training area of white-painted buildings in which the GE Group was sited, sitting in on each of the lessons given to officers and ratings and covering the complete spectrum of ships' electrical equipments. My teaching staff comprised 6 Engineer officers and 25 serving and retired Senior rates. This exercise enabled me to see the staff in action at the chalk face, to assess the quality of the syllabus and its delivery and to decide on my training strategy for the Group.

Whilst most of the existing courses were well prepared and put over I noted that many were not up to date with modern techniques taught by FOST and some were poorly presented from inadequate notes. Therefore I first set about re-writing the relevant course notes and went through them with the Instructors concerned, had them typed by my clerical staff and introduced them for the new classes going through the Group. Aware that every officer, senior rating and junior rate of any specialisation receiving training in Collingwood underwent at least some of its training in the GE Group, I then decided to revise all of the course notes for the rest of the classes. This took me the rest of the summer term to complete and implement.

During summer leave I again took the family on a riding holiday to Dartmoor where we stayed at a cottage near Two Bridges called Spaders. Sally, Paul and I rode from the Sherburton Pony Stud at Hexworthy every day with Eileen driving to the scheduled pub half-way round the day's ride to join us for lunch. Before our visit the year before, I had only had a few riding lessons, a pony trek in the New Forest and some tips from Sally. Then, on our arrival at the stables, our riding ability had been assessed but, as Sally and Paul were such good riders, the Coakers assumed that I must also be as competent in the saddle, so all three of us had been assigned to the 'A' ride. This included gallops, crossing rivers, jumps over low obstacles and went further and over more difficult terrain than the other three rides. Somehow, despite several suppressed anxious moments, I had managed to look confident, stay on the horse and keep up with the others, and had improved my equestrian skills sufficiently to be automatically included in this year's 'A' ride. We were picked up by a minibus at 0900 and prepared our mounts at

the stables run by Diana Coaker, a former National Hunt Point to Point Lady Champion, and her husband John, who were great characters, and tenants and friends of Prince Charles. By 1000 we were out on Dartmoor for a 24 to 32 mile ride, varied every day. Our landlady Mrs Webb was a great cook and we had a terrific breakfast, a nice hot bath on return and an excellent dinner, and once again thoroughly enjoyed this fun-filled and healthy outdoor family holiday during which we met a number of very interesting people. When we arrived home we were all delighted to learn that Sally had gained O levels in English Lit, English Lang, Maths, History, Biology and RE. Well done Sally.

On return from leave I learnt I had been given two extra jobs, that of WEO designate of the next Sultan and Collingwood Harbour Training Ship – HMS Diamond, and Course Officer of the class of newly commissioned Engineer Sub Lieutenants. The former entailed flying out to Gibraltar almost straight away to carry out Weapons and Electrical trials on the ship in the Mediterranean at the end of her last commission at sea, and to assess the work necessary to prepare her for early use as a training ship. On the flight out I met the Engineer Officer from Sultan designated to do the same job from the Marine Engineering angle. We looked each other up and down and realised that I had been his fag at RNATE Torpoint and hadn't met since he 'passed-out' 26 years ago. Gus Crane had been a kindly fag master and we again hit it off together. As we went to check in at the Hotel Bristol at Gibraltar we were handed a message saying we were to join HMS Diamond immediately as she had been ordered to sea. We did so and were soon out in the Atlantic meeting a Soviet fleet comprising a heavy cruiser, nine conventional submarines and a Depot ship, which were en route from Murmansk to the Black Sea. It was pretty rough when we met them and all of the submarines were on the surface and wallowing badly. We steamed close to them and, through binoculars we could see that they had had a rough passage and their crews were each being given a short break of fresh air. After exchanging friendly greetings, we 'fell-in' with them as they entered the Straits of Gibraltar and turned east to pass through the Mediterranean.

Then the propaganda war began. The Sverdlov class cruiser's band appeared on their Quarter deck and began to play lively music and seemingly, all of her ship's company, dressed in white trousers and blue tunics and caps, ran around the upper deck smiling happily. At our 0900 Armament Quarters every morning, having noted that all of the cruiser's guns remained firmly fore and aft all of the time, we let go a balloon away from the Russian ships and tracked it and moved all three turrets and the close-range guns. Then, at about 1100 we increased speed to 31 knots and dashed off to the East, had lunch and, then the traditional Med Fleet 'Hands to Bathe' so that when the Soviet ships caught up with us we were all enjoying a cool dip in the sea. The poor Ruskies, whose Captains probably feared that if they did the same, some of them might try to swim ashore, were denied this pleasure and clearly envied us. We shadowed them until we were relieved near Malta by another destroyer and after a further exchange of greetings we turned west and got on with the exercises we had planned. We prepared for and carried out an AA, surface and bombardment shoot, a damage-control exercise and a full-power trial on the way back to Gibraltar. Gus and I gathered enough data to be able to compile the minor refit defect list before Diamond became our responsibility, in the New Year.

After flying back to UK, I resumed my other two roles at Collingwood. The new class of Sub-Lieutenants was a keen, intelligent and lively bunch and I took them off once a week during their six month course, on a visit to one of the MOD research establishments, a tour of the local Dockyard departments, Whitehall, or the local Crown Court to broaden their minds. We took lunch together in a local pub and the visits were good for bonding. During a visit to Portsmouth court we were lectured by the senior Police Officer and given the low-down on crime in Portsmouth and, as we went up to the court above, we bumped into my Aunt, Helen Murdoch, who was Police Matron and was taking up a 'Lady of the Street' to face a charge of Prostitution. I introduced the class to my ebullient Aunt before we took up our very different positions in court. On all of these visits I had the students take notes and afterwards write a report, some of which were very entertaining.

Back at my proper job, I decided to personally take every class that passed through my Group, for at least one 55 minute instructional period during the course. This enabled me to meet each of the students, to teach them engineering topics not covered by any other course and to pass on some useful tips I had received during my career and particularly at FOST, whose very name inspired a degree of awe. I taught qualifying WE officers how to prioritise their work, to deal with emergencies like flooding, the importance of Running Machinery rounds, how to write their Night Order Book and how to support their senior ratings. I taught artificers how to realign the various elements of horizontally-mounted machines, sadly omitted from contemporary training, and how to restore a toppled gyro compass, data previously restricted to Gyro EAs. With the enthusiastic support of most of my staff, I had completely revised the classroom syllabus taught in the Group by Christmas, bringing it up to date with the latest techniques.

Eileen and I really enjoyed the Collingwood social life and never missed an event, and the children lapped up the Guy Fawkes night Fireworks Show and Christmas parties. Eileen and I were also the guests of the Chief POs Mess at their Christmas Ball, with the Captain and Mrs Bridle. We continued to enjoy frequent visits to the King's Theatre where we saw a number of plays and musical shows which were given a provincial showing with their star cast prior to their West End opening. About a third of these, including 'Boeing Boeing', 'Rattle of a Simple Man and 'Heloise' became hugely successful, another third had reasonably long runs in London and the rest flopped badly in the metropolis, but we had seen them all for a very modest cost. We also attended the plays operas and musicals put on by local amateur dramatic societies.

After spending 25 years in full or part-time study of the Sciences I had qualified academically to become a chartered engineer and, as

the past 3 years had been occupied in teaching practical engineering, I decided to change tack and devote my future leisure learning to the Arts. So, at the start of the 1969/70 academic year, I started an A' Level course in English Literature at Highbury College with Gillian Howarth, shown here, as my teacher.

The 20 strong class was made up of equal numbers of 30 /40 year old mature students of both sexes and 19/20 year old girls. Gillian not only managed to keep this disparate group focused on the subject, but set and marked lots of homework, and kept our interest growing throughout the course. She gave me a love of English Literature in general and of poetry, Shakespeare and Chaucer in particular, which I have never lost. In those days, Course Work didn't count towards one's exam result. Everything hinged on how one did in the two 3 hour papers, the first with compulsory questions on Chaucer's Wife of Bath's Tale, Milton's 'Paradise Lost Parts 1X and X, Shakespeare's The Winter's Tale, and George Elliot's Middlemarch. Next day we sat the 2$^{nd}$ paper with questions on Wilfred Owen's War Poems, TS Elliot's The Cocktail Party, DH Lawrence's Sons and Lovers and Virginia Wolf's To the Lighhouse. All of the class was still furiously writing when the time expired for each paper, and it speaks volumes for Gillian's teaching skills that all of us passed. I was glad to get a 'C' in what had been my worst subject at 'O' level.

In February 1970, HMS Diamond completed its short refit and was towed to a berth close to where the old Fisgard hulks had been moored off Elson, Gosport. I then spent a lot of my time getting it ready to take classes from Collingwood, before handing over the responsibility for the ship's WE equipment and on-board training, to a resident WE officer, appointed to the ship for that purpose.

By the end of the Spring term of 1970, I had settled down to the routine of spending 16 hours a week taking classes of officers, and ratings of all seniorities for a single instructional period; visiting HMS Diamond to monitor a damage-control exercise or the testing and tuning of a turret or the fire-control system, or chairing an examination board for the advancement of Electrical ratings. I then received an offer I couldn't refuse. The Appointer rang me and asked if I would like to join HMS Falmouth as WEO. The ship was in Portsmouth Dockyard undergoing conversion to a Leander type frigate fitted with the latest Gunnery Fire-control system, Sea-Cat missiles and a helicopter and, when commissioned in a year's time, and having worked-up, would be going to the West Indies for 8 months. As this guaranteed me another 14 months at home and a Charge job in a first-rate ship, I eagerly accepted the offer.

During my year in Collingwood, I was only required for duty every ninth night as the Duty Lt Cdr. in charge of the sizeable duty watch, and was not involved in any other ceremonial duties. I very soon regained the weight I had lost through the rather more strenuous regime at Portland and thoroughly enjoyed a very happy family life. I enjoyed the very different challenge the job represented and, with the help of a number of keen officers and senior ratings, made, I think, a reasonable job of running the biggest training group in the largest training establishment in the navy.

Sally's first love was riding, but she was also very handy with a tennis racquet and she and I often played in doubles matches. Despite my moderate standard of play, her accurate left-hand won many a game against friends and members of the family. Inevitably, but still ego-shattering, came the day when she asked me to book the court and when I asked who we were playing she replied, "Oh sorry Pa, you're not playing". I just wasn't up to her standard anymore!

When I arrived late at my 40th birthday party at Portland, I had been solemnly told by a rather tipsy older friend that,"Life really does begin at 40". That statement certainly proved to be "in vino veritas" for, in the following decade, I had a great time at home, at play and at work, though Sally and Paul's rising standards soon left me behind and I had to resort to playing games with my own age group.

# Chapter 19

## Weapons and Electrical Engineer Officer

## HMS Falmouth May 1970 – December 1972

I joined HMS Falmouth, a Type 12 Frigate, on the 27th May 1970, as her WEO. The ship was undergoing a major rebuild in Portsmouth Dockyard during which the latest semi-automatic gunnery system (MRS3 Mod3), the most modern long range and Navigational radars, a Seacat missile system and a hangar and an Anti-submarine helicopter flight-deck were being installed. When the ship was fully manned, I would have a staff comprising a Deputy WEO, a Warrant Officer, 20 Chief and Petty Officer Technicians, 29 junior technical ratings and 6 Seamen. It was a gem of a charge-job.

Engineer Sub-Lieutenant Mike Mugridge, a Radio specialist, who had served as the Deputy WEO in the ship's previous commission, and had 'stood-by' the ship whilst it was in dock, met me in the dockside office block assigned to the ship. He was a keen young Yorkshire man who, unable to bring his family south, commuted home every weekend. He showed me around the ship, nearing the completion of its modernisation, and we discussed the ship's progress and programme before apportioning the division of our responsibilities when the dockyard turned over the equipment to the ship's staff. I gave him the Electrics, Radio Communications, Ship's Radio Entertainment (SRE) and Divisional Officer of the Junior ratings, an arrangement with which he was happy. I retained overall charge of the department, and took over direct responsibility for Weapons Systems, Radar, DO of the Senior Ratings and Cinema Officer. Fortuitously, I had joined before the weapons installations and their alignment, and the radar installations were complete, and so I was able to supervise this painstaking and essential work.

During Summer Leave, The Murdoch's went to Dartmoor for another riding holiday. This time, because Mrs Webb was ill, we stayed at Huccaby Farm near the stables. The accommodation and food was not quite as good as at 'Spaders' in 1968 and 1969 but we all enjoyed ourselves. On the Monday, Eileen met us at the pub at Holne for lunch and, when I went to the bar to get the drinks, next to me was a cheerful face I recognised. It was the Archbishop of Canterbury, Michael Ramsey, whom I greeted and we shared a friendly and interesting chat. He was staying at the local hotel for a relaxing holiday and had dropped in for a pint. The equestrian highlight of the week, as in previous years, was the 'Warren House Gallop' at Friday lunchtime. The 16 members of the 'A Ride' lined up 1 ½ miles from the famous pub and, at the order "Go" all of us galloped as fast as we could across the moor to be the first to enter a bridle path between conifers, as it was only wide enough for two horses abreast. On this occasion Sally and Paul got there first and I was right behind Sally so I was bombarded with the clods from her horse for the last 2 furlongs. Sally won the race, Paul was second and I, covered in mud, came third with the other riders behind.

After summer leave, the ship's three technical officers, the Marine Engineer Officer, Engineer Lieutenant Peter Renson, who had also served at sea in Falmouth during its previous commission, and my deputy and I were joined by Lt. Cdr Richard Channon, formerly Captain of the submarine Olympus, as First Lieutenant.

During September and October 1970, the ship's complement was gradually built up, those living locally being able to go home every night and the others being accommodated in HMS Nelson. During this period, calling on my previous experience, particularly with FOST at Portland, I wrote and proved my departmental Standing Orders, including the instructions to men carrying out rounds, and was also able to incorporate a number of efficiency improvements which I had picked up earlier or devised myself. The voltage of the main generators was automatically controlled by very good electronic regulators so the first sign of a generator problem was a change in its speed and thus frequency output. By fitting main generator frequency meters in the Control and Communication Switchboard, it was easy to monitor the 440 volt main electrical supplies from a more congenial environment than the main switchboard in the boiler-room and, at the same time, keep check on all of the converted supplies. I also incorporated nine minor modifications to the Gunnery Fire-control system, the Radar systems, Sonar systems and Plotting tables and fitted Syntax Mod 1. All of these ten improvements were considered to have enhanced the ship's efficiency and were later approved by FOST.

By the time the new Captain, Commander Jeremy Dreyer joined, Peter Renson had been promoted Lt. Cdr and the ship's company had moved onboard, prior to going to sea for the first time. I felt we were in pretty good shape to face up to weapons and radio trials. It wasn`t long before I found that my confidence was misplaced. On the first day of sea trials, the Chief Electrician noticed the SRE was still playing music after we sailed, so he told one of the Electrical Mechanics to switch it off. I was on the enclosed Bridge as the ship approached the harbour mouth near HMS Dolphin, when the Captain and Navigating Officer came rushing in from their open Conning Position above, shouting "The 'Conning Intercom' isn't working" and ordered a course change via the voice pipe to the wheel house. I dashed along to the nearby Amplifier Compartment and found that all eight of the Intercom amplifiers were switched off. I switched them all on and reported to the Captain and then learnt that the young EM detailed by the Chief Electrician did not know which was the SRE amplifier and so had stupidly switched all of them off. This was a particular blow to my pride for here was I, head of department of a 'front-line' frigate on my first day at sea, after having regularly lectured Officers and Senior Ratings never to order anyone to carry out a duty he didn't understand, failing to ensure that one of my team knew what he was doing. This cock-up could easily have led to a serious mishap to the ship. Needless to say the Captain was not very happy and I had to guarantee that it would never happen again. The trials went well and to schedule and. with the ship looking like a warship, half the ship's company went off on Christmas leave at a time while the watch onboard prepared the ship for the commissioning ceremony programmed for 6<sup>th</sup> January 1971 when we would be berthed at the ceremonial South Railway Jetty.

When the ship was being complemented, she was destined to serve on the popular West Indies station for eight months and was heavily oversubscribed with volunteers. However, whilst undergoing our sea trials, 'My Lords', in their wisdom, decided to send us instead to the Far East for ten months. This change was very unpopular and extremely so with the ten West-Indians we had onboard. Eight of the Seamen and Stokers among them contrived by legal or other means to get off the ship, leaving only one of my PO Radio Electricians and an LREM to go East. These turned out to be two of my best maintainers, looking after the UHF radio and on-line crypto equipment respectively, and proved a great asset to the ship. The rest of my division, though also disappointed with the change of station, for all of us had been looking forward to a Caribbean cruise with visits to the USA, accepted their lot as part of the tradition exemplified by the naval adage, "If you can't take a joke you shouldn't have joined".

On the morning of the commissioning, as Wardroom Wine caterer, I thought I might need more bottles of Champagne than we carried for the party onboard afterwards. So I rang up the two nearest ships and persuaded them to let me have, on sale or return, two cases and took a steward with me to collect them. When we got back to the ship, the very smart band of the Coldstream Guards (the very one which played the music for the TV series 'Dads' Army'), was tuning up, a TV crew was setting up its gear, all the seating was in place and, sitting in the centre front rank of the VIP seats, was a woman wearing a head scarf from under which large round curlers were protruding. I drew the OOD's attention to this possible problem and it transpired that the lady concerned was the mum of one of the young lads onboard and had got there early to get a good seat. She was politely shown to another seat, also offering a good view of the proceedings. She continued to wear her curlers and scarf during the ceremony and we wondered what great social event, later in the day, she was preparing for. The ship's connection with the Coldstream Guards, signified by a red flash on the starboard side of the mast, to match the hackle on their bearskins, stemmed from the service rendered to the regiment by Lord Falmouth's family. The commissioning ceremony was splendid and was enjoyed by all, including Eileen and the children.

Soon afterwards £-s-d became history as the country's monetary system went decimal, and all retailers took advantage of this step change and rounded costs up. The price of my favourite tipple, a pint of draught Guinness went up from 3 shillings (15 p) to 17 new pence. At the same time, HMS Falmouth was undergoing extensive final weapons system Sea Acceptance Trials and, after their successful completion, began helicopter operating trials in the channel before embarking its own Wasp helicopter and air and ground crew. One of our Midshpmen, Chris Miller had a brother in the Royal Corps of Signals, the only soldiers who wore a plain dark 'woolly pullie'. Richard Channon thought this would make an ideal working dress for Falmouth's ship's officers and negotiated the supply of 16 from the army suppliers. Thus HMS Falmouth became the first RN ship in which officers wore this practical and inexpensive working rig, which was later adopted by the whole navy. With its management team sensibly dressed for the part, the ship felt ready to face a FOST staff work-up at Portland. I had been away from that frenetic scene for less than 2 years and, as the only one onboard who had previously served on FOST's staff, I was able to pass on to my fellow officers and to my own departmental senior and junior ratings, a number of tips on how to survive the pressure and get the most benefit from the training given during the next seven full weeks of intensive exercises. The work–up was, of course, very hard and exhausting work, but we survived and it sorted out the men from the boys. I was lucky to have a very good team, with only two exceptions, one of whom, who had passed the examination for promotion to Sub-Lieutenant, impressed both the staff and me for the wrong reason. Under pressure, he retired to the Chiefs' mess and left his busy team to get on with the work without his help or guidance. This dereliction of duty by an officer-aspirant was reported adversely by the staff and, after the work-up, he was drafted to another ship to give him a fresh chance of promotion, but he failed to improve his sense of responsibility under stress.

At last we reached the final week of the work-up and, after the final 'Thursday War' sea inspection, we were awarded the rare and highest possible distinction of a 'Good' pass from the Flag Officer Sea Training. For me the highlight of the work-up was our final AA 'shoot' when we achieved 100% hits, 22 Target-triggered bursts (TTBs) from 22 rounds, opening fire at 8000 yards. The whole ship did very well at Portland and came away in high spirits.

After a brief spell in Portsmouth, we sailed for a short home cruise incorporating some fleet exercises but including some treats. Fittingly, our first visit as a newly modernised and fully operational ship, was to the town whose name we bore and, after we berthed alongside, we received a warm civic welcome. The weather was good and the locals and grockles, (holidaymakers), made a fuss of us. Apart from official and private parties ashore and onboard, I managed a couple of rounds of golf with messmates and, like the rest of the ship's company, thoroughly enjoyed the social and recreational activities made available to us during an official visit to a friendly port.

*HMS Falmouth leaving Falmouth in June1971*

On our way to Rosyth, we picked up the Captain's father, Admiral Sir Desmond Dreyer, who had been my Captain in Saintes in the Med, 17 years earlier, and he took passage with us. The ship anchored for the night off Lindisfarne and we held our first wardroom mess dinner of the commission, with the Captain and his father as guests. The Admiral and I shared reminiscences during the dinner and before he was landed at Rosyth the next morning. There was just time for a quick visit to Dunfermline before we sailed for exercises of a somewhat lower key than we had grown used to at Portland. The ship then made a memorable visit to Dundee where we berthed alongside in the historic harbour, by then looking sadly underused, following the decline in the jute trade. We were entertained at a convivial civic reception given by the Lord Provost but, when a number of us, rather smartly wearing mess undress went to the 'Gents' at the town hall, we were horrified to find it full of drunks, and junkies injecting themselves. I visited Perth and enjoyed a tour of the city. However, I was disappointed to find how unimpressive the Tay Bridge of disaster fame was, after having heard so much about it from my grandmother. I managed to play, enjoy and lose a round of golf with my deputy Mike at a very good Dundee council-run course for only 50 pence a head, those were the days! On our last day there, the Captain asked me to co-host lunch in his cabin with the Lord Provost and three senior members of the Dundee city council. The Captain sat at the head of the table, two of the distinguished guests on each side and I sat at the other end. Jeremy Dreyer was an excellent raconteur and generous host and his chef had put on top class meal, which was enhanced by the best of wines and by lively, friendly discourse. At the end of lunch, Jeremy asked me to offer our guests their choice of post-prandial drinks so, standing in front of a sideboard groaning under the weight of a number of bottles of liqueurs including six excellent Malts, I turned to the principal guest and said, " My Lord Provost, which of the Captain's splendid malt whiskys would you like"?. Without hesitation he replied, "If it's all the same to you, Donald, I'll have a drop of Remy Martin". His fellow dignitaries followed suit and drank the brandy with relish. I wonder what the local press would have said about this apparent disloyalty to the local malt whisky industry, had they known?

Next morning we sailed eastward across the North Sea and through the Skagerrak and Kattegatt to the Danish mainland port of Arhus and berthed alongside in the inner harbour, within easy reach of the city centre. Like the Dutch, all of the locals were able to speak good English, and seemed to be anglophiles, so we thoroughly enjoyed their generous hospitality and reciprocated with onboard cocktail and children's parties. Our officers were given free membership of the local golf club and I enjoyed two days hacking my way around the course among local players of my lowly standard, and the subsequent 19th hole and wardroom socialising. Our first foreign visit proved to be a huge success all round and, as we steamed out of the harbour, we were given a rousing send off from the Danes as we set off to return to Portsmouth, to give leave and prepare for our deployment to the Orient.

My son Paul was a good cricketer who opened the bowling for his school X1 and was also a useful batsman. I was invited to play in the 'Fathers v Sons' match so, to avoid embarrassing Paul too much, I had some lessons from the ship's opening batsman in facing fast bowling. On the big day, the fathers went in first and weren't doing too well amassing only 67 runs by the time I went in at No 7. Paul, who had taken 3 wickets, was then brought back in to bowl to his Dad. As instructed, I pushed forward to his first ball, didn't see the ball, but somehow got a fine edge to the boundary. Paul clean bowled me with his next ball. However, having scored 4, I wasn't too ashamed of myself at the tea interval. During the boys innings, in which they were scoring freely, I was asked to bowl when Paul came in to bat at No 3 and he hit my slow bowling all over the place but, with a very flukey ball, I amazingly bowled the boys' best batsman for 44. Naturally the boys went on to win handsomely by 7 wickets. I was relieved not to have let Paul down in front of his chums.

On a Saturday afternoon in mid July, I had the great pleasure to be  present, with Eileen and Sally, when Paul became Victor Ludorum at his school Sports Day after he won the 100, 220, and 440 yards, High Jump, Rugby & Swimming Cups, Fencing Sabre, Cricket Cap and his Colours as team Captain for Rugby, Soccer, Fencing and Swimming. I was the proudest Dad there as he was repeatedly called forward to receive each trophy. I was embarrassed however, to receive the congratulations of the other fathers, for Paul had achieved an all round sporting standard way ahead of what I had ever reached in any sport.

Before the end of Paul's last term at Oakwood, we took him to see Bembridge School in the Isle of Wight and Embley Park School at Romsey and after a good look round and a chat with the scholars, mostly about sport, Paul chose Embley. His mother and Sally would have to take him there when he joined, because I would be at sea.

On 1st September 1971, HMS Falmouth left Portsmouth for the Far East via the Cape of Good Hope, briefly taking part in exercises off Portland as we passed, and joining up in the Bay of Biscay with HM Ships  Fearless and Phoebe to exercise our way to Gibraltar. We arrived at The Rock on 4th September, dressed in tropical rig, to share the colony with several other ships. During our four day visit, we suffered our first loss when two of our sailors fell into the huge empty graving dock, one being killed and the other seriously injured. On the 8th we sailed somewhat sadly south on the long haul to the Cape. The monotony of this long, lone passage was broken by a Syntax, rendezvousing with an RFA to refuel at sea and a Crossing the Line ceremony. The latter was made memorable by the arraignment before King Neptune of Petty Officer Nicholls. one of our two West-Indians, under the charge that he "Did appear on Divisions dressed as a negative". "PC was unheard of then and he took it all in good spirit.

We passed close to Cape Town and Table mountain before entering the harbour at Simonstown on the Cape of Good Hope peninsula and berthed alongside. We were immediately boarded by a number of uniformed and civilian officials and, as I had the only coloured ratings on the ship, I was introduced to the official concerned with non-white visitors. I had wondered how my two intelligent West Indian radio equipment maintainers would be treated in South Africa under their apartheid policy, but I needn't have worried for this official, who was 'cape-coloured' (of mixed race), outlined to me and the Petty Officer and Leading Hand concerned, a full programme of hospitality from wealthy non-white families, in fact they did rather better ashore than most of their shipmates.

This was my first visit to South Africa and on the first day I took the hour long train trip from Simonstown to Cape Town with several mess mates. We had a look at the department stores in the city and had a drink in a bar before going up Table Mountain in the cable car. This was a great experience particularly during the last 100 or so feet when, climbing vertically, it passed close to a narrow ledge on which mountain goats were munching grass quite unconcerned at the 1087 metres drop if they stumbled. The view from the top was spectacular and the 'table' was covered in beautiful spring flowers. There was however something missing. We had been advised that Cape Province was the most liberal part of the republic and, although apartheid was practised, it was so efficiently enforced that we hardly noticed it. Indeed, walking back through the naval dockyard that evening, one of my colleagues said, "I never saw a black man all day, what's the problem?" Passengers on the train were completely segregated, and the magnificent main station was entirely manned by whites, as were all of the nearby department stores and cafes. Furthermore, non-whites were not allowed in the cable car going up to the top of Table Mountain. During our week long visit I only saw one refreshing exception to the rigid separation of the minority whites from the blacks and half-caste South Africans and that was at mass on Sunday in Simonstown where apartheid was ignored, the choir and congregation being completely mixed. This single example of racial equality gave me hope that one day, a just society would emerge, but in the meantime, out of sight, out of mind, I shamelessly went along with our friendly white hosts and enjoyed a week of their most generous hospitality.

The South African Navy organised visits to vineyards, played games against our teams and laid on a golf tournament at a smart local course. Because the narrow fairway of the first hole was bounded by thick jungle-like woods, I addressed my ball on the first tee, close to the clubhouse, using my No3 iron. Suddenly, from a loudspeaker behind me, came the polite but firm voice of the club Secretary, a former British Lion Rugby player, telling me, and all within a nautical mile,

"We don`t drive off the first tee on this course with an iron"

Embarrassed, I took my wooden driver and promptly hooked the ball into the woods. My black caddie and that of my opponent went into the woods together to locate the ball but quickly came running out ashen-faced, shouting "Cobra". Conceding the hole, I started afresh at the second tee. Needless to say my charming South African opponent beat me easily but, despite my inauspicious start, I really enjoyed the game and the post match banter with him and the club secretary in the bar.

My final memory of this visit was going to an open air cinema and seeing a perfectly decent film that had been censored to ridiculous lengths by the puritanical censor, so that whenever a couple approached within a foot of each other, the scene was cut and the film jumped to a completely different scene, often with other characters. On the Sunday night, I put on 'Hello Dolly' for the wardroom's Sunday Night Cinema and our South African guests were delighted to see the civilised world's unexpurgated version of this great musical.

After leaving Simonstown and rounding Cape Agulhas we turned northwards into the Indian Ocean and hugged the coast all the way to Mozambique where we relieved HMS Juno on the Beira patrol. The task of this patrol duty, taken on by RN ships en route to or from the Middle or Far East, on behalf of the United Nations, was to deprive the illegal white government of Rhodesia of oil by blocking the only route available to their land locked country. The ship's Wasp helicopter flew many sorties to intercept possible blockade runners, and I accompanied Jeff Cowan on one of the flights, during which a sharp bank to port at 1600 feet with no doors on had me sweating. To while away the ten days we spent uneventfully maintaining this blockade in fine weather and a calm sea, we carried out gunnery exercises, A/S exercises using Syntax, played lots of onboard sport and, three times received an air drop of most welcome mail from home via an RAF Shackleton, before being relieved by HMS Zulu. We then set off northward for the Persian Gulf stopping for a couple of hours at Mombasa to embark the new MEO, Lt. Ray Perrett. We then set off for Bahrain, refuelling off Socotra before entering the Gulf to join HM Ships Intrepid and Minerva gathered at Bahrain to cover the British withdrawal from the Gulf where our influence had been exerted for 150 years.

We spent a week at Bahrain, at the start of which Peter Renson left the ship after more than two years. As Senior Technical Officer, I then moved from the 'Kasbah' on 2 deck into his well appointed cabin on the starboard side of 'Sea View Terrace', just below the bridge. The ship took part in the final sports matches held at HMS Jufair. I played in the final hockey match in which the last Senior Naval Officer Persian Gulf, Commodore Sir Peter Anson, whom I knew from FOST days, captained the RN team against an army team, and which we won. There was much nostalgic socialising as the base was winding down and, for those of us who had served in the gulf in earlier times, it was sad to see how quickly the facilities ashore were deteriorating. The ship then sailed south with Intrepid and Minerva to cover the RAF's withdrawal from the large Sharjah air base. Early one morning during a patrol out from Sharjah, we entered Elphinstone Inlet, reputedly the hottest place on earth, and steamed through shoals of fish. The week long annual Fleet Fishing Competition had just begun so the Captain decided to return to the mouth of the inlet that evening. Almost everyone onboard was on deck with their lines at dusk and lure lights were lowered but, in the 30 minute session allowed, not one fish was landed. The following night at anchor off Sharjah with HMS Minerva, her WEO Alex Barnett, my old chum from FOST's staff, challenged my division to a 30 minute WE fishing competition. His deputy came over to Falmouth to monitor his team and Mike Muggridge went over to Minerva. Both ships did well but his team won by total weight and number of fish caught. So, as previously agreed, I had to take a crate of beer over to Minerva as a prize. While I was there congratulating Alex and his team, as instructed by Alex, his deputy filled two 'met' balloons with water in my cabin so that access was more or less blocked. When I came to turn in later I tried to carry them out one at a time, to throw them over the side but each snagged on the cabin door, burst and soaked me and the carpet!

On the Thursday, the Officers of Falmouth were invited by the RAF to a golf match. The whole course was sand; one teed off as normal, but when the ball landed, it became buried in the sand so it was lifted and put on a tee stuck into a small cigar holder, to raise it to ground level. The 'greens' were made of heavily oiled sand which was rolled flat just before each pair played on to it and, naturally, one had to be careful not to tread on the sand between one's opponent's ball and the hole. Notwithstanding the rather strange conditions, it proved to be great social golf. Next morning, the RAF held their final ceremonial parade and that night their officers held a final mess dinner, to which we were invited. After a splendid meal, the mess games began and a heroic effort was made by all to polish off all of the mess's remaining stock of wines as it could not be left behind, in a Muslim country, when the last aircraft and officer left during the following week. When we returned to Falmouth at 0100, the farewell party was still going strong and after mass in the RAF chapel later that morning, attended by our doctor Chris Ashby and me, he was asked to help with an accident in the officers' mess. On arrival we found a very drunk RAF doctor had broken a leg trying to climb a monumental pile of empty bottles. Apparently he and a few stalwarts had carried on drinking all night!

Back onboard that afternoon, I was fishing from the flag deck when I caught a small ferocious-looking Catfish, all head and mouth with a short body and only six inches long. The landing of this mini-monster attracted the attention of the many other anglers on deck. I was advised by the experts among them that this catch was worthy of entry under the 'Ugliest Fish Caught' category in the Fleet Fishing Competition and so I had it photographed with a rule, to show its size, as it was not possible to send it back to the UK for judging. My elation at this catch, a rare piscatorial success for me, was suddenly terminated by the approach of my Gunnery Radar CPO who was clearly in great distress. To provide privacy we took cover in the small workshop under the Director where he broke down. We had been away from home then for three months and he couldn't stand being away from his wife any longer, was unable to face a further seven months away and wanted to go home. After two months away in the summer, he had thrown a minor 'wobbly' but this was a serious breakdown by a senior rating who had transferred from the RAF in which he had never been separated from his wife. I referred him to the Principal Medical Officer onboard the flagship HMS Intrepid, who sent the CPO home from where, and against his wishes, he was invalided out of the navy. This chap was a good example of a 'jolly good kid in harbour but no good at sea'. As a result of this, the ship was without a senior Surface Weapons Radar maintainer for the next six months whilst a relief was found and given the necessary training. In the meantime, as the only person left onboard who had done the relevant courses, I had to personally supervise the daily checks, setting-up, tuning and repair of the 903 Radar, the Gun- Direction System and the JYA Radar plotting tables as well as my overall charge responsibilities.

During daily checks two days later, a director system fault indicated we had developed a slip-ring defect which was overcome by using one of the spare rings but, after a different fault occurred a few days later, I realised we had a generic slip ring fault, and would have to change the whole unit. I signalled MOD and asked for a replacement to be air-freighted out to us. On a Sunday morning after a 10 day fleet exercise during which we had to utilise the remaining spare rings to keep the system operational, we anchored off Gan and were met by a boat carrying a crate containing a new unit. The replacement of this relatively complex unit was normally a specialist dockyard job undertaken alongside but, "Needs must as the Devil drives" so I and my small team of Gunnery maintainers, less the CPO who had gone home, tackled the job at anchor near the Equator. The old slip ring unit was disconnected and hoisted out of the director using a tackle and a tripod made from damage-control beams. We then saw, for the first time, that many of the delicate slip-rings were badly corroded. The new unit was lowered into position, connected up and tested and the whole director system proven. The defective unit was then packed in the supply crate and landed before dusk for return to the UK. That hard day's work was rewarded by a year of trouble-free service from the gunnery system, during which it achieved notable success.

Whilst acting as night and day 'plane-guard' for HMS Eagle during the aforementioned fleet exercise, I had a chat with the carrier's Executive Officer, Cdr. Murray Johnstone on the ship/ship phone. He had been the First Lieutenant of Nubian with me in 1962/4.

Having steamed over 24,000 miles in the 4 months since leaving home, we sailed east, rendezvoused with HMS Scylla and the submarine Finwhale, and exercised our way to Mombasa for a self-maintenance period. We berthed alongside HMS Truimph, a repair ship which was at anchor in the middle of the harbour and was en route home from Singapore. HMS Minerva was berthed on her other side. The three WEOs, Alan Western. Alex Barnett and I, were old friends from our time together as apprentices and later as Sea Riders at Portland. We had a photo taken taking notes on each other's ships and sent a copy to our old boss Don Fletcher. Alan and I went on station leave

*Alan Western, Alex Barnett and Don*

together for a week, going first to Nairobi on the famous overnight train, the African equivalent of the Orient Express. We had free first-class railway warrants and a sleeper each, enjoyed a superb 5 course dinner including a half Lobster Thermidor and a Filet Mignon steak (all for 25 Kenyan shillings, (£1.25) with wines at a very reasonable cost and very well served. At dawn we were awoken to see, to the south across a shimmering plain, the snow covered upper reaches of Mount Kilimanjaro. Whilst we were tucking in to an English breakfast, the train stopped to allow a herd of elephants to cross the tracks and as we approached Nairobi, we saw the very first Boeing 747 Jumbo jet landing in Africa. As temporary members of the Mombasa club we were entitled to stay at the famous Nairobi club so we took a taxi there and enjoyed a fabulous and luxurious three days in the Kenyan capital. One day we visited the parliament of this independent state and noted how well the members behaved compared with those of their mother parliament at Westminster! The club was across the central park from the city and, after an evening visit to the latter we walked back across the park without any sign of trouble. We also visited the Nairobi National Park and had a drink in each of the best hotels to see how the other half lived. On our last evening we dined in style in the club and enjoyed the company of several of the members. In December 1971 Kenya, after eight years of black rule, seemed to be a well run friendly ex-colony, with the two races getting on well with each other. We returned to Mombassa in daylight all the way and on arrival, went straight to Silversands a chalet style hotel for service personnel situated close to the beautiful sandy Nyali beach and to the home of

Jomo Kenyatta, the Kenyan President. We enjoyed a relaxing holiday of sun, swimming and cool drinks but I had a shock one night. I slipped out to the shower/lavatory, switched on the light and was horrified to see the whole place covered in creepy crawlies. I was glad to get back to bed and under my mosquito net.

The Chief GI Les Storr, edited a weekly humorous and somewhat defamatory magazine called UZZ which was published at noon every Saturday, reported jocularly on the incidents of the week, and was very well received by all onboard. The identity of the authors of the articles was never revealed and, in fact, I wrote a regular column and the odd article myself. This did not of course save me from being the subject of several unflattering cartoons, a fictitious 'Life Story' and various scurrilous stories, all obviously written by members of my division or the wardroom, all of which I enjoyed.

Paris People

HMS Eagle was also supposed to spend Christmas at Mombassa but, for political reasons she was diverted and the show that HMS Eagle, the RN's biggest warship, had arranged to entertain her crew, was watched, enjoyed and the cast hosted, by the smaller numbers aboard Truimph, Minerva and Falmouth. Two well-balanced shows were performed by a professional group on a stage in the Triumph's hangar with the audience, half of the complement of the three ships on each night, on the flight deck. The cast included Pan's People, Roger de Courcey, Johnny Ball, the Garland Sisters, Lee Leslie and the comedienne and impressionist Janet Brown. After the final show, Falmouth's wardroom entertained some of the cast to dinner and I found myself next to the charming and witty Janet Brown. After dinner I had a dance with her and also with Louise, the lead girl of Pan's People who signed the back of this photograph of her gorgeous group, which I sent home to Paul. He gained great kudos at school from having a Dad who knew Pan's People. The show and the socialising was a huge success and we were grateful to the absent HMS Eagle for having organised our entertainment.

Next morning as the Britannia airliner carrying the whole troupe back to the UK for the Christmas pantomimes roared down the runway, the pilot had to abort the take-off at the last moment and put the turbo props into reverse thrust. The aircraft ground to a halt just short of the boundary trees and a disaster was avoided. The very shaken passengers and crew escaped but, as the aircraft, and runway were now non- operational, the concert party were cared for by the RN until they caught the train for Nairobi and a flight home.

On 20<sup>th</sup> December, we went to sea for two days to prove all the equipment after our self-maintenance period but, on return, had to moor alone some distance from the other ships and a long boat trip from shore.  I went to Midnight Mass aboard Triumph and, after our onboard Falmouth celebrations and Christmas lunch; I went ashore, in seasonal, alcohol-enhanced, high spirits, to make the telephone call home I had booked. It was wonderful to be able to hear the family again after four months of separation.

We left Mombasa on 27<sup>th</sup> December for our second Beira patrol, relieving HMS Scylla. On New Years Eve, as the oldest man aboard the ship, I was asked to play Old Father Time at the ringing in New Year ceremony. Dressed appropriately and carrying a scythe and proclamation scroll, I waited behind the hangar with the youngest lad on the ship, a good looking 18 year old mechanic who, playing the role of the New Year baby, wore only a white towel as a nappy kept together by two large sick bay safety pins. On cue at 2359 I towed the young lad on to the flight deck where we were faced with most of the ship's company, all of whom were in a festive mood. Seeing us, they immediately began to sing Auld Lang Syne, until the MC told them to stop until the 16 bells had been struck, I then unrolled my parchment, read my spiel and rang the old year out with 8 bells before introducing the Babe and inviting him to ring 1972 in. In this high-spirited and boisterous atmosphere, the young lad grabbed the rope over-zealously, causing the clapper to detach from the bell and fly on to the deck among the revellers. Utter confusion reigned until the clapper was found, re hung and the last 8 bells were rung. In the front row of the assembly on the flight deck, the ship's renowned pessimist, a mournful Chief, proclaimed in a loud voice, "This interruption in the New Year Bell-ringing ceremony bodes ill for the ship in 1972". After a brief, embarrassing silence, the ship's band struck up and everyone sang Auld Lang Syne and drank a toast to the ship and the New Year.

Sadly, six months later, whilst on leave at home, Falmouth's New Year Babe was severely injured and disfigured in a car crash and was invalided from the service.

On the 4th of January our helicopter picked up a sick sailor from a giant tanker and landed him ashore in Beira for urgent medical attention but otherwise this 20 day patrol passed in a similar way to the previous one with sports on deck, an occasional dash off to check a tanker going too close to Beira and various exercises. The ship's immediate programme since we left the UK had frequently been changed at short notice for political reasons and though the ship's company had been kept informed by the 1st Lieutenant, they thought they had been kept in the dark and fed on manure, but had somehow flourished, so a wag devised a new RAS (Replenishment at sea) flag, a white mushroom on a black background. We were finally relieved of our patrol duties by HMS Achilles and, flying our own new RAS flag, fuelled from an RFA tanker, and at last were on our way to the Far East. However this was not to be direct, for we had to divert to the Seychelles to land one of our seamen suffering from appendicitis. We were only at Victoria, Mahé for 30 minutes but I noticed how much more 'touristy' it had become since I was last there. We then made for Gan to land and pick up personnel and mail before going on eastward. At Gan, I had time for a round of golf and to buy a duty-free automatic Seiko watch in the NAAFI, get back aboard and start reading the great pile of letters which had arrived for me while I was ashore, before we weighed anchor and set off for Singapore.

Besides about 30 loving letters from Eileen, and late birthday cards, there was a letter from Paul's housemaster at school. He reported that the school doctor and a consultant had diagnosed that Paul was Dyslexic and recommended that he had remedial tuition to correct this condition. After consulting our MO Chris Ashby, I wrote back to the school accepting their advice. This decision was to prove vital to Paul's future for he was able to continue with his sport and, at the same time gain 6 O levels and 2 A levels and to enjoy a career in leisure management and in rugby.

A defect on the turret prevented the guns being elevated to 5 degrees for our ceremonial entry to the Naval base so, dressed in whites with leather soled shoes I climbed into the turret to see what was wrong and promptly slipped on the oily deck and banged my knee against the fuze-setting machine. We managed to get the guns at the right angle in time. However, that evening whilst having a drink in the officers club with Mike Muggridge and his newly arrived relief, Lieutenant Bob Stevenson, an ordnance specialist, my knee suddenly 'blew up' and became full of fluid. I had to get a taxi back to the ship. Next morning, as Chris Ashby had already left for Hong Kong on another ship, I went to the Sick Bay in the former HMS Terror, now the tri-service ANZUK Woodlands Garrison Mess, and after a long wait, it being Saturday morning, I saw a young Australian Army doctor who, wearing a palm beach shirt, shorts and flip flops, told me the knee swelling fluid was blood. Wearing a face mask but no gloves and with flies buzzing around the wide open operating theatre, he cheerfully aspirated the blood and dressed the knee. I returned to the ship and later went into Singapore where I bought myself a full set of golf clubs, a new bag and a trolley and returned to the base ready to enjoy some golf during our three days in harbour. However, the knee became progressively more painful and my new clubs stood unused in my cabin and, when I finally saw an RN doctor, he said that the knee was badly infected. As we were sailing that day for competitive fleet gunnery exercises off the Malaysian coast against PTAs, surface and bombardment targets, I declined to go ashore for treatment and was able to play my part in the preparation for, and the firings. These proved very successful and, after various shoots by the rest of the RN fleet all over the world, HMS Falmouth was declared to have won the Fleet Surface and Bombardment trophies. We did pretty well too in the AA and Seacat missile firings and these counted towards our final position in the annual fleet Gunnery Championship. As we set off after the shoots towards Hong Kong our Wasp helicopter spotted a Soviet submarine, on the surface, presumably unable to dive because of a defect, being escorted by a Russian 'Spy' trawler. We closed and shadowed them as they made their way northward; their crews completely ignored our friendly waves.

Unusually, we entered Hong Kong harbour on 5th February 1972, via the Lamma Channel and, as we approached Stonecutters Island we passed close to the still smoking wreck of the liner Queen Elizabeth lying on her side like a great beached whale after the disastrous and very suspicious fire that destroyed her. On her quarter deck, looking like a gigantic Butler sink, was an empty swimming pool. It was sad to see this once great ship looking so forlorn. We berthed alongside in the tidal basin close to HMS Tamar and the China Fleet club. On the way to HK, I instructed our two Singapore-Chinese Artificer Apprentices, Lee and Goh to make a very large illuminated sign reading "Kung Hei Fat Choy" in Chinese characters and, with the Chinese New Year only ten days away, had them erect it along the upper deck on the shore- facing side. Local orders forbade flashing lights because of the proximity of Kai Tak airport, so the sign was left switched on at night and drew hoots of pleasure from passing taxi-drivers and other Chinese motorists. Soon after our arrival we held a Chinese mess dinner at a local restaurant, to dine out my deputy Mike Muggridge before he flew home to take up an appointment in shore wireless. Mike had been a loyal and hard working deputy, a popular member of the mess and a good partner on the tennis court and golf course.

Since we left Singapore my knee had been treated onboard daily by the Leading Medical Assistant but was still very painful, so Chris Ashby the MO took over its treatment and soon I was walking reasonably well, although still unable to christen my new golf clubs.

There were a number of RN ships in Hong Kong at that time and, for the first time, we met the leader of our squadron and, during three days alongside with her, her Cdr (WE) had a look over my department, expressed his satisfaction with it, and we enjoyed socialising onboard and ashore. I also took part, as a member of the board, in several examinations of senior ratings for advancement and a technical enquiry into an accident on one of the ships. After twelve days in Hong Kong, during which my knee was completely cured, we left harbour and made for Singapore with our leader for exercises on the way. On the Sunday before Lent, following a particularly good homily by the Padre during mass in the base Catholic chapel, and conscience-stricken after some over indulgence in the grain and grape at Hong Kong, Chris Ashby and I, decided we would join the chaplain in giving up alcohol for Lent. Normally the wardroom bar in Falmouth was closed at sea, except on Saturday evening, so our self-imposed pledge of abstinence began two days early. The ship then went north to Subic Bay in the Philippines where we joined a large SEATO fleet for three weeks of anti- submarine and air exercises with RAN, USN, Fillipno and Thai ships , at the end of which, in worsening typhoon weather, we returned to Hong Kong for a brief visit to spruce up with the help of Ah Soo and the girls of her side party. Chris and I were invited to dinner at the Jesuit College in Wanchai, by the Rector whom we had hosted onboard. When we politely declined the repeated offers of a pre dinner drink, because we had given up for Lent, the Jesuit teacher/priests asked the Rector if he would give us a mid-Lent dispensation so that we could drink wine with them during dinner. When we again refused, they said we were mad. Nevertheless we enjoyed a great, if dry, evening. The Senior Technical Officer ashore in Hong Kong was Commander Chesney Hallet, an ex-apprentice, a year ahead of me at Fisgard, who lived with his wife in a MQ on the Peak and, because I was the Senior TO afloat at that time at Hong Kong, he kindly let me have use of his official and very luxurious suite on the 5<sup>th</sup> floor of Tamar's Wardroom tower block. I had seven very comfortable nights of B&B in Tamar and

the rest of each day onboard the ship, which I could keep an eye on from the bedroom window as it lay floodlit in the dockyard basin below. If I looked out of the lounge window of the suite, I had a close up view of the 5 star Mandarin hotel, just across the road carrying the trams from Shaukiwan to Kennedy Town. I enjoyed a round trip on this route, riding upstairs in an ancient tram, seeing the Chinese families on the first floor of the buildings it passed eating meals, watching TV or playing Mah Jong. On 1<sup>st</sup> March, still in blue suits because of the unusually cool weather, we posed for the ship's company and departmental official photographs.

Incidentally, my cabin scuttle, (porthole) is the upper of the two dark circles immediately above the letter F of the pennant number on the ship's starboard side, shown in this photograph. The dark circle below it is the back of the floodlight.

*HMS Falmouth Ship'c Company, March 1972, Hong Kong*
*(Don is right of centre in front row)*

During our last two weeks in Hong Kong I managed to buy my home-coming presents for Eileen, Sally and Paul in what was then the best value shopping venue in the world, but a major defect just before we left prevented me getting in that first game of golf with my 2 months old clubs. We sailed on the Ides of March with the Australian fleet, led by the aircraft carrier HMAS Melbourne, had our successful inspection by the CinC and carried out gunnery, anti-submarine and tactical air exercises en route and, eventually arrived at Singapore naval base on 26th March for an assisted maintenance period, including 5 days of station leave before continuing our 4 month journey home. During this period, the annual ANZUK Forces 'Grimmy' competition was held to find which unit had a member who had dated the worst looking woman. A very good-looking AB from Falmouth, who had taken out a really hideous transvestite, won through to the finals and when the photo proving the ghastly mismatch was passed along the line of judges, including the Aussie Colonel, a Kiwi Army Matron, and the Senior RN Officer, the many Falmouths present cheered as each judge recoiled in horror before they unanimously awarded the trophy, a well worn Aussie army combat boot on to which was added, to the names of various Antipodean units, 'HMS Falmouth 1972'.

We had arrived just before Easter weekend and as I was pretty broke after my shopping spree in Hong Kong, I decided to take my leave first and to spend it in the mess ashore and to play a lot of golf. I began as I intended with a game on Holy Saturday morning. Never having been more than an enthusiastic hacker, I didn't play well but optimistically put this down to unfamiliarity with my new clubs and the fact I hadn't played since we left Gan two months earlier. Next morning after mass, having learnt that Chris and I had kept our Lenten pledge, the Padre invited us to a champagne breakfast which went on rather a long time so I blamed the chaplain for my abysmal performance on the course that afternoon. On Easter Monday, our new CO, Commander Gordon Walwyn, a gunnery specialist, joined and, in accordance with custom, took over command of the ship in a short turn-over from Jeremy Dreyer, who had already given all of his officers their 'flimsies'. I was very pleased with mine, which ended with a recommendation for promotion to Commander. That afternoon I played a slightly improved game of golf. Next morning I went to RAF Tengah with several messmates to see off our popular, generous and proficient former Captain, who flew home in a VC10, after commanding HMS Falmouth for 18 months. That afternoon I played rugby for what proved to be the last time. Normally the time of the daily 20 minute monsoon downpour could be predicted, but on this occasion, we had been playing about 50 minutes when a sudden storm brought bolts of lightning all around the ground which were rather frightening, so the referee blew his whistle and abandoned the game as we all ran for shelter from the lightning and torrential rain. On the Wednesday I played golf in the morning and was pleased with my round but this moderate success was my undoing for, in my state of elation I was persuaded to play soccer for the wardroom in the ship's 7-a-side knock-out cup competition beginning at 1630. Quite incredibly we progressed to the floodlit final which was held before a crowd. In the second half, with the score at 1 all, I was tackled by a pair of 19 year old backs and, in the words of the subsequent Hurt Certificate, was brought heavily to the ground and suffered the violent displacement of three vertebrae. The two lads picked me up but I was in such pain that an ambulance was called and I was carted off to the ANZUK military hospital at Changi. The orthopaedic consultant, an RAF Wing-commander, met the ambulance at the hospital and, after the X-rays, had me placed on a slightly backward tilted board and put in traction. I was destined to remain there under this remedial treatment for 13 days. My bed was at one end of the officers' ward on the top floor of the hospital. Most of the occupants were young Australian army officers who had been wounded in the Vietnam war, there was one young New Zealand subaltern who was not only wounded but also had malaria and was being barrier nursed at the other end of the ward. Next to me was a Canadian Flight Lieutenant pilot who had flown a Phantom jet aircraft in a squadron formation non-stop from the UK, refuelling several times in flight, despite unknowingly having a broken rib and punctured lung. I felt humble at being among these guys for, in a sense my problem was self inflicted, trying to play young men's contact sports at the age of 43. The nursing sisters were formidable Australian army ladies of my age who had their work cut out trying to control the Aussie walking wounded who had chums outside the hospital smuggling in lots of beer to them. They were a lively and very friendly crowd and generously gave me beer, but it was quite difficult drinking the stuff with my head lower than my legs. The Canadian pilot in the next bed and I were the only patients receiving the tender loving care of a beautiful Eurasian physiotherapist, much to the envy of the Aussies. My very able deputy Bob Stephenson visited me, bringing me up to date with the news and, when I heard that the ship was finally leaving Singapore on 25th April, after a 3 day visit to Penang, I resolved to be out of hospital by then and, to this end, carried out my regime of exercises religiously. Although I still had a certain amount of back pain, which I omitted to report, I was discharged on the 22nd and driven to the naval base where I did some last minute shopping while awaiting sea transport out to the ship. I will always associate the song 'I was born under a wandering star' with my spell in that hospital for, while I lay in traction, the film Paint Your Wagon was shown to the staff and up patients in the open-air cinema nearby, I heard every word of that great musical without being able to see it. I boarded RFA Stromness on Sunday 24th and after24 hours aboard a ship run by a martinet of a Captain, who looked and acted like James Robertson Justice, was feared by all his officers and crew and whose officers' mess was dominated by the Medical Officer's veritable dragon of a wife, I was relieved to transfer back to HMS Falmouth, my own, friendly, male only ship.

After gunnery and missile firings, we set sail for Ceylon. I still had some back pain so I got OEA Brian Sheppard to make a set of pulleys and weights so that I could give myself 30 minutes of traction after lunch every day. I was feeling completely fit by the time we reached Colombo on 3rd May. We berthed just astern of two Soviet guided missile destroyers one of which was the flagship of the Russian Pacific fleet. Then began the propaganda war, first we challenged them to a soccer match but they, suspecting we had brought the RN team with us, declined, earning some derision from the local press. Then they gave a very good band concert but the locals preferred our ship's amateur pop group to their classical music. Our ship's company went ashore in plain clothes singly or in small groups and seemed to have plenty of money, theirs went in uniform in larger groups, oddly holding hands like children, and in the charge of an officer or NCO, and had little money to spend.

Falmouth was open to visitors but the locals were only allowed on the Russian ships' upper decks. To finally clinch this political victory, we took the local VIPs and press to sea for a day and gave them a demonstration of our capabilities including weapon firings and helicopter flying which received glowing praise in the local media. The two modern and very well armed Russian ships never moved any of their weapons or aerials during the 10 day visit or transmitted their radar or sonar suggesting that the need to keep electronics going in the tropics had not yet been grasped by the Ruskies. The Russian Admiral invited our Captain, First Lieutenant and one other officer to their official cocktail party and Gordon Walwyn, in an apparent show of egalitarianism, took Midshipman Tony, later Vice-Admiral Sir Anthony, Dymock, who had a degree in Russian and afterwards he regaled us with hilarious things he saw and heard at that party, particularly at the sight of successive Russian Officers being carted away paralytic and being instantly replaced by fresh host officers. Our stay at Colombo was extended because the proposed visit to Bombay was cancelled when we refused to answer the Indian questionnaire regarding carrying nuclear weapons by neither confirming or denying we had any. I played a couple of rounds of golf and toured the rather shabby city that had clearly been quite imposing in the days of the Raj but now lacked investment. However, the locals were friendly towards us and though poor, appeared to be happy with their independence.

After finally leaving Colombo. we proceeded straight to the Gulf and paid official visits to Dubai, Abu Dhabi and Kharg Island where we exercised with the Iranian navy for a week and were then lavishly entertained to a caviar party by the Crown Prince who had earlier flown his private helicopter on to our flight deck at sea. I was asked by the Iranian flagship to loan them one of our films but, as this was illegal, I offered to send them my operator with a projector and film. Their rigid, feudal two-class system, (officers and the rest of the populace), stopped them having a rating in their wardroom so, in protest I declined to show the film to them myself. Small wonder, that the Shah and his ruling class were later overthrown in a revolution. We then went south to Bahrain where we were dismayed to see how the shore facilities had deteriorated in the 6 months since our last visit, even the swimming pools were out of action. On then to Sharjah where all the local traders seemed to be driving around in RAF lorries left behind when we withdrew, and the once busy air base, now somewhat pretentiously called Sharjah International Airport, had only one listed arrival and departure in a week. Before leaving the Gulf, we visited Muscat a place I had visited and have written about in a previous chapter, and then set out for Mombasa, fuelling en route.

During our brief stop at Mombasa, I met John Wiseman, an old chum, and we played golf. Halfway round the course, a police car loudspeaker message called for Lieutenant Wiseman, so we walked to it and he was asked to go to the local hospital to give blood to a sick woman who had the same rare blood group as he had. When he returned he said how great it was to give blood direct to someone in great need. We carried on playing and he beat me.

We steamed non-stop then to Simons Town for a three- day visit, I took the Captain and two other newly joined officers to Cape Town in plain clothes one day, in the staff car kindly loaned to us by the SA navy. We also went up Table Mountain and, while walking back to the cable car and admiring the view, we met my two Chinese Apprentices, who, as usual were very smartly dressed, in uniform. They joined us for the descent and chatted with us without causing any concern to the white South Africans present and, at the bottom of the mountain, calmly sat in the White Only seats of a bus with no adverse reaction. It appears that the South Africans considered the Japanese, alone of all Asians, to be 'honorary whites' and thought that Goh and Lee must be Japanese. On the 2nd evening, I went to a party at the home of Captain Dieter Gerhardt, and entertained him onboard afterwards to a lengthy nightcap, (see Chapter 17). On the last night, a SA navy sentry reported seeing a frogman near one of their submarines and set off an alarm which had us, and all the ships in the harbour, going to Action stations for real. After a whole night closed up taking the prescribed labour-intensive counter measures, the port authorities finally concluded the sentry had seen a seal.

We broke the long haul north with two days at Freetown Sierra Leone and I attended a reception at the British embassy and was given a tour of the city. I can understand why it was known as the 'white man's grave' for the climate was very hot and humid.

On the night we passed Madeira en route to Gibraltar, we held a mess dinner to dine out the five officers leaving the ship on arrival home. As the 1st Lieutenant was one of these, and I was the next in seniority, I became Mess President for the occasion and had to give a welcome to the Captain and a valediction for each of the leavers. I scripted and gave a short light hearted anecdotal description of each of them, starting with Surgeon Lt. Chris Ashby, who had looked after us so well, then Lt. 'Jamey' Jameson the Navigating Officer, for accurately piloting us for over 70,000 miles since leaving home , Lt Jeff Cowan MBE, who had driven the Wasp Helicopter without a prang and gained his Bridge Watch-keeping ticket, old Etonian, Lt Tim Jones, one of the very best Gunnery Officer I ever worked with, and finally No 1, our outstanding old Rugbeian, First Lieutenant, Lt Cdr Richard Channon, who had run the most friendly and happy wardroom and the cleanest, and happiest ship in which I had ever served and, despite our mushroom flag, kept the ship's company and their families better informed than all the others. I concluded my eulogy by saying, and meaning,"That Falmouth is an efficient warship, which has met all of the CinC Fleet's requirements of her throughout the past 18 months, is due, in no small measure, to the enthusiasm and professional skill of the officers we are dining-out tonight. We have enjoyed their company, learnt much and benefited greatly from their presence. Will you all now join me in wishing them a fond farewell and good luck in their new appointments".

Next morning we carried out an AA shoot against a target towed by a Canberra aircraft and then had a brief stop at Gibraltar before sailing north in company with HM Ships Cleopatra and Zulu to Plymouth where, in the Sound, we embarked HM Customs on the evening of the 19th July. Once cleared, we set off on the final leg to Portsmouth, arriving alongside next morning, to a great welcome from our families. Again I find it difficult to express the joy and happiness I felt, at being reunited with Eileen and the children.

We had been kept in touch not only by our daily letters and phone calls from Subic Bay and Mombasa, but by the regular issues of the informative and descriptive Falmouth Packet, edited by the First Lieutenant. I paraphrase a passage from his last edition, to describe some of the feelings I shared with many of my shipmates as we were reunited with our wives that morning. 'I am truly grateful to you my dear Eileen, for coping alone with two teen-age children, the school-run, house and garden and all the things husbands do as a matter of course, and still finding time to write me a loving letter every day. I take off my hat to you and to all naval wives. As Jane Austen wrote," She gloried in being the wife of a naval man, but she must pay the penalty of quick alarm for belonging to that profession which is if possible more distinguished in its domestic felicity than in its national importance." - God Bless You Eileen.

We had a simply wonderful time together during the children's summer holidays and my foreign service leave, although this time, I was grounded from riding, and we stayed at home, travelling daily in the car to the beach and to the local countryside.

When I returned from leave I was delighted to find that my formal application to join the Institution of Marine Engineers had been accepted, but most surprised and honoured to have been elected a Fellow, rather than a Member. I could only guess that this was on the strength of a published thesis on the restoration of sea-water-flooded electrical equipment. My status as a Chartered Engineer was to prove most beneficial when I entered civilian life seven years later. Almost all of my very good team of maintainers and my first rate deputy and friend, Lt Bob Stephenson were still aboard and, with the exception of the new First Lieutenant, Lt. Cdr Tony Light, a pleasant fixed-wing Pilot, the new officers were younger and rather less experienced than their predecessors. They were however, a keen and friendly bunch. To ease them in to their new duties, we went to sea for a shake-down cruise, including a second visit to Falmouth, before returning to Portsmouth for a few days, berthing on Fountain Lake Jetty. I have two personal memories of this period. The CinC Fleet announced that HMS Falmouth were the 1971/72 Fleet Surface Weapons Champions by winning the Surface Gunnery and Bombardment trophies, coming second in the AA and third in the Sea Cat Missile firing competitions. Not bad for an Anti-Submarine Frigate, in a fleet totalling 72 surface combatant ships, including 2 cruisers, 10 large destroyers and 60 frigates, most of whom took part in the fleet competition. It is also worth mentioning that Falmouth's ship's staff had changed a major gunnery component at anchor, alone in the Indian Ocean without outside help, just before the competition started. Unsurprisingly, when the trophies were presented that week, none of the WE division, which alone maintained and manned the semi-automatic Gunnery tracking system, Computer and Director, and partially manned the Turret, and provided the Blind-fire Safety Officer (me), were invited to the ceremony. The group photograph taken at the ceremony showed only Seamen and the new CO and Gunnery Officer, both of whom joined the ship after the firings which won the title.

At home, Molly, the dear lady we 'inherited' from the previous owners of our house, retired after four years with us, to live with her son in Southsea. She had done a great job looking after us and we wondered how we would ever be able to manage without her. However, we were soon extremely lucky to find her successor, a real treasure. Eileen Clarke, settled down quickly and proved to be a tower of strength and indispensable to all four of us for the next 32 years, until she retired in 2005. During her long reign, she and her husband Bob became members of the family and remain our very good friends. Sally and Paul still affectionately call Eileen, "Auntie Clarke".

Back onboard, about this time, I overheard one of the young first commission officers still onboard, telling the newcomers to the wardroom that, as a result of my back injury at Singapore, "The WEO is past it and couldn't run to save his life". Incensed, I challenged the 24 year old Lieutenant, (who later became a Commodore), to a 100 metres race along the jetty. Although I was wearing overalls and he was in sports rig, I beat him by a yard, proving to him, and all of the mess who were watching and cheering, that there was still life in the old dog. Shortly afterwards we went to Portland for a short work-up during which the newcomers learnt a lot and the ship performed well, earning a 'Good' report, and we had another 100% TTBs AA shoot. We then went to Plymouth for the weekend before taking part in a 14 day NATO fleet exercise in the Atlantic. On our return to Portsmouth, my relief, Lt. Cdr Barney O'Carroll joined and, 5 days later, just before the ship sailed to Antwerp for the first foreign visit of the second commission, and with Barney champing at the bit to take over, I left the ship, to join HMS Collingwood as 2i/c of the Control School, ostensibly my first non-technical posting.

From the technical sea charge-job standpoint, HMS Falmouth was the pinnacle of my naval career and I thoroughly enjoyed being head of her WE department. During my 2½ years in her, I was successively blessed with two good, kind, considerate and proficient Captains, two hard working and able deputies, a very good Warrant Officer and, apart from two exceptions, less than 4% of my total staff, a first rate set of senior and junior ratings who were loyal, hard working and behaved well onboard and ashore.

**The Weapons Electrical Engineering Division of HMS Falmouth March 1972 at Hong Kong**

*Rear:* REA/A Goh, OEA/A Lee, CEM Brown, O'S Raynor, CEM O'Keefe, REMn/A Muscroft
    LCEM Billaney, LREM Lopez, OEM Smallshaw. LREM Dean, REM Main, REM Newsom
    LEM Ryland, AB Swadling, LOEM Kinally, CEM Morrice, CE Rawlings, CPO Rootes
*2nd:* CEA/A Key, POCel Orr, PORel Fitzjohn, POrel Nicoholls, PO West, POCel Magennis,
    POOEL Stead, POOel Wattam, OEA Price, POCel Acons
*Ist:* CREA Linfield, OEA Ma ,kenzie, CRel Jordan, COEL Ranshaw, REA Hall, CEMech Barker
*Front:*            FCCEMech Jordan, Lt Cdr Murdoch, Lt Stephenson.
*Absent:*      CE Mech Thomas, POOel J ohnstone, POoel Whitehead,REA ERdwards,
           LREM Hallam OEM Hannah,OEM Gardiner, CEM Britten, REM Butler

I also had a comfortable cabin, friendly mess mates, none of whom, smoked, quite incredible in the early 70s, another example of Falmouth being way ahead of its time. I look back nostalgically with pride at having been part of a great ship's company of a very efficient, well led, trend-setting and most successful front-line ship.

# Chapter 20

## Control Electrical School Staff Officer
## HMS Collingwood

### December 1972 – December 1974

The Control Electrical School was headed by a Commander, who was responsible for the training, welfare and discipline of the staff of 36 Officers, one Warrant Officer, around 50 Chief and Petty Officers and civilian Instructors and 640 students. Like the Commanders i/c of the other three autonomous schools, (the Ordnance Electrical, Radio Electrical and Common Training Schools), he reported directly to the Captain of HMS Collingwood, the navy's largest training establishment. I relieved an old friend Lt. Cdr, George Pincott, who had been a year ahead of me at Fisgard and with whom I had served in HMS Theseus in 1949-51. George gave me a good turn-over during the week before the school went on Christmas leave, including the ceremonial and disciplinary responsibilities I would have as deputy to the School Commander, Jack Howard, an ebullient, ex- rugby hero, Instructor Commander.

The Control school, as the CE school was generally known, was accommodated in 3 new 4-storey blocks flanking a quadrangle which served as the school assembly area and deck hockey/volley ball pitch. This whole complex was situated near the western fence around Collingwood, about a mile from the main gate. The school's own administrative offices and, in 4-berth cabins, all junior CE ratings who were awaiting draft after having completed course, were accommodated in Plate block, CE Apprentices in Saintes Block and Junior CE ratings in Matapan block. Leading CEMs, CEAs and Mechanicians acting as leading hands of a floor, occupied single cabins whilst other Leading Hands shared 2 or 3 berth cabins.

Chief and Petty Officers of the Control school lived in all-Collingwood messes. All junior Control ratings fell in on the quadrangle by class, before and after instruction, marching to and from their classrooms and demonstration rooms in the technical training areas of Collingwood. Every Friday morning the whole school, with the other 3 schools and the ship's company, took part in Collingwood's ceremonial divisions on the main parade ground,

On return from a happy traditional family Christmas at home, I found myself doing the job of the First Lieutenant in a ship. First thing every morning, before morning divisions I de-briefed the duty Chief and then took charge of the parade, inspected them and then called on the Commander to come and take the salute as his school marched off for the first session of instruction. I then briefed the Commander on any overnight incidents or problems before carrying out an inspection of the accommodation areas with the CE School Fleet Chief, who was like a Guards RSM, tall, smart and a strict disciplinarian. I then studied the list of defaulters with whom I would have to deal after the end of morning classes. The Fleet Chief stopped them from dashing off to lunch when they fell-out from the parade and the Regulating Petty Officer arraigned them individually before me to answer the relevant charge(s). I had to hear all of the charges and, if they were serious, I had to decide whether there was a case to answer. If I passed the case on upwards I had to act as the prosecutor at the School Commander' table and, if very serious, at the Captain's table. At 1210 every day, after hearing the serious cases, I then had to deal with a string of minor offences. After the charges were read out by the RPO, I asked the accused if he understood the charge, before solemnly intoning the following:

"I shall try this case myself, if I find you guilty, I may punish you myself or pass you on to the Commander for sentencing, depending on your record. Do you plead Guilty or Not Guilty?"

This daily ritual led to the award of minor punishments, ensured that the defaulters had Hobson's choice from the menu in the dining hall, and lost me the chance of a pre-prandial drink.

One morning, I was informed by the duty Chief that he had found a young local woman in bed with one of the Leading Hands. Pending my arrival, he had told the woman to get dressed and had detained her under watch in his office. Aware that the woman concerned was not subject to the Naval Discipline Act, and that if news of this incident reached the salacious press it would lead to unwelcome and embarrassing publicity for the school and Collingwood, I recorded her personal details and had her quietly escorted to the main gate and on to a bus to Fareham. The L/H was then charged with improperly keeping a female in his cabin overnight and ended up before the Captain, and was disrated. No details of this case ever appeared in the local or national press.

Later, in 1974, the new Fleet Chief, Barry Vernon reported that he had caught an Apprentice writing graffiti and asked me if he could punish the lad himself, as the punishment I or the Commander could award was unlikely to act as a deterrent. I agreed to turn a 'Nelson's eye' to this slightly illegal course of action. That lunch time, before the parade was dismissed, the young lad was pulled out in front of the school and was invited to write in chalk in large letters, "I hate the Fleet Chief " and anything else he felt, while his schoolmates scampered off laughing to lunch. After 15 minutes of graffiti writing, the lad was told to scrub it all off again and, only when the Fleet Chief was satisfied that the parade ground was spotless, by which time his clean up activity had been seen and jeered at by his satiated chums, was he allowed to go to lunch and have the last remaining choice of meal. After three days of this humiliating, but entirely appropriate punishment, he was reprieved. We never had anymore graffiti in the Control School.

The incidence of minor offences early on highlighted the absence of a clear, concise set of standing orders such as FOST had required every ship's WE department to have. So I decided to write a set for the school which I would require all members of the school to read, and to sign that they had done so. I didn't expect this would stop minor wrongdoing but thought it should reduce the scale and would certainly eliminate the old excuse of ignorance of the rules.

In May 1973, whilst unwisely leaning over to cut a wide section of my long garden hedge, I suffered a slipped disc and, in considerable pain was taken by ambulance to Haslar hospital, where I spent 10 days in traction. This time I had morale raising visits from Eileen and the children and, as I was not tilted backwards, I could write, so I took this opportunity to draft the set of Standing Orders for the school. Unfortunately I also had to write a 'Much regret unable' response to a Royal Garden Party invitation Eileen and I had received. After a warning from the Orthopedic Specialist not to be so dam stupid in the future, to act my age, regularly do my daily exercises and never ride, or play games of uncertain reaction, I returned to work.

The Control School competed with all the other schools in HMS Collingwood in all forms of sport, and other competitive activities and did very well in all of them. These activities fostered an esprit de corps among members of the Control Electrical branch of the Royal Navy's Weapons Electrical specialisation. To further enhance this pride in their branch, I designed a Control School logo and a template was made. The new logo, showing a Seacat launcher and missiles, 4.5 inch Mk8 gun , A/S 170 transducer and an Exocet missile in flight,  was used on

all school paperwork, plaques, school 'colours' awarded for sport and for the school tie which was sold for just £1 to those entitled to wear it. As the official logo of the CE school, then bigger than HMS Dryad and almost as big as HMS Excellent and HMS Vernon, it soon became the official badge of the CE specialisation which, at that time, had more ratings than the TAS branch. I took a lead from the Fleet Air Arm, adapting their great PR 'Fly Navy' idea, and had car stickers made in blue and white saying, 'Control Navy' and sent a free copy to the Controller of the Navy, in case he thought we were trying to usurp his position. The Admiral didn't object.

In July 1973, we held the CE School Sports day and I couldn't resist the temptation to take part in the Veterans Race, in  which I officially came second to my boss, although this photograph suggests a dead heat. Jack was a genial laid-back character and a popular School Commander who went on to reach Flag rank. In September 1973, Jack was relieved as Commander of the school by another outgoing officer, Anthony (Taff) Davies, a Guided Weapons specialist who, having spent time at Whale Island, was more at home with ceremonial parades than his predecessor, was smart, keen and full of progressive ideas. He soon initiated a school and branch newsletter called the CE Bulletin, and appointed me its editor. This magazine reported twice a year on past school activities, publicised future events, and disseminated drafting and advancement information to all CE ratings in the navy. Taff also persuaded the HMS Collingwood Welfare Fund to pay for the renovation and furnishing of an empty hut near the Control School, which was then equipped with leisure equipment from the school's own funds, and was named the CE Club. This was the first such club in Collingwood and proved a popular facility for junior livers-in and a venue for all rank school get-togethers and 'hoolies'.

The longest term students of the Control School were Control Electrical Artificer Apprentices, who spent a total of 2 ½ years in residence. They were accommodated in 4-berth cabins by classes, and ranged in age from 17 to 19 ½ years. When the Captain carried out his annual inspection of the CEA Apprentices' cabins, his wife, acting like the Headmaster's wife of a boys' public school, came along to check on the lads' welfare. Taff Davies the School Commander accompanied the Captain and I escorted his wife, who showed great interest and asked many questions. She was especially intrigued by the pin-ups displayed in the cabins. The most junior apprentices favoured near-pornographic pictures of nude or semi-nude young ladies; those in their second year in Collingwood preferred fully clothed ladies emerging soaking wet from the sea; whilst apprentices in their final year, apparently grown fed up with sex, went for posters of powerful motor bikes or sports cars. I was asked what minimum standard of decency I imposed on the pin-ups displayed. I told her that any picture of a lone female, dressed or naked was all right, providing she was not posing pornographically. Pin-ups that did not meet this specification were removed. The CO's wife, who had two sons, thought for a moment, and agreed.

In an effort to boost their congregations, the three oddly sourced Chaplains, a Welsh Church of England, an Irish Free Church and an English RC padre respectively, persuaded the Commanders of the four schools to sponsor church services in Collingwood once a month. The sponsoring school's Commander and his Deputy and their families were expected to attend and to encourage the rest of their school to do likewise. Taff and his wife and family were keen church goers and though normally, the Murdoch's went to church at St Colman's in Cosham, we went to Collingwood once a month where we first went to mass in the RC Chapel, and then attended the COE service with Taff and his family, before having drinks and lunch in the wardroom. On the first occasion, the RC padre had just acquired the services of an organist and had decided to introduce the singing of hymns to the mass. The Captain's wife entered the chapel with her two sons and three other boys she had collected from their local Prep School and, during the opening hymn, led by a nervous priest and discordantly sung by a tone deaf congregation, one of the boys began to titter. The CO's wife's commanded him to behave, but this only resulted in all five boys bursting into loud giggling, at which she heavily hand-bagged her nearest son. He promptly broke into unrestrained laughter which soon spread to the other boys. The padre finally accepted defeat, the hymn was abandoned and, eventually, the boys' wild merriment subsided. Collingwood's First Lady was not best pleased with the conduct of her sons and their friends. However, the RC Chaplain persevered in his effort to bring the mass alive with the sound of music and, after a few months the congregation managed to produce a reasonably melodic mass and the boys learnt to behave in the house of the Lord.

Nominally, my job in the CE school was non-technical but I was able to keep my hand in because, as an FIMarE who had experience in simulators, I was appointed as the electrical engineering member of the board overseeing the design of the simulator for training RN Marine Engineers in the operation and maintenance of the new ships' Gas Turbine propulsion units. This entailed several visits to the firm constructing the simulator and later to HMS Sultan during its installation and commissioning. I also had a break from checking the cleanliness of cabins and lavatories, when I chaired several boards examining candidates for Chief Control Electrical Artificer and was also a standing member of the WE Officer selection board.

At about this time came the sad news that my step-brother George, who had been my buddy in our teenage years, tragically died of kidney failure aged 48, after returning sick from a work assignment in Italy. I missed him very much though, due to our divergent travels, I had seen little of him in recent years.

Although I had to be in the CE school every weekday before 0800, worked most of every lunchtime and seldom left before 1800, I was still required to act as Duty Lt. Cdr (virtually CO) of Collingwood every 13th night. Just before midnight on the 4th November 1973, a spoilsport set fire to the carefully prepared Guy Fawkes bonfire and it proved incredibly difficult to extinguish the fire at that unsocial hour. That was the only noteworthy incident I was called upon to tackle during my last two years in Collingwood.

In August 1972, I had enrolled for an A level course in History at Highbury College. I missed a number of lessons while Falmouth was away from Portsmouth but Veronica Nethercott, the teacher kindly set me the syllabus and, as I had purchased the text books covering English and European History during the 16th and 17th centuries, I was able to keep abreast of the class whilst at sea. When I left the ship, I resumed the one evening per week lessons at college, took the examination in June 1973 and gained my second A level at C grade. I then resolved to take up French again, enrolled for the 1973/4 course in spoken French and passed the Linguists Intermediate exam and took and passed, as the only RN candidate, the O level. I then enrolled, for the 1974/75 A level French course with the same lovely French teacher, known as 'La belle Brigitte'.

In the autumn of 1974, I was found to have an ear infection caused by a nostril blocked by the delayed effect of a diving stunt in Bahrain ten years earlier. This necessitated a hand-drill, bore-out operation in Haslar, a mile or so of gauze being stuffed up my nose, a drip tray affixed below it, and a grommet passed through my eardrum. Whilst looking as if I had heavily lost a boxing match, I was visited by my former Captain, who, now a retired Admiral was in Haslar hospital recuperating from a knee operation. Bill O'Brien was in great spirits and we had a good old chin wag. I was back to duty three days later.

The Commander of Collingwood, President of the

wardroom, kindly allowed me to hold therein the first reunion of my 1944 entry of artificer apprentices, on 2nd August 1974 to commemorate the 30th anniversary of our joining the Royal Navy. Twenty four of the original seventy eight members of the class thoroughly enjoyed the dinner and reminiscing after in the bar.

## Anson 1944 - 74

*1944 Anson 30th Anniversary 2nd August 1974 – HMS Collingwood*
*Reunion Chairman at Head of table (rear cente): Terry Liming*
*Left from front: John Turner, Dennis Taylor, Rodney Tudor, Ken Oram,*
*Phillip Wooden, Peter West, Fred Staker, Willy Powell,*
*Sydney Wakeham, Mike Roberts, Charlie Poole,*
*Right from front: Don Murdoch, Jack Palmer, Joe Nicholson, Ernie Ware,*
*Rodney Pill, Phillip Snell, Gerry Barker, Eric Ball, David*
*Rowlands Peter Hodges, Harry Edwards, Barry Partridge*

This successful event was the first of many reunions of 1944 Anson held at Portsmouth, Plymouth and Exeter in the following 30 years.

After it had provided 10 years of loyal and self-maintainable  service to the Murdochs, I decided, to the dismay of Eileen and Sally that our old Morris 1000 Traveller would have to go and be replaced by a more comfortable car. Eileen and Sally were in tears when the new owner came to take away the car they so loved and in which Sally had passed her test, but Eileen liked the luxury of the relatively new Triumph 2000 which replaced it. Sally, whose 21st birthday party was held in the wardroom in May 1974 and who was then, an instructor at a

riding school in Denmead, bought an old Morris 1000 saloon which she hand- painted bright yellow and named Snoopy.

Paul had made his mark at Embley Park, on the sports field and, spent all of his 1974 summer holidays working as a pool attendant at the brand new Havant swimming pool and bought a 'trials' motor bike in anticipation of his pay. Next day, after I had just completed marking out the badminton court, Paul, who was practising a 'scramble' around the apple trees, lost control and ploughed into and wrecked the brand new net I had just put up ready for the next day's family Badminton tournament and garden party Family legend has it that this was the only time I ever lost my temper with Paul!

Eileen and I enjoyed the social life which continued apace in HMS Collingwood throughout this period, although a new wardroom was being built to replace the temporary war-time structure. We went to all the summer and Christmas Balls, Ladies Nights, Control School social outings, amateur plays, shows and musical concerts put on by talented shipmates. Sally and Paul also enjoyed parties put on in the mess and social events run by the school.

Fitness tests were introduced in the navy at this time and were very keenly enforced in the Control School. I had no difficulty meeting the standard for a 45 year old and settled down to keeping myself fit until the next test with a leisurely round of golf at Southwick Park, where I was a founder member. Despite playing every weekend and most recreational afternoons, occasionally with low handicap players like Fleet Chief Barry Vernon, of graffiti stopping fame, I failed to achieve a handicap better than 23.

During the last few months of this 7th and last spell in Collingwood, I received a polite letter from the Admiralty telling me that I would not be promoted to Commander as, having been promoted Lt Cdr. at the age of 38, I had run out of zone for years in the rank, on the same day as I entered it for minimum age. In my time, having had no chance of earlier transferring to the General list, despite being the first of my class to be promoted Lieutenant and to Lieutenant-Commander, I had come second to an exceptional Ordnance Officer, 3 years older than me, in the selection for the only Weapons, Electrical or Air Engineering Commander promoted that year. I was of course disappointed but, shortly afterwards, was rewarded with a plum job as the first Engineer Officer to lead an XP

Weapons Trials Team, until then the exclusive prerogative of senior experienced Gunnery Officers.

On the 2nd December 1972, just before I left Collingwood, nine members of my apprentice entry who were still serving, had notched up a total of 300 years service between them. They lunched together in HMS Nelson wardroom and posed for this picture.

*Top Peter Alp, Don Murdoch, Philip Wooden, Sydney Wakeham, Gus Simpson, David Rowlands, Derek Smith, Joe Nicholson, Peter Hodges*

In a strange way, for an engineer, I have to say I enjoyed my two years as the Staff Officer ie, Executive Officer, of the Control School. I left it with a greater appreciation of the broad picture of 'whole man training' and its importance to the navy. I have many fond memories of ceremonial drill successes and cock-ups, having to bellow out orders to the whole school when leading the march off at ceremonial divisions on the biggest parade ground in the service, trying to look serious at hearing for the umpteenth time, the same lame excuses from young defaulters for their misdemeanours and, as a onetime ill-disciplined apprentice myself, dealing firmly but, I trust fairly, with wayward youths without showing them any empathy. I was given a kind send off by the Control School and my

messmates, the cartoon shown here and a pencil vase, the underside of which is shown below, Looking back I consider myself lucky to have had the loyal support of a great team of officers and senior ratings, two convivial COs and the best Fleet Chiefs in Collingwood. Together, I like to think, we ran a happy boarding school of lively, intelligent young men.

# Chapter 21

## Type 21 Surface Weapons Trials Team Leader
## Captain Weapons Trials (XP)

### January 1975 - March 1977

I joined HMS Excellent immediately after Christmas leave and made my way to XP, the section of the Whale Island Gunnery School responsible for 'Experimental' trials on naval gunnery, whose alumni, as former Experimental Lieutenant-Commanders, according to their honours board, included Admirals of the Fleet Lord Jellicoe and Sir Michael Le Fanu.

Suitably impressed and humbled, I met Lt Cdr Peter Goodman, a renowned Gunnery Officer whom I was to relieve as Trials Team Leader for Surface Weapons, Radio and Radar trials on the new 'state of the art' Type 21 frigates. I was briefed on my role as a Trials Team Leader by Commander XP, a senior Gunnery Officer, who pointed out that I was the first non Gunnery Officer to head a trials team responsible for Gunnery systems and their acceptance. I was also briefed by the Captain Weapons Trials, (CWT), who also headed Underwater Systems Trials, based at HMS Vernon.

There were 8 Type 21 Frigates:- HM ships Amazon, Antelope, Ambuscade, Arrow, Active, Alacrity, Ardent and Avenger in various states of completion when I joined XP. I was just in time for the final sea trials in HMS Amazon, took charge of the Harbour and Sea Acceptance trials in HMS Antelope, the Installation Inspections and HATs and SATS in Ambuscade, the whole gambit of all of the Inspections and trials including the Marking-Out and Installation Inspections, HATs and SATs, including those on the Exocet system in HMS Arrow and those Inspections and trials for which the last 4 of the class were ready by March 1977.

The Type 21 frigates weighed 3250 tons, were propelled by 2 Olympus and/or 2 Tyne gas turbine engines giving, a top speed of 32 knots, were fitted with the first RN digital Surface Weapons System WSA4, an automatic 4.5 inch Mark 8 gun in an unmanned mounting, a quadruple GWS 24 Sea Cat missile launcher, four GWS 50 Exocet launchers, 3 inch Rocket launchers and two 912 Radar auto-follow directors. They were also fitted with the latest Early Warning and Gun Direction Radar and Radio Systems.
Because of the technological quantum leap that the Surface weapon systems of the Type 21s represented, I was afforded a long learning curve, during which I had a good turn-over from Peter Goodman on my new executive duties, whilst spending all my spare time studying the advanced electronic techniques involved with the equipment, a technical feature he had not been required to master.

During my first two months in XP Peter took me, with the

team, on Contractor's Sea Trials on HMS Sheffield from Barrow in Furness and HMS Antelope from Woolston, during which we carried out the first firing of their 4.5 inch Mk 8 gun off Eskmeals and Portland respectively. I also shadowed him on Inspections in Antelope and Ambuscade, held in their builders' yards at Woolston and Scotstoun. On the first trip up to Glasgow in the shuttle, one of the Trident's three engines shut down as we took off and the fully loaded aircraft had to return to Heath Row pdq and make an emergency landing. As we touched down, we had fire-engines running along on both sides of us and Peter, sitting next to me, declared that I must be a Jonas as the team had never before had such a fright!

On another occasion we flew to Edinburgh from Gatwick to carry out Acceptance trials on the Sea Cat system in HMS Norfolk at Rosyth so that I would know how to conduct them on Antelope and other ships. Peter Goodman proved a good instructor, a witty companion, and gave me sound advice on running a trials team eg, always carry out a wash-up at the end of the working day, write up the report and decide the pattern of the next days work, whilst all the team were together, before relaxing. He taught me a lot in the two months we overlapped, before he left XP, and I was left in charge of the Type 21 Trials team. This comprised Lt Cdr Jack Kyle, a  Gunnery Officer, Lt Alan Palmer a Gunner, Lt Tony Turner a WE Officer trained in WSA4, Lt David Redwood a radio/radar specialist and Lt Tony Collingswood a 4.5 Mk 8 specialist, and, for Exocet trials only, Lt Boyd Crawford. I also had two Chiefs, Brian Branch and Jack Frost who were Ordnance and Control Chief Artificers respectively. We worked very well together, enjoyed each others company socially, only wore uniform whilst working on commissioned ships, and travelled to, and worked at, Yarrow's and Vosper Thorneycroft's shipyards in plain clothes, where we were given a good lunch in the managers' restaurant. All officers were entitled to 1st class rail travel and I persuaded the XP Admin authorities to allow our Chiefs to also travel 1st class because we worked as a team on the train, on our classified preparations for, and reports on, a trial. We also stayed at the same hotels, being driven in RN transport to and from the hotel to the shipyard and airport.

We always travelled to Devonport, Southampton and Heath Row or Gatwick airports in three of our own cars, in rotation, including my own Triumph 2000, which carried 4 of us  comfortably, and our trials equipment and luggage easily. The wash-up and compilation of the day's report, and the preparations for the next day's work were carried out straight away. When this was complete we went to the bar for a pre dinner drink before dining and then going to the cinema, a show or football match together, or had a quiet evening in. Five of the 21s were built at Yarrows shipyard in Scotstoun, Glasgow and, at first, the team was booked into the RNVR club, a floating hulk in the centre of Glasgow. The single cabins were tiny and poorly ventilated and had no portholes. Trials team members were paid a small lodging allowance which was just enough for bed, breakfast and dinner at the club, but my predecessor believed in the old 'Canteen Messing' idea, not favoured by me or most of the team, of saving on a proper dinner to fund drinking, and making do with take-away meals such as fish, sausages or haggis and chips for supper every night. One weekend, shortly after he left, the old vessel sank in a storm and thereafter we were always accommodated for bed, breakfast and dinner at a comfortable hotel run by two middle-aged sisters from Northern Ireland. Within the team we had a wealth of talent for doing the odd maintenance and repair jobs on plumbing and electrics and the two dear ladies came to rely on us to fix most of their hotel defects. Indeed they used to meet us on arrival with a free pint of our preferred tipple and the hotel defect list. They also provided us with complimentary tickets to the Scottish Opera and Ballet, to top class plays and shows and to mid-week football Internationals at Hampden Park, all of which were enjoyed.

On 10<sup>th</sup> April 1975 , Eileen and I celebrated our Silver Wedding Anniversary with a splendid dinner party in the brand new Trafalgar Room of the recently built wardroom of HMS Collingwood, booked before I joined HMS Excellent Most of the family attended and thoroughly enjoyed the occasion, not least Sally and Paul who appreciated the company of their cousins, their grand parents and aunts and uncles. The wardroom staff really did us proud

I soon gained a great deal of respect for Yarrow's shipyard. It was the only surviving ship-building yard on the Clyde and its management and workers were the pick of those previously employed by John Brown, Fairfield and other legendary builders of great RN and commercial ships. All five of Yarrow's Type 21s were at various stages of construction on site when I took over as Trials Team Leader. Each of them had a Foreman in charge who really knew everything about his ship and had the knowledge and authority to ensure that the ship was ready for the programmed Marking-out and Installation Inspections, Contractors Sea Trials and Harbour Acceptance Trials. Most of the deficiencies noted during the day's inspection or trial were remedied overnight and were re-presented to us the next morning. It was a wonderful experience to carry out all of the Inspections and Trials from the initial marking out of compartment layout, carried out just after the ship was launched, right through the installation, commissioning, harbour and sea acceptance trials and finally, to be able to tell her Captain at sea in the Mediterranean, that the necessary standards had been achieved and the ship was materially ready to join the fleet or, as happened twice on one ship, had not been achieved, and the SATs would have to be repeated. This particular ship, whose build at Woolston had fallen behind because some of the shipyard work force had been moved to other ships, had an uncompromising Captain whose officers and senior ratings clearly feared him and lacked self-confidence. When, after their third attempt, I told him that that the ship had passed SATs, he gave me a ship's tie and said he was glad to see the back of me. Thereafter, whenever we travelled to a potentially difficult trial, I wore that tie, to indicate that we faced a troublesome time.

The WSA4 digital fire control computer had an inbuilt facility to carry out an analysis of the whole system's performance and produce records of the standard hitherto made, after the Trials teams return, by the analysis group back in Whale Island. At the end of the SATs of the second Type 21 to complete them, I was able to tell her Captain and, by signal, CWT, the MOD and CinC Fleet, that HMS Ambuscade had achieved the standard, without adding the traditional rider, "subject to analysis", because we had done the analysis onboard after the final shoot and produced the records. This was a 'First' in the history of XP and after our return from Gibraltar, my decision was upheld by Commander XP and CWT.

One Monday morning I was called to Haslar to have the grommet in my left ear checked, six months after its insertion during my nose operation. A would-be specialist peered at it and, declaring that it had been extruded naturally, grabbed it with a pair of tweezers. Unfortunately it was still firmly rooted and his pull perforated the ear drum, causing me to yell in pain. He apologised and, putting some drops into the ravaged ear, cheerfully assured me that the drum would soon heal. I returned to Whale Island and next day flew out with the team to carry out trials on a ship off Gibraltar. On the  Friday evening, returning by air with the team after a successful trial, I could still hear the noise of the jet engines in my left ear long after I entered the terminal building at Heathrow. The noise persisted the whole weekend and, on the Monday, after handing in my trials report I went to the surgery where the MO took one look at my eardrum and sent me to Haslar. The following day, the senior ENT specialist, carried out an inner ear operation to repair the damage done to the hearing mechanism. When I came to, he was sitting on the end of my bed and told me regretfully, that the operation had failed, the ear was irreparably damaged, a hearing aid would be no help, I now had only one ear, was unfit for the naval service and would be invalided. I was absolutely devastated and said something to the effect that "If someone has thick glasses because of an eyesight problem, he is thought to be clever, but if one has a hearing problem, people think he's daft". The Surgeon Captain replied, "Too many people think that way, deafness is only another disability". He then offered me a life-line, telling me that if my Captain wrote to the Second Sea Lord and stated that I could carry out my duties with only one ear, the head of naval personnel might give me special permission to remain in the RN until I reached 50 in 4 years time. Next day, back at Whale Island, CWT, Captain Ken Croydon, with whom I got on very well, kindly wrote to 2SL and within a week, to my great pleasure and relief, the Admiral's affirmative reply was received. I soon learned how to position myself so that I could hear what was going on, conduct trials, chair meetings and carry out my other tasks, with only one ear. It also came in handy when someone said, "It's your round Don".

I was blessed with a great team of professionals who, like FOST staff Sea Riders, not only completely knew their job and carried out all of their tasks diligently, but also helped the shipbuilders and ship's staff to repair and prepare the equipment when necessary. All of the team relished the ships' successes and were deflated by the very few failures.

Vickers, the manufacturer, presented me with a 4.5 inch Mk 8 tie, for diagnosing the cause of the contamination of the hydraulic system of HMS Ardent's gun control system, curing it before the first scheduled firing of the gun, and also for showing the Vickers installation team how to align the high grade pump with its motor, a procedure I had been taught as an apprentice and had used several times at sea with horizontally-mounted machines. One of the brass 4.5 inch cartridge cases used in Ardent's successful 20-round burst during her acceptance firing, was given to me, suitably engraved.

Normally I spent Mondays in the office at Whale Island, discussing my report on the previous week's trials with Cdr XP, claiming my modest expenses for car mileage, hotel bill etc, - all backed up by receipts, and preparing the paper work and schedules for the week's trials with the team, We generally left around 1600 for the airport or Plymouth in a convoy of three cars, laden with our luggage and test equipment and reached the hotel in Glagow, Plymouth, Gibraltar or Fishguard in time for a late dinner and ready to start the trial next morning. When there were no Type 21 trials scheduled, we undertook trials on county class destroyers in commission, at Devonport and, once in a Leander class frigate in Portsmouth. However, these trials became few and far between as the Type 21 build programme progressed. We were booked into flights and modest hotels by a very good administrative team in XP, led by a retired Gunnery officer, Frank Swift, who really looked after the various trials teams. Somehow, our three or four day Type 21 trials seemed tailored to allow us to attend the more prestigious social events back in the wardroom of HMS Excellent.

Eileen, Sally, Paul and I thoroughly enjoyed HMS Excellent's wardroom social events including the pre- Royal Tournament Portsmouth Field Gun run with its great Strawberries and Cream Tea, the fantastic fireworks shows and the summer and Christmas Balls.

Paul continued to shine on the sports field at Embley Park and at the age of 17, gained his Duke of Edinburgh Gold award. He was only allowed to take one parent to the palace for the presentation so he took his mother and this more than made up for Eileen missing  the royal garden party the year before. Sally and I visited the Tate while Eileen and Paul were in the palace and she says Paul was very blasé about the whole thing until the Duke spoke to him and then he became tongue-tied. In the photo shown here before he and Eileen went into the Palace, Paul seems quite unexcited at the prospect of meeting the Duke of Edinburgh. In August, four months before his 18th birthday, Paul was invited to join the England Schoolboy Rugby team squad for a week of training at the national sports centre at Bisham Abbey prior to selection of the national team. After seven days of invaluable coaching by the England trainers, Paul played Fly-half for the England Schoolboys XV 'Possibles' against the 'Probables'. In a nice touch by the RFU, the Possibles wore the England colours of white with a red rose. Paul was advised that he was too small to be a fly-half in senior rugby and, after he switched to wing three-quarter he went on to be capped for Hampshire and to play for Havant First XV for 14 years.

My WSA4 expert, Tony Turner, whose wedding the whole team attended, completed his two years with XP, half-way through my term, and was relieved by another clever young Lieutenant. Wayne Wiseman. The rest of the team stayed with me throughout my two years as Team Leader, and consistently provided me with loyal, professional help, advice and friendly company. I still have many fond memories of those two years, including, in no particular order:

Counting each shot of the first 4.5 Mk 8 automatic 20 round burst and cheering if it succeeded and groaning if it failed.

Quickly calculating, with my slide rule, if the tracking parameters had been met, while the towing aircraft flew back to start the next run, and giving Jack Kyle the go-ahead to bring it in for a firing run in which a string of TTBs was achieved.

Receiving a daily 'Hard Lying' allowance for living onboard an unfinished ship at sea for Contractor's Sea Trials when the accommodation was superior to much I had earlier experienced at sea as normal conditions.

Locking the for'd 912 Radar on to the target at     the end of the range at Aberporth and watching the first frigate - launched     Exocet running straight to and hitting the target in a force 6 wind.

Witnessing, with Yarrow's Managing Director, the Friday noon dash of some

*HMS Arrow's first Exocet passing over the 4.5 Mk 8 gun*

of his workers to the pub, 50 yards from the gate of the shipyard at Scotstoun, in which a team of barmaids had lined up numerous glasses of Whisky and Chaser for this weekly ritual.

The wind rattling the rigging of the sailing dinghies moored close to the XP building on the south side of Whale Island.

Running around the island in the annual personal fitness test, encouraged by Gunnery and PT Instructors.

Flying over my house and Whale Island on a clear morning at 25,000 feet, on my way to Gibraltar with the team, for the Sea Acceptance Trials on a Type 21 frigate.

Informing the Captain that his ship had achieved the required standards and observing his delight at the news.

Being dined out in HMS Excellent's wardroom and being presented by my trials team with an engraved tankard, and the distinctive XP tie with its camel and gun motif. I am proud to wear that relatively rare tie on appropriate occasions.

Later, during a visit to XP, I was delighted and humbled to see that my name had been added to the Experimental Lieutenant-Commanders honours board that had so impressed me on the day I joined the navy's august 'Camel corps', so named because their time was spent humping test gear around to test the navy's guns.

In February1977, with my two years in XP expired, the Appointer offered me the post of WEO of the reserve aircraft carrier HMS Bulwark, then in a state of Preservation by Operation, (P by O) at Portsmouth. He told me that my job would be to bring all of the ship's WE equipment up to operational standard and keep it ready to go to sea at short notice and added that, if the ship was brought forward to rejoin the fleet, I would take her to sea. This sounded to me, to be a pretty good last appointment in the navy and I jumped at the chance.

Shortly afterwards, my relief, Lt Cdr Peter Sibley, a WE officer with a Cambridge MA, joined to relieve me in XP and he accompanied me and the trials team to Scotstoun and Woolston for all of the inspections and trials carried out during our three-week turn-over period.

I thoroughly enjoyed my plum job as the Leader of a trials team at the cutting-edge of weapon system technology, with a very good team, considerable responsibility, authority and great job satisfaction.

# Chapter 22

## Weapons Electrical Engineer Officer

### HMS Bulwark
### March 1977 – June 1979

HMS Bulwark was berthed stern-to in a non-tidal basin in Portsmouth dockyard and, as I came up the gangway for the first time I saw a huge painted notice boldly declaring:

"HMS Bulwark Will Sail Again"

The Captain was Commander Arthur Carpenter MBE RN, a Marine EngineerOfficer, who, as an apprentice 2 ½ years senior to me, had won fame at Fisgard by knocking-out the reigning heavyweight boxing champion in the finals in 1944. The ship's MEO Lt Cdr Paul Marshall, also an ex apprentice, had been the ship's Senior Engineer during the prevous commission at sea and had put the ME department into reserve in 1976. Both he and I had deputies and there was a Seaman Lt who was First Lieutenant and another Lt who was Supply Officer, all of these officers had also served on board Bulwark at sea. As I was 2 months senior to Paul, I became the second in command. My department comprised my deputy, Lt John Lindfield, 4 CPOs, 8 POs and 40 ratings, all of whom had recently served at sea in Bulwark or other ships. The total ship's company numbered around 200.

The Lt Cdr I relieved had been the Deputy WEO in the previous commission, but had since decided to leave the service and left the ship a few days after I joined. All of the officers except the Captain were required to carry out the duty of Officer of the Day, remaining on the ship overnight. This duty came around every six days and the OOD slept in an extraordinarily large and very comfortable bed in the Captain's spacious suite. When not duty OOD I worked on weekdays from 0800 to 1600, and then went home.

The ship received supplies of 225 volt dc elecricity and low pressure steam for domestic purposes, from ashore. None of the electrical machinery was cocooned and all of it was available for use. as was all of the Radar, Radio and internal communications, gyro-compass and navigational aids and both aircraft lifts, the bomb lift and all of the boat and ammunition hoists. Because the twin 40 mm gun mountings were exposed to the elements, they had been cocooned.

Built by Harland and Wolff Ltd in Belfast and launched in 1948, HMS Bulwark had been first commissioned, as a fixed wing aircraft carrier in 1954 and was almost 30 years old when I joined her. All of her electrical, radio, radar and weapons equipment was of the same vintage as that in HMS Theseus in which I had served in 1949-51. My job thus posed no technical problem, but, with a small team and the age of the equipment, was unlikely to be a sinecure, for the equipment needed a fair amount of tlc to keep it going.

*Centre: WEO,(Don), CO , MEO*

At the first Heads of Department (HODs) meeting, I attended; the CO said that the ship would not be towed out to Spithead for the Silver Jubilee Fleet Review in June, to swell the numbers, as had reportedly happened to some reserve ships in earlier fleet reviews. However, since everyone coming down the motorway into Portsmouth would see the ship, he wanted it dressed overall to look like a tiddly warship. We had two ship's motorboats which were berthed nearby on the tidal jetty and these were also to be spruced up and would be used to go out to Spithead during the review. We did not expect or receive any outside help for this task, so the junior ratings were kept pretty busy painting during the next two months.

For four days, commencing on the 10th May 1977, I was a member of a Court Martial board held in HMSNelson to try three Royal Marines, a Warrant Officer and two Sergeants on a total of ten charges of theft and falsifying accounts. The three marine NCOs, who were represented by QCs, were very smart throughout the trial. We four officers on the board, lunched in the Victoria and Albert suite quite separately from the defence counsel who ate in the wardroom. At the end of each day's hearing, after the court adjourned, we went through the evidence in detail and it was continually stressed by the Judge Advocate that, if we had the slightest doubt, we must acquit. However, we were convinced by the weight of evidence which we all fully understood, that all three of the accused, who ran the CinC's Printing Office, had been running a racket and found them not guilty of theft, but guilty of falsifying accounts. The WO was reduced to the rank of Corporal, and he, and the two Sergeants were deprived of their Long Service and Good Conduct medals and badges. This was the first time I had sat in judgment and found it a very interesting experience that left me with the firm opinion that a naval court martial was very much fairer to the accused and to justice, than a civil court.

The Queen's Silver Jubilee was celebrated throughout the country in June 1977, and in Widley, then a village with a full range of shops, the local Ironmonger, Frank Mills, organised a street party which was held in a field behind our house for all of the residents of the London Road. This memorable and happy occasion was fated to be the last such gathering for soon afterwards the demise of the village shops began as the out-of-town supermarkets took over.

On the night before the Silver Jubilee Fleet review was due to be inspected by Her Majesty, our very smart Captain's Motorboat took the Captain and the non-duty officers and their wives along the lines of RN, Commonwealth and foreign ships assembled at Spithead and we all enjoyed the spectacle. Next morning at 0800 the ship was dressed overall with flags and looked very smart to all of the many visitors coming into Portsmouth.

This ceremonial event and the marked improvement in the ships outward appearance, was soon followed by media speculation that, because of delays in the building of the 'Through-deck-cruiser', HMS Invincible, later re-designated as an aircraft carrier, the MOD was considering bringing HMS Bulwark forward. This would allow her to join her younger sister ship HMS Hermes in filling the gap in the fleet's air support at sea, resulting from the demise of the last big fleet carrier, HMS Ark Royal. These rumours were neither confirmed nor denied by the MOD but, as I was the only officer onboard who had not already served in her for two years, I was nominated as 'Bring-Forward Co-ordinator' for the whole ship, in addition to my duties as head of the WE department. I was given the task of producing a plan to get the ship to sea in six months. Suddenly, the 'quiet number' I had been given as my last posting in the RN, became rather more demanding. I sat down with the Captain, MEO, 1$^{st}$ Lt, and Supp;y Officer to plan the outline of a Bring Forward operation for all departments including a huge build-up in the size of the ship's complement. After receiving their inputs, I took the details home and produced Issue 1 of an integrated plan on my drawing board, with the week by week sequence of events, minus of course, the actual dates. It was printed by a Dockyard Drawing office and copies went to the CO and HODs onboard the ship to help them formulate their own detailed plans. At the same time I decided to test the readiness of my own department by carrying out, in a month's time, without actually leaving our berth. a 'Fast Cruise', an exercise used after a maintenance period, to run up and prove all of the WE equipment needed to get the ship to sea, and to remain there operationally,

My small but keen and competent team worked very hard to prepare for the Fast-Cruise and, on the scheduled date, the exercise was witnessed by our own Captain and the Chief Staff Officer to the Admiral i/c of Reserve Ships', who was impressed by the success of the simulated sailing, and reported glowingly to the MOD that the WE department was in good shape and the whole ship's company in confident mood. However, the rumours of the ship's impending return to sea, soon dried up and, for the last three months of 1977, we relaxed. I went sailing once a week in one of our four Bosun dinghies and also played a round of golf. Although I failed to lower my high golf handicap, I did manage to win a 4-boat 'Pub Crawl' sailing race around Portsmouth harbour, with one of my young CEMs as crew. The race, carried out during the Saturday opening hours of 1000 to 1400., involved downing a ½ pint at the Coal Exchange, Fareham, the Cormorant, Portchester, Pubs at Flathouse, and Old Portsmouth, and Hornet Sailing Club and finishing at the Jolly Roger at Elson. A couple of weeks later, we won the Three Harbours race which started at Hornet, Gosport, went along Southsea and Hayling fronts, into and up Chichester harbour to the Ship Inn at Langstone, where all the dinghy crews had a pie and a pint before lowering the masts to pass under Hayling Bridge. The second half of the race was started by the judge in the ship's motor boat/cum/safety boat. The dinghies then raced down Langstone harbour, out to sea, around Spit Sand fort, into and up Portsmouth harbour, around No 3 buoy and back to Hornet. Although only four dinghies and 8 men competed, I mention these two races, solely because they were the only, albeit modest, sporting successes I ever had in my life. I loved sailing, often took a dinghy out on my own during the light evenings and one Saturday took Eileen to Cowes. Unfortunately she didn't enjoy it as I had hoped and Sally was still wrapped up in riding and tennis, but Paul enjoyed sailing and my brother-in-law Jim, and nephew Andrew, also came with me on several occasions.

During this period it was not all fun. I had to continually refine the draft Bring Forward programme, and I also took the opportunity to up date the departmental Standing Orders including in them, for the first time, instructions to personnel carrying out rounds of running machinery and Compartment Instructions for all of the many WE compartments. I also ensured that the daily checks and maintenance on all of the equipment were carried out, but the panic was off, for the time being at least. To show the local populace that we were still alive and kicking, I had a flashing 5-pointed Christian star made onboard, anyone can produce a 6-pointed star of David, and it twinkled from our high masthead throughout 1977 Christmas.

Around this time, my dear Mother-in-law became ill and was soon unable to look after herself. Sally and Paul were living at home with us and the house was full but, Eileen and I realised we should care for her. We therefore applied to the local council for formal permission to put a residential caravan in our fairly big back garden so that she would have a degree of privacy and we could look after her. Eileen duly entertained a deputation of councillors and council officers, who all seemed to think it was an ideal site, but the council rejected the plan on the grounds that, it would be an undesirable backland development. We were furious. However,

 after a rethink, we decided that, in any case, it would be better solution if we built an extension on to our house. I drew up the plans, which were approved, and we had a granny annex built in the same style as the house. The builders made a good job of it and Eileen's mother moved in before Christmas 1977. Eileen Clarke looked after Mum during weekdays while Eileen was at work and she was very happy there, but, sadly her condition deteriorated, and she died in April 1978 at the age of 73. She had been a loving Mother-in-law to me and I missed her very much, as did Eileen, Sally and Paul.

On 23rd January 1978, the official announcement was made that HMS Bulwark would be brought forward to rejoin the fleet for two years, in early 1979, after a three month long docking and the repair of essential defects (code-named a DED). This would be the first time the ship had been in dock since 1974, and would include some modernisation to facilitate her new role as an Anti-Submarine Aircraft Carrier, as well as retaining an alternative Amphibious capability. After a meeting with the CO and HODs onboard, I updated the Bring Forward Plan to Issue 2, putting real dates to the integrated sequential programme and promulgating it to them, the Dockyard authorities and the staff of the CinC Fleet. We were informed that the budget for the DED and modernisation was limited to £5,000,000 of which the WE department's share was only £1.25 million. During the previous year, the MEO and I had compiled a defect list, but, in view of the budgetary limitations we had, perforce, to scrutinise this list and, after personally looking at each task, take off all jobs that the ship's staff could undertake with assistance from the local Fleet Maintenance Unit, when available, leaving to the Dockyard only the work beyond our capability. Because their main steam machinery had lain unused for 2 years, and would, of course, by its very nature and size need dockyard help on most of its defects the ME department was allotted £2.5 million. In the first week of the pre-DED period, a potential programme-stopper emerged when the bulkheads between the messdecks and hangar were discovered to have been insulated with Blue Asbestos. The ship was evacuated to allow a private specialist contractor's team aboard to seal it and make it safe. This unexpected work delayed the progress of the onboard work planned for all departments by two weeks. All 200 of us who had slept onboard her in the previous year, were X-rayed and placed on the 'At risk of Asbestosis' list, although many of us had already been subjected to very much closer contact with asbestos in other ships.

I was due to leave the service the day before my 50$^{th}$ birthday in January 1979 but was asked by the Appointer if I was prepared to extend my service by 6 months and take the ship to sea. He added that a Commander would be joining the ship to take over as WEO and I would become his deputy. I also learnt that the new Captain would be George Brewer with whom I had enjoyed serving before, and he would join in July, so I agreed. In the event, the Commander(WE), Tony Wardale, an ex-submariner who would not join until August, turned out to be the best boss I could possibly have had and he and I have remained friends ever since.

On 5$^{th}$ August, with the arrival of Tony Wardale, I stepped down from being head of the WE department to become DWEO, though still carrying out the duties of Bring-Forward Coordination Officer for the whole ship. We entered the three month long DED on 17$^{th}$ August, with my final BF plan, Issue 7, dated 10$^{th}$ May 1978 which measured 6 feet by 3 feet. The detailed sequence of the integrated activities of all of the ship's activities in those hectic 12 months, shown on this plan, was thereafter closely followed, right to the final event on that giant bar chart. This was HMS Bulwark's first operational requirement, her participation in a major NATO Anti-submarine exercise in the North Atlantic in May 1979, as planned a year earlier. There was some slippage in the intermediate milestones due to the asbestos hiatus and uncharacteristic dockyard industrial (in) action. The success of the Bring Forward programme indicates the determination of all involved in getting a 30 year old ship, laid up for two years without having been fully refitted back to sea as a fully operational ship, at minimal cost, in a short time.

Apart from attending progress meetings, I spent most of the next five months in overalls supervising the work being done by the WE department in place of unaffordable dockyard personnel. My excellent Chief Electrical Mechanician Tony Mc Dermott and I were the only WE personnel who had previously served in a big dc ship, so he led one team of Artificers and Mechanicians and their mates and I another similar team, in undertaking the refit of the many large motors and other major items of electrical equipment. At the same time, the similarly skilled ratings of the ME department were also carrying out tasks normally done by dockyard personnel. Repair by replacement was hardly an option for a ship of Bulwark's age and almost every job undertaken by the ship's staff and the RN Fleet Maintenance Group, required the skills of an old fashioned Artificer, with which the ship was, fortuitously well provided. Without their sterling work, the tight programme would not have been met.

Every ship has radio maintainers who are never happier than when they are working aloft. My daring 'steeplejacks' soon realised that I didn't like going up the mast and often delighted in calling me to come up and inspect a defect on a UHF aerial out on the yard arm or on a radar waveguide, and to decide how it should be repaired. This had me sweating, especially when we were docked down in C Lock, whose dock bottom was 130 feet below. The DED ended in mid November and the ship was moved to Pitch House Jetty on the sea wall where the full ship's company moved onboard and began the massive, labour-intensive task of painting the whole ship inside and out, storing ship and carrying out Harbour Acceptance trials on all of the equipment. One day, the car owned by the ship's 2ic, Commander Mike Howitt, and also my beautiful Triumph 2000, parked close to the ship, was accidentally sprayed with grey paint when the wind gusted. The lads concerned cleaned off the paint.

Berthed on the sea wall, we kept a full watch of officers and some 300 ratings onboard every night, under the command of the Duty CO, a Lt Cdr known as the DLC. As the senior Lt Cdr onboard, I organised the duty DLC's roster of nine Lt Cdrs holding a Bridge Watchkeeping Certificate. One November Sunday, I was duty DLC when, at around 2300, I had a phone call from the MOD police at the Dockyard Main Gate reporting that a man with an Irish accent had telephoned a warning that he had "placed a bomb in the Tiller Flat of HMS Bulwark". The police informed me that their senior officer and an Intelligence Officer were on their way to the ship. I ordered the whole duty watch, many of whom were in their bunks, to muster on the flight deck in 10 minutes time. By the time the MOD Police and MI5 arrived, I had gathered the Duty officers and the duty watch together and had outlined the threat and our likely action. I told the Police that our Steering Gear Compartment, had been locked since 1600 on Friday and the keys had, ever since, been safely stowed in the manned Damage Control HQ. I added that the term Tiller Flat was normally only used on smaller ships. The Intelligence Officer said that IRA bombs were normally triggered by a 12 hour clock fuze. These two factors suggested that the bomb warning was a hoax. The Captain was ashore for the weekend so I had to decide on the action. I chose to carry out a thorough search of the alleged bomb location, with which I was familiar, having just refitted the steering motors. We found nothing untoward during this search but, bearing in mind that the IRA often gave incorrect or misleading information on the location of planted bombs, I ordered the duty watch to carry out a systematic search of every one of the many compartments in the ship. This was controlled from DCHQ from where the keys of compartments were drawn. This whole operation took until 0230, before I was satisfied that we had searched everywhere and that there was no bomb onboard. The Police and I concluded that the warning had been a time-wasting hoax, perpetrated by a mischievous sailor, probably from a destroyer or frigate, after a few pints in one of the pubs on Portsmouth Hard. I explained this to the duty watch and congratulated them all on carrying out a thorough search on a cold night. I have to say, I was also proud of the way they took the news that it had been a hoax, especially considering their night's sleep had been ruined. I told the Captain on his return aboard later that morning. To avoid giving the oxygen of publicity to the hoaxer, and to lessen the chance of copy-cat action by other would-be hoaxers, the news of this incident was not given to the media and never appeared in the local or national press. The next really eventful duty I had was my last duty in the RN, in Bulwark at Rosyth, on a Sunday in May 1979.

One of the Sea King helicopters due to join the ship in the New Year landed aboard and was used to prove the new hangar stowage arrangements. When these were completed, the pilot took the ship's Commander, who was an aviator, myself and several other officers closely involved with the ship's programme, to a planning meeting at Culdrose in Cornwall to discuss the move onboard of the Air Group. The Pilot was Richard Shultz a German Kapitan-Lieutenant (Lt Cdr) who wore a rakish U-Boat Captain's style cap and joked all the time. On the way back to Portsmouth, he carried out a sonar-dunking to show us how the aircraft responded in the hover.

By Christmas 1978, the WE department totalled 143, including four Officers, one Warrant Officer, seven CPOs, twelve POs and 119 ratings. The dockyard's contribution to getting Bulwark ready to join the fleet having been completed, the new ship's company set about the task of turning the 'Rusty B', by now re-nicknamed the 'Incredible Hulk', into a habitable floating home for 2000 men.

HMS Bulwark's WE Department at sea in the Irish Sea, April 1979
*Don is 6th from left in front row centre*

I spent the weekend of the 1978 England v Wales rugby match at the Prince of Wales' Hotel in London on a course for officers about to leave the service. As I expected to be at sea until I began my terminal leave in June 79, I opted for this particular course and was told to arrive at the hotel before 1900 and to bring my CV. I didn't have one as such, but did have a blurb written about my career by the Admiralty a couple of years earlier, for the purpose of recruiting Artificer Apprentices. I thought that this professionally produced spiel would be suitable. On arrival at the hotel we had to hand in our CVs. After dinner, the mixed bag of officers of the three services and all ranks up to Brigadier, all in plain clothes, assembled for the first session of the resettlement course. The lecturer told us that the staff had read all of our CVs and first, he was going to show us all, how not to write a CV if we wanted to impress a civilian employer and get a good job. He then projected on to a screen a well typed A4 sheet, the title of which had been blacked out, to save the blushes of the author. He then sarcastically read out what he called the Yo Ho, Boys Own adventure story of - my life! The class laughed as he mocked each sentence and I prayed that no one guessed it was my entry for the worst CV of the year. However, I kept mum and, with the embarrassing prose still on the screen, he wrote on the blackboard, a

- 411 -

proper CV, based on the data contained in my original, and invited us all to copy it and to rewrite our CVs in a similar format. I happily took this officially recommended version back to the ship for future use. All day and after dinner on the Saturday, and on Sunday morning, after a sleepless night due to the revels of the Welsh fans celebrating their unexpected victory at Twickenham, we were lectured at, and interviewed by, a team of business experts and consultants and on the Sunday afternoon were each given, one to one, recommendations for our particular route to success in civilian life. For some reason I had told one of the earlier interview boards that I fancied becoming a Probation Officer. The board advised me that this would be the wrong career move for me as I was, by nature, too cynical and would be too intolerant of ne'er-do-wells. They strongly advised me to stick to engineering, where I had done pretty well. I returned to the ship with the ideal CV and a clear idea on where I should seek my second career.

During Christmas leave, I was reading the newly arrived copy of the Marine Engineers' magazine in bed one morning, when Eileen drew my attention to an advert on the recto page, calling for ex WE officers with trials experience, to join the new Sting Ray Torpedo project in Marconi Ltd at Portsmouth. I read it with interest but told her that I had been advised in London, not to apply for a job until I had less than six weeks left in the service. However, Eileen persuaded me to have a go. Remembering an important piece of advice from the resettlement course, I sent my application direct to the Managing Director and not the Personnel Manager, as directed in the advert, told him I would not become available until mid July and, of course, enclosed my new professional CV. On the last evening of my leave, as Eileen and I were going out to dinner, I received a phone call from the Sting Ray Project Manager at Portsmouth, asking me if I could come in for an interview on the following morning. I was questioned by three senior managers, none of whom I had ever met before. Although I later learnt that two were ex-Captains (WE) and the other an ex Commander (WE).

The interview lasted about 40 minutes and seemed to go well. I then went straight back to the ship where we were undergoing the last harbour trials before going to sea. A week later I received a letter from Marconi offering me a post as a Trials Manager, starting in July and asking me if I was interested in the post. Needless to say, I said yes.

I celebrated my 50<sup>th</sup> birthday on 18<sup>th</sup> January 1979, in the nearly finished wardroom ante-room of the Bulwark, first with pre-lunch drinks for all of my messmates, a rather costly gesture in a, by then fully manned, aircraft carrier. That evening I entertained some of them again with their wives, and also my friends and family, to a party in the same venue, with a buffet supper dance. Very few RN engineer officers get to celebrate their half-century birthday in the ship in which they are about to sail. Shown below are Eileen and me and some of the guests, including, bottom right, the President of the mess Commander Mike Howitt and my boss' wife, Sue Wardale, both of whom are clearly in party mood.

Next day, it was back to the final harbour trials. 'A' Boiler Room was flashed up for the first time since March 1976, and was taken up to full pressure. 'B' Boiler room followed and we carried out steam generator trials, loading them through plates

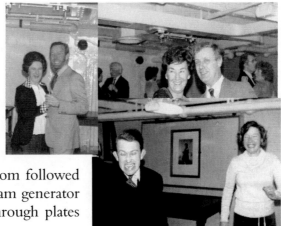

lowered over the side into the harbour. Everything was coming together nicely and the morale of the whole ship's company rose a notch every day, as yet another milestone was passed. In mid February we carried out the full 'Preps for Sea' and then carried out a 'Fast Cruise', involving all of the ship's departments. For two hours we simulated going to sea with all of the ship's propulsion, weapons. Radar radio, internal communications, navigational, air department, boats and the seamanship equipment, working and manned. This exercise highlighted a few minor shortcomings, but was a success.

Form and

Order of Service

to be used in asking

The Blessing of Almighty God

upon

Her Majesty's Ship BULWARK

in the presence of
His Royal Highness Commander The Prince of Wales
K.G., K.T., P.C., G.C.B.

at Portsmouth                    Friday, 23rd February, 1979

On the morning of 23$^{rd}$ February 1979, the Bulwark's 1200 strong ship's company, and 1500 guests were packed into the hangar when, to the stirring sound of a fanfare from 8 Dragoon guards, the Royal guest of honour entered via the starboard after access. I was fallen-in in front of the WE division, as an immaculate Prince Charles, passed inches in front of me, followed by Lord Louis Mountbatten but, incongruously preceded by a scruffy crowd of TV cameramen, microphone carriers and photographers, walking backwards, only a few feet in front of him. Obviously used to purposefully wallking, without apparently noticing the media rag bag so close to him, he inspected the front rank of the divisions, the Royal Marine band and the ship's guard drawn up in front of the VIP's position. This area contained, I was happy to see, Eileen and Sally, Arthur Carpenter and Paul Marshall and their wives, as well as the CinC Fleet and the Commandant of the Royal Marines and their wives. The Prince congratulated all concerned with getting the ship ready for sea trials, and said he was impressed by the ship's cleanliness and the smartness of her ship's company. He then cut the commissioning cake with the youngest sailor onboard, 16 year old JMEM Dwyer, The Prince of Wales then attended a reception in the wardroom during which Eileen and Sally were delighted to meet him. This Royal pre-prandial drink before HRH lunched with the Captain, is amusingly illustrated by Tugg's cartoon, shown below, the original of which, presented to the Prince by the officers of HMS Bulwark, now hangs in the cloakroom of HMS Nelson's wardroom.

After the pomp and partying of the ship's rededication ceremony, we had our last weekend in Portsmouth for 3 weeks before leaving for Sea Acceptance Trials of all of our equipment. On Monday 26th February, we carried out our final 'Fast Cruise' exercise and all was well, so we remained 'flashed-up' and all of our equipment running and manned overnight, ready to sail on the next afternoon tide.

My Special Sea Duty post was on the bridge and I was there next afternoon when, with two big tugs secured to the ship to turn her round to face south and the harbour mouth, the Captain ordered "Obey Telegraphs" and "Let go for'd and aft". As the tugs started to turn us to port an agonised shout came from the Navigating Officer on the port wing of the bridge, reporting that the compass repeater was going the wrong way. I looked at the Bridge master Pelorus and steering tape repeater and noted both were showing the ship turning to port. I rushed to the port wing and, sure enough it was indicating a turn to starboard and was showing a false ship's head. I always carried a pocket screwdriver on me so I quickly removed the terminal cover and swapped over two of the three lines to the repeater and, when the ship was on a steady southerly heading, realigned the repeater with the pelorus. The Captain ordered slow ahead both engines and after disengaging from the tugs, ordered "Half-ahead both engines", increased speed and made for the harbour entrance – panic over! A few minutes later the iconic picture shown below was taken as we passed the Round tower and fulfilled the prophecy that "HMS Bulwark Will Sail Again".

*HMS Bulwark leaving Portsmouth on 27th February 1979*

As we passed along Southsea front, I carried out a transit check on St Jude's Spire in line with the Naval War Memorial and the port wing compass repeater was spot on. The reversal of two of its connections was not picked up earlier because the ship remained firmly alongside during the Fast Cruise Exercise. An amendment of the drill stopped this embarrassing event ever happening again.

The ship anchored for the night at Spithead and everyone aboard was highly delighted that the 'Incredible Hulk' had made it back to sea. After a celebratory nightcap in the mess, with my colleagues, I retired to my largish, newly refurbished and comfortable cabin, positioned vertically above the port propellor, and slept like a top.

During the next three days we carried out Sea Acceptance trials of our radar and radio communications and, at the same time, SATs of the auxiliary machinery and drills involving the steering gear, anchors and boats. All went well and we proceeded to Plymouth where we spent the weekend embarking spare gear from HMS Ark Royal which was paying-off. As we left Plymouth Sound at dusk on the Sunday evening and passed Cawsand doing 15 knots, a trawler appeared from around Penlee Point on a collision course with us. Captain Brewer calmly ordered, "Full Astern both engines" and the ship slowed promptly enough to narrowly miss the fishing boat as it cut across our bows. The Signal officer asked the Captain whether he should send a terse signal to the fishing boat, but the Captain replied, "No, he has had a big enough fright already!"

Throughout the next two weeks, we operated in the South Western approaches, carrying out SATs of the propulsion machinery and flying trials and DG and sound ranging in the Plymouth areas. The highlight of this period was a most successful four hour full power trial, out into the Atlantic when the 'Old Girl' actually achieved the highest speed in her 31 years. With the permission of the Commander (E), I took parties of junior WE ratings, who had never before experienced a full power trial at sea, down below so that they would not miss the chance of witnessing, from the engine room, a steam driven capital ship going like the clappers. They were all very impressed, and some a trifle scared at the noise down below, but had something to tell their children, long after steamships had completely disappeared.

The Wardroom had purchased a large TV set which was situated in the Ante room. As we were seldom likely to berth alongside, the TV aerial was temporarily mounted, after anchoring, on one of the 40mm gun directors and the director aligned with the transmitter. As the ship swung at anchor, the aerial was kept aligned automatically and we enjoyed pretty good reception. On Wednesday nights, at that time, there was a programme, introduced by the song "We are Sailing" which featured HMS Ark Royal and examined the role at sea, of different members of her crew. Captain Brewer was invited each week to view the episode and we always conveniently anchored in good time and ready to watch. The episodes showing the Ark's Captain and the Master at Arms were well received by all, not least our Captain. However, the third episode concerned the Ark Royal's Chaplain who tried too hard to be 'one of the lads' and resorted to effing and blinding. At this, George Brewer, who was a staunch Christian and abhorred swearing, angrily stood up, and announced, "If that Chaplain was aboard this ship, he would be off it on the next boat". He then stormed out of the mess. I have to say that all of the officers present were also disgusted at the chaplain's language and I suspect that the lads were not impessed either!

Bulwark was the only remaining RN warship whose main electrical supply was 220 volts dc. In all of the 440 volt ac ships, the maintenance of the electrics, including the generators and all of the engine-room electrical equipment, was the responsibility of the ME department, but in Bulwark it remained with the WE department.
All of the original wiring was lead-cased and, over the years, it had suffered surface damage, which occasionally resulted in a fire. During our sea trials, and in the rest of my time aboard, we averaged one such minor fire every two weeks. My Action/ Emergency station was in DCHQ, just 2 minutes dash from my cabin, and as I was completely deaf on my left side, I always tried to sleep on my left side so that I could hear the telephone. However, I had an

arrangement at DCHQ and the main switchboard next door, that if I didn't answer the phone, to send a messenger hot foot to shake me. Naturally the fortnightly fire generally occurred at night, but we soon had the best fire-fighting organisation at sea. Mind you, the call out for a fire certainly got the adrenalin running but we managed to keep the damage done down to an acceptable level.

After 17 days of successful sea trials , which culminated in SATs (Air), the ship returned to Portsmouth on Friday 23rd March 1979. That very evening the ship held a Ball in the hangar to celebrate the ship's recommissioning exactly a month earlier. Bulwark was

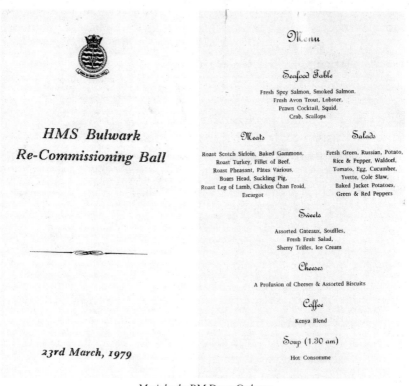

**HMS Bulwark**
**Re-Commissioning Ball**

*23rd March, 1979*

Menu

Seafood Table

Fresh Spey Salmon, Smoked Salmon,
Fresh Avon Trout, Lobster,
Prawn Cocktail, Squid,
Crab, Scallops

Meats

Roast Scotch Sirloin, Baked Gammons,
Roast Turkey, Fillet of Beef,
Roast Pheasant, Pâtes Various,
Boars Head, Suckling Pig,
Roast Leg of Lamb, Chicken Chan Froid,
Escargot

Salads

Fresh Green, Russian, Potato,
Rice & Pepper, Waldorf,
Tomato, Egg, Cucumber,
Yvette, Cole Slaw,
Baked Jacket Potatoes,
Green & Red Peppers

Sweets

Assorted Gateaux, Souffles,
Fresh Fruit Salad,
Sherry Trifles, Ice Cream

Cheeses

A Profusion of Cheeses & Assorted Biscuits

Coffee

Kenya Blend

Soup (1.30 am)

Hot Consomme

*Music by the RM Dance Orchestra*

blessed with two champion CPO Cooks, both of whom had very recently won Olympia Gold medals, and the standard of cuisine onboard, for the ship's company and the officers was very high.

As we had been at sea all week, the mail had arrived onboard after I went home in order to escort Eileen to the Ball. After we arrived onboard with my sister and her husband and two friends, we sat at our allocated table in the hangar and began to enjoy ourselves. I then thought I had better check the letter rack in the wardroom and when I did, I found I had a letter from Marconi Ltd. It contained a formal offer of a Trials Management position at Portsmouth beginning on 2nd July 1979 at a starting salary 60% higher than I was led to expect. On the way back to my guests at the table, I happily ordered Champagne. My guests and I thoroughly enjoyed that splendid evening.

A few days later HMS Bulwark, all signs of the Ball removed, and the ship cleared away for action, sailed for her short work-up at Portland and next morning, was boarded by the whole of FOST's Staff, for their Sea Check. On completion of this three-hour-long inspection, the ship anchored in Weymouth bay and began the Harbour drill and exercise phase of the work-up. As the boat trip from Portland naval base to the anchorage took a long time and the ship carried 6 Wessex transport helicopters, Bulwark's own aircraft did most of the conveyance of the staff to and from the ship. The wife of one of the Aviators had pre-recorded a series of airport announcements and the appropriate message was broadcast for the information and the amusement of the Admiral's staff and the ship's company. Broadcasts such as,

"Bulwark Air Lines announce the imminent departure of Flight BK 13 to Portland, passengers for this flight should go to the Flight Deck immediately;" and,

"Bulwark welcomes the passengers of Flight BK 14 from Portland and hope you enjoy your stay".

These and other examples of being a 'quick flip to the front' during the harbour week and the sea weeks at Portland, earned many 'Brownie Points' for the ship. The ship's helicopters also proved invaluable during the Disaster and 'Aid to Civil Power' exercises carried out ashore in the fictional country of Portlandia. On the second Sunday at Portland, officers' guests were invited to Pimms on the quarter deck at noon. While ashore for Mass in the RN Chapel, I rang my niece Mary at Piddletrenthide in Dorset, with whom Eileen and my sister Eileen were staying for the weekend, and invited them to come out on the MFV leaving Portland at 1130. Although the trip was a little bumpy, they enjoyed the party and Mary loved being the centre of the attentions of a number of our dashing young aviators.

A ship of Bulwark's size requires a huge staff to cover all of the intensive exercises encountered in the sea weeks and the staff and ship's company were pretty exhausted by the time we anchored late every night. The electrical aspects of our damage-control exercise were restricted to the after section of the ship, larger than a whole destroyer, because there was insufficient staff to monitor the whole ship. Fortunately the after DC party did very well. My favourite memory, of the work-up was the morning when, surrounded by a bevy of ant-submarine frigates who were all unsuccessfully pinging away with their sophisticated sonars, our antiquated WW2 sonar, operated by one man in the bowels of the ship, detected a submarine inside the screen. To the amazement of our escort, and FOST's staff, Bulwark hoisted the black flag to show she had a firm submarine contact, told them where the submarine was and then scrambled a Sea King helicopter to attack it. This supreme example of one-upmanship came about because the submarine was just below that morning's surface acoustic layer and the frigates' sonar beams were being deflected away from the submarine, while Bulwark's ancient transducer was below the layer and able to send her sonar beam straight at the target. The old adage, "Many a good tune is played on an old fiddle", seemed appropriate.

As always, the Work-Up was hard, indeed fatiguing work for everyone but, as usual we all learnt a lot and, having approached the whole thing in the right manner, even enjoyed the challenge. After surviving a final 'Thursday War', in which we were the principal target for sustained attacks from above, below and on the surface, and during which our response was monitored by the entire corps of FOST Sea Riders, we were declared by the Admiral to be fit to join the active fleet. A few days later the ship set off northward to join RN and Allied ships for a major NATO Anti-Submarine exercise.

As I had learnt 30 years earlier in HMS Theseus, an operational carrier is a floating airstrip whose ship's company's role is to keep the principal weapons, ie the aircraft and their armament, flying, by providing a secure, mobile and sustainable platform from which they can operate. During our passage to the North Atlantic between Iceland and the Orkneys, every day, except Sunday 22nd

*Irish Sea April 1979. Lt Alan Barton, Cdr Tony Wardale and Don,(wearing track suit)*
April, was dedicated to an intense programme of day and night flying. On the day of rest, Sunday divisions were held and while we were smartly dressed the photograph shown on page 411 was taken,

just before the ship 'Blew soot' and we had to scarper to save our No 1 suits. During the early days of the passage, the flight deck was occasionally available to all, for sporting activities and was put to good use for deck-hockey, volleyball and circuit training,

As we approached the 'War zone' the tempo of flying, particularly by the Sea King A/S helicopters, increased and involved night flying in darkened ship conditions. I had done quite a bit of flying at Portland in 1967-69 and thought I'd like one more helicopter flight before I left the navy, so I persuaded Jock English, CO of 826 (Sea King) Squadron, to allow me to accompany the crew of one of them during a practice A/S patrol, just before the start of the NATO exercise. I attended the briefing with the air crews and heard I was flying with Richard Shultz, who was chatting with his neighbour when this was announced. The CO said, "Did you get that Richard?". The German pilot stood up, clicked his heels and said. "As zey say in ze English war films, 'Jawohl mein Kapitan'", and sat down to a roar of laughter.

To increase their flight endurance, it was normal practice aboard Bulwark for A/S helicopters to take off like a fixed-wing naval aircraft, with the ship steaming into the wind, rather than to rise vertically. Two hours before dusk, we sped forward along the flight deck after the other chopper in our patrol, took off effortlessly, and made our way at 180 knots to our first sonar dunking position. I was seated in the spare seat alongside the sonar operator who had, on his other side, the Observer, responsible for the aircraft's navigation. Up front were the two pilots, Richard and a young Sub-Lt. A Sea King in forward flight flies as smoothly as a fixed-wing aircraft, but when it hovers to lower and operate its sonar transducer in search of a submarine, as it does frequently during a patrol, it has a tendency to vibrate. The next 4 hours seemed endless to me and I was very relieved when we made our landing approach from the port quarter of the ship, lit only by dim landing lights. After the de-briefing I was relieved to stagger back to my cabin absolutely exhausted, but full of admiration for the crew. Richard the pilot was 28, but the rest of his crew were 21, 20 and 19 years old and, at the age of 50, I was clearly too old for this sort of flying. My respect for the skill and stamina of the aircrews was further enhanced, during the subsequent NATO exercise held in pretty heavy weather, when the sonars of at least two of our 18 Sea Kings were 'in the dip' day and night at all times during the 15 day 'war' in the North Atlantic, when other ship's helicopters were occasionally grounded by the sea conditions. Our Wessex 5s also did sterling work evacuating injured sailors and ferrying stores and personnel between ships.

During the exercise, the ship's routine Daily Orders were enlivened by a humorous 'useful phrase' in German to stimulate anticipation of the ship's forthcoming first foreign visit. Written by our German joker Richard Shultz they included such vital German expressions as, "Don't worry, my friend will pay". I have mentioned Richard Shultz several times and the reader may think he was the only non RN character among Bulwark's aviators. In fact there was another pilot named Shultz, a Lt Cdr in the Canadian navy, A USN Pilot and a giant blond haired Aussie Wessex pilot named Wong who, naturally, was known as Suzie and took it in good spirit, although a more macho-looking guy would be hard to find. All of these chaps were on exchange duty with the RN and seemed to be enjoying their secondment, and the company of the 70 similarly skilled and lively RN pilots and Observers we carried.

The NATO exercise ended on 15th May and, en route to Scapa Flow, a mess dinner was held in the wardroom, at which I had the honour and distinction of being dined out of the ship and the navy at sea. The meal was of course superb and the President said some kind and humorous words, and presented me with a fake hearing trumpet, before inviting me to say a few words. After thanking him and the mess for dining me out, I said that my mess mates probably expected me to tell them how much the navy had changed during my 35 years service but, instead, I pointed out that very little had changed, eg. my first ship Theseus was almost identical to my last, Bulwark. I ended my short farewell speech with a salute to the greatest single change in those years, the fantastic improvement in the standard of food served in RN ships. Finally I wished the ship a happy commission. The aviators, released from Cdr (Air)'s two month long

*High Jinks after Dinner 16th May 1979 Don is at right of 3rd row from front*

embargo on their drinking during flying operations, really went to town in the bar after dinner.

Next morning I underwent my pre-Discharge Medical and Dental examinations, normally carried out in a shore establishment but, since we had a Surgeon Commander MO and a Dentist onboard, and I was going on terminal leave straight from the ship, these were carried out onboard. Despite a bit of a hang-over, not noticeable in the official mug shot taken that day and shown here, my final RN 'medical' was no problem and neither was the oral check. However, when I sat in the dentist's chair and looked up, I was horrified to see the deck-head close above me, was covered in incredibly explicit  pornographic pictures, presumably, to take the patients mind off the pain. I asked the Dentist when his surgery was due for Captain's Rounds. He wasn't sure and hadn't seen the Captain's reaction to the Chaplain of HMS Ark Royal on television, similarly trying to be 'one of the lads'. I strongly advised him to get rid of these pictures pdq before the 'old man' saw them, or else he would be 'on his bike'. I later learnt that he had left the ship suddenly. That evening, whilst en route from Scapa Flow to Rosyth, I enjoyed a farewell drink or several in the Chief's mess with my very good Warrant Officer and the WE Chief POs.

Early on the morning of Saturday 18th May, HMS Bulwark passed under the rail and road bridges and secured to a buoy in the Forth, opposite Rosyth Dockyard. The ship was to be open to the public for three days, including the Bank holiday Monday, as the principal attraction of Rosyth Navy Days, starting at 1400 that afternoon. The morning was taken up in ranging the aircraft on deck, sprucing up the guns and trying to eradicate the stains left by the North Atlantic. However, I was excused these tasks because I attended the exercise wash-up held ashore in Rosyth. The COs and Navigating Officers of all the NATO ships that took part in the exercise brought their charts and logs and went through the whole exercise together. I recall that at one time during the 15 days, the Anti-submarine forces were in firm sonar contact with nine submarines. There were only 8 NATO subs in the exercise, 3 RN, 2

USN, and I each Canadian, Dutch and German so it was concluded that a Soviet Submarine had joined in the fun. The Captain of the German U-Boat showed the meeting a photograph of Bulwark, taken through his periscope. He told us that, just after taking the photo, the carrier had turned towards him and he had to dive deep to avoid being sunk. We had no idea of how close the U-boat had come to us. That afternoon I intended to take one of the Bosun dinghies for a last sail as the ship's sailing officer, but my relief came aboard with his wife and we had a chat and tea together before they went ashore saying he would be back on Monday morning to join.

I was Duty DLC next day, my last Sunday on the ship. Half of the ship's company had been ashore the day before; their first time on terra firma for six weeks, and the other half went ashore on Sunday morning. The ship was open to visitors and I invited aboard my friend from HMS Falmouth days, Bob Stevenson and his wife Betty, who lived locally, and we enjoyed a very pleasant lunch together. It was a relatively quiet duty until 1700, when the last boat loads of visitors left for Rosyth and South Queensferry, despite the efforts of some of the public to carry away bits of the ship as souvenirs. Then it all became a little hectic. Captain Brewer insisted that the DLC personally checked all of the myriad secret signal crypto equipment inserts and documents, rather than allow him to delegate this irksome task to one of his many other duty officers. As we had just been involved in a major NATO exercise, there were more than the usual number of these and it took over an hour to complete. Then the first boat load of returning libertymen arrived and disgorged a number of drunken sailors. We only had 4 cells onboard and these were soon filled so I had to arrange for the overspill to be accommodated in their own messes, in the care of the Leading Hand of the mess. I also arranged for them, and the occupants of the cells, to be personally checked every 15 minutes by one of the duty officers and hourly by me, to ensure they had come to no harm.

The Captain and Commander were ashore and though I had several duty officers and midshipmen, I was in charge and responsible for the ship and for around 1000 men aboard. I met every boat returning to the ship to decide what action to take with each libertyman returning aboard drunk, to ensure his safety. The last boat reached the ship about 0015 and after sorting out its cargo of lads, I made another rounds of the cells and the drunks farmed out to their messes and then retired to my cabin, I was shaken 30 minutes later to take an urgent radio telephone call from the police at Inverkeithing. They reported that they had in custody one of our sailors whom they had charged with murder. The police alleged that the sailor had kicked a civilian to death in a drunken brawl, and wished to bring him aboard to collect his gear before jailing him to await trial. I dressed, called the Master at Arms and together we met the police launch and took the accused, who was very drunk, handcuffed, and shoeless, under escort to his mess deck where, when his locker was opened, it was found to contain items of property belonging to some of his messmates. After a detailed investigation of these findings. the sailor concerned, still stoned out of his mind, was handed back to the police and, after the relevant paperwork was completed, he was taken ashore by them. This whole hiatus took about three hours and, after making another rounds of the cells and other places with drunks in my care, I only managed a catnap before it was time to meet the Captain and Commander returning aboard at 0715. They both went straight to their cabins and I next saw them on the after end of the flight deck just before Colours. In accordance with naval practice, the duty Signalman loudly reported to me "Eight O'clock Sir" and I gave the traditional and strange response, "Make it So"; the Royal Marine band struck up the National Anthem and the White Ensign began its ascent of the staff while we all duly saluted her Majesty. After the band, fallen in on the after lift, had descended to the hangar and dispersed, the Captain turned to me and asked if I had had a quiet duty. I gave him a short resume of the unusual event of my last naval duty and went below to hear the charges against about a score of ratings who had returned aboard drunk. Considering some 1000 had gone ashore for the first time in over a month, 2% coming back smashed wasn't bad, and none of them, apart from the one charged with murder, had caused any real trouble on board, and as far as I knew ashore, before staggering back to the ship. This compares very favourably with civilian lads of their age. Mercifully all survived the night without coming to grief, an ever present possibility with drunken sailors. When they faced me next morning, though still pretty hung-over, none was physically worse off but, when weighed off by the Captain, they would feel it in their pockets.

The ship was open to visitors that afternoon, so I retired to my cabin and later had a quiet evening onboard, as we were leaving for Hamburg next morning. My relief, a pleasant fast-track graduate Lt Cdr who, 20 years younger, cleverer and seemingly more laid back than me, joined the ship at breakfast time and told me that his wife was on her way to Hamburg by air and would meet the ship on arrival, and that he would be living ashore with her throughout the visit. He joined me as I conducted the WE Preparations for Sea and then, after the ship left Rosyth, we spent most of the 350 mile passage, together, carrying out the turn-over. This painstaking exercise was continued during the 60 mile journey up the narrow Elbe from Cuxhaven to Hamburg, during which I was a Special Sea Dutyman on the bridge. The WE office writer brought each of the many documents requiring signatures to us and when this task was completed, my relief left me with the clear impression that he was confident he could crack the job he was taking over.

HMS Bulwark berthed alongside in the St Pauli district of Hamburg, on the afternoon of 23rd May, in walking distance of the city centre and directly opposite a large Blohm and Voss floating dock. We were given a full ceremonial and musical welcome. That night the ship held an official Cocktail party in the hangar and afterwards the jollity continued in the wardroom as a spontaneous and friendly Anglo-German party. Next morning I was relieved of my duty as Senior Catholic, responsible for organising boats ashore for the disappointing number of the 80 Catholics onboard wishing to attend mass, by a professional, when a Catholic Chaplain joined. That night, the eve of my departure, Tony Wardale and his three other WE Officers, took me on my final run ashore in the navy- a 'Creep up the Reep' as a tour of the Reeperbahn, the notorious red light, bar and club district was known. This culminated in a lengthy visit to the city's biggest Beer Cellar where the foaming steins were served by pretty frauleins and where, if you were prepared to buy the Oompah band a round of drinks, you could conduct the music. I have a vague memory of several of our young aviators making a terrible hash of this, much to the amusement of all the patrons, which included most of our wardroom. I was safely brought back to the ship by my colleagues in the small hours and slept soundly in my cabin for the last time. During the morning I had my farewell meeting with the Captain who thanked me for my part in getting the ship back to sea, gave me a pleasing 'flimsy' and wished me a happy second career. At 1145 I was asked to go up to the flight deck where I found the whole WE department assembled. Tony Wardale gave a kind valediction and then presented me with a plaque, made in the ship's WE workshop onboard by one of the WE Artificer Apprentices and listing all of my naval appointments from 1944 to 1979. At lunchtime in the wardroom I enjoyed the traditional leavers' Vin d'honneur and, at 1400, I was driven to Hamburg airport from where I took off in a BA airliner in a real donner und blitzen storm for London. With a fairly high level of alcohol content, I slept until we were passing Southend and then enjoyed the view as we slowly descended while flying up the Thames to land at Heathrow.

On the way home by train, I looked back fondly on my time in Bulwark and concluded that I had been extremely lucky to have had such an interesting and rewarding last job in the Navy. I had been blessed with an excellent Captain, a kind and most considerate Commander (WE), a challenging task and a largely supportive department, staffed with keen, competent and loyal senior ratings. I had also enjoyed the company of a particularly happy wardroom. In fact I could scarcely have had more job satisfaction than I did in helping get the Incredible Hulk back to sea as an operational A/S Carrier. However, it was now time to settle down at home and embark on a new career, but first I owed Eileen a good holiday.

Next morning I went to Thomas Cook's at Cosham to pick up the air tickets, hotel and hire car reservations and dollars I had already arranged by post, for a four week free-lance visit to the west and east coasts of the USA. During my time in the navy I had served three long spells in the Far East, two in the Gulf and one in the Mediterranean, and been all around Africa, but had never been to America, and Eileen and I had never had an accompanied foreign shore posting, so I was determined to take her to the country of her choice for my terminal leave.

On Monday 27th May, Eileen and I left the house in the care of our adult daughter Sally and son Paul and flew in a Pan Am Jumbo to Los Angeles. After a refueling stop at New York we were told that our luggage appeared to have been inadvertently taken off and put on the wrong plane at JF Kennedy and this caused us some worry during the flight across America but fortunately this was not  true and we were reunited with it at LA. We eventually reached our first hotel, at Anaheim at 0300 local time and turned in, only to wake up, due to jet lag time shift, at 0700. After a quick dip in the pool and breakfast, we went for a day trip to Hollywood and our holiday was off to a great start. The whole of the next day we spent in nearby Disney Land and rounded off a great time with dinner in a Mexican restaurant. On day 3, we picked up our pre-booked hire car, a 3.5 litre, automatic, air-conditioned Chevrolet and set off for San Diego along the coast road, lunched and spent a delightful afternoon in La Jolla and then on to the hotel in San Diego. During our three days there, we spent one memorable day in nearby Tijuana, leaving the car, on advice, parked on the US side of the border. We loved San Diego and its people, which both of us thought had more than the edge on our home town. We then motored north along the US 1 coast road on our un-planned itinerary to San Francisco stopping overnight at motels in Long Beach, Santa Barbara, San Luis Obispo, a charming town with which we fell in love, Carmel and Pacifica. Eileen and I swam every day in the warm sea, and every night in the motel pools but when we dashed down the beach at Pacifica on our daily "last one in the water is a cissy" challenge, we found the sea was bitterly cold and noticed that though the beach was crowded, no one else was in the water. The Aleutian current, which makes the Pacific too cold for bathing as far as 60 miles south of San Francisco, had not swung westward out to sea! The rooms in all of the 5 motels we stayed in were large, clean and comfortable, had a bathroom, TV and refrigerator and an ice cube dispenser. All of the motels had a pool, a good and reasonably priced diner next door and friendly staff. With the exchange rate of $2.14 to the pound, the average cost to us was only £11 a night for the room including use of the pool. We thoroughly enjoyed the freedom of this phase of the holiday and met nothing but friendliness from the local inhabitants.

As we approached San Francisco, only the top of the Golden Gate was visible above the fog which enveloped the city but, by the time we had checked into our hotel in Market Street, the sun had broken through showing all the vibrant colours of this cosmopolitan city. Eileen and I set out straight away to see every sight and to sample all of the many exotic cuisines available, enjoying three splendid days in so doing.

All too soon we found ourselves aboard a United Jumbo jet on the way to Toronto, via Chicago, to have a look at Canada and then the eastern states. A few days earlier, the US media had been saturated by the death of John Wayne, but this was replaced by the tragic crash of a DC 10 airliner which lost an engine on take-off from Chicago and her last few seconds of flight was repeated on every TV news bulletin. This caused us some apprehension as we winged our way across the states. Incidentally, the only piece of UK news we read or heard during our four weeks in the states, was a report on a scandal involving the Liberal leader Jeremy Thorpe.

We arrived in Toronto in time for dinner and I was pleased to see that the hotel foyer displayed a portrait of the Queen. The next three days were delightful as we toured this beautiful city with its blend of modern architecture and a historic quarter. The local

people seemed to be very pro British and were very friendly and helpful as we explored all of the famous sights, including the Toronto tower, the world's highest structure, from the top of which we had a magnificent view

of the impressive city and its environs. We then travelled by coach to Niagara, via Hamilton and admired the Ontario countryside but found the world's honeymoon capital too sickly and were glad that we were booked into a hotel

on the USA side of the border on the river bank almost immediately upstream of the Niagara Falls. We swam in the hotel pool close to the fast running river and in earshot of the roar of the adjacent falls and afterwards enjoyed a Happy Hour with Tapas, followed by dinner on the riverside patio. Next morning we crossed back to the Canadian side, which affords a more spectacular view of the falls, before re-crossing the border bridge and making for Buffalo, a large and unattractive industrial city, to catch a coach to Pittsbugh.

While I was planning our holiday, onboard HMS Bulwark several months earlier, I had been advised that it was best to hire a car to tour California but to get weekly bus tickets when traveling in the eastern states and to go by Greyhound bus. I took this advice and at midnight, after enjoying a first rate open air evening opera performance in the surprisingly pleasant city of Pittsburgh, we were near the front of the queue when the Greyhound bus for Richmond in Virginia, pulled into the bus station. Eileen and I were laden down with a case and hold-all each, and were rudely swept aside by the most ill-mannered crowd we have ever seen, who were hell bent on getting the best possible seat. By the time we staggered on to the bus, there were only two seats left and they were at opposite ends of the vehicle, which had started its 1400 mile journey at Portland in Oregon and was going to Tallahassee in Florida. Eileen had sitting next to her, a huge dirty, obese, middle-aged coloured man wearing a pork pie hat and a string vest, who looked as if he had just left the field he worked in; I had a filthy junkie next to me who gave himself a 'fix' just after the bus moved off. I could see Eileen was terrified at the thought of a night on the bus in such unsavoury company and was close to tears. We both had aisle seats so I was able to keep an eye on Eileen and I visited her several times but she was pretty upset, particularly when I came back from a reconnaissance of the loo to warn her not to use it as it was absolutely revolting. After 4 hours of misery, the bus pulled into the Washington bus station where we had a merciful comfort stop and a coffee and, when we anxiously returned, we were relieved to find that Eileen's neigbour had left the bus to grace the capital with his presence. After dusting down his seat, I joined Eileen and the two of us slept most of the 100 miles to the old Confederate capital. On arrival, at about 0700, the surly driver took our luggage out of the hold and, after totally ignoring my adverse comments on the state of the onboard loo, promptly plonked the cases down on an oil slick and drove off. We had the bus station Ladies and Gents to ourselves and were able to clean the oil off the cases and leave them in the left-luggage store, have a wash and brush-up, change and eat a good breakfast and were touring the historic city by 0900. We enjoyed a look at Richmond and, in particular a visit to the old Confederate Parliament buildings where the guide, a charming Southern Belle, made a fuss of us because we were the only English couple on the guided tour. Richmond seemed to us to be almost completely inhabited by Afro-Americans and I mused that Jefferson Davis would have been turning over in his grave. After lunch in a good restaurant, we boarded a clean Greyhound coach and had a comfortable journey, sitting together in polite company, for the journey back to Washington DC. The penny then dropped, only the very poorest Americans travelled by bus at night when the fares were lowest. Passengers with weekly tickets avoided overnight travel like the plague!

We arrived at our hotel at 1800 and, after dinner, went for a stroll around the nearby Capitol, and enjoyed a pleasant evening in an Irish pub which sold draught Guinness, Although this was near a charity shop raising money "to free Northern Ireland from the British yoke", and we were clearly English, we were well received by all of the staff and patrons, most of whom seemed to have relatives living in England, in places like Surrey! We thoroughly enjoyed the company of these fervent Irish Americans who were rather less closely linked with the old country than I, who had an Irish mother.

Next morning after breakfast as we were getting ready to attend mass, we received an unexpected phone call in our hotel room. It was Sally who, knowing we would be then at that particular hotel, rang and said. "Happy Father's Day and congratulations, you have been awarded the MBE in the Queen's Birthday Honours List." I was flabbergasted. In those days, unlike those receiving civil awards, recipients of military decorations were not informed beforehand and Sally's news, learnt from the TV and press and a number of phone calls received at home, was a complete and very pleasant surprise. What a Father's day present!

After mass in the biggest Catholic Church in the USA, we had a coffee in the cafeteria in the crypt and in the shop there saw an LP record of the choir of St John's Catholic Cathedral Portsmouth.

It's a small world! It was raining for the first time in the three weeks of our holiday, so I hailed a taxi and, after sitting in the back and telling the overweight Afro-American driver, who was wearing a baseball cap and a string vest and smoking a big fat cigar, where we wanted to go, Eileen asked the driver, "Do you often get bad weather in Washington?". He took the cigar out of his mouth, spat out of the window and said, "Lady, there aint no such thing as baaaadd weather, there's rainy weather, sunny weather, snowy weather, and windy weather, but there aint no such thing as baaadd weather". He then spat out of the window again, wound up the window, put his cigar back between his lips and drove us back to the hotel. Ever since then, if anyone mentions bad weather to us, we always reply, "There aint no such thing as baaaddd weather". That afternoon the sun came out again and we took a boat trip up the Potomac to George Washington's house. Next morning we visited Arlington National cemetery where, it struck me, the roar of jet aircraft taking off from the nearby National airport every 30 seconds and passing over the massive graveyard at 200 feet at full throttle, with their wheels still down, surely must prevent America's heroes from Resting in Peace! We witnessed a military funeral but couldn't even hear the funeral volley of shots, let alone the words of the service. We spent a very interesting afternoon in some of the Smithsonian museums flanking the Mall. During the day, the centre of Washington is attractive and lively but after the museums and government buildings close, it is dead; for bars, theatres and clubs, one has to go the suburbs for any form of nightlife. On the Monday evening we visited George Town, the old colonial district, and the next night, Arlington, enjoying both evenings immensely.

Next morning, after three wonderful days in Washington, we set off in a bus for Philadelphia via a rather run down Baltimore, whose street corners seemed occupied by large groups of unemployed men. We checked in to our main street city centre hotel, the Penn Center Inn, the best hotel of our USA tour, early in the afternoon and straight away went out on a tour of the historic city. This included seeing the cradle of USA's independence and the Liberty Bell. The multi-storey, state of the art hotel, with its open air swimming pool on the 5th floor, cost us only £32 a day for the luxurious room we had on the 8th floor, with in-built luxuries which still hadn't arrived in British hotels 20 years later. We strolled out after dinner and had a delightful evening in local clubs.

The following morning we took the bus to New York and enjoyed the 100 mile trip through New Jersey. By lunchtime we had checked into our pre-arranged hotel in West 46th Street which, though very handily situated

Don, Uncle John Reagan, Eileen, cousin Jack

within walking distance of the highlights of Manhattan, was the least good hotel we stayed at in the USA. However, we were soon out enjoying the Big Apple, had several very good meals in restaurants and visited Macys, Central Park and Broadway. We spent a day in Ridgefield New Jersey with Eileen's Uncle, whose family made a great fuss of us and gave a party in our honour. All of his neighbours were so friendly and we felt most welcome in this part of small town America.

It was our original intention to return to England on a Laker  shuttle after 3 days in NY but the earlier DC10 disaster had grounded all of Fred Laker's aircraft and had affected BA and other airlines and there were no spare seats on any flights to the UK until 3 days after our planned departure date. We didn't have a credit card in those days or enough cash to pay for 3 more days accommodation and meals and a more expensive flight home. We therefore had to dash down to Wall Street, to the only branch of Lloyds bank in NY. The manager kindly let us have $400 from our UK account and also suggested some of the sights we should make certain to see, during our extra 3 days in the city. On the way back to the hotel, a relieved Eileen said to the taxi-driver, "I love this city". Recognising her accent, the ex-GI, who had been in England before landing in Normandy in 1944, replied, "Lady, you gave it to us, you can have it back anytime you like!" He then went on to moan about how New York had gone to the dogs since its pre-war days. After booking a BA flight to London on Monday 25th June, and extending our hotel booking, we set about making the best use of our longer spell in probably the most lively city on earth. We took a most interesting boat trip around Manhattan Island, walking through the West Side, of Bernstein fame, to catch the boat; visited Harlem, Radio City, the Rag Trade area, Rockefeller Center and the Waldorf Astoria, (for a drink). On Midsummer's Day, our last full day in the USA, we strolled to nearby St Patrick's Cathedral for Sunday mass. The famous church, although huge, is dwarfed and lost between two skyscrapers, and as we approached we were amazed to see a line of priests standing on the top of the flight of steps up to the entrance, each holding aloft a banner reading, "Hands Off Gay Priests" and, at the end of the line, a bearded young man wearing a black hat carrying a banner saying, "Hands Off Gay Rabbis". As we walked past the line to enter the cathedral they handed us a leaflet. I thought, "This could only happen in America!" However, on reading the handout, it appeared that this was Day 1 of the first International Gay Week. No mention was made of the picket outside, during the well attended and uplifting mass. We lunched in another of the thousands of very good and reasonably priced restaurants in Manhattan and, in the afternoon visited the United Nations building where, among other features, we admired the huge carved ivory tableau of Chinese life, presented to the UN by China. That evening we dined in a smart Italian restaurant whose walls were adorned with pictures taken of previous celebrity diners. The meal lived up to its promise.

We made a last visit to Central Park next morning, enjoyed another good lunch at a nearby restaurant, returned to check out of the hotel and took a taxi to JFK airport. Our flight arrived from Miami and left for London, dead on time and we said a fond farewell to the USA after the best holiday we had ever had, among the friendliest local people, and at the most reasonable cost.

Our four weeks in America had been a wonderful experience. Those unlucky enough never to have visited the States are given a misleading and generally unfavourable impression of life there. Films tend to show only the worst features of society and to exaggerate their impact on life in the USA. We stayed in the centre of several great cities, but saw no crimes being committed and the only policemen we saw were polite young men having breakfast next to us in dinettes. We found the local people, on both sides of the states and Canada, had a particular fondness for the British perhaps, but not entirely, because they understood us. Practically everything for sale, ie, clothing, books, souvenirs, food, alcoholic drinks, hotel and motel accommodation, petrol, theatre tickets, and tours were less expensive than in the UK and property, was much bigger, better and cheaper than in Britain. I like the Americans' positive response to "How are you?" Even if clearly unwell, they reply "Fine". In Europe people usually say "Not too bad", "Pas mal" or "Nicht so Schleck", even if they are quite well.

The overnight flight to London was smooth and uneventful and we arrived home at 1100, to a welcome from Sally and Paul and found a large postbag awaiting.

Lt-Commander Don Murdoch R.N. (left), of Widley, Portsmouth, looks at a plaque listing all his naval appointments from 1944 to 1979, presented to him by Commander A. Wardale, R.N., before he left the anti-submarine aircraft carrier H.M.S Bulwark to retire.

Awarded the M.B.E. in the recent Birthday Honours List, the Lt-Commander has a reputation as an inventor and, during his service, received three Herbert Lott awards, including a major award of £600 for a ship-borne tactical teacher.

Lt-Commander Murdoch, who joined the Navy as an electrical artificer apprentice in August, 1944, spent two years as trials team leader for the Type 21 frigates, with responsibility for inspections and trials in the eight ships in the class.

He was appointed weapons electrical officer in Bulwark in March, 1977, when the carrier was in Portsmouth Naval Base in a state of preservation by operation.

He was then responsible for bringing the department to a fully-operational state.

*28th May 1979 at Hamburg – Portsmouth News*

Next day, I visited HMS Bulwark which was back alongside in

Portsmouth for a week, to pickup the heavy items of my kit. I had a farewell drink with my ex-messmates and then effectively, left the navy after 35 years unbroken service. Thus, ended my first and principal career, one which nearly ended very prematurely, due to my youthful folly.

I served in the RN at a time of great social change that encouraged men from less affluent backgrounds than before, to carve out a career without feeling it necessary, to hide, deny or invent their origins, adopt a hyphenated name or assume an affected accent. I never saw any class distinction during my 22 years as an officer, and met nothing but friendliness from officers of all backgrounds in any of the many wardrooms in which I messed.

*Lieutenant Commander*

*D. W. Murdoch, M.B.E.*

*Royal Navy*

46 London Road,
Widley, Hants.

Chartered Engineer                    Cosham 370662

Success in any career, particularly in the armed services, requires a great deal of luck. I had more than my fair share of good fortune in the Royal Navy and this helped give me a modestly successful, very happy and rewarding career and a blissful family life. In addition to Lady Luck, I am eternally indebted to others for helping me enjoy my chosen vocation:

My mother who, after 3 ½ years of my apprenticeship, made me pull up my socks and stop swimming against the tide of discipline my wife Eileen, who proved to be the perfect naval wife, loving, loyal, dependable and capable of running a home and family alone.

The Drafting and Appointment Officers who consistently sent me to interesting, demanding, satisfying and rewarding sea and shore jobs; but not those who failed to give me an accompanied foreign posting ashore at anytime during my naval service!

All of my Commanding Officers and most of my bosses, who were professional, kind and considerate and encouraged me to gain the necessary qualifications for, and to seek, promotion.

My very many loyal, keen and hardworking junior officers, Warrant Officers, Chief and Petty Officers and junior ratings.

I thoroughly enjoyed almost all of my 35 years in the Senior Service, made a lot of friends and, inevitably a few enemies, and trite as it may sound, I really loved the navy, its traditions, its innate fairness and the sense of humour and comradeship of mess and shipmates. I will always be thankful that I made the right choice back in 1944, saw the light in 1948, married the right girl in 1950 , that we adopted two babies in the 1950's and I was commissioned in 1957.

On Monday 2nd July 1979, though technically still serving in the RN until 17th July, I began my second career at Marconi Space and Defence Systems Ltd at Browns Lane, Portsmouth, just two miles and only 20 minutes from home.

After working for MSDS for two weeks, in lieu of my entitlement to four weeks Educational and Vocational Training (EVT), I had the opportunity to take Eileen to one last great social event as a serving officer before I retired from the navy.

On the penultimate day of my 35 continuous years of service, Eileen and I attended HMS Nelson's Summer Ball. It was another splendid occasion and brought back to both of us many happy memories of similar great events in this august venue, stretching back through 22 years to our first Ladies Guest night there.

On the following morning I marked my last day in the Royal Navy by hanging up my ceremonial sword at home.

Thereafter it was only used to cut the cake at family weddings and significant anniversaries and birthdays.

# Chapter 23

*Marconi Space and Defence Systems (MSDS)Ltd and Marconi Underwater Systems (MUSL)*

*Professional Engineer and Manager July 1979 – January 1993*

At 0850 on Monday 2nd July 1979, I clocked-in at Reception at the Broad Oak works of MSDS at Hilsea and, together with three other 'joiners', began my induction training, given by an old colleague from Fisgard, Charles Cole. This short course explained most of the differences between the navy and working for a civilian firm, not least of which apparently, was the importance of filling in the weekly Time Sheet! I learnt that I was joining the company as a PE3, (Professional Engineer Grade 3) and would be entitled to overtime pay. During the medical examination, necessary for me to join the attractive sounding pension scheme, I told the company doctor that I had only one ear and, after a few tests he certified that I was fit to carry out my new duties but advised me to position myself at meetings so that I could hear what was going on. I was then escorted to the adjacent Browns Lane site, HQ of MSDS' Underwater Division and to the Sting Ray project offices, where I met my new immediate boss, Ron Short, who had interviewed me six months earlier, was shown the layout and my office and met my secretary and team. I then began the learning curve, made shorter by the previous trials experience I had gained in the RN.

The Sting Ray torpedo is an autonomous light-weight homing torpedo capable of launch from a helicopter or light aircraft or from a surface craft of any size. The torpedo carries a shaped charge that could punch a hole through the hull of any submarine, inflicting almost certain mortal damage. This revolutionary torpedo was in the advance stages of design by MSDS in Stanmore Middlesex and at Portsmouth and was undergoing early sea trials at the British Underwater Trials Evaluation Centre, (BUTEC) in Raasay Sound, NW Scotland. The trials vehicles, as the torpedoes used during the design phase were known, had their explosive section replaced by a Recovery Section which, not only brought them to the surface after a run but also carried a comprehensive recording system which monitored and recorded all of the torpedo's movements and target tracking data. Sea Trials were carried out on batches of torpedoes to evaluate every change in the design of the homing head, propulsion plant or recovery/ recording system found necessary from previous trials. Batches of torpedoes were modified, assembled and tested at Browns Lane and flown to Broadford on the Isle of Skye in the Inner Hebrides by private or contracted aircraft. They were then transported by road to BUTEC where they were launched on the range, recovered and taken to the MSDS base at Kyle of Loch Alsh for data retrieval and de-preparation before being flown back from Broadford to Eastleigh for Portsmouth.

My first few weeks were fully occupied in drawing up the plans for the next Sting Ray trials due to be held in Raasay Sound, and in arranging the necessary material and personnel support. I went up to the trials range with Ron Short for a few days to sight all of the facilities, including the base workshop and hotel facilities.

I then began work on the Sting Ray Master Trials Schedule to cover development of the torpedo right through until its acceptance into service by the RN.

I had a day off to take the family up to London for my investiture at Buckingham Palace when Her Majesty the Queen presented me with the MBE. It was a truly memorable occasion. I was very surprised at how short she is, and pleased that she asked me a second question, based on my answer to her first one. The whole ceremony was very well conducted and Eileen, Sally and Paul also enjoyed it, although Eileen and Paul had been to the Palace five years earlier when Paul received his Duke of Edinburgh Gold award from Prince Philip. On the way home that night, we celebrated with a dinner at Hindhead.

After working for MSDS for about six weeks, I was called by the Personnel Manager and asked if I had noticed that my Secretary, showed a tendency to go sick on a Friday or Monday, or both. The lady in question was the first female I had ever had working for me and when I tackled her about this, probably a little brusquely, she burst into tears and insisted that she really hadn't felt well on those occasions. Oddly, this bout of sick-extended weekends suddenly stopped. The PM also mentioned that one of my peripheral staff had often been seen to be the first one in the Broad Oak Bar at noon and the last one to leave at 2.30pm. I gave him a dressing down and threatened him with an official warning if it happened again, These two incidents were my first experience of civilian workplace malpractices, without having the support of the regulations and powers of the Naval Discipline Act.

Back at work, the next major planning task was to organise the logistic support and trials plan for the deep water trials at the USN-run Atlantic Underwater Evaluation Center (AUTEC) on Andros Island in the Bahamas. As a prelude to this, I flew out to AUTEC by RAF VC10 via Ottawa and , Washington, and West Palm Beach and Miami by commercial airways to sight the facilities, with a couple of Sting Ray Trials Engineers. The journey out took three days. Whilst this was all very relaxing, and I was able to show my colleagues a bit of Washington, including the Aero Space Smithsonian Museum, it struck me that my

budget, and thus the company's, was paying our salaries for three days lost in travel each way, that could have been avoided if we had flown direct from London to Miami by a commercial airline.

I was accommodated in the USN Batchelor Officers' Quarters and though I shared a pretty basic hut with the MSDS on-site manager, (an ex RN WE officer), and a serving RAF officer, the food was very good. During my 2 ½ days at AUTEC, I witnessed a dummy-run of the preparations for a Sting Ray torpedo trial and the post trial analysis and left Andros on the Friday morning with a good idea of the logistic requirements of a series of Sting Ray trials. The two guys who came out with me, stayed on to complete the 12 strong on-site Sting Ray trials team. As my RAF flight from Washington to Lyneham was not until the Tuesday night, I spent most of the Friday and all of the Saturday and Sunday touring South Florida, including Miami, the Florida Keys and the Everglades in a hire car, before catching a morning flight back to Washington, spending the day and night in the city and going out to Dulles for the RAF VC10 flight to Lyneham.

Just before I arrived, Andros Island, had been struck and damaged by the 1979 hurricane and was probably the least attractive island in the Bahamas. Furthermore, having enjoyed 15 days in

California with Eileen, only 5 months earlier, I was not so taken with Florida, with its very flat terrain, but the natives were friendly and I enjoyed my short freelance holiday, despite being bitten in

*Miami Beach to myself after breakfast on a Saturday*  the eye by a mosquito in the Everglades, and I loved revisiting Washington, and completing my tour of the Smithsonian.

I arrived back in the UK on the Wednesday and, having

drafted my report and recommendations, during the journey home, I handed them to my secretary to type and on the Friday night was on my way to Esbjerg in Denmark with my sister and her husband Jim to pick up Andrew their son, who had broken his arm. I took my car and on the way to pick him up from a farm at Hadsund in Jutland near Arhus where the accident occurred, we paused at Frederica in the middle of a busy Saturday afternoon!

We stayed overnight in Arhus, were shown around the chicken farm and entertained by the farmer and his charming wife on the Sunday morning before dashing back to Esbjerg with Andrew to catch the ferry back to Harwich. So ended a mobile 15 days in North America and Denmark in October 1979.

Apart from 2 or 3 more visits to the Kyle and one to Falmouth to iron out pre-trial logistic problems, I remained anchored at Browns Lane for another five months, enjoying going home every night to Eileen and the family. By March 1980, the revised trials programme was up and running to the new Master Trials Schedule. At the same time the company began bidding for the development of a new, deeper running and autonomous heavyweight torpedo to be submarine-launched and designated 7525 – Spearfish. This new torpedo, intended mainly for use against surface targets but also submarines, would be driven faster than any other torpedo in the world, by an engine powered by a new fuel mixture. Ron Short was appointed to run the 7525 Trials part of the Development Cost Plan, (DCP) and asked me to go with him to Chaucer House in Portsmouth city centre, to formulate and cost the trials programme. I happily agreed for he was such a good boss. The Spearfish contract turned out to be the biggest single British defence contract ever, when it was awarded to the company, but did not include the cost of the safety trials which could not be defined until the design of the propulsion system had been finalised. I did not realise then that I would later become responsible for this contract.

The DCP team at Chaucer House was led from the front by our fearsome Welsh Managing Director Don Evans, an ex RN EA Apprentice who had left the RN as a Captain with a CBE. During the early stages of the design submission, he held brain-storming sessions at which some of the most renowned scientists and engineers in the country examined the design options. I recall that at one such session, two of Britain's top Hydro-dynamicists showed by sketches, that it would be impossible for a torpedo to meet Don Evans' bottom line requirement of a speed in excess of 70 knots. Our Welsh wizard, or Dragon, an Electrical Engineer, took a piece of chalk, made a new sketch and said "What if we did this?". The two top underwater propulsion specialists guardedly said that it might do the trick, but they doubted it. Later, when the first Spearfish in-water trial, embodying Don Evana' suggestion, was carried out, his minimum top speed requirement was well achieved.

On the 4th June 1980, I was called to Browns Lane where I was interviewed by John Wright the General Manager and three senior managers, for progression to the grade of Professional

Engineer Grade 4. As I recall, most of the searching 30 minute interview was related to the costing of work. I was informed shortly afterwards that I had been advanced to PE4 and though this meant I would no longer be paid overtime, this new status placed me in a higher pay scale, gave Eileen and me free private medical assurance, and was a pre-requisite for promotion to a senior management post.

In November 1980, my darling daughter Sally married Brendan, a boy she had started school with as an under 5 year old and had known and been a friend of, all her life. The wedding, with a Nuptial Mass, was held at St Colman's Cosham, the parish church attended by both families, and the reception took place in the wardroom of HMS Collingwood. The newly weds soon bought a new house in what is now known as North Harbour, just 2 miles from both family homes.

The production of the detailed DCP for the £500 million Spearfish contract took a tremendous effort on the part of the regular MSDS staff members of the team, and a number of temporary ancillary sub-contractors, to complete by the required submission date of January 1981. For the first 2 months afterwards, I was engaged in answering follow-up enquiries during the MOD's scrutiny of our DCP, but in March 1981, Don Evans formed a new group to iron out technical problems highlighted by the Sting Ray Trials. This unit, headed by David Disley from Stanmore, known as the Sting Ray Trials Assessment Group (STAG), was based at Browns Lane and was staffed by some of MSDS' top design engineers from Stanmore and Portsmouth. As Deputy Head of the group, my role was mainly administrative, ensuring the hardware and software requiring analysis and/or modification was made promptly available to the right expert and keeping the work going to a tight timetable. This entailed much unpaid late evening and weekend work by the whole team, for all of us were PE4s or PE5s.

During my year at Chaucer House, I had enjoyed a good lunch every day at the Civic Offices' Restaurant with Eileen, who worked for the City Engineer, although I was often late home with the pressure of work on the DCP. At Browns Lane, now that I was a PE4, I had a very good lunch in the Senior Managers' Restaurant. This surviving example of class distinction provided a starter, main course, dessert or cheese and biscuits and coffee, accompanied with a beer and all waitress-served, for the princely sum of £1.

In March 1981, the father figure of our family, Uncle Fred Coombs, died at home of a heart attack. He was a great guy in all respects, had a distinguished war record at sea as Chief Yeoman of Signals in HMS Nelson during WW2, where he won the BEM. He was a kind and gentle giant who was always willing and eager to help anyone, especially a member of his extended family. A lovely man who was devoted to his wife, he loved life and everyone. He never had a bad word to say against anyone and was always cheerful. Auntie was devastated at his passing as were Eileen, Sally Paul and I who missed him very much.

After 3 months of sustained effort, the back of STAG's task was more or less broken, the Sting Ray development programme was back on track, and some of its members returned to their previous posts or were allowed to take overdue leave. Having been unable to take my full holiday entitlement in 1980, due to pressure of work I was permitted to take 3 weeks off in June 1981.

Eileen and I had visited France for short breaks of five to seven days several times by car in the 1970s, staying at small hotels in Brittany, Normandy and Paris, Rouen and Versailles, crossing the channel to St Malo, Cherbourg, Le Havre and Calais respectively. So, having been well and truly bitten by wander lust during our great freelance American tour of 1979, we decided to venture into mainland Europe and to make a 24 day independent tour of the continent in my new coupé. After sharing out my duties between my kindly colleagues, on Friday 5th June, I attended the moving 40th anniversary memorial evening mass at St Colman's church for my former mentor, Fr Frederick Freeley. This service was served by my son-in-law Brendan, and the gathering of the revered priest's friends in the hall afterwards, organised by Danielle Miles, author of the saintly priest's biography, was well attended. Eileen and I then set off about 2100 for Dover for a night crossing at the start for our European odyssey, armed with a set of Michelin maps, which gave distances in Kilometers and place names in the local language, as shown on sign posts, and a multi-language phrase book.

We had a nap in the car at St Omer before driving to Laon, halfway between Brussels and Paris, where we stayed for the rest of Saturday sightseeing and dined and slept at a hotel. As in the USA, we then left after breakfast and leisurely followed our pre-planned route, driving only during the morning, admiring the scenery, and visiting places of special interest en route to our next intended overnight stop, generally picnicking for lunch and spending the afternoon and evening sightseeing around the new town and later dining at the hotel in which we were staying. Again, benefiting from our earlier visits to France, we always checked in to our hotel before 1400, and, almost always, were able to choose the best room.

Avoiding motorways, we traveled down through eastern France, overnighting in hotels at Vitry le Francois and Pontarlier before crossing into Switzerland and driving to Fribourg where, after being

shown over the town, and Fr Freeley's links, by Danielle Miles' Aunt, Madame Remy, we stayed overnight at her lovely home and enjoyed a splendid dinner party. Eileen was sat between our hosts and, as several of the guests did not speak English, I was able to practice some social French at the table. Eileen and I thoroughly enjoyed the evening among delightful company.

Next morning we bade farewell to M. Jacques and Mme.

*Eileen&Déde at Fribourg*    Déde Remy, crossed into France and continued with our itinerary, staying overnight at Chambery and, via the famous Route Napoleon, at Castelaine.

From the latter, we diverted to visit the quite spectacular Gorge du Verdon, France's Grand Canyon, before making our way to Cannes via a world famous perfumery at Grasse. It was pretty hairy driving up to Le Point

Sublime of the Gorges du Verdon, when    *Le Point Sublime, Gorge duVerdon*
I had to back on to a narrow lay by with a sheer drop of 1200 feet, to allow a huge French Army Alpine Corps lorry, driven by a young learner driver, to slowly squeeze past me on the safe side of the narrow road. The view from the Point was worth the sweat on my palms getting there, but Eileen, my very good navigator, who looks quite relaxed in the photo, was close to this monster lorry as it inched past and was less sure. As we didn't reach Cannes until 1800, there were no vacancies at the first three hotels we tried and we had

to take pot luck. The room in the hotel close to the lovely sandy beach to the east of the famous harbour was OK, as was dinner, but after we returned from a midnight swim in the sea and popped into the bar for a night cap, we witnessed the proprietor having an obviously unwelcome visit from the local Mafia boss and his 'heavies' who did not discourage us from retiring somewhat expeditiously to our room. After breakfast we spent an hour or so strolling around the harbour, eyeing the yachts before driving to Nice and picnicking on the pebble beach and then moving on to Monaco. The winding road down from the Corniche to Monte Carlo is spectacular and we also enjoyed viewing the harbour and the Casino, but didn`t try our luck at the gaming tables.

After driving back up to the Riviera Corniche, we sped along this beautifully engineered international coast road into Italy alternately passing through lengthy tunnels and crossing long viaducts for 200 Km. When we crossed the border I did not understand the road warnings in Italian and, as it was quite warm that evening, I had my window down and, after about 50 Km, I developed a sore throat and began to feel drowsy before realising that the warnings were telling me to keep my windows closed while passing through the tunnels-I was suffering from carbon monoxide poisoning! We stopped close to a magnificent viaduct high above the sea, took great gulps of air and then happily continued on our way.

The first stop we planned in Italy was Chiavari, a resort on the Italian Riviera, between Genoa and La Spezia and we chose a nice hotel close to the beach, parked and entered. I had an AA book with a basic set of phrases in several languages but, since we were only 130 Km from France, I expected the Receptionist to speak French if not English. Big mistake! In fact, we were the only English speakers in the hotel and, seemingly even in the small town, and very few spoke French. Using the phrase book, I painfully mispronounced my way through booking us in for the night with dinner and breakfast, with the patient phonetic assistance of the

charming receptionist. At dinner we were the centre of interest of all of the Italian guests and waiters as, unable to recognise a Bill of Fare that didn`t include the word spaghetti, we struggled to understand the friendly waiter's miming of the menu, even getting a clap from everyone when we got it right. Despite my embarrassment, it was a memorable meal and a most enjoyable evening for Eileen and me and apparently the local residents. That night, I studied the phrase book and wrote a crib sheet of the most important phrases I would need during the coming eight days touring Italy. Fortunately everyone we met was happy to politely correct my pronunciation and we had no more real language problems in Italy We spent the morning on the pebbled beach at Chiavari, before driving to Pisa

where we booked into another delightful hotel before walking to view, admire and climb the leaning tower. The tilt is noticeable when ascending and Eileen felt unable to reach the top so I escorted her down to the ground before climbing to the top and gingerly circling the top level. I have to admit I found the experience a bit nauseous, like sea sickness, but I couldn't resist the temptation to do it. We tried to visit the adjacent cathedral but were prohibited because Eileen's arms were uncovered.

Next morning after encountering the worst urban driving we have ever experienced, we visited Florence - why don't we call it by its Italian name Firenze? - and, besides touring the historic and cultural sights and marveling at most of them, we shopped in a leather market where Eileen purchased a stylish handbag and I bought a very smart briefcase, before returning to the striking Tuscany countryside and journeying to Sienna. We stopped at the Tourist Information office to seek advice on where to stay and were advised by an Italian speaking English woman working there, who recommended a gem of a hotel close to the famous Campo, and added to my sparse Italian, the phrase "Letto Matrimoniale" to be used when asking for a double bed. Sienna was superb, lovely shops, a wonderful hotel and a great atmosphere in the town.

Off next morning to the Eternal City via Lake Bolsena and a motel we checked into, 12 Km north of Rome. After quickly unpacking, we drove to the city and, at about 1500, we achieved the principal objective of the holiday, when we reached St Peter's and parked in front of the Basilica. We toured St Peter's, the Vatican Library, and the Sistine Chapel and Eileen, who had done all of the navigating, during the 1600 mile journey thus far, is shown in this photo looking as pleased as punch to have reached her goal. During the evening, exhausted and delighted, we drove back through some horrendous traffic, to the very good motel where we had a swim in the pool, before changing and enjoying a first rate dinner. Next morning after breakfast, having quite miraculously avoided damage to our new car in the race tracks of Florence and Rome, we decided to use the very good bus service and went into Rome for a whole day of happy sightseeing. I had visited Rome 25 years earlier but enjoyed this visit more, not least since it thrilled Eileen so much. It was quite warm and during the course of seeing every great sight, we ate plenty of delicious ice cream to keep cool. That night, at dinner back in the

Bela Motel at La Storta, a television company filmed a scene for an Italian 'Soap' while we were having dinner so we were accidental extras. It was all quite amusing. On our third and last day in Rome we took in all of the tourist spots we had missed, like the Spanish Steps and the Trevi fountain. We loved the tasteful architectural mix of buildings of ancient Rome and of the XV1th century, though we thought that the latter, though endowed with beautiful classic sculptures and pictures, were more for the glory of the Bishops of the time, than for God.

Next morning, on the first stage of our journey home, we drove first to Perugia and then to Assisi where we attended a mass in English at the cathedral. We found this very spiritually uplifting and much more moving than mass in the tourist-filled churches of Rome. We then crossed the Apennines to Fano on the Adriatic coast, had a swim at Cattolica and, after visiting the oldest Christian church and admiring its magnificent mosaic covered walls, as well as the museum dedicated to the poet Dante at Ravenna, we stayed there in a hotel overnight.

On the morrow, we drove the 130 Km to Venice and checked in to a mainland hotel close to the Lido for two nights. We then spent the whole of the time on the islets of ancient Venice visiting St Mark's Square, the Doges Palace and the canals, and enjoyed several great

meals in good restaurants. I recall being amazed at how small the soldiers of old Venice must have been to have worn the suits of armour and helmets displayed in the palace. We thoroughly enjoyed seeing all of the prescribed places of interest and, of course, enjoyed a romantic tour of the canals and under the bridges of Venice in a gondola, as shown here.

We next drove east to Trieste and, after a tour of the city; turned south to Koper in Slovenia, then part of Yugoslavia. It was a hot day and we fancied a swim in the sea but every beach we passed was privately owned by a hotel. Can you believe it, no public beach in a communist country! At Koper we went into a supermarket to buy our picnic fare and at the checkout, I was angrily harangued by the woman behind me for daring to buy a bottle of Italian wine rather than a bottle of the local vintage. Out in the main street a policeman stopped me taking a photograph of the local memorial to the WW2 fallen and, when we were made to feel rather less than welcome in a local tavern, we decided to return to happy, friendly Italy and enjoyed a swim and picnic from the first beach after we crossed the border back into free Europe. We then set off via Udine for Tarvisio in the Dolomites where we spent our last night in Italy in a friendly family-run hotel.

Next morning we drove north, climbing all the way, to the Austrian border and then, on the Summer Solstice, down the mountain road through falling snow, which had turned to rain by the time we entered Salzburg. We spent a couple of hours sightseeing in the unfriendly weather before moving off to Rosenheim in Bavaria

where we spent the night at a good, modern hotel, before crossing back into Austria to tour picturesque Innsbruck. There we enjoyed an Austrian tea with wonderful cakes, Oberamagau of Passion Play fame and visited Neuschwanstein and King Ludwig's fairy-tale castle. We then drove up the Romantische Strasse to Schongau where we booked into another well appointed new hotel for the night. In the bar before dinner, the local Germans were quite friendly and on the TV, a recent BBC TV version of Daphne Du Mauriers, 'Rebecca', dubbed into German, was being shown; we were impressed at how well it lip-synchronised. During our last night in Italy, with seven days in Austria and Germany ahead of us, I had compiled a crib sheet of essential German phrases and these proved invaluable.

Next morning we made our way to Augsburg and after a tour of the city went on to Donnaworth on the upper reaches of the Danube, and Noordlingen, to the walled town of Dinkelsbuhl. There was no sign of war damage or restoration along the very attractive Romantsiche Strasse, which seemed happily locked in a medieval time warp. Our next visit was to Heidelberg where we toured the famous university and raised a stein of beer to 'The Student Prince' at one of the open air student bars, before moving north along the east bank of the Rhine and crossed it at Bingen. The riverside road, on both sides, gives a fascinating view of this great international waterway and we enjoyed watching small laden tankers stemming the flow on their way to Switzerland, passing empty vessels in ballast trying to keep a steady course northwards with the flow. We stopped for a picnic on our way to Koblenz and Eileen is seen here having a siesta on the river bank. We toured the city and then took the road along the south bank of the Mosel through steep banks of vineyards to the picturesque town of Bernkastel where we spent a delightful last night in Germany at the attractive Hotel Zur Post whose picture has graced our dining room ever since. After breakfast we diverted from our  plan, to visit Luxembourg and then went to the last great battle scene of WW2 at Bastoigne, and to the ultimate battle site of the Napoleonic wars at Waterloo, before checking in to a hotel in the southern suburbs of Brussels. Leaving the car there we took a tram into the centre of the city and toured the Belgian capital, having a drink outside a café in the Grand Square, before returning to our hotel for dinner, in a double deck tram. The first few kilometres of the journey, in the city centre, were underground.

The last day of our European tour was spent visiting Ghent and the scene of the last major naval engagement of WW1 at Zeebrugge, before visiting Bruges and then spending the last night there at a hotel. I made the mistake of asking for a room in French instead of English, and was received coldly. I had absolutely no knowledge of Flemish and Bruges was in their part of Belgium. Next morning we made our way to Ostend and boarded a ferry to Calais.

We reached home early in the afternoon of Sunday 28th June

1981 having driven 3640 miles in 24 days, and were in high spirits having had a really wonderful holiday, and then came the bad news!

Paul welcomed us home before telling us the staggering news that Sally had walked out on Brendan and that after only 7 months their marriage was over. Eileen and I were dumbfounded for, on the night we left on our tour of Europe, Sally and Brendan appeared to be quite happy. Earlier, I had done several jobs in their house and all seemed normal, so we had no inkling of disharmony between the couple everyone considered to be an ideal match. It transpired that, shortly after we went to France, Sally told Paul that she wanted to leave Brendan and persuaded him, and his cousin Andrew, to move all of her belongings from the marital home while Brendan was at work and to put them in storage and left a letter for Brendan before coming back to the family home. Sally was at a friend's house when we returned home but, after being advised by Paul of our arrival and now knowledge of the break up of her marriage, she came home. After a long discussion with Sally, Eileen and I accepted that her marriage had irrevocably broken down and that her separation from Brendan was a fait accompli.

Next morning, I was back at work at Browns Lane and had plenty to do taking over the group as Dave Disley was soon due to go on holiday himself and some modifications needed proving. At the end of July 1981, the government awarded a fixed-price contract to MSDS to develop the Spearfish torpedo in the face of competition from the American firm Gould's Mark 48 torpedo.

In November 1981, its task completed, the STAG group was finally wound up and its members redeployed, generally to more senior positions. I was appointed Sting Ray Design Control Manager i/c of a Professional Engineering group comprising 5 PE4s, 3 PE3s, 3 PE2s, 4 non graduate Engineers and 2 Admin grades, my first real technical job since leaving the navy.

In this senior management post I was responsible for the assessment and clearance of Sting Ray defect repairs, modifications and the updating of assembly and test schedules, was Chairman of the Torpedo Modifications committee and the Automatic Test Equipment (ATE) Prime Contractor's Modifications committee. I was also the company's Acceptance Authority for the Sting Ray ATE. I later learnt that the senior of my five PE4s had been offered the position but had declined the promotion because he, "didn't want the hassle, the responsibility, travel and the long hours!" All of my graduate engineers were clever chaps but most of them were happy to do the more mundane tasks, as long as they went home every day at 1630. I relied on the PE3s and Technicians, who were paid for overtime, to work off site and out of hours. After six months in the job I was given a large pay rise to bring my pay above that of the guy who turned the job down.

At this time, the advanced development trials of Sting Ray had been completed and the final design changes, resulting from their analysis were being processed prior to design freeze. My top priority was the completion and acceptance of the ATE for the warshot torpedo, from the sub-contractor. Therefore, in addition to my Design Group management responsibilities in Browns Lane, I was required to travel to Donibristle in Fifeshire at least twice a month for three or four days, where the first Warshot ATE was being built. The acceptance trials were successfully completed on Friday 2nd April 1982 and I signed MUSL's acceptance of the ATE from the Sub Contractor, subject to the rectification of a few minor defects, and happily left with my small team for Portsmouth. We flew down to Heathrow and on arrival at Waterloo to catch the Portsmouth train, noticed the London evening newspaper posters were announcing that Argentina had invaded the Falklands. On the Saturday morning I was telephoned by Andrew Glasgow, the company's Design Director and asked if the Sting Ray Warshot ATE was ready to be installed at an RN Armament Depot. I said yes, with a bit of work, which could be completed in the RNAD.

I attended a meeting hastily convened and chaired by Don Evans and attended by Andrew Glasgow that afternoon, at which it was decided to have the fairly extensive ATE packed and sent from Donibristle forthwith. I was tasked to arrange its expeditious installation, testing and presentation to the MOD, for acceptance, and for providing support to the RNAD staff during the subsequent testing of a batch of warshot Sting Ray torpedoes, for delivery to the RN Task Force assembling to liberate the Falklands.

On Sunday 4th April, we visited RNAD Frater to sight the layout of the Weapon remote control facility built for testing live Sting Ray torpedoes. From the morning of Monday 5th April all through that week and the following (Easter) weekend to Tuesday 13th April, we toiled day and night to meet this extraordinary requirement, and managed to deliver the live Sting Ray torpedoes to the fleet on time. A few of the memories I have, of that exciting period are:

The civil servant RNAD technicians refused to fit the warheads to the torpedoes so this was carried out by MUSL

Receiving a complaint from their Union. for telling the RNAD personnel to get back to work when they dallied too long in the canteen after their midnight meal break.

Driving back to the Test complex after a late meal and seeing a vixen and her cubs transfixed by my headlights.

The cheer from the control room when the first live Sting Ray passed its comprehensive pre-delivery weapon test.

The MOD signing their acceptance of the ATE, installed, set to work and in use, in record time over a holiday period.

Andrew Glasgow was subsequently awarded an OBE and I

received the thanks of the Managing Director and a handsome bonus, for our part in what was known by the MOD as 'Operation Corporate' and by the company as, 'The Sting Ray Special Exercise'.

I remained in that post for a further 18 months and apart from a number of visits to Donibristle to carry out acceptance trials on new ATEs, and to chair modification meetings, and to MSDS at Neston in Cheshire to carry out similar tasks, I was pretty firmly based at Browns Lane. On one occasion, as I was required at Neston early one week and later at Fife I had a hire car and took Eileen with me and she enjoyed a day in Chester and a night with me at the Blossom hotel, I paid for her, and the journey to Edinbugh. This was Eileen's first visit to Scotland and she was not impressed with the capital or Dunfermline. We drove back via the East coast.

In June 1982, we went on another motoring tour, this time going to Spain, via the Loire valley, the Dordogne, Lourdes, Bayonne and Biarritz, staying overnight at Chartres, Poitiers, Perigeux and Tarbes. At dinner in the latter, I was tackled by several French pilgrims en route to Lourdes, in a lively discussion in French over Les Malvinas. I pretended I didn't know what they were talking about until someone said "Les Iles Sud Atlantique" I then said," Ah! You mean Les Isles Britannique- the Falklands".

When another guy said that the islands were closer to Argentina and so belonged to them, I suggested that they would not have been happy if an Italian army landed in Corsica one morning and took it over because it was nearer Italy than France, despite the local inhabitants being, and speaking, French. The pilgrims seemed to  take my point and we all enjoyed a convivial evening. Eileen and I were moved by a visit to the shrine at Lourdes, set in a beautiful park and thronged with pilgrims from all over the world. The town of Lourdes however, was full of shops selling religious kitsch with which we were not impressed. We toured Bayonne and stayed at Biarritz, enjoying swimming in the sea and the taste of the large golden sardines served at dinner as the fish course. Next morning we crossed into Spain and visited Loyola, the rather run-down birthplace of St Ignatius, before turning eastward to Pamplona. Out of the famous Bull-run season, this was a rather ugly and dusty city,

 so we made for Olite in Navarre and booked into its X11th Century castle-cum-luxury Parador, where we were the only non-Spanish guests and none of the regionally-dressed staff spoke English, so we had to try our hand at Spanish from a phrase book. We had a super day and night there, and at a former Convent at Alcaniz, and two nights at a new Parador in Benicarlo on the Mediterranean coast near Peniscola, before turning north towards the Costa Brava. At Sitges, we made the mistake of staying in a seafront café-hotel which turned out to be the noisiest and grottiest hotel we have ever stayed in, so we spent the next night in the best hotel the seaside resort could offer, only to be plagued and bitten by mosquitoes. We moved on then after a quick tour of Barcelona, to Tossa de Mar where we booked in to a delightful Spanish hotel fairly close to the sandy beach and enjoyed three blissfully happy days. Again, we were the only British guests but there were some Germans and Swiss guests as well as Spanish. We had Dinner, Bed and Breakfast there and the meals and room were first rate, and the staff and guests very friendly. On the first day I bought the local daily newspaper whose headline announced that the 14,000 Argentinian soldiers in the Falklands had surrendered to the British Task Force. This great news further lifted our spirits and

my obvious pleasure is visible in the next photo. We had planned to go on to the French Riviera but there were not enough days of holiday left, so we drove back to Le Havre stopping en route and visiting Nimes, Clermont Ferrand, Orleans and Liseux, where we heard mass in St Therese's resting place, before driving to the Channel ferry.

In March 1983, my step-father died suddenly in his sleep at the age of 83. Charlie, as we knew him, was a kind, pleasant, quiet, shy and very methodical man, who liked a flutter on the horses. For ten years or so, he and Mum had led a quiet life, occasionally going on short holidays and attending all of the family parties and events.

During his last two years, he had acted as her guardian as she became more and more forgetful whilst cooking, shopping and doing the housework, it was clear that she could not live alone so, after the funeral, my sister Peggy offered to take her to Somerset and look after her. While my other sister and I, and our two better halves were clearing the house prior to forwarding all of Mum's treasured belongings on to her,

*Mum & Charlie in 1980*

we found, just inside the trapdoor to the loft, a raffia bag I had made while at Futcher's school 55 years earlier, stuffed full of small bundles of £5 and £10 notes held together by elastic bands, and some bags of silver. We took the bag to our house and counted its contents and were astonished to find it contained a total of £5400 Three of us travelled to Somerset that weekend and on the Saturday morning, took Mum and Peggy to Langport to bank Mum's hoard in her building society deposit account. The local branch of the society only had one clerk who rented a desk in an estate agent's office in this small market town. We arrived less than an hour before the office closed and when we plonked down piles of bank notes and silver coins and asked to deposit the lot in Mum's book, the poor girl , who had no computer terminal and had to do the whole transaction by hand in ink, was astounded. I wonder what she told her family when she got home!

For some time, Mum and Charlie had a relatively small joint savings account in the Abbey National BS, but no current account. It seems that they managed to live happily, if thriftily, as was their wont, on his RAF, MOD and State pensions and, most weeks, to put away 'for a rainy day', Mum's state pension on the day she drew it from the post office. They could have afforded to have travelled more in their retirement but were happy to choose to stay at home. In the event, all of the money put aside in the loft, funded the annex built on to Hugh and Peggy's 300 year old cottage which provided sizeable and comfortable accommodation with privacy when she so wished, but assistance close at hand when necessary for Mum for the next ten years.

Eileen and I were thrilled on the 26th of May 1983, when Paul's partner Karen Marrs, gave birth to Victoria, our first granddaughter, to the great delight of both of the families. The young parents, shown here after the baby's christening, bought a cosy little house in Stamshaw and we were ever willing and able, when not on holiday abroad, to baby-sit for them.

Back at work, with the pressure of work as Design Control Manager, reduced I spent much of my time correcting the English in reports and documents written by some of my clever graduate Engineers who had managed to get a degree without the help of grammar. Gradually, all of the loose ends of the complex Sting Ray design were tied up, the design was frozen and the development programme of this advanced light-weight torpedo, which we all considered had great sales potential to NATO and of course to the MOD , drew to its conclusion. We then awaited the government's award of the production contract, and began looking at other aspects of underwater warfare which merited improvement.

A month after Victoria arrived, Eileen and I set off for ten days holiday at the hotel in Tossa we'd visited the year before. We drove down the east side of France visiting Versailles, Nevers, Lyon and Perpignan en route, and back up the west side via Toulouse, Bordeaux and Rennes to Caen. Whilst at Tossa we toured the Costa Brava and Barcelona and were sickened by a Bull fight we saw.

In September, Eileen and I thoroughly enjoyed seven days holiday in a Gite near Jonzac in La Charente Maritime, with my sister Eileen and her husband Jim. On the pen-ultimate evening, our friendly farmer landlord threw an enjoyable party for us. Whilst there, we toured the Dordogne visiting St Emilion and Bergerac. On the way to the Gite we had visited the U-Boat pens at St Nazaire and stayed overnight at a hotel in Vendee and, on the way home, visited Saintes, toured a brandy distillery at Cognac and stayed at Royan. We were amazed to see a war cemetery there, with hundreds of graves all dated April 1945. The Germans had held the town to deny access to Bordeaux, for long after the rest of France was liberated. Only a few weeks before VE day, President De Gaulle decided to storm the town, "pour la gloire de la France", rather than wait until the German surrender, which Britain did in order to free the Channel Islands without the loss of life and total destruction suffered by Royan.

In the autumn of 1983, Don Evans assembled all of the Underwater Division of MSDS at Browns Lane to announce that the company had hit the jackpot. We had won the contracts for the updating of the Mk 24 torpedo, the production of the Sting Ray torpedo and the development of the Spearfish torpedo. This great news for the company, led to the Underwater Division of MSDS being set up as a separate entity, Suggestions were invited for a name for this company and, after rejecting a proposal to call it, Marconi Underwater Developments, presumably because we didn't want our name shortened to MUD, we became Marconi Underwater Systems Ltd, MUSL, pronounced Mussel, more appropriate for a company dealing with the sea, with Don Evans as its first MD. The future looked rosy. He also announced that the company would be moving within a year to new premises at

Waterlooville. In November 1983, Ron Short was appointed Spearfish Project Manager and he kindly appointed me to be Assistant Manager. My role for the next year was similar to my original job with the company, the planning and logistic support of development Torpedo trials, but this time with Spearfish.

In April 1984, Paul and Karen were married at St Joseph's church. Both of the families were highly delighted to see them formalise their partnership.

Two months later, Eileen and I crossed to Le Havre for our summer holiday in Tossa de Mar, taking in a tour of the Auvergne on the way to Spain and the Dordogne on the way home. We again enjoyed a week at the Hotel Avenida in Tossa and stopped overnight en route in Logis de France at Brionne, Beaugency, St Gervais D'Auvergne, Brioude, St Chely D'Archer and St Jean Du Gard, On the way home, we stayed in similar small hotels, rightly renowned for their regional cuisine, at Albi, St Cirq Lapopie, Les Eyzies, Saujon, Amboise and Pont Leveque, taking the opportunity to tour each of the areas around these attractive venues. Again, we travelled in the mornings and did our sightseeing after lunch.

In September of the same year, Eileen and I took Karen, Paul and Victoria for a 7 day Gite holiday in the Dordogne. On the way from St Malo, we had a swim on the beach at La Baule and stayed at Pornic and La Rochelle en route, during which the four adults enjoyed a huge Fruits de Mer, comprising a lobster, two crabs, oysters, mussels prawns, cockles and winkles. The Gite was lovely and all five of us had a great time  Every morning I took Victoria into the village in her pushchair, to buy the bread and croissants for breakfast and the local women made a great fuss of her Paul and Karen went riding and we all went to the beach, several times. On the overnight ferry back to Portsmouth, Karen, Paul and Eileen suffered from mal de mer, but Victoria thought the ship's movement was great fun.

Later that year the company moved to the brand new site at Brambles Farm at Waterlooville, just 12 minutes drive from my home and I was given my own office on the top floor, next door to the Spearfish Project Manager. I was destined to continuously occupy this pleasant office until I retired more than eight years later.

At Christmas 1984, all 1900 members of the staff of MUSL were given a splendid Christmas box, in the shape of a sumptuous hamper, with the compliments of the Managing Director, to mark an excellent year for the new company. We also had a Christmas lunch in the smart new restaurant, paid for by the company, and a formal dinner and dance at a hotel on Hayling Island, which was a great success. MUSL was on a high, with three major projects in hand and strong rumours of two more in the offing, so we all looked forward to 1985 with confidence.

Les Ball, one of my engineers and an ex RN WE officer, told me that he had received compensation for a partial loss of hearing and, knowing I only had one ear, asked if I received a disability pension. When I said no he gave me an application form and advised me to apply. Because I had been allowed to stay in the navy for four years after losing the hearing of one ear, I had naively thought I was not entitled to a disability pension and, having undergone my final

medical examination before discharge, at sea in May 1979, by a doctor unfamiliar with pension entitlement, I had not been advised to apply. I sent off the form and was subsequently examined by an ENT specialist. He was in possession of the report of the operation at RNH Haslar in 1975, which had failed to repair the damage done to my left ear in a simple check carried out by a trainee RN doctor.
A year after my application, I was awarded a 20% Disability Pension, back dated one year. This brought my total naval pension up to that of a Commander and though my naivety in 1979 cost me 7 years of this tax-free 'War pension', I was delighted, and called on Les bringing him a bottle of Glen Livet, his favourite malt whisky.

I spent the first two months of 1985 preparing for and carrying out the trials on the prototype Spearfish Overall weapon ATE, prior to its in-house ATE Bonus demonstration to the MOD. I also attended trials held in Scotland, together with engineers from the American company manufacturing the torpedo engine. By the end of February, the trials had provided enough experience and data on the running of the high speed Spearfish torpedo on its unique fuel mix, to be able to specify the necessary safety trials. On 7th March I was invited by Ron Short to draw up the trials schedule and specifications for a Development Cost Plan (DCP) for the MOD and Ordnance Board Safety Trials required to clear the Spearfish torpedo for use by the RN.

During the two months before the MOD accepted this proposal, the company began to tender for a contract to develop a 'Continental Shelf Mine' (CSM). Although still responsible for the organisation of Spearfish trials and, working from my office, I was seconded to the team putting together the DCP for the CSM, to produce and cost the development trials for this 'clever', pro-active anti-submarine and anti-surface ship mine. I completed my part of this submission just as my costed proposal for the Safety Trials on Spearfish was accepted and given a fixed-price contract.

On 29th May 1985, I was delighted when Ron Short made me Manager of this new project, worth at the beginning, £5 million and, with the numerous and inevitable Changes of Requirement, (CORs) made by the MOD during the remainder of the Spearfish development programme, over £13 million by the time I retired almost eight years later. In 1992, I was appointed Spearfish Project Safety Officer, in addition to my Project Management duties.

On 14th May 1985, Eileen received a phone call from Karen saying that she had just been delivered of a second daughter, who would be called Charlotte, and asking Eileen if she would pick her and the baby up in an hours time, after she had showered and changed, to take them home from the hospital to their new house in Havant. Thus our fit as a fiddle daughter-in-law, took the arrival of her second child in her stride.

In 1986, Don Evans reached the GEC's, (MUSL's parent company) compulsory retirement age of 65 and, though he had built the company from scratch into the leading British Underwater Research and Development company, employing 1900 people, he had to leave. On his last day, this Captain of Industry and holder of both a Military and a Civil CBE, drove to work as usual in his company MD's Jaguar XJ6 but had to hand in the keys. After making his farewells, he was driven home in one of the ordinary fleet cars. Subsequently a new Managing Director was appointed.

My job involved many two day visits to the Explosive Test Ranges at Shoeburyness with my MOD and Ordnance Board opposite numbers, Cdr Chris Howe, Lt Cdr Derek Rowland, my Quality Assurance Controller, Bill Hall and a team of Engineers from the Design Authority of the relevant part of the torpedo being subjected to safety trials, plus of course the torpedo hardware. We normally stayed at a hotel in Southend and travelled in a hire car from Waterlooville. I also made several visits to the RNAD in Ayrshire during the Automatic Test Equiment acceptance trials.

Whilst staying at a hotel near the depot, I visited my grandfather's home town Kilwinning and can understand why he moved south!

The safety of a weapon is, of course, paramount particularly when embarked in a submerged submarine. This concern has also to be tempered with ensuring that the warhead will detonate when it is ordered so to do, whilst remaining perfectly safe at all other times. This requirement also applies to bi-propellant fuels and to the transport of live and fuelled torpedoes which might be involved in an accident.

Throughout my 13½ years with Marconi, we enjoyed a happy social life. I joined the Portsmouth Retired Naval Officers' Association, was a life member of the Wardrooms of HMS Nelson and Collingwood and Eileen and I attended the Summer and Christmas Balls, Cocktail Parties and Ladies' Night Dinners. I was also a member of two London monthly dining clubs, the Anchorites who dined at the Café Royal and the Seven Seas Club which dined at the Corn Exchange. Paul regularly played for Havant First XV from 1975 to 1989 and I attended all the home games and many away fixtures. I particularly enjoyed basking in his reflected glory after the Hampshire Cup Final at Basingstoke in 1988. Havant won and Paul was Man of the Match, after tackling Basingstoke's winger to prevent a certain try, and later scoring two tries himself.

During our 1986 summer holidays, touring the south of France, Eileen 'froze' on several occasions and was unable to move her legs for several seconds. On our return home this phenomenon became more frequent and, after a series of tests at various medical centres, her consultant diagnosed that she was suffering from Parkinson's Disease. This chronic condition receives much adverse and demoralising publicity and, for a woman who had never had a day's illness in her life, and was a bundle of energy, the news was devastating. However, Eileen took it bravely and resolved to live as normally as she could. Having given up her job with Portsmouth

City Council five years earlier, she was able to adjust her activities as necessary. At first, the onset of other symptoms of the disease was distressingly rapid but after the optimal dosage of drugs was found, her condition stabilised. For the next five years, with the aid of drugs, though exhibiting tremors and some freezing of motion, she was still able to drive a car and to live a fairly normal life.

During the evenings of the summer of 1987, I built the first and

lower of two tree-houses for Victoria (4) and Charlotte (2) in my garden and clad it in what Victoria insisted was 'tree-wood', ie still had the bark on it. Shaped like Noah's Ark, it was 18 feet long and had a 3.5 foot beam and was named by the two children,

HMS Squirrel since a family of them frequented the garden. I attached a slide from the Quarter Deck and a figurehead on the bows. On 16th October that year, a hurricane struck the south of England and though it destroyed the roof of the nearby summerhouse and the front doors and roof of the garage, the tree house was undamaged.

In April 1988, Eileen and I attended the 30th Anniversary of the commissioning of HMS Cheviot at Singapore, as Captain D8 with Admiral Sir William O'Brien, the then Captain, and most of the officers of the 8th Destroyer Squadron. The dinner, arranged by Roger Doherty, our doctor in Cheviot, was held at the British Medical Association in London and was a splendid affair; it was great to see my old messmates again.

On the 10<sup>th</sup> April 1990, Eileen and I celebrated our 40<sup>th</sup> wedding anniversary with a dinner for friends and family at the Havant Conservative Club. Sally and Paul presented us with a framed photograph of the family on canvas taken two weeks earlier by David Streten. We were delighted with this portrait, which hangs in pride of place at home. The whole family enjoyed the evening.

We continued to take our car to the continent every year for our long summer holiday and also for a couple of short breaks and, after having completed a pretty comprehensive tour of the whole of la belle France during more than 30 visits, we took advantage of the course in German the company had encouraged me to take, and in 1990, 1991 and 1992, did the same in West Germany, staying at delightful family-run hotels. After the last of these great free-lance motoring holidays, Eileen's condition began to deteriorate and she could no longer be left unattended, or drive a car. I therefore gave notice of my intention to retire a year early in January 1993.

I had reached A/S level in French before leaving the navy and underwent a 'Technical French' course and German to level 4 under the company's auspices, whilst at Waterlooville. The only use I made of these modest linguistic skills, on behalf of the company, was to give a short unclassified talk to visiting French and German visitors telling them what great torpedoes we designed and made. I was also invited to attend the local college annual pre-GCSE lunch to try to get the students to practise their linguistic ability before the exams. One of my last extraneous tasks was to produce a fairly comprehensive illustrated description of the workings of Spearfish and each of its sections for VIPs. This was published in glorious technicolour and made me feel quite proud. Unfortunately, it was classified as Secret and I was unable to have a copy.

Auntie May, Eileen's mother's sister, was a very sprightly, smart and kind lady who doted on Eileen and me and our children and grandchildren. It was a great shock to us all when, unable to contact her during our regular morning telephone call one day, I rushed down to her flat to find she had collapsed and was in a coma, I called 999 and accompanied her to the hospital but she never regained consciousness and passed peacefully away that evening at the age of 89 whilst all of us were visiting her. Even in her 90th year, Auntie was always busy, with her housework, her family and helping friends and neighbours, by whom she was much missed After Requiem mass at a crowded St Colman's church, she was laid to rest with her beloved husband Uncle Fred, in Kingston cemetery.

*Auntie May is seen sitting in a chair here with Mum and the family in 1987*

The management of all aspects of the Spearfish Safety project had provided me with complete job satisfaction for the last eight years of my working life, or rather the remunerated part of it and, I am proud to say, provided over 20,000 man days of work for the MUSL personnel at Waterlooville, Neston and Croxley whom, as Project Manager, I employed to do the work. I am also pleased to say that all the work detailed in the original safety trials contract and the many Changes of Requirement (CORs) later added and agreed with the MOD, was completed on time and within budget.

During my last five years with MUSL, there were five savage culls of staff which I thought were most insensitively instigated and executed by top management. The company lost many good, keen and loyal servants as it shrank from 1900 to 450. I cannot envisage this happening if Don Evans had still been in control of the successful company he had built up.

Some of my abiding memories of MUSL are:

The first thing all employees did every morning was to make themselves a cup of coffee.

The very good and reasonably priced one-class MUSL restaurant, normally attended by less than 50% of the staff, being packed when the lunch was free at Christmas.

Being asked by an aspiring Trials Engineer during a job interview, what sort of company car went with the job and telling him the Manager running a half-billion£ contract only got a Cavalier and everyone else bought their own!

Giving a dinner party at home for Ron Short and his charming wife Tessa and Dave Disley and nearly asphyxiating them after the meal when I passed around cigars and four of us lit up in an unventilated room. This was before I became responsible for safety!

The pretentiously named Broadford International Airport, on the island of Skye off NW Scotland, run by a lass called Jeannie who was the Air Traffic Controller, Ticket clerk, Baggage loader, Met and Security officer and rode her bike to and from the airport.

Being offered a senior management post by the MD of MSDS at Donibristle and, without thinking, blurting out, "My father's family spent a millennium trying to get out of Scotland and I'm not reversing that decision". He laughed.

Don Evans, a twice decorated former RN Captain knew every one of his huge staff by name, 'kicked ass' when he thought necessary, but insisted on being called Don; his successor knew few of his diminishing workforce below the level of Director and hardly ever walked around the site.

When I joined the company most of the senior managers were ex naval officers but, during my time, the ratio of ex RN to civilian managers became evenly balanced. However, as in my naval career, I was extremely lucky throughout my second and final career, with thankfully only two brief exceptions, to have been blessed with proficient, good, kind and considerate bosses, whom I respected and with whom I got on well. I am particularly grateful to the energetic, innovative and convivial Ron Short, for whom I happily worked most of my time with the company, and Dave Disley, Rick Carey, Frank Whiley, Graham Holt and Frank Simm for whom I also enjoyed working. I was fortunate to have the professional services of several brilliant young engineers like Kevin Walsh, and of Bill Hall my Quality Assurance officer. I must also pay tribute to the patience and professionalism of Chris Howe and Derek Rowland of the MOD and Ordnance Board respectively, with whom I worked closely.

The company's third Managing Director in seven years, Andy Williams presented me with a splendid set of stainless steel garden implements and said a few kind words when the Spearfish project said their official farewell to me. This was followed by a convivial liquid farewell at the nearest pub.

It is a paradox that I began my working career hoping to look after torpedoes, only to join the first class of Electrical Artificer Apprentices not to be trained in their maintenance, and yet came to dedicate the final years of my working life to their development. I don't think I could have chosen a more varied, interesting, and rewarding second career than I enjoyed with Marconi. I had a succession of managerial posts, most of them demanding and all of them satisfying. I was treated well by my superiors and was loyally supported by my colleagues and assistants. Under the wise and paternal guidance of the GEC Chairman Lord Weinstock, the company paid well. On my retirement, I benefited from its very good, final salary pension scheme, from having been enrolled in SERPS and from having received a generous number of Management issue shares in GEC. As a result, when I left MUSL in January 1993, Eileen and I became 'comfortably off' pensioners.

**Marconi**

Underwater Systems

Marconi Underwater Systems Limited
Elettra Avenue, Waterlooville
Hampshire PO7 7XS, England
Telephone: Waterlooville (0705) 260886    Telex: 869233
          Facsimile: (0705) 260246

**DONALD W. MURDOCH** M.B.E., C.Eng., F.I.Mar.E.
Project Manager

*Eileen and Don going to a Ball 1981*

Looking back on all of my working life, and despite the long forced separations experienced during my first career, I will always consider myself to be a former naval person rather than an ex-employee of Marconi, perhaps because the Royal Navy was a complete way of life and not just a good job, and it gave me the experience to tackle the second with confidence.

# Chapter 24

## In Retirement

### January 1993 to December 2009

I began my retirement by ignoring the previously eagerly anticipated first benefit of not having to go to work on a Monday morning. I was persuaded by my parish priest to take up the job of counter of the Sunday collection in place of an elderly chap who had been doing it for years and wished to retire. The task, including the paperwork and banking of the money was not onerous but it occupied the whole of every Monday morning and delayed my long dreamt of Monday morning lie-in, for 16 years until, on my 80th birthday, a kind newly retired chap stepped forward to relieve me.

I had built up a modest portfolio of shares in each of the de-nationalised industries, in a Building society and also had a considerable number of shares in MUSL's parent company GEC. On the Ides of every month I checked their market value and boasted to Eileen how well they were doing. However she was not impressed when the dividend payments were fairly minimal and, after a few months, she persuaded me, against my inclination, to sell the lot while they were highly priced, and to buy high-interest savings bonds. We made a good profit on the sale of the shares and amassed a goodly sum in bonds, but in the next few months, the GEC shares rose further and I moaned, "it was a mistake my Dear, selling our shares," (or words to that effect). A few months later, GEC shares slumped catastrophically from £12 to 06 pence a share and the others went well below the price we received for them. Many of my former colleagues at MUSL lost a fortune during that crash. I ate humble pie for several days and had to bow to woman's intuition.

There must be a grapevine which provides details of newly retired people for, within a few months, I was besieged with requests from worthy charities asking for my services as an unpaid helper. In the first flush of enthusiasm to put something back into the society that had been so very kind to me, I refused none of these earnest pleas and soon found myself engaged in some seven or eight different jobs which together, I suppose, occupied me for an average of about 15 hours a week, mostly close to home. Later, when I joined the 20th century, just before it ended, and bought myself a Personal Computer and could work at home, I reached a peak of 14 non-remunerative jobs, before I finally retired in 2009.

When Sally and Paul were young children, I was away at sea for much of the time and had been unable to make the sort of play facilities that a garden of the size of ours would allow. So in the Spring of 1993, not only was I able to put the splendid garden tools given me on leaving MUSL, to good use, but to continue to turn the far end of the garden into a playground for my granddaughters. I erected a set of swings and climbing frame and constructed a second, tree-house, 15 feet up another apple tree near the Noah'a Ark I had built 6 years earlier when they were small. I also made a colourful roundabout based on a car's half shaft and wheel. Victoria and Charlotte often used their 'park' as they called their part of my garden, and also held all of their parties in it.

During my first five months of retirement. Eileen's condition showed some improvement and, after enjoying a short holiday in Brighton, we decided to embark on another freelance motoring tour of up to 28 days of eastern France and Germany.

On 22nd June we took the ferry to Caen and are shown on the next page boarding the Ro-Ro at Portsmouth that morning, bent on enjoying another leisurely continental tour. On the way over the channel, although it was quite calm, Eileen was unwell and on arrival at Ouistreham, she was very poorly, so I tried to return on the same ferry returning that evening but it was fully booked.

So we checked into the nearest hotel for the night and Eileen went to bed. I hoped she would be well enough by the morning to continue the holiday but she awoke suffering badly from her Parkinsons' symptoms and so we caught the ferry back that morning and returned home.

After a further adjustment of the drugs regime, her medical condition stabilised. However, as a result of her PD, she then suffered three falls about six months apart, separately breaking each wrist and an ankle respectively. requiring hospital treatment on each occasion. When I retired from MUSL, the company's free Medical Insurance offered to continue to cover me for a modest premium but, as Eileen's falls resulted from her chronic problem, they would not cover her. I therefore pulled out of the scheme myself and we set aside a regular sum for her to 'go private' if necessary. Eileen was declared unfit to drive a car and it soon became clear to us both that our tours of the continent, or indeed holidays of any kind, were a thing of the past and so we adjusted our life-style, contenting ourselves with short trips, with an occasional overnight stay at a hotel. We still attended Ladies Night Dinners at HMS Nelson and Collingwood but no longer took to the floor. We were however able to attend all of the grandchildren's school fetes and sports days and the displays put on in the gym and pool in which they played a prominent part.

On 13th October 1993, my dear Mother passed away peacefully at my sister Peggy's home in Somerset, at the age of 93½. Mum had suffered from dementia for about 10 years and Peggy had done a great job caring for her, Mum was always smart, ever cheerful and, though she had no recent memory, she could remember her childhood in Ireland and, in her own way, clearly enjoyed life to the end. She had a way of humorously associating words in a peculiarly Irish manner, for example she once said, "Auntie Nell

would have turned over in her grave if she had known they were going to cremate her"; "Mary shouldn't have called then, she knows I religiously go to mass every Sunday morning", and, on another occasion, "You should have been at Mrs Hannibal's funeral, it was out of this world". Mum worked hard

*Eileen, Simon, Mum, Peggy and Hugh* and enjoyed travelling until she was in her 70s, but always put her family first. She gave up much to give her children a good start in life and it is only fitting that her last ten frail years were spent in the loving, happy, and comfortable care of her eldest daughter Peggy and her husband Hugh, and not in a care home. She enjoyed visits     from her family and attending family parties as the aged benign Matriarch, known as 'Little Nan". She loved seeing, and playing with her many grandchildren and great grandchildren. It was her wish that she be buried with my father in Portsmouth and so, after a service at the local church at Langport, and a Requiem Mass at St Colman's in Cosham, in the presence of her family, she was laid to rest with Dad, 50 years after his death.

On 2$^{nd}$ August 1994, I travelled to Plymouth in a coach full of local Portsmouth members of my class of 1944, to attend the 50$^{th}$ anniversary of our joining the RN at RNATE Torpoint as Artificer

Apprentices.

*Fraser, Westlake, Oram, Cann, Barker, Cook, Smith, Edwards, Buckingham*
*Pritchard, Field, Carpenter, Ware, Hodges, Hoskins, Taylor, Ball, MurdochT,urner*
*Muller, Ruse, Staker, Wakeham, Weedon, Bodt, Butler, Powell, Snell, Alp*
Roberts, Tudor, Partridge, King, J.Palmer, Teasdale, Simpson, Cross, Liming, Prout.

During the Autumn of 1993, our beautiful, athletic

daughter-in-law Karen was diagnosed as having cervical cancer and began a long course of radio and chemotherapy treatment. Her intense treatment culminated in a spell in the Royal Marsden hospital in London and when she left this world famous cancer treatment centre in June 1994, she was told that there were no residual cancer cells in the affected area, and we brought her home to a great welcome from the family. At around the same time, Victoria passed the entrance exam and won an assisted place at the Portsmouth Grammar School and prepared to join this prestigious school. The Murdoch family was in very high spirits and, during the 1994 summer holidays, we all enjoyed the spectacle of the Tour de France as it twice passed along the top of Portsdown hill.

Just before Victoria joined her new school, Karen became ill again and had to go back into hospital. She was let out for the day to

take Victoria to the PGS on her first day, but she looked very poorly and returned to hospital. Eleven year old Victoria had a long bus journey every day from Warblington to Old Portsmouth and her anxiety about her Mother prevented her from settling down properly at the school. To cheer her up, I began to take her there and back every day in my car, but she became more and more unhappy. At the half-term holiday, Victoria begged her parents to let her move to Warblington Comprehensive School, close to home and though clearly disappointed at this, Karen and Paul, (and Eileen and I), understood the situation and concurred with Victoria's wish.

Karen's condition further deteriorated, and just before her birthday in December, she was told that her illness was terminal. Notwithstanding this terrible news, Karen and Paul bravely attended the children's school open day that evening. After Christmas, she and Paul attended a special counselling course at Bristol that gave them both some consolation but, on the first Friday of March, Karen's consultant gave her the dreadful news that she had only a few days to live. Paul drove her to our house and Karen herself broke the tragic news to us, before she and all of us burst into tears. Karen quickly regained her composure and bravely began to make her final plans. She asked me to arrange a farewell lunch in two days time on the Sunday for all of the family, and then calmly started to make the funeral arrangements. On the Saturday she underwent an operation recommended by her GP, which extended her life by a week and she spent the time teaching Paul how to cook and look after the children. When she arrived for the lunch on the Sunday, she had disguised her pallor and put on a brave face, took charge of the proceedings, played the perfect hostess, and was up-beat with all 28 of the extended family, including a number of children who attended. I had left my credit card behind the counter before she arrived but at the end of the meal, she came with me and insisted that the proprietor give me back my card saying that it was her party and she wanted to pay for it. Karen was offered a place in the local Hospice but declined saying she wished to die at home and early on the following Sunday morning, the 12<sup>th</sup> of March 1995, a few hours after Eileen and I last saw her, and in the presence of Paul and her doctor, she passed away at the age of 34. Paul and the children, then only 11 and 9 years old, were devastated as were we and the rest of the family.

In accordance with her wishes, Karen's funeral service was conducted at the Warblington parish church, jointly by the Rector and the Parish priest of St Colman's. At Karen's request, after the service, all of the very many floral tributes were taken by the men of the family, for processing in aid of the Rowan's Hospice. Some time after the cremation, a requiem mass was held at St Colman's, at which Victoria bravely read a lesson, and Karen's ashes were then formally buried in her grave at Warblington cemetery.

Eileen and I saw a lot of Victoria and Charlotte during the following months and they often spent weekends with us when they were taking part in Gymnastic or Trampoline competitions or in Ballet performances, especially when Paul, who was then Deputy Manager of the Havant Leisure Centre, was busy at work with a major event and unable to take them. The girls were competitive performers and enjoyed the support of their grandparents and we of course were delighted with their successes.

Sally had joined MENSA in 1990 and, in mid 1994, without warning me, she arranged for a MENSA entry 'Home Examination Pack' to be sent to me and persuaded me to take this pilot exam. I reluctantly agreed and sent off the papers. A month or so later I was told that I had reached the required entry standard and was invited to sit the proper entry exam, Sally again persuaded me to have a go, " You can do it Pa", said she. Early one Saturday in November 1994, I found myself in a large room at the Ibis Hotel Portsmouth, with about 20 other candidates and 5 invigilators. My fellows were of both sexes and three types, 18 to 24 year old students, 25 to 50 year old teachers and other graduates, and 50 upwards working or retired teachers and engineers. I appeared be the oldest. We were all told to sit at well separated single desks and the first of the three papers were handed out face down. At 0900 we were told to turn over our question papers and commence. When the bell sounded at 0955, we were all still writing furiously. Our answer papers were collected and a new set placed face down and, at 1000, off we went scribbling like mad again. The same happened with the third paper and, after these were collected we were invited to go to the restaurant for a coffee before going home. Over coffee it seemed that although all of us had seen many exam papers before, this had been the hardest we had ever faced, given the limited time to complete, and which none of us had achieved with any of the three papers. I was surprised and delighted to learn, just before Christmas, that I had been elected a member, with an IQ of 148, one less than my brainy daughter, but notably higher than I was given by the RN.

In September 1996, Bruce Balmain of 1941 Grenville entry, organised a buffet supper reunion at Portsmouth of Royal Naval Artificer Apprentices who had trained at the Artificers' school at Torpoint, during WW2. Around 100 'ex-boys' attended and many had expressed a desire for the formation of an Association for all who had undergone an apprenticeship at Fisgard Portsmouth, Chatham or Torpoint. This first gathering of over 65 year old veterans proved successful, and a catalyst for an old school association. Nine of them, plus one older ex-boy, met at the ERA's Club in Southsea on 15th November 1996 and founded the Fisgard Association, electing Bruce Balmain as Founder Chairman.

Bruce owned a portable word processor and 79 year old Fred Lewis, who had joined Fisgard in 1932, was the only founder member who owned a personal computer. Fred agreed to run the membership register and Bruce took on all of the other secretarial duties. An ad hoc committee of eight, including Bruce and Fred, was formed by volunteers from the original 10 founders and we decided to hold a formal Dinner and Dance at a hotel during the

# Time to renew friendships and remember the old days

**Dear ex-apprentice,**

There must be thousands like you living in the Portsmouth area who, since its foundation by the legendary Admiral Sir John 'Jackie' Fisher in 1905, spent up to four and a half years of your youth and early manhood under training in HMS Fisgard.

In exchange for a 'sixth-form' academic education, training as a skilled craftsman, the considerable development of your sporting prowess and true comradeship, you suffered 19th-century public-school-like living conditions, long working hours, ridiculously low pay, insufficient victuals and penurious liberty.

Nevertheless, I wager you look on your alma-mater with pride and affection – perhaps because the Fisgard ethos lives on in you?

I am sure you will agree that the academic and professional training you received at Fisgard proved invaluable to you during your time in the navy and perhaps more so since leaving the service.

Many of the 200-plus, 70-80 strong divisions who trained at Fisgard hold class reunions on significant anniversaries. Maybe you have attended one?

However there was no 'old school' association until the 'Fisgard Association' was formed in November 1996 following a very successful reunion held at Portsmouth in September 1996, (organised by the Grenville 1941 entry), for anyone

**HMS Terrible and HMS Hercules, two of the Fisgard ships in 1932**

who had trained at Fisgard during World War II.

The aim of this new association is to organise social events and the first of these is a reunion planned for Tuesday, September 16th 1997 at the Portsmouth Marriott Hotel.

Membership of the Fisgard Association is available (at no cost – entry or subscription) to anyone who has undergone training as an artificer apprentice, for any length of time, at HMS Fisgard, Portsmouth (1905-30); Chatham (1930-39); Torpoint (1939-83) or in the Fisgard Squadron of HMS Raleigh at

Torpoint since 1984.

So if you'd like to meet your old classmates and pals and sportsteam mates, join the 200 plus members of the association by sending your details (and SAE) quoting your division and date of entry/leaving to Fred Lewis BEM, 93 Kimbolton Road, Portsmouth PO3 6DA.

**Don Murdoch**
Anson Division,
HMS Fisgard '44-'48

London Road,
Widley

following September and to launch a Newsletter, a Membership Directory and an old school tie for members. All 10 of us agreed to try to recruit as many members as we could and my appeal was published in March 1997, the local newspaper. The initial income available to launch this enterprise came from the raffle held at the earlier reunion buffet supper, and the class who sponsored it, augmented by donations from the enthusiastic founder members,

We had no joining fee or annual subscription so the committee agreed to consider this and other proposals and to bring their suggestions to the next committee meeting. As a result of the recruiting efforts of all of the founder members during the Spring of 1997, the membership total grew rapidly and with this, an increase in postage and other expenses. It became obvious that approval would have to be sought, at a General Meeting to raise a regular income by levying an annual subscription. At the next committee meeting, responsibility for all of the different activities of the Association was shared between the 8 members. By then I had bought a PC and was able to take some of the 'office' weight off Bruce. The Association's first formal Dinner and Dance, held at the Marriott Hotel at Portsmouth on 16$^{th}$ September 1997, and attended by 98 members and 54 guests was a huge success and demonstrated that the fledgling association had got off the ground. This event was reported on, and the General Meeting and lunch advertised in Issue 1 of the Fisgardian, produced by Bruce. Seventy members attended and 110 sent their apologies together with their voting preferences for the agenda items at the first General meeting of the Association in November 1997. Thus 40% of the then 460 strong membership, played an active role in deciding the future shape of the Association – a very creditable proportion and a solid mandate for the decisions made at the meeting. My position as acting Secretary, and Editor of the Fisgardian was confirmed.

In June 1998, Eileen and I spent a weekend in Brighton at the Ship Inn on the front and on the Saturday evening entertained my great niece Holly and her fiancé, who were undergrads at the nearby Sussex University. We all enjoyed the evening, but sadly it was to prove the last time Eileen and I ever went away for a break as, shortly afterwards, her condition took a turn for the worse.

At the 1998 AGM of the Fisgard Association, I regretfully had to step down from the posts of Secretary and Editor due to the need to actively care for Eileen. However, working at home, I was able to continue as an Assistant in the Secretariat run by David Gutteridge and local Assistant to the new volunteer Editor Trevor Scantlebury, who lived in Bristol. I also continued to write regular articles for the Fisgardian under different pseudonyms. At the 1999 AGM, I volunteered for the Post of Treasurer when Ivor Parker stood down, and remained in this post until the 2008 AGM.

In 2001, the post of Editor became vacant and the task was carried out by an Editorial committee, of which I was a member for several years. I was able to do all of the editorial work involved, and my job as Treasurer, on my PC at home. The editorial meetings for the Fisgardian and for the book 'Second to None', commemorating the Centenary of the RN Artificer Apprentice, published in 2003, were held at my house. The whole edition of 1500 copies of this book was sold, giving the Association a modest profit and the members who bought it, a souvenir of the history and ethos of their artificer apprenticeship. By then, the total world wide membership had stabilised at around 1500 with new members replacing those 'crossing the bar' or lapsing. Under Bruce Balmain's inspirational leadership and, with the dedicated efforts of successive keen, competent and hardworking committee members, the Association continued to provide a first class social service to its members. 754 members and guests celebrated the Centenary of RN Artificer Apprentices in 2003 at the biggest formal dinner ever held in Portsmouth Guildhall. My contribution to the combined efforts of all of the committee during that splendid weekend of celebrations was to produce on my PC, the large displayed seating plan for the Centenary Banquet and place cards, and to have written Chapter 1, (History of Artificer Apprentices), and most of 3, (Folklore). I also helped edit the other three Chapters of 'Second to None', a copy of which was handed to every member who attended the banquet.

A replica of the seating plan formed the centre-fold of Issue 12 of the Fisgardian, a bumper illustrated edition issued three weeks after the memorable event, and dedicated to reports on the celebrations.

*Cook, Simpson, Roberts, Tudor, Murdoch, Barker, King, Edweards, Westlake.*

I spent my 70th birthday in January 1999, having my prostate gland reamered out in St Mary's hospital Portsmouth. I was the first and eldest of four guys being operated on that day and we all got on well together, before and after our operations. In fact, the whole three days was a bit of a hoot, largely due to the humorous up-beat attitude of the patients and staff. I came-to after my op with a very beautiful Eurasian anesthetist gently waking me and a greetings card from an old friend who had undergone the same operation some years earlier, welcoming me to 'the golden handbag club'. This name referred to the requirement of new members to carry around, for two or three days, a transparent bag containing their waste bodily fluid, of that approximate colour. Despite dreading the very sensitive finale, the connecting tube was painlessly removed on the last day and I suffered no further problems with my 'waterworks'.

In the Spring of 1999, my younger sister and I responded to an advert in the Portsmouth News asking former evacuees to send in the stories of their evacuation during WW2. The bulk of our two stories was subsequently published in a magazine commemorating the 60th Anniversary of the outbreak of the war. We were later asked by the Head of the Social History faculty at Reading

University if we would provide him with a copy of our original manuscripts for the archives, which we did. A request was later made by a Professor of a similar faculty at Lancaster University. As a former pupil for two years, I was also persuaded to write of my experiences at a local school for 'delicate children', and this story, with a lead in on how I had come to be sent to this special school in the first place, was locally archived, after I had given it as a lecture to the school.

I was evacuated twice, first from September 1939 to July 1940 and later from September 1941 to July 1944. I went to school in Eastney, Portsmouth between those two evacuations and the archivists were also interested in my story of life at school during the blitzes on Portsmouth. Together, these archived stories of my unusual life from 1929 to 1944, constituted a social commentary on a part of local society, which the archivists thought was worth recording.

In August, 1999, Victoria passed 11 GCSEs, 3 at A★, 5 at A , one at B and 2 at C grade. We were all thrilled especially as her best grades were in 'difficult' subjects such as Science, Maths, English, French and Spanish. In September she enrolled at Havant College to study Maths, English, Spanish and General Studies at A level.

We celebrated the Millenium quietly at home and on the 10th April 2000, held a Golden Wedding Anniversary luncheon party at the Lord Romsey restaurant at Highbury, close to our first home, Eileen and I were feted by our family and friends and the staff of our favourite restaurant pulled out all the stops to make it a great occasion.

During the year, I accompanied Victoria when she visited some of the Universities which offered her a conditional place to study Mathematics. These included Bristol, Bath, Royal Holloway London, Reading and Surrey. In August she achieved a Grade A in her A level Maths, a B in Spanish, a C in General studies and a D in English Literature,  and had met the conditions of each of the universities she had visited, but, as she wanted to go to one with a campus, Bristol and Southampton were ruled out. She chose to read Mathematics and Statistics with Spanish at Surrey. One evening, shortly afterwards she called on me in high dudgeon, because she had received a letter from the MOD offering to sponsor her through university, if she would agree to join the RN as an Engineer Officer on graduation, having attended Dartmouth for training during the summer vacations. Victoria assumed I had put them up to this offer and was not best pleased. I had absolutely no connection with this proposal and eventually convinced her so. I assume that a recruiter with access to UCAS thought that, having the right qualifications, she might like to join the RN. At the end of her first year at Guildford, where she lived in University Court, she spent a month at Valencia University, living with a Spanish family, but when she returned to Surrey after the summer break, she decided to drop Spanish and concentrate on Mathematics and Statistics. During her time at Surrey, we visited her several times and took her to lunch in the university's very good lakeside restaurant.

Although I live next door to a pub, my favourite watering hole for many years was 'The George', a 300 year old tavern, half a mile away on the top of Portsdown hill, one of the very few local 'proper' pubs remaining. Every Saturday at noon a group of retired ex-servicemen, including two pilots, one the secretary of the Battle of Britain Pilots' Association and the other ex Fleet Air Arm, three ex navy and one former soldier met there for a lively hour of putting the world to rights in what was known, after a TV curmudgeon, as the 'Victor Meldrew Appreciation Society. Sadly by 2008, most of these local characters had passed on.

On Good Friday 2003, Eileen fell down the stairs and suffered a broken elbow. I took her to the A&E department of

Queen Alexandra Hospital where she underwent an operation, to join the fractured joint with wires. This was carried out by an RAMC Captain who was one of a team of Army surgeons gathered there prior to being shipped out to Iraq for the second Gulf war. The operation was a huge success and her arm, still 'wired up' six years later, is working perfectly. However, during the week she was in hospital, Sally and Paul redecorated and re-furnished our dining room and converted it into a bedroom and, when Eileen came home she found we were effectively living in a bungalow and she need never go upstairs again. Her fall had also shaken up a latent arthritic condition in her right hip that made walking very painful so I bought her two wheel chairs, one for indoors and the other for carrying in the car. I also had a swivel seat fitted in the passenger front seat and this proved invaluable for taking Eileen about.

The following year, my left knee began to give me problems and an X ray showed I had osteoarthritis, as forecast in 1972 when I injured it. During the six months I waited for a knee replacement, the right knee also became painful and, since my mobility priority was to be able to wheel Eileen about in the house and out of doors, I decided to give up my charity jobs involving walking or going out in the evenings . Thus, after years of making regular door to door collections for the Rowan's hospice, and 'Relate', the annual street collections for Christian Aid, the delivery of literature for the Conservative party, and membership of the committee and Treasurer of the ecumenical Churches Together in Cosham, an organisation dear to my heart, that regularly met in the evening, and which, by 'Buggins turn' I had actually chaired for a year in the 1980's, I restricted my 'outside activities' to those I could carry out on my PC at home. I continued to run the local area Christian Aid collection through my regular team and the actual collecting in two roads I had looked after for 25 years.

Captain Jeremy Dreyer kindly gave a dinner party for his officers of HMS Falmouth's 1970-72 commission, and their wives, at his home in Droxford in the summer of 2004. Unfortunately Eileen was not able to attend but I did. Jeremy, who was at that time in charge of the Ascot Race course, and his wife Toni, together the perfect host and hostess were in great form, the meal was superb and, as all of the Falmouths moved left after each course, we all met each other at the table and enjoyed reminiscing on our particularly happy wardroom and a memorable and successful commission. Richard Channon the former First Lieutenant, and later Captain i/c Submarines, gave the thank you speech after dinner. He began his witty address with the observation, "Looking around the table, I am delighted, in this day and age, to note that all of us are still happily married to the same girls as we were in 1972, we have all kept our hair and have been promoted or decorated. This must be a record and once again proves Falmouth was a unique ship!" When Paul came to pick me up at the end of this splendid reunion of old friends, our generous host asked if he could sit in the driver's seat of my son's Alfa-Romeo 'Spider', for old times sake, as he had loved owning and driving one when he was Naval Attaché in Rome.

Because of my relative, and Eileen's total, immobility, we spent rather more time at home than hitherto and so, in my spare time, I wrote a detailed account of my Artificer apprenticeship entitled 'A Trevoliers`s Tale'. In the Spring of 2006, the editor of the `Fisgardian` magazine began publishing a serialised version of this story in 12 parts. This proved popular with readers and led me to think that if I added this story to the parts detailing my pre-navy life, already published/archived, I had the first 5 chapters of my life story, and the foundations of a personal social history. If I went on to complete this, it might prove useful to future students of history in their studies of a period which saw sweeping changes in British social attitudes and society in general. I therefore embarked on writing a chronological account of my life in the navy and in civilian industry, from the completion of my apprenticeship onwards.

In January 2005 I had my left knee replaced at Royal Haslar

hospital and, four months later, the right knee. On both occasions I was out of hospital in 6 days and after three weeks in the Gorseway nursing home on Hayling Island in which Eileen lived whilst I was in Haslar, I was able to look after her again and we returned home. Both operations were successful and I had no adverse after effects. Much has been said in support of Haslar hospital and I must say the professionalism of all of the staff including the cleaners, was first class. However the hospital itself was in a poor state of repair and the wards were little different from the 'Scutari-like' layout when my grandfather died there in 1903, were very noisy, and the food. like that in all of the local NH hospitals, was of 1960 RN standard.

In June 2005, just after recovering from my second knee op, Victoria took her proud Dad and me to Guildford Cathedral for her graduation ceremony. There was inevitably lots of hanging around before the dignitaries began their slow entry. By then, I could stand no longer and exhaustedly sat down on the aisle side, mid way down the nave. As the Chancellor and Professors in their splendid multi-coloured gowns and head gear, processed solemnly past me. I was intrigued, from my seated position, to see how terribly scruffy the footwear and, in most cases, the trousers, worn by the males, were, compared with the attire of the females. This was also evident as the new graduates brought up the rear, some of the lads wearing dirty trainers and jeans under their gowns and most of them unfamiliar with a tie. At long last, the 5 seconds dedicated to the focus of my presence arrived when Victoria was called and stepped up to receive her higher 2.1 BSc Hons from the Chancellor. At the party afterwards in a huge marquee on the lakeside, she found me a seat and the staff kept topping me up with Pimms. It was a memorable occasion and I was very proud of Victoria, who had worked her way through university, by teaching gymnastics for 20 hours a week at the local Leisure centre, but Victoria's most cherished claim to fame was that she was the limbo dancing

champion of UNIS. Shortly afterwards, she gained a position with a firm of accountants and began her 3 year 'apprenticeship' to become a chartered accountant. As a reward for achieving this status in 2008, her company seconded her to an affiliated company in Melbourne for 4 months, with her fare and accommodation paid. She had a whale of a time in Australia, and whilst there she met her boy friend Troy Petrie.

Meanwhile, her younger sister Charlotte, who has a natural flair with children, studied child care at South Downs College after getting her GCSEs and, armed with an NVQ3 in the subject, the equivalent of A levels, worked in Spain for 15 months as a crèche supervisor for a holiday tour company. During this period, she met Kyle Conway, a sports coach for the same company. They fell in love and, at the end of the season, returned to Portsmouth and set up home together. Charlotte became Deputy Manager of a Day Nursery at Titchfield. She continued to practise her skills as a fully qualified trampoline teacher by taking two evening classes of young children every week at Havant Leisure Centre. Kyle secured a local

*Guests at Charlotte's 21<sup>st</sup> Birthday Party May 2006, viewed from Treehouse*

*Victoria, Charlotte, and their cousins Michael and Stephen reunited with Treehouse*

post in young persons' welfare management.

In 2007, my regular autumnal 'leaf mould' asthma persisted throughout the winter and following Spring, leaving me breathless after the least exertion, I was subjected to a number of different tests including X Rays and blood tests, after which the consultant said.

"The good news is that you haven't as suspected got Asbestosis. The bad news is that you have Emphysema" He went on to say that my 10 years of smoking, which ended in November 1954, had done the delayed damage and I was now diagnosed as having COPD - Chronic Obstructive Pulmonary Disease. Needless to say I was somewhat shaken by this dread news but he reassured me, with an upbeat prognosis, saying that if I took his prescribed treatment, the deterioration of my lung power would be slowed or even halted. He prescribed the use of a steroid inhaler and two other inhalers.

At the time of writing, I am happy to say that two years on, my breathlessness, though still happening after any sort of exertion, is quickly relieved by the appropriate inhaler and I have been able to live a reasonably normal life, for an unfit old man of my age. With the help of several mechanical aids, I have continued to care for Eileen without outside help, except for 3 weeks after I injured my left arm, during which, two care assistants visited Eileen thrice daily.

By September 2008, I had completed the draft of the first 12 of the projected 24 illustrated chapters of my 'social history'. For convenience, Chapters 6 to 12 were given the title of the ship or shore establishment in which I was serving at the time and, together with the aforementioned five chapters, covered my whole life up to when I joined my first ship as a commissioned officer in 1958. The whole file, provisionally and unimaginatively titled 'Don's Story', was stored on my PC and I made a back-up CD to transfer the file, and other data if my computer became corrupted. My daughter Sally asked if she could borrow the CD so that she could read my story and, after she had transferred the story to her laptop to read it at leisure, she returned the CD. Unknown to me, but agreed with her brother and nieces, she began to correct the mistakes in my draft story and prepared and arranged for its publication, as a surprise present for my 80<sup>th</sup> birthday in January 2009. The kind thought behind this unique present was much appreciated when I opened a box containing 10 professionally printed copies of the book, which the family had kept secret from me. The early publication was clearly intended to spur me on to finish the whole story and. in fact, by then, I had completed the draft of Chapters 13 to 18 and decided to stick with the temporary title, 'Don's Story'.

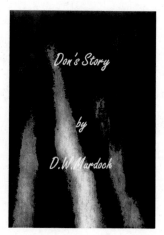

On 1<sup>st</sup> October 2008, Charlotte gave birth to Chloe, her first child, in hospital at Petersfield. The whole family was thrilled, not least Kyle and Charlotte, the happy affianced parents. Eileen and I visited our first great-grandaughter only hours after her birth and we were entranced with her.

Having given notice 12 months earlier, I retired from my long held position as a member of the committee and Treasurer of the Fisgard Association and, at the 2008 AGM, was presented with a handsome engraved glass plaque by David Eaton, the Chairman.

By my 80th birthday, a relief was found to take over and I stepped down after 16 years service, from my Monday morning income accounting job at St Colman's church. At the same time a former Christian Aid employee in Africa, kindly stepped forward and volunteered to take over the post I had held with my favourite charity for 15 years and been actively associated with for 32 years.

On 11<sup>th</sup> July 2009, Chloe was baptised at St Colman's church at 1130 and, after the ceremony, all of the witnesses repaired to our house, where they were joined by other guests at a combined party to celebrate Chloe's christening and Eileen's and my joint 80th birthday party, held in our garden. Prudently, Paul, Sandra and Troy had erected three gazebos the day before, as it drizzled practically all afternoon. However, despite the inclement weather, all of the 96 guests seemed to enjoy themselves, the caterers did a good job, Chloe's christening and our birthday cakes were ceremonially cut, Paul gave an entertaining speech, toasts were made, and the champers was quaffed. Then, stepping forward and uncovering the family's surprise 80<sup>th</sup> birthday present for Eileen, Charlotte presented the special gift she had devised, Sally organised and Victoria and Charlotte painstakingly put together. Eileen was absolutely delighted when she opened it to find her whole life recorded in beautifully arranged and captioned photographs. The family had again co-operated secretly to produce a memorable and most welcome present for an octogenarian grandparent.

Meanwhile, the 14 children present ignored the weather and happily, if muddily, played in the garden and up the tree houses, and reportedly slept all the way home.

All my life, I have been an avid reader and, since I retired from MUSL, spent most of my leisure time, reading classic literature, at first, revisiting some of the great works I had read in my childhood and at sea, and then reading many more for the first time. These included the works of Trollope, Tolkien and Joyce, and all of the sea novels of Patrick O'Brian. I also have 'The Times' delivered daily.

*Back Row:Troy, Sally,Don,Kyle,Paul,.Front Row: Victoria, Eileen & Chloe. Charlotte*

My Scottish paternal great-grandmother, Irish Grandma and her daughter, my mother, all lived to a great age but, in their later years, developed Dementia. None of my male ancestors, on either side, lived long enough to suffer from this affliction, but it seemed possible, as I entered my dotage, that I might finish up with the same problem. I therefore decided to monitor my mental health by doing the Times general knowledge crossword puzzle, and later the Su Doku, every day and have become hooked on this daily exercise of my little grey cells. If I fail to complete the puzzles by 1000, I become concerned that my brain decay rate is increasing. The X-word checks my memory and the Su Doku exercises the lg cells. The absolute certainty of the only possible correct answer proves that mathematical logic could not just have evolved in a random fashion, it must have been created by a superior being and, in my considered opinion, proves there is a God.

Since 2007, Eileen and I have perforce, led a pretty quiet life, never straying far from home. We go out locally shopping two or three mornings a week, and to pub/restaurants for lunch, and every Friday we enjoy lunch out with my sister Eileen and her husband Jim. We also attend luncheons run by ex RN organisations, Probus and Eileen's old school. Eileen has to take a large number of drugs including pain-killers, which together make her rather sleepy by early afternoon, so we are always home by 3pm. We live downstairs and have had the house specially adapted so to do, with a walk-in shower, portable hoist and lifting chair. Despite her problems, Eileen remains in good spirits and enjoys visits from friends, reading, and some TV. The twice daily phone calls from Sally, the many from Paul, and frequent visits from all of the family, act as a tonic for both of us and fortunately, we always seem to have something special to look forward to, and to plan. Our next major event of this kind is, DV, our Diamond Wedding Anniversary on the 10th April 2010 followed, two months later by Charlotte and Kyle's wedding. Milestones like these, add spice to our life. I spend much of my time pottering around taking ten times as long to complete jobs I found easy only a few years ago. I happily listen to Classic FM while I am doing the household chores. Eileen was a very good cook and, over ten years ago, taught me how to rustle up a number of different dishes. I even manage to do a Sunday roast for the family once a month and quite enjoy donning my blue and white apron and getting cracking. Bless them; the family always do the washing-up afterwards.

During the past 80 years, society in Britain has changed beyond recognition. The standard of living and expectancy of life have improved immensely, the air breathed in our cities is clean, life is fairer, the old class divisions have more or less disappeared and, with the availability of cheap travel and television, people have generally become more aware and tolerant of those from other cultures or creeds. Young people nowadays are more aware of the poverty prevalent in the Third World and more likely to do something about it. Unfortunately, these welcome signs of social progress have, for no clear reason, been accompanied by a decrease in moral standards, a drop in the proportion of children enjoying the love, security and guidance of a happy family, an increase in verbal, physical and sexual violence and in vandalism and litter. At present the justice system seems to be more concerned with the welfare of the criminals than their victims.

I would like to see the BBC live up to its proud motto and charter, "To educate" and to lead the rest of the responsible media away from its current obsession with the promotion of greed, violence, marital infidelity and promiscuity and bring back a Polite Society. Historically, civilisation's pendulum must be due to swing the right way sooner or later.

Despite the many and varied experiences in life that have challenged my religion, I still believe that the simple rules of Christianity, the Ten Commandments, inherited from Judaism and largely supported by all of the other great religions, still offer the best guidelines for an ordered and harmonious society. The fact that ever more and more people ignore these rules does not mean they are bad laws. Eileen and I hold dear the Nicene Creed and get great spiritual comfort from mass at the local friendly, multi-racial Catholic churches and their inspirational priest Fr Sean Tobin.

Within the constraints lately placed upon us by our relative immobility, Eileen and I enjoy life as much as we can. We cherish countless wonderfully happy memories of our life together and of Sally, Paul, Victoria, Charlotte and Chloe. We are also thankful that, while we were able, we took every possible opportunity to travel far and wide. We have been extremely lucky in love and life and Thank God for this great blessing.

*Eileen and Don at 'le dix avril' 19th September 2009*

# List of Illustrations

# Abbreviations

| | |
|---|---|
| AA | Anti-Aircraft |
| AB | Able Seaman |
| ac | Alternating Current Electricity |
| AE | Air Engineering branch prefix |
| AKA | Also Known As |
| AME | Admiralty Mining Establishment |
| ANZUK | Australian,NewZealand,United Kingdom |
| A/S | Anti-submarine |
| ATE | Automatic Test Equipment |
| ASUAT | Anti-Submarine Universal Attack Teacher |
| CEM | Control Electrical Mechanic |
| CO | Commanding Officer |
| CPO | Chief Petty Officer |
| CYS | Chief Yeoman of Signals |
| dc | Direct Current Electricity |
| DCP | Development Cost Plan |
| D/F | Direction Finding equipment |
| DO | Divisional Officer |
| DV | Deo volente (God willing) |
| ENT | Ear, Nose and Throat |
| ENSA | Entertainments Association {for armed services) |
| EO | (Marine) Engineer Officer |
| FAA | Fleet Air Arm |
| FMG/U | Fleet Maintenance Group/Unit |
| FOST | Flag Officer Sea Training |
| GI | Gunnery Instructor |
| GO | Gunnery Officer |
| HF | High Frequency radio |
| HMUDE | Her Majesty's Underwater Detection Establishm't |
| JB | (Electrical ) Junction Box |
| JTS | Junior Technical School |
| (L) | Electrical Specialisation |
| MAA | Master at Arms (Senior policeman on ship) |
| ME | Marine Engineering branch prefix |
| MF | Medium Frequency radio |

| | |
|---|---|
| Med | Mediterranean |
| M/G | Motor Generator (dc) |
| MO | Medical Officer |
| MOD (N) | Ministry of Defence (Navy) |
| MQ | Married Quarter |
| MRS | Medium Range (Gunnery) System |
| No 1 | First Lieutetenant (2i.c) of Destroyer or Frigate |
| No 1s | Best uniform suit |
| Oggin | Water, Sea, harbour, |
| OCRM | Officer Commanding Royal Marines |
| OOD | Officer of the Day |
| OOW | Officer of the Watch |
| OPL | Off Privileged Leave (No shore leave) |
| Oppo | Opposite Number, team mate, friend |
| PC | Personal Computer: Politically correct |
| pdq | Pretty dam quick; straight away |
| PIA | Pakistan International Airways |
| PO | Petty Officer |
| PTI | Physical Training Instructor |
| QD | Quarter Deck |
| (R ) | Radio (and Radar) Specialisation |
| RFA | Royal Fleet Auxiliary (Supply ship or tanker) |
| RATOG | Rocket-Assisted Take-Off Gear |
| RN | Royal Navy |
| RNDQs | Royal Naval Detention Quarters |
| RNH | Royal Naval Hospital |
| RPO | Regulating Petty Officer (Naval policeman) |
| SEATO | South East Asia Treaty Organisation |
| SRE | Ship's Radio Entertainment |
| S &S | Supply and Secretariat branch |
| SYNTAX | Synthetic Tactical Exercise |
| TAS | Torpedo Anti-Submarine (branch) |
| TLC | Tender Loving Care |
| TS | (Gunnery) Transmitting (and Computer)Station |
| TTB | Target Triggered Burst ( by close-proximity fuze) |
| UHF | Ultra High Frequency radio |
| VHF | Very High Frequency radio |
| WE | Weapons Electrical (&Radio) Engineering prefix |
| WEO | Weapons Electrical Engineer Officer |
| YMCA | Young Men's Christian (Temperance) canteen |

# *Glossary of Terms*

| | |
|---|---|
| Adrift | Late back onboard from ashore |
| Airy-fairy | Name given to Fleet Air Arm by sailors |
| Art-App | Atificer Apprentice |
| Asdic | Anti-Submarine Detection equipment |
| Ashore | Off the ship or out of the establishment |
| Banyan | A beach picnic with beer |
| Boy Art | Traditional name for Artificer Apprentice |
| Browned-off | Detailed by authority to do something |
| Caboosh | Equipment room also used as cabin |
| Captain (D) | Captein i/c of Squadron of Destroyers |
| Coxswain | Senior CPO on ship. Helmsman in Action |
| Crusher | Regulating Petty Officer (ship's policeman) |
| Cushy number | Quiet, easy job |
| CW Candidate | Candidate for Commission as a Sub Lt. |
| Dabtoe | Name given to Seamen by other branches |
| Defence Watches | All weapons manned, Crew in 2 watches |
| Dhobey | Washing, laundry |
| Ditched | Crashed in sea, or thrown overboard |
| Donkey Boiler | Aux.Boiler used when not flashed-up |
| Ex- Boy | Artificer who has been an RN Apprentice |
| Exped | Organised Expedition |
| Fishead | Name given by Fleet Air Arm to sailors |
| Flashed up | With main steam raised |
| Flyco | Flying Control Position on Bridge wing |
| Gash | Waste put down gash shute, surplus |
| Gobby | Pensioner mess attendant for apprentices |
| Go Dutch | Share the cost evenly |
| Guard Ship | HQ and Safety ship for a Sailing Race. |
| Greenie | Name given to Electrical branch |
| Hard Lyers | Extra pay for arduous living conditions |
| Heads | Ship's lavatories |
| Hook Boy | Petty Officer Apprentice (Prefect) |

| | |
|---|---|
| Hurt Certificate | Proof of injury when on duty |
| Jankers | Strenuous drills or exercises as punishment |
| Jaunty | Master at Arms, senior policeman on ship |
| Jolly | A visit to an attractive place |
| Junior ship | Ship with most junior Captain |
| Keyham Stag | Candidates for Engineer Officer Cadetship |
| Kiwi | New Zealander |
| Legal Eagle | Naval Officer who is a qualified lawyer |
| Lobs | Look out Boys, a warning |
| Logged | An official warning reported in ship's Log |
| Mess Undress | Officer's Evening dress |
| Native | Sailor who lives locally |
| Night Clothing | Change into clean clothing after work |
| No 1 | First Lieutenant, 2nd in Command |
| Noggin | A quick drink |
| Pom | Australian name for a Briton |
| Pompey | Portsmouth; Portsmouth division of RN |
| Pongo | Sailor's name for a soldier |
| Pusser | Srictly in accordance with orders |
| Pussers | Naval Issue |
| Rabbit | Present either made or bought |
| Rec Room | Recreation Room |
| Rig of Day | Style of uniform to be worn |
| RN | Royal Navy |
| Royal | Sailor's name for a Royal Marine |
| Sailor | Anyone serving in the Royal Navy |
| Shakedown | Go to sea to try out equipment and crew |
| Sick Bay Tiffy | Sick Berth attendant (dressed like tiffy) |
| Skate | Apprentice often under punishment |
| Skipper's Lobs | Captain's Warning |
| Slop Room | Naval Clothing Store |
| Sonar | NATO name for A/S (in place of Asdic) |
| Sprog | Newly joined apprentice or rating |
| Strine | Australian as spoken |
| Square-Bashing | Repetitive Marching Instruction |
| STAAG | Stabilised Tachometric (auto) AA Gun |
| Stand Easy | Short break at work; Relax when on parade |
| Stroppy | Cheeky, disrespectful of authority |
| Thunder Box | WC overhanging the water |
| Tiddly | Smartly dressed; smartly turned-out. |
| Tiffy | An RN Artificer or Artificer Apprentice |

| | |
|---|---|
| Typex | Electro-mechanical Coding machine |
| Up-'omers | A girl friend whose mother is a good cook |
| Upper Yardman | Rating candidate (22-23) for a commission |
| Weigh | Weigh Anchor, Hoist anchor and proceed |
| Weighed-off | Awarded punishment |
| X Craft | 3-man Midget Submarine |
| Work-Up | Intense period of warship training |